STUDENT BOOK

STECK-VAUGHN

REASONING THROUGH
LANGUAGE ARTS

TEST PREPARATION FOR THE 2014 GED TEST

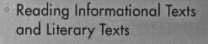

- Reading Informational Texts and Literary Texts
- Writing an Extended Response
- Using Standard English Grammar, Usage, and Conventions

POWERED BY
PAXEN

Houghton
Mifflin
Harcourt

POWERED BY
PAXEN

Acknowledgments

For each of the selections and images listed below, grateful acknowledgment is made for permission to excerpt and/or reprint original or copyrighted material, as follows:

Text

2 From "Sleep Research in the Blind May Help Us All" by Steven Lockley, PhD. © 2012. **3** From nationalgeographic.com "Wind Power" © 2013. Ng Staff/National Geographic Creative. **4** From USA Today – (Academic Permission), 9/15/2010 © 2010 Gannett-USAToday. All rights reserved. Used by permission and protected by the Copyright Laws of the United States.The printing, copying, redistribution, or retransmission of this Content without express written permission is prohibited. **5** From American Rhetoric, www.americanrhetoric.com. "Checkers" by Richard Nixon, 1952. **6** From www.historyofvaccines.org "The Scientific Method in Vaccine History" accessed 2013. **7** Excerpt from *Savage Inequalities: Children in America's Schools* by Jonathan Kozol, copyright © 1991 by Jonathan Kozol. Used by permission of Crown Books, an imprint of the Crown Publishing Group, a division of Penguin Random House LLC. All rights reserved. Any third party use of this material, outside of this publication, is prohibited. Interested parties must apply directly to Penguin Random House LLC for permission. **8** From *The New York Times,* 6/6/2012 © 2012 The New York Times. All rights reserved. Used by permission and protected by the Copyright Laws of the United States. The printing, copying, redistribution, or retransmission of this Content without express written permission is prohibited. **9** From *The Wall Street Journal,* December 8 © 2007. **10** Used with permission of The Associated Press Copyright © 2015. All rights reserved. **11** From *The New York Times,* 7/24/2008 © 2008 The New York Times. All rights reserved. Used by permission and protected by the Copyright Laws of the United States. The printing, copying, redistribution, or retransmission of this Content without express written permission is prohibited. **13** From *The Wall Street Journal,* June 20 © 2012. **14** From *The Washington Post* 12/5/2010 © 2010 Washington Post Company. All rights reserved. Used by permission and protected by the Copyright Laws of the United States. The printing, copying, redistribution, or retransmission of this Content without express written permission is prohibited. **15** From *The New York Times,* 6/10/2008 © 2008 The New York Times. All rights reserved. Used by permission and protected by the Copyright Laws of the United States. The printing, copying, redistribution, or retransmission of this Content without express written permission is prohibited. **16** Used with the permission of *The Atlantic* © 2008. **17** Reprinted by permission of International Creative Management, Inc. Copyright © 1990 by Barbara Ehrenreich. **18** From American Rhetoric, www.americanrhetoric.com "Democratic National convention Keynote Address" by Barbara Jordan © 1976. **19** From huffingtonpost.com "NBA Officiating Has Gone Kindergarten" © 2013. **20** From *The New York Times,* 6/29/2008 © 2008 The New York Times. All rights reserved. Used by permission and protected by the Copyright Laws of the United States. The printing, copying, redistribution, or retransmission of this Content without express written permission is prohibited. **21** Used with the permission of Susan Estrich. Originally published in *The New York Times,* May 22 © 1994. **22** From *Forbes,* "Failure to Launch: Adult Children Moving Back Home" © 2012. **23** From *Newsweek,* December 11 © 2007 IBT Media. All rights reserved. Used by permission and protected by the Copyright Laws of the United States. The printing, copying, redistribution, or retransmission of the Material without express written permission is prohibited. **24** From *The Washington Post,* December 5 © 2010. **30** Copyright © 1961 Tillie Olsen from *Tell Me a Riddle* reprinted by permission of the Frances Goldin Literary Agency. **31** "Why I Like Country Music", from *Elbow Room* © 1972 by

James Alan McPherson, is used with the permission of James Alan McPherson and Little Brown and Co. and the Faith Childs Literary Agency, Inc. There shall be no unauthorized use or quotation from this excerpt without the express, written permission of the Author or his agent. **36** "Blood-Burning Moon", from CANE by Jean Toomer. Copyright 1923 by Boni & Liveright, renewed 1951 by Jean Toomer. Used by permission of Liveright Publishing Corporation. **37** Reprinted by permission of International Creative Management, Inc. Copyright © 1940 by Walter Van Tilburg Clark. **41** "The Circling Hand," from *Annie John* by Jamaica Kincaid. Copyright © 1985 by Jamaica Kincaid. Reprinted by permission of Farrar, Straus and Giroux, LLC. **45** © 1988 Bobbie Ann Mason. Used by Permission. All rights reserved. **46** "In the Gloaming" by Alice Elliott Dark, *The New Yorker* © 1993 Alice Elliott Dark. Reprinted with permission by Dunow, Carlson & Lerner Literary Agency. **49** From "Healthy Landscape with Dormouse" by Sylvia Townsend Warner © 1966. **50** From the *Los Angeles Times,* July 14 © 2012. **60** Reprinted with permission from MayoClinic.com. **61** From CNN.com, 1/17/2013 © 2013 Turner Broadcast Systems, Inc. All rights reserved. Used by permission and protected by the Copyright Laws of the United States. The printing, copying, redistribution, or retransmission of this Content without express written permission is prohibited. **63** From Huffingtonpost.com "The Affordable Care Act: Good News for Former Foster Youth," © 2012. **66** Reprinted with permission from MayoClinic.com. **67** From the pamphlet included in the *Oregon Almanac,* "The Land of Opportunity" by Oswald West, © 1912. **71** From apsofdurham.org "Why Adopt a Shelter Pet?", accessed 2013. **73** Reprinted with permission from MayoClinic.com. **75** Albert A. Gore's Nobel Lecture © The Nobel Foundation (Oslo, December 10, 2007); Source: Nobelprize.org. **76** From "Kikuyu Binds" by Michele Graves, Courtesy of the Peace Corps, © 2010. **77** From "Kikuyu Binds" by Michele Graves, Courtesy of the Peace Corps, © 2010. **79** From *Soul of a Citizen* © 2009 by Paul Rogat Loeb. Reprinted by permission of St. Martin's Press. All rights reserved. **82** From *The Wall Street Journal,* May 19 © 2013; From cleanwaterportland.org "12 Reasons to Vote No" © 2013. **83** From *The Wall Street Journal,* May 19 © 2013; From cleanwaterportland.org "12 Reasons to Vote No" © 2013. **84** From the Facts On File and Issues and Controversies On File "NFL Head Injuries," accessed 2013; "10 Point Plan to Save Football" © 2009, reprinted with permission from Christopher Nowinski, Sports Legacy Institute, www.sportslegacy.org. **85** From the Facts On File and Issues and Controversies On File "NFL Head Injuries," accessed 2013; "10 Point Plan to Save Football," reprinted with permission from Christopher Nowinski, Sports Legacy Institute, www.sportslegacy.org. **86** Reprinted with permission from the Natural Resources Defense Council, www.nrdc.org; from pmel.noaa.gov "Carbon Dioxide and Our Ocean Legacy" © 2006. **90** From "The Future of Light is the LED," *Wired* © 2011; from energy.gov "Frequently Asked Questions: Lighting Choices to Save You Money," accessed 2013. **92** From CNN.com, 5/28/2013 © 2013 Turner Broadcast Systems, Inc. All rights reserved. Used by permission and protected by the Copyright Laws of the United States. The printing, copying, redistribution, or retransmission of this Content without express written permission is prohibited. **96** From "I'll Never Do It Again" from *The Chronicle of Higher Education* © 2009. **97** From "I'll Never Do It Again" from *The Chronicle of Higher Education* © 2009. **112** From *Current Health Teen* "DN'T TT N DRV: Why You Should Disconnect While Driving" by Nancy Mann Jackson © 2011. **114** From "Is Bullying Going Digital? Cyber Bullying Facts" by Yalda T. Uhls © 2010. **116** From *USA Today Magazine* "Saving Our Space Program" by Bob Deutsch © 2010; "The Space Race is a Pointless Waste of Money" by Gerard DeGroot © 2009. **118** From "Raise the Minimum Wage to $10 in 2010" by Holly Sklar © 2009.

Images

cover (bg) © chinaface/E+/Getty Images; **cover** (bg color) ©Roman Okopny/E+/Getty Images; **cover** (inset) © Peter Mukherjee/Vetta/Getty Images. **BLIND** Corbis Entertainment © Fairchild Photo Service/Condé Nast/Corbis. **1** iStockphoto © Alejandro Rivera. **58** © Xavier Collin/Celebrity Monitor/Splash News/Corbis. **59** iStockphoto © CostinT. **78** whitehousemuseum.org **94** Frazer Harrison/Getty Images **95** iStockphoto © aldomurillo. **120** Fred Prouser/Reuters/Corbis. **121** iStockphoto © subman

Reasoning Through Language Arts

Table of Contents

About the GED® Test

Welcome to the first day of the rest of your life. Now that you've committed to study for your GED® credential, an array of possibilities and options—academic, career, and otherwise—awaits you. Each year, hundreds of thousands of people just like you decide to pursue a GED® credential. Like you, they left traditional school for one reason or another. Now, just like them, you've decided to continue your education by studying for and taking the GED® Test.

Today's GED® Test is very different from previous versions of the exam. Today's GED® Test is new, improved, and more rigorous, with content aligned to the Common Core State Standards. For the first time, the GED® Test serves both as a high-school equivalency credential and as a predictor of college and career readiness. The new GED® Test features four subject areas: Reasoning Through Language Arts (RLA), Mathematical Reasoning, Science, and Social Studies. Each subject area is delivered via a computer-based format and includes an array of technology-enhanced item types.

The four subject-area exams together comprise a testing time of seven hours. Preparation can take considerably longer. The payoff, however, is significant: more and better career options, higher earnings, and the sense of achievement that comes with a GED® credential. Employers, colleges, and universities accept the GED® credential as they would a high school diploma. On average, GED® graduates earn at least $8,400 more per year than those with an incomplete high school education.

The GED® Testing Service has constructed the GED® Test to mirror a high school experience. As such, you must answer a variety of questions within and across the four subject areas. For example, you may encounter a Social Studies passage on the Reasoning Through Language Arts Test, and vice versa. Also, you will encounter questions requiring varying levels of cognitive effort, or Depth of Knowledge (DOK) levels. The following table details the content areas, number of items, score points, DOK levels, and total testing time for each subject area.

Subject-Area Test	Content Areas	Items	Raw Score Points	DOK Level	Time
Reasoning Through Language Arts	**Informational Texts—75%** **Literary Texts—25%**	*51	65	80% of items at Level 2 or 3	150 minutes
Mathematical Reasoning	**Algebraic Problem Solving—55%** **Quantitative Problem Solving—45%**	*46	49	50% of items at Level 2	115 minutes
Science	**Life Science—40%** **Physical Science—40%** **Earth and Space Science—20%**	*34	40	80% of items at Level 2 or 3	90 minutes
Social Studies	**Civics/Government—50%** **U.S. History—20%** **Economics—15%** **Geography and the World—15%**	*35	30	80% of items at Level 2 or 3	70 minutes

*Number of items may vary slightly by te

Because the demands of today's high school education and its relationship to workforce needs differ from those of a decade ago, the GED® Testing Service has moved to a computer-based format. Although multiple-choice questions remain the dominant type of item, the new GED® Test series includes a variety of technology-enhanced item types: drop-down, fill-in-the-blank, drag-and-drop, hot spot, short answer, and extended response items.

The table to the right identifies the various item types and their distribution on the new subject-area exams. As you can see, all four tests include multiple-choice, drop-down, fill-in-the-blank, and drag-and-drop items. Some variation occurs with hot spot, short answer, and extended response items.

2014 ITEM TYPES

	RLA	Math	Science	Social Studies
Multiple-choice	✓	✓	✓	✓
Drop-down	✓	✓	✓	✓
Fill-in-the-blank	✓	✓	✓	✓
Drag-and-drop	✓	✓	✓	✓
Hot spot		✓	✓	✓
Short answer			✓	
Extended response	✓			

Moreover, the new GED® Test relates to today's more demanding educational standards with items that align to appropriate assessment targets and varying DOK levels.

- **Content Topics/Assessment Targets** These topics and targets describe and detail the content on the GED® Test. They tie to the Common Core State Standards, as well as state standards for Texas and Virginia.
- **Content Practices** These practices describe the types of reasoning and modes of thinking required to answer specific items on the GED® Test.
- **Depth of Knowledge** The DOK model details the level of cognitive complexity and steps required to arrive at a correct answer on the test. The new GED® Test addresses three levels of DOK complexity.
  - **Level 1** You must recall, observe, question, or represent facts or simple skills. Typically, you will need to exhibit only a surface understanding of text and graphics.
  - **Level 2** You must process information beyond simple recall and observation to include summarizing, ordering, classifying, identifying patterns and relationships, and connecting ideas. You will need to scrutinize text and graphics.
  - **Level 3** You must explain, generalize, and connect ideas by inferring, elaborating, and predicting. For example, you may need to summarize from multiple sources and use that information to develop compositions with multiple paragraphs. Those paragraphs should feature a critical analysis of sources, include supporting positions from your own experiences, and reflect editing to ensure coherent, correct writing.

Approximately 80 percent of items across most content areas will be written to DOK Levels 2 and 3, with the remainder at Level 1. The extended response item in Reasoning Through Language Arts (45 minutes) is considered a DOK Level 3 item.

Now that you understand the basic structure of the GED® Test and the benefits of earning a GED® credential, you must prepare for the GED® Test. In the pages that follow, you will find a recipe of sorts that, if followed, will guide you toward successful completion of your GED® credential.

GED® Test on Computer

Along with new item types, the 2014 GED® Test also unveils a new, computer-based testing experience. The GED® Test will be available on computer and only at approved Pearson VUE Testing Centers. You will need content knowledge and the ability to read, think, and write critically, and you must perform basic computer functions—clicking, scrolling, and typing—to succeed on the test. The screen below closely resembles a screen that you will experience on the GED® Test.

The **INFORMATION** button contains material vital to the successful completion of the item. Here, by clicking the Information button, you would display a map about the American Revolution. On the Mathematical Reasoning exam, similar buttons for **FORMULA SHEET** and **CALCULATOR REFERENCE** provide information that will help you answer items that require use of formulas or the TI-30XS calculator. You may move a passage or graphic by clicking it and dragging it to a different part of the test screen.

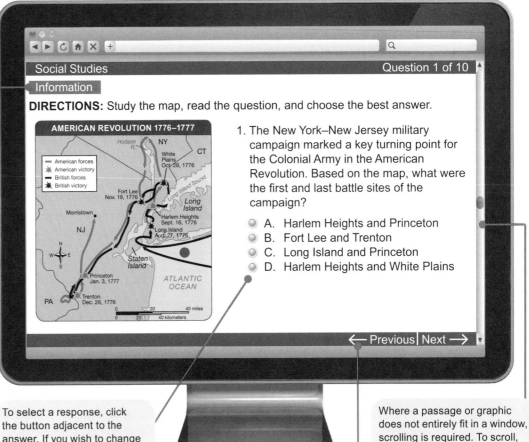

To select a response, click the button adjacent to the answer. If you wish to change your answer, click a different button, thereby clearing the previous selection.

Where a passage or graphic does not entirely fit in a window, scrolling is required. To scroll, click the scroll bar and drag it downward to display the appropriate part of the text or graphic. The light gray portion of the scroll bar shows the amount of text or graphic that you cannot presently see.

To return to the prior screen, click **PREVIOUS**. To advance to the next screen, click **NEXT**.

Some items on the new GED® Test, such as fill-in-the-blank, short answer, and extended response questions, will require you to type answers into an entry box. In some cases, the directions may specify the range of typing the system will accept. For example, a fill-in-the-blank item may allow you to type a number from 0 to 9, along with a decimal point or a slash, but nothing else. The system also will tell you keys to avoid pressing in certain situations. The annotated computer screen and keyboard below provide strategies for entering text and data for fill-in-the-blank, short answer, and extended response items.

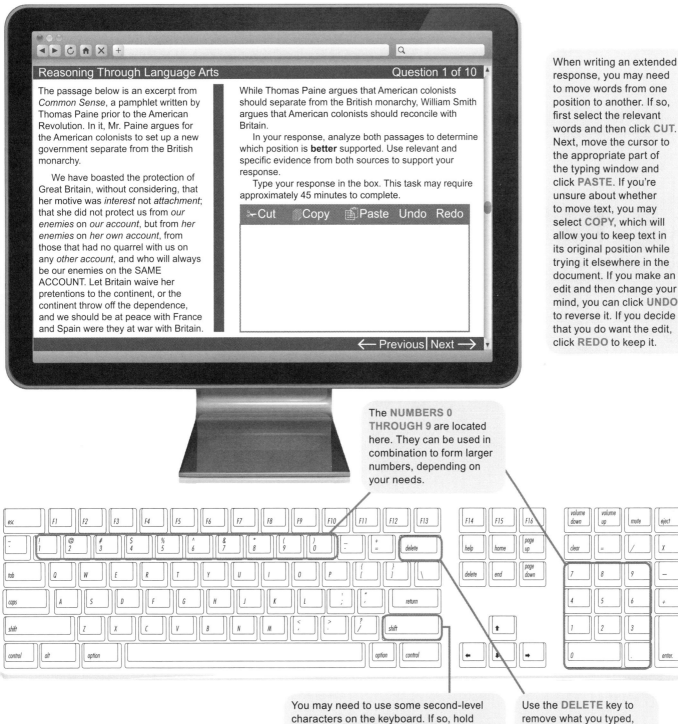

When writing an extended response, you may need to move words from one position to another. If so, first select the relevant words and then click **CUT**. Next, move the cursor to the appropriate part of the typing window and click **PASTE**. If you're unsure about whether to move text, you may select **COPY**, which will allow you to keep text in its original position while trying it elsewhere in the document. If you make an edit and then change your mind, you can click **UNDO** to reverse it. If you decide that you do want the edit, click **REDO** to keep it.

The **NUMBERS 0 THROUGH 9** are located here. They can be used in combination to form larger numbers, depending on your needs.

You may need to use some second-level characters on the keyboard. If so, hold down the **SHIFT** key and type the second-level key, such as a question mark.

Use the **DELETE** key to remove what you typed, and then type in a new answer.

About *Steck-Vaughn*
Test Preparation for the 2014 GED® Test

Along with choosing to pursue your GED® credential, you've made another smart decision by selecting *Steck-Vaughn Test Preparation for the 2014 GED® Te.* as your main study and preparation tool. Our emphasis on the acquisition of key reading and thinking concepts equips you with the skills and strategies to succeed on the GED® Test.

Two-page micro-lessons in each student book provide focused and efficient instruction. For those who require additional support, we offer companion workbooks, which provide *twice* the support and practice exercises. Most lessons in the series include a *Spotlighted Item* feature that corresponds to one of the technology-enhanced item types that appear on the GED® Test.

The **LEARN THE SKILL** section provides information about the skill to be studied.

Each lesson includes correlations to **ASSESSMENT TARGETS** that will help focus your studies.

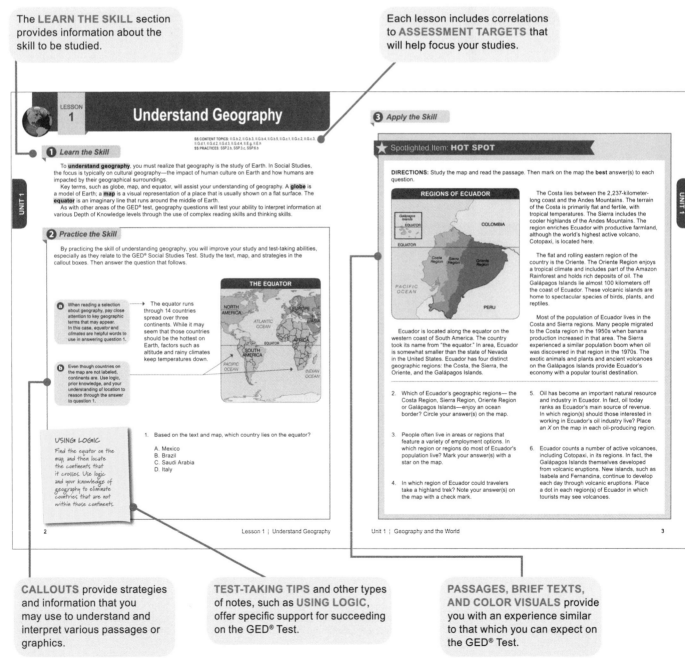

CALLOUTS provide strategies and information that you may use to understand and interpret various passages or graphics.

TEST-TAKING TIPS and other types of notes, such as **USING LOGIC**, offer specific support for succeeding on the GED® Test.

PASSAGES, BRIEF TEXTS, AND COLOR VISUALS provide you with an experience similar to that which you can expect on the GED® Test.

Every unit in *Steck-Vaughn Test Preparation for the 2014 GED® Test* opens with the feature GED® Journeys, a series of profiles of people who earned their GED® credential and used it as a springboard to success. From there, you receive intensive instruction and practice through a series of linked lessons, all of which tie to Content Topics/Assessment Targets, Content Practices (where applicable), and DOK levels.

Each unit closes with an eight-page review that includes a representative sampling of items, including technology-enhanced item types, from the lessons that comprise the unit. You may use each unit review as a posttest to gauge your mastery of content and skills and readiness for that aspect of the GED® Test.

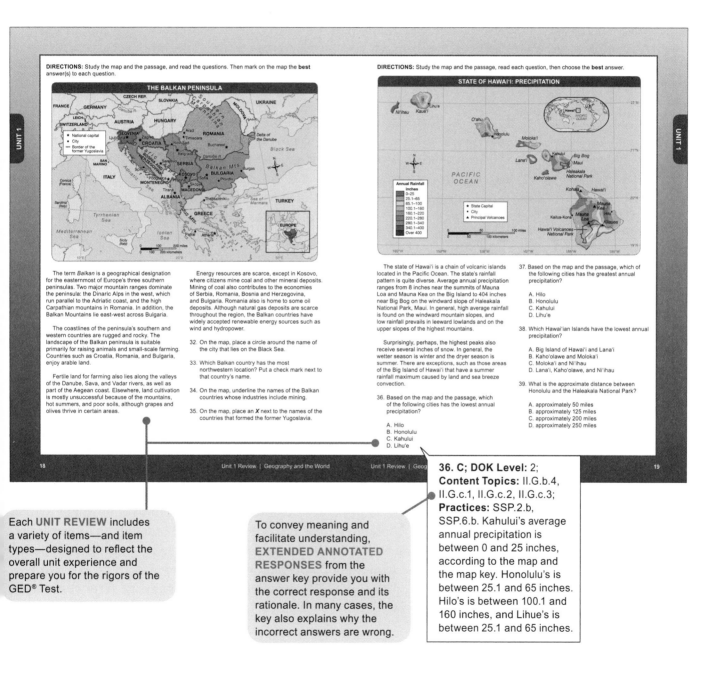

Each **UNIT REVIEW** includes a variety of items—and item types—designed to reflect the overall unit experience and prepare you for the rigors of the GED® Test.

To convey meaning and facilitate understanding, **EXTENDED ANNOTATED RESPONSES** from the answer key provide you with the correct response and its rationale. In many cases, the key also explains why the incorrect answers are wrong.

36. C; DOK Level: 2; **Content Topics:** II.G.b.4, II.G.c.1, II.G.c.2, II.G.c.3; **Practices:** SSP.2.b, SSP.6.b. Kahului's average annual precipitation is between 0 and 25 inches, according to the map and the map key. Honolulu's is between 25.1 and 65 inches. Hilo's is between 100.1 and 160 inches, and Lihue's is between 25.1 and 65 inches.

About the GED® Reasoning Through Language Arts Test

The new GED® Reasoning Through Language Arts Test is more than just a collection of words. In fact, it reflects an attempt to increase the rigor of the GED® Test to meet the demands of a 21st-century economy. To that end, the GED® Reasoning Through Language Arts Test features an array of technology-aided question types. All questions are delivered via computer and reflect the knowledge, skills, and abilities that a student would master in an equivalent high school experience.

Multiple-choice questions remain the majority of items on the GED® Reasoning Through Language Arts Test. However, a number of technology-enhanced items, including fill-in-the-blank, drag-and-drop, drop-down, and extended response questions, will challenge you to master and convey knowledge in deeper, fuller ways. For example,

- Multiple-choice items assess virtually every content standard. In contrast to the previous GED® Test, multiple-choice items on the new series include four answer options (rather than five), structured in an A./B./C./D. format.
- Fill-in-the-blank items allow you to demonstrate vocabulary skills at a higher cognitive level by requiring you to provide your own synonyms or definitions. Fill-in-the-blank items also may require you to write a short phrase or sentence in response to a question.
- Drag-and-drop items involve interactive tasks that require you to move words, phrases, or short sentences into designated drop zones on a computer screen. You may use drag-and-drop options to classify and sequence information, analyze an author's arguments, and edit to re-order sentences within a paragraph.
- Drop-down items include pull-down menus of response choices directly embedded within the text. You may use drop-down items to demonstrate mastery of language skills, such as conventions of Edited American English and standard usage and punctuation. Such items are designed to mirror the editing process.
- An extended response item on the GED® Reasoning Through Language Arts Test is a 45-minute task that requires you to analyze one or more source texts in order to produce a writing sample. The source text will not exceed 650 words. Extended response items will be scored according to how well you fulfill three key traits:
  - analyzing arguments and gathering evidence found in source texts
  - organizing and developing your writing
  - demonstrating fluency with conventions of Edited American English

You will have a total of 150 minutes (including a 10-minute break) in which to answer about 51 items. A total of 75 percent of texts on the exam will be drawn from informational sources (including nonfiction passages from science, social studies, and workplace contexts). The remaining 25 percent will come from literature. All told, 80 percent of the items on the GED® Reasoning Through Language Arts Test will be written at Depth of Knowledge Levels 2 and 3.

About *Steck-Vaughn Test Preparation for the 2014 GED® Test: Reasoning Through Language Arts*

Steck-Vaughn's student book and workbook help unlock the learning and deconstruct the different elements of the test by helping you build and develop core reading and thinking skills. The test itself will require you to read closely, to write clearly, and to edit and understand standard written English in context. The content of our books aligns to the new GED® language arts content standards and item distribution to provide you with a superior test preparation experience.

Our *Spotlighted Item* feature provides a deeper, richer treatment for each technology-enhanced item type. On initial introduction, a unique item type—such as drag-and-drop—receives a full page of example items in the student book lesson and three pages in the companion workbook. The length of subsequent features may be shorter depending on the skill, lesson, and requirements.

A combination of targeted strategies, informational callouts, sample questions, assorted tips and hints, and ample assessment help focus study efforts in needed areas.

In addition to the book features, a highly detailed answer key provides the correct answer and the rationale for it so that you know exactly why an answer is correct. The *Reasoning Through Language Arts* student book and workbook are designed with an eye toward the end goal: Success on the GED® Reasoning Through Language Arts Test.

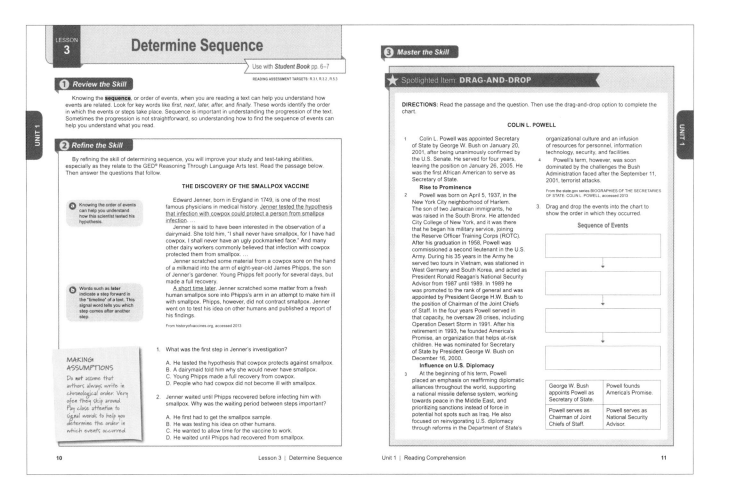

Test-Taking Tips

The new GED® Test includes more than 160 items across the four subject-area exams of Reasoning Through Language Arts, Mathematical Reasoning, Science, and Social Studies. The four subject-area exams represent a total test time of seven hours. Most items are multiple-choice questions, but a number are technology-enhanced items. These include drop-down, fill-in-the-blank, drag-and-drop, hot spot, short answer, and extended response items.

Throughout this book and others in the series, we help you build, develop, and apply core reading and thinking skills critical to success on the GED® Test. As part of an overall strategy, we suggest that you use the test-taking tips presented here and throughout the book to improve your performance on the GED® Test.

> **Always read directions thoroughly so that you know exactly what to do.** As we've noted, the 2014 GED® Test has an entirely new computer-based format that includes a variety of technology-enhanced items. If you are unclear of what to do or how to proceed, ask the test provider whether directions can be explained.

> **Read each question carefully so that you fully understand what it is asking.** For example, some passages and graphics may present information beyond what is necessary to correctly answer a specific question. Other questions may use boldfaced words for emphasis (for example, "Which statement represents the **most** appropriate revision for this hypothesis?").

> **Manage your time with each question.** Because the GED® Test is a series of timed exams, you want to spend enough time with each question, but not *too* much time. For example, on the GED® Mathematical Reasoning Test, you have 115 minutes in which to answer approximately 46 questions, or an average of about two minutes per question. Obviously, some items will require more time and others will require less, but you should remain aware of the overall number of items and amount of testing time. The new GED® Test interface may help you manage your time. It includes an on-screen clock in the upper right corner that provides the remaining time in which to complete a test.

Also, you may monitor your progress by viewing the **Question** line, which will give you the current question number, followed by the total number of questions on that subject-area exam.

> **Answer all questions, regardless of whether you know the answer or are guessing.** There is no benefit in leaving questions unanswered on the GED® Test. Keep in mind the time that you have for each test, and manage it accordingly. If you wish to review a specific item at the end of a test, click **Flag for Review** to mark the question. When you do, the flag will display in yellow. At the end of a test, you may have time to review questions you've marked.

> **Skim and scan.** You may save time by first reading each question and its answer options before reading or studying an accompanying passage or graphic. Once you understand what the question is asking, review the passage or visual for the appropriate information.

> **Note any unfamiliar words in questions.** First attempt to re-read the question by omitting any unfamiliar word. Next, try to use other words around the unfamiliar word to determine its meaning.

> **Narrow answer options by re-reading each question and re-examining the text or graphic that goes with it.** Although four answers are *possible* on multiple-choice items, keep in mind that only one is *correct*. You may be able to eliminate one answer immediately; you may need to take more time or use logic or make assumptions to eliminate others. In some cases, you may need to make your best guess between two options.

> **Go with your instinct when answering questions.** If your first instinct is to choose **A** in response to a question, it's best to stick with that answer unless you determine that it is incorrect. Usually, the first answer someone chooses is the correct one.

Study Skills

You've already made two very smart decisions in studying for your GED® credential and in purchasing *Steck-Vaughn Test Preparation for the 2014 GED® Test: Reasoning Through Language Arts* to help you do so. Following are additional strategies to help you optimize your possibilities for success on the GED® Test.

4 weeks out ...

> **Set a study schedule for the GED® Test.** Choose times in which you are most alert and places, such as a library, that provide the best study environment.

> **Thoroughly review all material in *Steck-Vaughn Test Preparation for the 2014 GED® Test: Reasoning Through Language Arts*.** Use the *Reasoning Through Language Arts* workbook to extend understanding of concepts in the *Reasoning Through Language Arts* student book.

> **Keep a notebook for each subject area that you are studying.** Folders with pockets are useful for storing loose papers.

> **When taking notes, restate thoughts or ideas in your own words rather than copy them directly from a book.** You can phrase these notes as complete sentences, as questions (with answers), or as fragments, provided you understand them.

2 weeks out ...

> **Review your performance on the unit reviews in the student book, noting any troublesome subject areas.** Focus your remaining study around those areas. For additional test practice, you may also wish to take the GED Ready™ practice tests or the *Pretests and Posttests for the Steck-Vaughn Test Preparation for the 2014 GED® Test.*

The days before ...

> **Map out the route to the test center, and visit it a day or two before your scheduled exam.** If you plan to drive to the test center on the day of the test, find out where you will need to park.

> **Get a good night's sleep the night before the GED® Test.** Studies have shown that students with sufficient rest perform better in testing situations.

The day of ...

> **Eat a hearty breakfast high in protein.** As with the rest of your body, your brain needs ample energy to perform well.

> **Arrive 30 minutes early to the testing center.** Arriving early will allow sufficient time in the event of a room change.

> **Pack a sizeable lunch.** A hearty lunch is especially important if you plan to be at the testing center most of the day.

> **Remember to relax.** You've come this far and spent weeks preparing and studying for the GED® Test. Now it's your time to shine!

GED® JOURNEYS

Fran Lebowitz

Fran Lebowitz studied hard to learn how to write and to obtain her GED® certificate.

For Fran Lebowitz, reading was the key to good writing. Lebowitz truly began to hone her craft after she left high school without her diploma. She learned the mechanics of strong story-telling by reading the work of others. As she notes, "Until I was about 7, I thought books were just there, like trees. When I learned that people actually wrote them, I wanted to, too."

Lebowitz ultimately pursued and obtained her GED® certificate and worked a number of odd jobs before landing a position as a columnist at the magazine *Interview*. She also wrote for other magazines, such as *Mademoiselle*, before venturing into books. Her first book, a collection of essays called *Metropolitan Life*, was published in 1978. That effort was followed by *Social Studies* in 1981.

Through those works and others, Lebowitz became known for sharp-witted commentaries on human nature. Reviewers referred to her dry and sarcastic style as "urban cool." However, for more than a decade, Lebowitz suffered from writer's block. During that time, she gave lectures and even guest-starred on television series such as *Law & Order*. In 1994, she returned to writing with the release of her first children's book, *Mr. Chas and Lisa Sue Meet the Pandas*. For Lebowitz, the book was a labor of love. As she says, "To me, nothing can be more important than giving children books."

"Until I was about 7, I thought books were just there, like trees. When I learned that people actually wrote them, I wanted to, too."

CAREER HIGHLIGHTS: *Fran Lebowitz*

- Born October 27, 1950, in Morristown, New Jersey

- Worked as a magazine columnist at *Interview* and wrote for *Mademoiselle*

- Wrote best-selling books that reflect her sharp wit and sarcastic style

- Wrote a children's book called *Mr. Chas and Lisa Sue Meet the Pandas*

Reading Comprehension

Unit 1:
Reading Comprehension

You most likely read something every day: information on a Web site, an e-mail, an employee manual, or a magazine article. Many of the texts you read are nonfiction pieces whose primary purpose is to inform and educate. You may also read fiction, such as novels, short stories, or comic books. These entertain with tales of adventure, romance, and mystery. Regardless of what you read, good reading skills are important to daily life as well as to success in work and in higher education.

The nonfiction and fiction selections that follow are similar to those you will see on the GED® Reasoning Through Language Arts Test. As with other areas of the GED® tests, questions about these works will test your ability to read and interpret passages through the use of various reading skills. In Unit 1, you will practice key skills related to reading both nonfiction and fiction works.

Reading and writing are closely connected. People read what others write, and people write for others to read.

Table of Contents

Determine Main Idea and Details

❶ Learn the Skill

The **main idea** of a passage is the most important point the author wants to make. Paragraphs, too, have main ideas that support the main idea of the passage. The main idea of a paragraph is stated in its topic sentence, which may appear at the beginning, in the middle, or at the end of the paragraph. **Supporting details** provide more information about, or support, the main idea. These details may include facts, explanations, statistics, examples, or descriptions.

Main ideas may be stated directly or implied. When a main idea is implied, think about what the details mean in terms of the paragraph or the passage.

❷ Practice the Skill

By practicing the skill of determining main idea and details, you will improve your study and test-taking abilities, especially as they relate to the GED® Reasoning Through Language Arts Test. Read the passage below. Then answer the question that follows.

LIGHT AND CIRCADIAN RHYTHM

We live in an increasingly 24/7 society, with work, family, and social pressures all chipping away at our sleep. Couple this with long work hours, shift-work, chronic caffeine use and exposure to the glow of computer screens late into the night, and it may be much more than sleep that suffers. We may also be throwing off the body clock, or circadian rhythm, and its control of hundreds of body processes that keep us healthy and feeling well. While much is yet to be learned, there is growing evidence that a misaligned body clock can contribute not only to sleep problems, but also increase risk of developing diabetes, depression, obesity and even some forms of cancer.

For the past 60 years, neuroscientists have been studying the role of light in regulating the body's circadian rhythm. Since the early days of studying sleep in caves and underground laboratories, we've been able to determine that light exposure is the great circadian regulator. Most of us naturally have a body rhythm a little longer than 24 hours—and light is the major environmental time cue that resets the clock in our brains each day so that we remain synchronized with the 24-hour day. In turn, the clock regulates our sleep and wake cycle, our mood, alertness and performance patterns, hormones, heart rate, and many other functions.

From SLEEP RESEARCH IN THE BLIND MAY HELP US ALL by Steven Lockley, Ph.D., © 2012

a By reading the underlined text, you know the main idea is that throwing off the body's circadian rhythm may affect a person's health.

b The topic sentence makes a broad statement about scientific study of the circadian rhythm. The rest of the paragraph supports the topic sentence by providing more information about what scientists have found in their studies of the circadian rhythm.

INSIDE THE ITEMS

Questions may include other words or expressions that ask you to find main ideas or supporting details. For example, you may be asked "What does the author want to say?"

1. Which detail **best** supports the idea that disrupting the body's circadian rhythm can have a negative effect on a person's health?

A. We live in a world in which work, family, and social pressures chip away at our sleep.
B. A misaligned body clock can increase the risk of developing diabetes, depression, obesity, and cancer.
C. Chronic caffeine use interferes with the body's ability to regulate the circadian rhythm.
D. Long work hours and shift-work can disrupt sleep patterns.

DIRECTIONS: Read the passage, read each question, and choose the **best** answer.

BENEFITS OF WIND ENERGY

1   Ancient mariners used sails to capture the wind and explore the world. Farmers once used windmills to grind their grains and pump water. Today, more and more people are using wind turbines to wring electricity from the breeze. Over the past decade, wind turbine use has increased at more than 25 percent a year. Still, it only provides a small fraction of the world's energy.

2   Most wind energy comes from turbines that can be as tall as a 20-story building and have three 200-foot-long (60-meter-long) blades. These contraptions look like giant airplane propellers on a stick. The wind spins the blades, which turn a shaft connected to a generator that produces electricity. Other turbines work the same way, but the turbine is on a vertical axis and the blades look like a giant eggbeater.

3   The biggest wind turbines generate enough electricity to supply about 600 U.S. homes. Wind farms have tens and sometimes hundreds of these turbines lined up together in particularly windy spots, like along a ridge. Smaller turbines erected in a backyard can produce enough electricity for a single home or small business.

4   Wind is a clean source of renewable energy that produces no air or water pollution. And since the wind is free, operational costs are nearly zero once a turbine is erected. Mass production and technology advances are making turbines cheaper, and many governments offer tax incentives to spur wind-energy development.

5   Some people think wind turbines are ugly and complain about the noise the machines make. The slowly rotating blades can also kill birds and bats, but not nearly as many as cars, power lines, and high-rise buildings do. The wind is also variable: If it's not blowing, there's no electricity generated.

6   Nevertheless, the wind energy industry is booming. Globally, generation more than quadrupled between 2000 and 2006. ... Germany has the most installed wind energy capacity, followed by Spain, the United States, India, and Denmark. Development is also fast growing in France and China.

7   Industry experts predict that if this pace of growth continues, by 2050 the answer to one third of the world's electricity needs will be found blowing in the wind.

From the nationalgeographic.com article WIND POWER, © 2013

2. In paragraph 1, the author writes, "wind turbine use has increased at more than 25 percent a year." Which main idea does this detail support?

    A. "Ancient mariners used sails to capture the wind and explore the world."
    B. "Farmers once used windmills to grind their grains and pump water."
    C. "Today, more and more people are using wind turbines to wring electricity from the breeze."
    D. "Still, it only provides a small fraction of the world's energy."

3. The main idea of paragraph 4 is implied. Which sentence **best** states the implied main idea?

    A. Many governments offer tax incentives to spur wind energy.
    B. Wind energy produces no water pollution and no air pollution.
    C. Operational costs of wind energy are low.
    D. Wind energy is environmentally friendly and relatively inexpensive.

4. Which implied main idea do the details in paragraph 5 support?

    A. People complain about the noise from turbines.
    B. Blades should move faster to avoid killing birds and bats.
    C. Wind energy has some negative aspects.
    D. Wind power is becoming more popular.

5. How is the information in paragraph 6 related to the information in paragraph 5?

    A. The word *Nevertheless* in the topic sentence contradicts the details in the previous paragraph.
    B. The details in paragraph 6 support the main idea of paragraphs 5 and 6.
    C. The details in paragraph 6 directly support the topic sentence of paragraph 5.
    D. The word *Nevertheless* in the topic sentence indicates that the details do not support the main idea.

UNIT 1

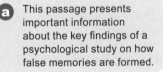

❶ Learn the Skill

When you **summarize**, you restate the main points of the text in your own words. The first step in summarizing is to locate the main ideas. A summary should include all of the main ideas, assertions, or findings, as well as other significant information the author provides. Questions that begin with *who*, *what*, *when*, *where*, *why*, and *how* can help you identify ideas to include.

❷ Practice the Skill

By practicing the skill of summarizing, you will improve your study and test-taking abilities, especially as they relate to the GED® Reasoning Through Language Arts Test. Read the passage below. Then answer the question that follows.

a This passage presents important information about the key findings of a psychological study on how false memories are formed.

b Judgments about the study are provided as quotations by the author of the passage and by an expert on the subject, not by the writer of the summary.

HOW A FALSE MEMORY CAN BE CREATED

Psychological research has shown various ways "false memories" are created, such as through the power of suggestion or through vivid imagination. Now scientists studying imagination have found that people who watched a video of someone else doing a simple action often didn't remember and thought they had done it themselves when asked about it two weeks later.

"This is a completely new type of false memory," says Gerald Echterhoff, a psychology professor at the University of Muenster in Germany and co-author of the paper published in the September issue of the journal *Psychological Science*.

"This is a false memory from just observing someone," he says.

Psychologist Daniel Schacter of Harvard University in Cambridge, Mass., who has edited a book on false memories, says ... it "sounds like an extension of earlier work that has shown imagining you'd done something can result in false memories."

From *USA Today*'s article FALSE MEMORIES: DID YOU LOCK THE DOOR OR JUST IMAGINE IT?, © 2010

TEST-TAKING TIPS

News articles often summarize important events, including studies and new discoveries. As you read a news article, think about what is the key piece of new information. The title can give you clues.

1. Which sentence **best** summarizes the new study's conclusion on false memories?

A. The powers of suggestion and imagination create false memories.
B. Researchers and psychologists have concluded a new study on false memories.
C. Watching a video of someone performing an action can result in a false memory.
D. The study is an extension of earlier work on false memories.

DIRECTIONS: Read the passage, read each question, and choose the **best** answer.

RICHARD NIXON DEFENDS HIMSELF

1   I come before you tonight as a candidate for the Vice Presidency and as a man whose honesty and integrity [have] been questioned.

2   Now, the usual political thing to do when charges are made against you is to either ignore them or to deny them without giving details. I believe we've had enough of that in the United States, particularly with the present Administration in Washington, D.C. To me the office of the Vice Presidency of the United States is a great office, and I feel that the people have got to have confidence in the integrity of the men who run for that office and who might obtain it.

3   I have a theory, too, that the best and only answer to a smear or to an honest misunderstanding of the facts is to tell the truth. And that's why I'm here tonight. I want to tell you my side of the case. I'm sure that you have read the charge, and you've heard it, that I, Senator Nixon, took 18,000 dollars from a group of my supporters. …

4   The question is, was it morally wrong? I say that it was morally wrong—if any of that 18,000 dollars went to Senator Nixon, for my personal use. I say that it was morally wrong if it was secretly given and secretly handled. And I say that it was morally wrong if any of the contributors got special favors for the contributions that they made.

5   And now to answer those questions let me say this: Not one cent of the 18,000 dollars or any other money of that type ever went to me for my personal use. Every penny of it was used to pay for political expenses that I did not think should be charged to the taxpayers of the United States. It was not a secret fund. …

6   Do you think that when I or any other Senator makes a political speech, has it printed, should charge the printing of that speech and the mailing of that speech to the taxpayers? Do you think, for example, when I or any other Senator makes a trip to his home State to make a purely political speech that the cost of that trip should be charged to the taxpayers? Do you think when a Senator makes political broadcasts … that the expense of those broadcasts should be charged to the taxpayers? Well I know what your answer is. It's the same answer that audiences give me whenever I discuss this particular problem: The answer is no. The taxpayers shouldn't be required

to finance items which are not official business but which are primarily political business.

From CHECKERS by Richard Nixon, 1952

2. Which statement **best** summarizes Nixon's reason for making this speech?

    A. He wanted to question the charges made against him.
    B. He wanted to do the "political thing" by ignoring or denying charges.
    C. He wanted to accuse the present administration of wrongdoing.
    D. He wanted to present details about his side of the charges.

3. Which statement **best** summarizes the last sentence in paragraph 2? Nixon believes that

    A. he should be elected Vice President.
    B. people should trust those who hold the important office of Vice President.
    C. he has the integrity and inspires the people's confidence to be Vice President.
    D. the Vice Presidency is an important office.

4. Which statement **best** summarizes Nixon's view about what would make taking the money morally wrong? Taking the money would be wrong if

    A. it were used personally, contributed secretly, or guaranteed special treatment for some.
    B. the taxpayers of the United States had paid the money.
    C. it were used for printing and mailing political speeches or making political broadcasts.
    D. he did not declare the money on his tax returns.

5. Which statement **best** summarizes Nixon's explanation of why he took the money?

    A. He took the money as the result of a misunderstanding among contributors.
    B. He needed the money to cover certain personal expenses.
    C. He knew that nothing was morally wrong in taking the money.
    D. He took the money for political expenses, which taxpayers should not have to cover.

Determine Sequence

READING ASSESSMENT TARGETS: R.3.1, R.5.3

1 Learn the Skill

A passage's **sequence** is the order in which events or steps occur. Following events in chronological, or time, order is important to help you understand the relationships between these events. Following steps in sequence will help you understand a process. For example, if you understand the order of events in a newspaper story, you will be better able to analyze how one event may have led to another. Similarly, if you follow the steps in changing a tire, you will do the job correctly.

If an author does not use dates or numbers, he or she may use signal, or transition, words, such as *first*, *next*, *then*, and *finally*. Signal words may indicate chronological order or a series of steps. Identifying signal words can help you follow or order sequence.

2 Practice the Skill

By practicing the skill of determining sequence and the skill of answering questions that require you to drag and drop words or phrases into a specific location, you will improve your study and test-taking abilities, especially as they relate to the GED® Reasoning Through Language Arts Test. Read the passage below. Then answer the question that follows.

a When the author refers to the *steps* of science, you should expect a sequence to be described. As you read, try numbering the steps in this sequence.

b Notice the signal words, such as **after**, **began**, and **led to**. These can help you determine the sequence of events in the passage.

THE SCIENTIFIC METHOD

What we think of today as the "steps" of science have developed over time, and they may differ according to the type of investigation being conducted. Generally, though, the steps involve making an observation, forming a hypothesis … conducting a test, and making a conclusion.

Scientific investigations usually begin with an observation that points to an interesting question. One famous example of an observation that led to further investigation was made by Scottish biologist Alexander Fleming in the 1920s. After an absence from his lab, he returned and began to clean some glass plates on which he had been growing a certain kind of bacteria. He noticed an odd thing: one of the plates had become contaminated by mold. Curiously, the area around the mold looked free of bacterial growth. His observation indicated that a causal relationship might exist: the mold or a substance produced by the mold might prevent bacterial growth. Fleming's observation led to a series of scientific tests that resulted in new knowledge: Penicillin could be used to treat bacterial infections.

From the historyofvaccines.org article THE SCIENTIFIC METHOD IN VACCINE HISTORY, accessed 2013

TEST-TAKING TECH

When taking the computer-based test, use the electronic highlighting feature. The highlighted sequence words will help you follow the order of steps or events.

1. According to the passage, which step in the scientific method occurs **before** forming a hypothesis?

   A. conducting a test
   B. making an observation
   C. reaching a conclusion
   D. gaining new knowledge

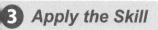

★ Spotlighted Item: **DRAG-AND-DROP**

DIRECTIONS: Read the passage and the question. Then use the drag-and-drop option to complete the chart.

INEQUALITIES IN AMERICA'S SCHOOLS

1   I had begun to teach in 1964 in Boston in a segregated school so crowded and so poor that it could not provide my fourth grade children with a classroom. We shared an auditorium with another fourth grade and the choir and a group that was rehearsing, starting in October, for a Christmas play that, somehow, never was produced. In the spring I was shifted to another fourth grade that had a string of substitutes all year. The 35 children in the class hadn't had a permanent teacher since they entered kindergarten. That year, I was their thirteenth teacher.

2   The results were seen in the first tests I gave. In April, most were reading at the second grade level. Their math ability was at the first grade level.

3   In an effort to resuscitate their interest, I began to read them poetry I liked. They were drawn especially to poems of Robert Frost and Langston Hughes. One of the most embittered children in the class began to cry when she first heard the words of Langston Hughes. ...

4   The next day, I was fired. There was, it turned out, a list of "fourth grade poems" that teachers were obliged to follow but which, like most first-year teachers, I had never seen.

From SAVAGE INEQUALITIES: CHILDREN IN AMERICA'S SCHOOLS by Jonathan Kozol, © 1991

2. Drag and drop the events into the chart to show the order in which they occur in the passage.

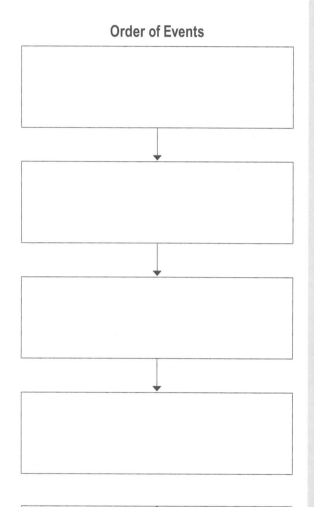

Order of Events

The author reads poetry to his students.	The author is fired.
Rehearsals for the Christmas play begin.	The author is shifted to a different fourth-grade class.

UNIT 1

Categorize

READING ASSESSMENT TARGETS: R.2.1, R.2.3, R.2.5, R.5.1, R.5.2, R.5.4

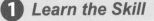

UNIT 1

1 Learn the Skill

Categorizing can help you organize information into groups. You can sort various elements, such as people, events, places, and even texts, into groups according to their similarities or differences. Categories may be broad, such as *Regions of the United States,* or narrower, such as *Foods That Contain Vitamin A and Vitamin B.*

2 Practice the Skill

By practicing the skill of categorizing, you will improve your study and test-taking abilities, especially as they relate to the GED® Reasoning Through Language Arts Test. Read the passage below. Then answer the question that follows.

a The first line refers to data about "who tends to vote." From this statement, you know that you will be categorizing voters.

b In this paragraph, the words **age** and **race** describe categories of voters. These categories predict how likely someone is to vote.

WHO VOTES IN THE UNITED STATES

The Census Bureau ... released data showing who tends to vote in the United States. ...

Some of the results are not surprising: age, sex and education are all reliable indicators of national voter turnout trends, according to the report. And Americans vote more, on average, when a president is on the ballot.

But buried in the report are some revealing tidbits. Minnesotans tend to post among the highest general-election turnouts in the nation (including a whopping 79.2 percent in 2004). Residents of Texas and West Virginia, on the other hand, tend to occupy the lower end of the voter-participation spectrum. In the 1996 presidential election, for example, voter turnout scarcely hovered above 50 percent in both states.

Certain motifs are constant regardless of who is running in a national election. Unsurprisingly, perhaps, age is often a predictor of whether someone will vote; older Americans are most likely to show up to the polls, while voters ages 18 to 29 are the most disengaged. Voter behavior varies by race, too, with white voters most likely to cast their ballots, and Hispanic voters most likely to stay home.

That pattern does not hold in some of the swing states that could help decide the presidential election this year.

From *The New York Times*'s article CENSUS DATA FINDS WHO VOTES, AND WHO DOESN'T by Rebecca Berg, © 2012

USING LOGIC

When reading, you may come across an item or an idea that you think belongs in a category. Clues from the sentence can indicate the correct category.

1. The author places voters ages 18 to 29 in

    A. an age group most likely to vote.
    B. an age group less likely to vote.
    C. a group representing swing states.
    D. a growing segment of the voting population.

DIRECTIONS: Read the passage, read each question, and choose the **best** answer.

A NEW TASTE SENSATION

1   Americans are taught from an early age that there are four basic tastes—sweet, salty, sour and bitter. But what describes the taste of chicken soup?

2   To an increasing number of chefs and food-industry insiders, the answer is "umami," dubbed "the fifth taste." First identified by a Japanese scientist a century ago, umami has long been an obscure culinary concept. Hard to describe, it is usually defined as a meaty, savory, satisfying taste.

3   But now, in the wake of breakthroughs in food science—and amid a burst of competition between ingredient makers to create new food flavorings—umami is going mainstream. … Packaged-food companies such as Nestle, Frito-Lay and Campbell's Soup are trying to ramp up the umami taste in foods like low-sodium soup to make them taste better, while the nation's mushroom farmers are advertising their produce to chefs as an ideal way to get the umami taste.

4   The food industry is embracing umami as part of an effort to deliver highly flavored foods to consumers while also cutting back on fat, salt, sugar and artificial ingredients. At the same time, more consumers are scrutinizing food labels for chemical-sounding words and unhealthy ingredients.

5   To understand the taste of umami, imagine a perfectly dressed Caesar salad, redolent of Parmesan cheese, minced anchovies and Worcestershire sauce; or slurping chicken soup; or biting into a slice of pepperoni-and-mushroom pizza. The savory taste of these foods, and the full, tongue-coating sensation they provide, is umami.

6   While umami is a relatively new concept in this country, it has been well known in parts of Asia for nearly 100 years. It was identified in the early 20th century by Kikunae Ikeda, a Japanese scientist who coined the name umami (pronounced "oo-MA-mee") using the Japanese term for "deliciousness." He found that foods with the umami taste have a high level of glutamate, an amino acid and a building block of protein. Mr. Ikeda developed and patented a method of making monosodium glutamate, or MSG, a processed additive that adds umami taste to food, much as sugar makes things taste sweet.

From *The Wall Street Journal*'s article A NEW TASTE SENSATION by Katy McLaughlin, © 2007

2. Why is umami categorized as the "fifth taste" in this passage?

    A. The Japanese have different categories of taste.
    B. Umami is a new, healthful type of food and needs a new taste category.
    C. The artificially created tastes of umami do not fit the natural taste categories.
    D. Umami does not fit into the four basic taste categories.

3. According to the author, the taste of umami **best** fits within the

    A. salty category.
    B. low-sodium category.
    C. savory category.
    D. chicken soup category.

4. In paragraph 5 the author helps readers understand the taste of umami by

    A. describing tasty foods that fall into the taste category of umami.
    B. naming all possible food combinations that contain the taste of umami.
    C. repeating how delicious umami can taste.
    D. recommending pepperoni-and-mushroom over other kinds of pizza.

5. How does the author categorize foods with the umami taste?

    A. They contain high levels of MSG.
    B. They contain high levels of glutamate.
    C. They are rarely packaged or processed.
    D. They are basic Japanese dishes.

Identify Cause and Effect

READING ASSESSMENT TARGETS: R.2.1, R.2.2, R.2.3, R.3.4, R.5.1, R.5.2, R.5.3

UNIT 1

① Learn the Skill

A traffic accident blocks the road you travel to get to work. You choose to take another route. This is an example of cause and effect in action. A **cause** is an action or situation that makes another event happen. A cause may be stated or implied in a text. An **effect** is something that happens as the result of a cause. In the example above, the traffic accident is the cause, and having to find a new route is the effect. Effects, too, may be stated or implied.

Signal words such as *accordingly, because, consequently, as a result, therefore, so, then,* and *to this end* can help you identify a cause and its effect.

② Practice the Skill

By practicing the skill of identifying cause and effect, you will improve your study and test-taking abilities, especially as they relate to the GED® Reasoning Through Language Arts Test. Read the passage below. Then answer the question that follows.

WARNING ON CLIMATE CHANGE

ⓐ An author often will explain a cause and likely effects. In this passage, the author lists several effects before the cause.

ⓑ A cause may have more than one effect, and a single effect may have more than one cause. The effects listed in the passage are all results of one cause.

As the world gets hotter by degrees, millions of poor people will suffer from hunger, thirst, floods and disease unless drastic action is taken, scientists and diplomats warned Friday in their bleakest report ever on global warming.

All regions of the world will change, with the risk that nearly a third of the Earth's species will vanish if global temperatures rise just 3.6 degrees above the average temperature in the 1980s–90s, the new climate report says. Areas that now have too little rain will become drier.

Yet that grim and still preventable future is a toned-down prediction, a corporate compromise brokered in a fierce, around-the-clock debate among scientists and bureaucrats. Officials from some governments ... managed to win some weakened wording. ...

And while some scientists were angered at losing some ground, many praised the report as the strongest warning ever that nations must cut back on greenhouse gas emissions.

From the Associated Press's article DIRE WARNING ON CLIMATE, © 2007

USING LOGIC

Authors may use cause-and-effect signal words to guide your reading. However, when these words are not present, you can find a cause or an effect by connecting key ideas or details to one another.

1. Which statement **best** explains the connection between greenhouse gas emissions (fourth paragraph) and the information in the first and second paragraphs?

A. Greenhouse gas emissions cause increased rain and flooding.
B. Endangered species would survive if greenhouse gases were reduced.
C. Losing ground does not result from greenhouse gas emissions.
D. Greenhouse gas emissions cause global warming.

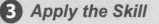

❸ Apply the Skill

DIRECTIONS: Read the passage, read each question, and choose the **best** answer.

EFFECTS OF HIGH-FRUCTOSE CORN SYRUP

1   High-fructose corn syrup is a sweetener used in many processed foods ranging from sodas to baked goods. While the ingredient is cheaper and sweeter than regular sugar, new research suggests that it can also make you fatter.

2   In a small study, Texas researchers showed that the body converts fructose to body fat with "surprising speed," said Elizabeth Parks, associate professor of clinical nutrition at the University of Texas Southwestern Medical Center in Dallas. The study, which appears in The Journal of Nutrition, shows how glucose and fructose, which are forms of sugar, are metabolized differently.

3   In humans, triglycerides, which are a type of fat in the blood, are mostly formed in the liver. Dr. Parks said the liver acts like "a traffic cop" who coordinates how the body uses dietary sugars. When the liver encounters glucose, it decides whether the body needs to store it, burn it for energy or turn it into triglycerides.

4   But when fructose enters the body, it bypasses the process and ends up being quickly converted to body fat. ...

5   The researchers found that lipogenesis, the process by which sugars are turned into body fat, increased significantly when the study subjects drank ... drinks with fructose. When fructose was given at breakfast, the body was more likely to store the fats eaten at lunch.

6   Dr. Parks noted that the study likely underestimates the fat-building effect of fructose because the study subjects were lean and healthy. In overweight people, the effect may be amplified.

7   Although fruit contains fructose, it also contains many beneficial nutrients, so dieters shouldn't eliminate fruit from their diets. But limiting processed foods containing high-fructose corn syrup as well as curbing calories is a good idea, Dr. Parks said.

From *The New York Times*'s article DOES FRUCTOSE MAKE YOU FATTER? by Tara Parker-Pope, © 2008

2. What is the **most** likely reason that high-fructose corn syrup is used in processed foods instead of sugar?

 A. It is sweeter and more nutritious than sugar.
 B. It is cheaper and sweeter than sugar.
 C. It is easier to obtain and has more calories than sugar.
 D. It is a natural sweetener and, therefore, more nutritious than sugar.

3. How did high-fructose corn syrup in drinks affect the bodies of the people in the study group?

 A. Overweight people gained weight.
 B. Lean people gained no weight.
 C. Sugar turned into fat more rapidly when fructose was present.
 D. Sugar was digested with more difficulty than fructose was.

4. What does paragraph 6 explain about the results of the study?

 A. It explains that the study was limited in scope.
 B. It suggests that the results would be the same for a larger group.
 C. It contradicts the findings of previous studies on sweeteners.
 D. It confirms the benefits of eating natural fruits.

5. In paragraph 7, the author notes that fruit contains fructose. How might this information affect a dieter's food plan?

 A. Dieters should eat fruit so that they do not lose important nutrients.
 B. Dieters should eat fruit in small quantities because it contains fructose.
 C. Dieters should eat processed foods instead of fruit because they do not contain fructose.
 D. Dieters should cut calories by eliminating all foods containing fructose.

UNIT 1

Compare and Contrast

READING ASSESSMENT TARGETS: R.2.1, R.2.4, R.3.2, R.3.3, R.3.4, R.5.1, R.5.3

UNIT 1

1 Learn the Skill

Authors often compare and contrast to make or strengthen a point. To **compare** is to look for similarities between at least two things. You might explain how an orange is like an apple—both are fruits, both are round, and both have outer skins. To **contrast,** however, is to look for differences. When contrasting, you might explain that an orange has a tough outer skin, but an apple's outer skin is thin and easier to tear.

Certain words, such as *in addition to* and *likewise*, can help signal similarities. Other signal words, such as *however*, *whereas*, *on the other hand*, and *in contrast*, signal differences. A Venn diagram is useful in showing how two or more objects or ideas are similar and different.

2 Practice the Skill

By practicing the skills of comparing and contrasting, you will improve your study and test-taking abilities, especially as they relate to the GED® Reasoning Through Language Arts Test. Read the passage below. Then answer the question that follows.

METHODS OF OPPOSING GENERALS

a The first paragraph compares Lee and Sherman on the basis of their significance in U.S. history. Later paragraphs contrast the generals by giving examples of actions they took during military advances.

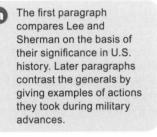

b The passage identifies the generals' differing strategies for winning the war. From this information, you can identify not only differences between the generals but also a goal they shared.

Generals Robert E. Lee and William T. Sherman both secured their places in U.S. history as a result of their efforts during the U.S. Civil War. Lee rose to become general-in-chief of all Confederate armies, and Sherman led Union troops in crucial battles at Shiloh, Chattanooga, Atlanta, and Savannah.

Believing that the means to ultimate success was to defeat Union troops on Northern soil, Lee led his Army of Northern Virginia into Pennsylvania in early June 1863. Lee's aim was to capture the railroad hub at Harrisburg, Pennsylvania, and force Union troops in Virginia to move north to engage him. While marching through the fields of Pennsylvania, Lee forbade his troops from looting the farms or destroying any homes. The Confederate troops used useless Confederate money to pay for the food they took to support their army.

Nearly a year later, in May 1864, Sherman began his march through Georgia to the sea. Unlike Lee, Sherman encouraged his men to take all the food and livestock from the farms they passed. Sherman needed food because he was cut off from Union supplies. He also burned homes and barns. Sherman's aim was to demoralize the South and destroy supplies that could be used to aid the Confederates. He was certain that not only defeating the Confederacy but also obliterating the southerners' will to wage war was vital in preserving the Union after the war's end.

MAKING ASSUMPTIONS

Do not assume that a text only compares or only contrasts. Most details in this passage focus on contrasting the generals. However, the passage provides clues to ways in which the generals were alike as well.

1. What ultimate goal did both generals share?

   A. Both wanted to control new territories.
   B. Both wanted to take food and livestock from farmers.
   C. Each wanted to destroy the fighting spirit of the other side.
   D. Each wanted the war to end with victory for his side.

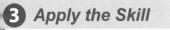

3 *Apply the Skill*

DIRECTIONS: Read the passage, read each question, and choose the **best** answer.

MINNESOTA TWINS STUDY

1   When identical twins are raised apart, you can disentangle nature and nurture for a given characteristic by simply measuring how similar the twins are. You can double-check your answer by comparing the similarity of identical twins (who share all their genes) and of fraternal twins (who share only half their genes).

2   The Minnesota researchers tracked down every pair they could find—and measured traits related to almost every aspect of life: health, cognition, personality, happiness, career, creativity, politics, religion, sex and much more. The Minnesota study reveals genetic effects on virtually every trait. The breakdown between nature, nurture and everything else varies from trait to trait. But Ms. [Nancy] Segal emphasizes the uniformity of the results—the consistent power of genes, the limited influence of parenting.

3   Some findings go down easy: As most would expect, identical twins raised apart have virtually identical heights as adults. Some findings seem obvious after the fact: Genes, but not upbringing, have a pretty big effect on personality traits like ambition, optimism, aggression and traditionalism. Other findings perennially cause outrage: The IQs of separated identical twins are almost as similar as their heights. Critics of intelligence research often hail the importance of practice rather than inborn talent, but a three-day test of the Minnesota twins' motor skills showed that how much you benefit from practice is itself partly an inborn talent.

4   Many of [the study's] findings are bipartisan shockers. Take religion, which almost everyone attributes to "socialization." Separated-twin data show that religiosity has a strong genetic component, especially in the long run: "Parents had less influence than they thought over their children's religious activities and interests as they approached adolescence and adulthood." The key caveat: While genes have a big effect on how religious you are, upbringing has a big effect on the brand of religion you accept. Identical separated sisters Debbie and Sharon "both liked the rituals and formality of religious services and holidays," even though Debbie was a Jew and Sharon was a Christian.

From *The Wall Street Journal*'s article O BROTHER, WHO ART THOU? by Bryan Caplan, © 2012

2. How does comparing identical twins who are raised apart help scientists understand the importance of nature and nurture?

A. Because these twins have the same genes but different upbringing, scientists can determine the extent to which upbringing and genes affect traits.
B. Scientists can determine whether genes affect upbringing.
C. Scientists can compare identical twins raised apart with fraternal twins raised together.
D. Because these twins have the same genes and similar upbringing, scientists can compare the effects of genes and upbringing.

3. In paragraph 2, the author says that the study compared different traits in the twins raised apart. What did researchers find the twins had in common?

A. Genes had the greatest effect on a person's health.
B. The effects of nature and nurture were the same for each trait.
C. Parenting had no effect on traits.
D. Genes had the most effect on traits.

4. In paragraph 3, which contrast do the signal words **but not** make?

A. Genes have a big effect on personality traits, but upbringing does not.
B. Some findings are obvious, but others are obvious only after the fact.
C. Genes have a big effect on ambition but less of an effect on aggression.
D. Some findings are easier to understand than other findings.

5. What was surprising about the comparison of religion in identical twins raised apart?

A. Genes did not have a big effect on how religious the twins were.
B. Upbringing had a big effect on how religious the twins were.
C. Genes had a big effect on how religious the twins were.
D. Genes had an effect on the religions that the twins chose.

UNIT 1

Determine Author's Point of View

READING ASSESSMENT TARGETS: R.2.7, R.4.1/L.4.1, R.4.3/L.4.3, R.6.1

UNIT 1

❶ Learn the Skill

Nonfiction texts are written from different **points of view**—the perspectives and purposes with which an author writes a particular piece. A reader can determine an author's point of view on the basis of clues from the text, such as details that point out what the author likes or dislikes; vocabulary, particularly adjectives and words with strong impact; and the author's interests or background. Also, the magazine, newspaper, or Internet site may reveal something about the author's political or other views.

❷ Practice the Skill

By practicing the skill of determining an author's point of view, you will improve your study and test-taking abilities, especially as they relate to the GED® Reasoning Through Language Arts Test. Read the passage below. Then answer the question that follows.

A MYTH ABOUT FEDERAL EMPLOYEES

a Words that have positive or negative meanings, such as **fair**, may help indicate the author's point of view.

The notion that federal workers consistently earn higher salaries than comparable private-sector workers has become an accepted truth. Conservative think tanks, including the Cato Institute, make much of data that does not offer fair comparisons of similar public-sector and private-sector jobs or account for how experience and education affect pay. A pediatrician with a small practice in Des Moines and a doctor at the National Institutes of Health who is leading a team of 50 researchers trying to cure cancer both provide health care, for example, but we shouldn't expect that they be paid the same.

Though some critics question their accuracy, government analyses show that federal employees make on average 24 percent less than their private-sector counterparts. … In addition, the average private-sector salary in 2010 for a recent college graduate was $48,661. Entry-level federal workers start at $34,075, or $42,209 for candidates with superior academic achievement.

b The byline tells you that this passage comes from a newspaper opinion piece.

From *The Washington Post*'s opinion piece FIVE MYTHS ABOUT FEDERAL WORKERS by Max Stier, © 2010

TEST-TAKING TIPS

Some questions might ask you to consider an author's purpose. The author's **point of view** is often related to his or her purpose for writing. An editorial or opinion piece presents an opinion on a current issue.

1. Which sentence **best** states the author's point of view?

   A. Federal employees need to be paid more for their work.
   B. Government analyses of federal pay are inaccurate.
   C. Federal employees should be paid the same as private-sector employees.
   D. Federal employees are not overpaid compared with private-sector workers.

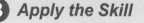
DIRECTIONS: Read the passage, read each question, and choose the **best** answer.

BUDGET FOR NATIONAL PARKS

1   One piece of legislation that deserves a serious push is the National Park Service Centennial Initiative. A brainchild of Dirk Kempthorne, the Interior secretary, the initiative would use the years leading up to the park system's 100th birthday in 2016 to raise $1 billion in private money and match that with $1 billion in federal money—above and beyond normal appropriations—to rejuvenate the national parks.

2   As recent visitors can attest, the parks need all the help they can get. Stingy budget appropriations and decades of deferred maintenance have taken a toll on everything from park roads to day-to-day operations. In his brief tenure, Mr. Kempthorne has done several good things for the parks—including killing a potentially harmful rewrite of the service's management policies that would have promoted inappropriate commercial and recreational activities at the expense of conservation. He wants now to provide a special revenue stream by using the promise of a federal match to entice private donors to help underwrite vital projects.

3   The idea was so appealing that the House Natural Resources Committee approved it by a voice vote. It has languished ever since. …

4   The solution seems ridiculously obvious. The budget office should find the offsets (an increase in park concession fees would do the trick), and the Democratic leadership should schedule a vote. We predict that the verdict would be overwhelmingly positive, and the Senate would follow suit. The parks and their millions of visitors would be the winners, and Congress could show that it can get things done—even in an election year.

From *The New York Times*'s editorial HELP THE PARKS, © 2008

2. What does the use of the word **stingy** (paragraph 2) reveal about the author's point of view about the budget appropriations for the national parks.

   A. The author believes that the appropriations have been unfairly small.
   B. The author believes that the appropriations have been delayed too long.
   C. The author worries that the appropriations will be potentially harmful.
   D. The author worries that the appropriations have been misused.

3. According to the passage, the author of the editorial believes that the legislature should

   A. withhold voting on the park initiative until after the election.
   B. find the money to back the National Park Service Centennial Initiative.
   C. hold another committee meeting and vote again on the issue.
   D. demonstrate the importance of the National Park Service by campaigning for conservation.

4. Which statement **best** expresses the author's overall point of view?

   A. Representatives are doing all they can to help the National Park Service.
   B. The National Park Service Centennial Initiative deserves positive attention.
   C. Management polices of the National Park Service need to be rewritten.
   D. The National Park Service has an above-average budget that should be maintained.

5. According to the passage, with which statement would the author **most** likely agree?

   A. The federal government works quickly to help the programs it oversees.
   B. The Democratic leadership should not vote on the proposed bill.
   C. The National Parks Service needs more support from the federal government.
   D. National parks should rely on visitors to get the funding for upkeep.

UNIT 1

Make Inferences

READING ASSESSMENT TARGETS: R.2.3, R.2.4, R.4.1/L.4.1, R.4.3/L.4.3, R.5.3

UNIT 1

❶ Learn the Skill

When you read, you may find that the author has suggested, or implied, some of the information necessary to understand the piece. When an author does not directly state ideas, you combine what is stated, or explicit, with your prior knowledge to **make an inference**. The facts, suggestions, clues, or language in the passage must support your inferences.

❷ Practice the Skill

By practicing the skill of making inferences, you will improve your study and test-taking abilities, especially as they relate to the GED® Reasoning Through Language Arts Test. Read the passage below. Then answer the question that follows.

THINKING IN THE AGE OF THE INTERNET

a You can figure out what *silicon memory* means. To search the Internet, you use computers, which have silicon chips that store memory.

b The word **but** signals a shift in the author's attitude. The author's main idea follows this transition.

For me, as for others, the Net is becoming a universal medium, the conduit [path] for most of the information that flows through my eyes and ears and into my mind. The advantages of having immediate access to such an incredibly rich store of information are many, and they've been widely described and duly applauded. "The perfect recall of silicon memory," *Wired*'s Clive Thompson has written, "can be an enormous boon [advantage] to thinking." But that boon comes at a price. As the media theorist Marshall McLuhan pointed out in the 1960s, media are not just passive channels of information. They supply the stuff of thought, but they also shape the process of thought. And what the Net seems to be doing is chipping away my capacity for concentration and contemplation. My mind now expects to take in information the way the Net distributes it: in a swiftly moving stream of particles. Once I was a scuba diver in the sea of words. Now I zip along the surface like a guy on a Jet Ski.

From *The Atlantic*'s article IS GOOGLE MAKING US STUPID? by Nicholas Carr, © 2008

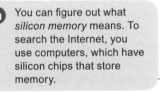

MAKING ASSUMPTIONS

Clues to the author's meaning come in both the passage's title and byline. On the basis of these, you can assume that this passage will explore how the Internet changes ways that people think.

1. Which is the **most** accurate inference to make from the statement "Once I was a scuba diver in the sea of words"?

A. The author took his time to delve deeply and process information.
B. The author moved quickly through vast quantities of words.
C. The author lost sight of how information should be obtained.
D. The author used the Internet to find information about scuba diving.

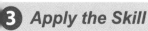

★ Spotlighted Item: **DRAG-AND-DROP**

DIRECTIONS: Read the passage and the question. Then use the drag-and-drop option to complete the web.

COUCH POTATOES

1   Someone has to speak for them, because they have, to a person, lost the power to speak for themselves. I am referring to that great mass of Americans who were once known as the "salt of the earth," then as "the silent majority," more recently as the "viewing public," and now, alas, as "couch potatoes." What drives them—or rather, leaves them sapped and spineless on their reclining chairs? What are they seeking—beyond such obvious goals as a tastefully colorized version of *The Maltese Falcon?*

From SPUDDING OUT by Barbara Ehrenreich, © 1990

2. Drag and drop the three **most** logical inferences from the table into the web.

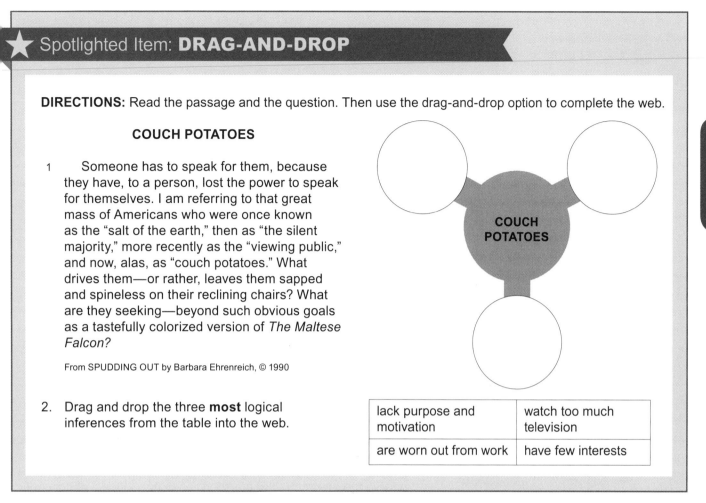

lack purpose and motivation	watch too much television
are worn out from work	have few interests

DIRECTIONS: Read the passage, read each question, and choose the **best** answer.

SPUDDING OUT

1   My husband was the first in the family to "spud out," as the expression now goes. Soon everyone wanted one of those zip-up "Couch Potato Bags" to keep warm in during David Letterman. The youngest, and most thoroughly immobilized, member of the family relies on a remote that controls his TV, stereo, and VCR, and can also shut down the neighbor's pacemaker. ...

2   But we never see the neighbors anymore, nor they us. This saddens me, because Americans used to be a great and restless people, fond of the outdoors in all of its manifestations, from Disney World to miniature golf. Some experts say there are virtues in mass agoraphobia, that it strengthens the family and reduces highway deaths. But I would point out that there are still a few things that cannot be done in the den, especially by someone zipped into a body bag. These include racquetball, voting, and meeting strange people in bars.

From SPUDDING OUT by Barbara Ehrenreich, © 1990

3. What is the **implied** main idea of this passage?

A. It is difficult to understand why people want to watch old movies on television.
B. Too much attention to televised sporting events causes problems.
C. Arguing over television program choices can strain family harmony.
D. Watching too much television can lead to decreased physical activity.

4. Which is the **most** logical inference to make from the information in paragraph 2?

A. People do not go out of their homes as much as they did in the past.
B. Families spend more quality time together.
C. Because families stay at home more, there are fewer car accidents.
D. Strangers now have television-related topics to discuss when meeting for the first time.

Analyze Style and Tone

READING ASSESSMENT TARGETS: R.4.1/L.4.1, R.4.2/L.4.2, R.4.3/L.4.3, R.5.1, R.5.4, R.6.1, R.6.4

1 Learn the Skill

Authors have specific writing **styles**, or ways in which they use words to communicate thoughts or feelings. An author may use short sentences to emphasize certain ideas or long sentences to describe a scene or explain information. A style is often determined by the type of writing, the author's purpose, and the audience. For example, the style of a political speech to supporters may differ from one to opponents.

Style is closely related to an author's **tone**, which shows the author's attitude toward the topic. An author's choice of words creates the tone. An author may use words that have strong connotations, or meanings beyond their dictionary definitions. For example, a *small* room (no connotation) might be called a *cozy* (positive connotation) or a *cramped* (negative connotation) room.

2 Practice the Skill

By practicing the skill of analyzing style and tone, you will improve your study and test-taking abilities, especially as they relate to the GED® Reasoning Through Language Arts Test. Read the passage below. Then answer the question that follows.

THE DEMOCRATIC PARTY

a This author uses repetition as a style to emphasize the points that follow the repeated words.

b The author's tone emphasizes the Democratic Party as one to which people can turn for change.

Throughout–Throughout our history, when people have looked for new ways to solve their problems and to uphold the principles of this nation, many times they have turned to political parties. They have often turned to the Democratic Party. What is it? What is it about the Democratic Party that makes it the instrument the people use when they search for ways to shape their future? Well I believe the answer to that question lies in our concept of governing. Our concept of governing is derived from our view of people. It is a concept deeply rooted in a set of beliefs firmly etched in the national conscience of all of us.

From the DEMOCRATIC NATIONAL CONVENTION KEYNOTE ADDRESS by Barbara Jordan, © 1976

USING LOGIC

When reading a passage, identify the emotions that the words might evoke. You can often determine the tone, or author's attitude, this way. Having an idea of tone helps you understand the text.

1. In which statement does the language **best** reflect the author's attitude toward the Democratic Party?

   A. "Our concept of governing is derived from our view of people."
   B. "They have often turned to the Democratic Party. What is it?"
   C. "Well I believe the answer to that question lies in our concept of governing."
   D. "It is a concept deeply rooted in a set of beliefs firmly etched in the national conscience of all of us."

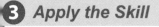

DIRECTIONS: Read the passage, read each question, and choose the **best** answer.

NBA OFFICIATING GOES KINDERGARTEN

1 While the 2013 NBA Playoffs have certainly been entertaining for the thousands of basketball fans across the world, I have found myself constantly turning away from the television during many a game.

2 Don't get me wrong; I have loved watching the Golden State Warriors and Denver Nuggets race up and down the court and share the ball. I love how evenly matched and physical the Los Angeles Clippers and Memphis Grizzlies are. And, I truly enjoyed watching the Miami Heat and San Antonio Spurs dismantle the Milwaukee Bucks and Los Angeles Lakers, respectively.

3 But, every double foul, ridiculous flagrant and soft technical that these officials call makes me sick to my stomach. This isn't playoff basketball, it's kindergarten basketball.

4 The National Basketball Association is not a league where everyone deserves equal opportunity and fairness. One guy in a team's locker room can make $16 million and have a locker next to a guy who makes $85,000. But, the new NBA officiating rules have been created in order to forge a game where everyone can be safe, where a 6-3 shooter can fearlessly drive at a 7-1 behemoth because he knows he'll be protected by the refs.

5 It's bogus. …

6 When you look at documentaries that show basketball from the '70s, '80s and '90s, the game has completely changed. The playoff series between the Knicks and Reggie Miller's Pacers could never happen in today's league. Larry Bird and Dr. J could never have gotten into fights in today's league. Guys like the bad boy Pistons, Bill Laimbeer, Kurt Rambis and Kevin McHale could never exist in today's league. And, it's a shame. …

7 I will continue to watch the NBA playoffs and be invested in who is crowned the next world champion, but I will also continue to be peeved at this fake brand of officiating.

From huffingtonpost.com's article NBA OFFICIATING HAS GONE KINDERGARTEN by Jake Fischer, © 2013

2. In the first sentence of paragraph 3, the author uses the phrase **sick to my stomach**. How would the tone of this sentence change if he had used the word **upset** instead the phrase?

A. The tone would be less upbeat.
B. The tone would be more threatening.
C. The critical tone would be softened.
D. The harsh tone would become sarcastic.

3. What does the author's word choice in paragraph 3 reveal about his purpose?

A. He exaggerates his feelings to emphasize his attitude toward playoff officials.
B   He uses jargon to show his familiarity with the sport.
C. He mentions "kindergarten basketball" to appeal to elementary school coaches.
D. He writes in a detached, academic style that indicates research and knowledge.

4. Paragraph 5 consists of two words: **It's bogus.** Which statement **best** explains the impact of this short paragraph?

A. The short paragraph prevents it from having a strong impact on the passage.
B. The short paragraph and the word *bogus* emphasize the author's dislike of NBA officiating.
C. The word *bogus* emphasizes the author's frustration with unequal pay for NBA players.
D. The short paragraph and the word *bogus* subdue the angry tone of the passage.

5. On the basis of the author's word choice in paragraph 6, which statement **best** describes his attitude toward NBA basketball during previous decades?

A. He appreciates the playing style but thinks that the players took advantage of lax officiating.
B. He respects the players and playing style but understands why the game had to change.
C. He is ashamed of the players and the playing style.
D. He admires the players and idealizes the playing style.

Draw Conclusions

READING ASSESSMENT TARGETS: R.2.1, R.2.5, R.2.8, R.3.4, R.5.2, R.5.4

1 Learn the Skill

Drawing conclusions is similar to making inferences. As you know, an inference is an educated guess based on facts or evidence and on your own prior knowledge. By combining several inferences to make a judgment, you **draw conclusions**. Determining a cause and its effect, categorizing, and comparing and contrasting also can help you draw conclusions.

2 Practice the Skill

By practicing the skill of drawing conclusions, you will improve your study and test-taking abilities, especially as they relate to the GED® Reasoning Through Language Arts Test. Read the passage below. Then answer the question that follows.

a The text points out that Americans pay three kinds of taxes. Finding explanations for facts within the text can help you draw conclusions.

b The last paragraph presents facts about the price of oil rather than gas taxes. So this paragraph supports a conclusion that is different from the conclusion in the first paragraph.

GASOLINE TAXES AND PRICES

Americans pay, on average, 49 cents per gallon in gasoline taxes, according to the Lundberg Survey released last week. That includes federal, state and local charges.

Canadians pay more than double that amount, $1.26 per gallon. And up it goes, with the Dutch among the most taxed: They are paying $5.57 per gallon this month, according to the survey, for a total pump price of $10.05 per gallon.

Gas taxes are used to encourage conservation, to finance roads and transit, and to fill other government coffers. Higher rates tend to insulate drivers from price spikes. On a percentage basis, Europeans have had to absorb far smaller increases in gas costs than Americans in recent years. They're used to paying double what Americans do—or more—and they live accordingly.

On Friday, the price of oil traded above $142, a new record, suggesting that more increases at the pump are coming.

From *The New York Times*'s article SAVORING BARGAINS AT THE AMERICAN PUMP by Bill Marsh, © 2008.

TEST-TAKING TIPS

Working backward is often helpful. Look at what the question asks. Change the wording to a fill-in-the-blank statement: "_____ can be concluded." Then find the most logical choice.

1. What is the **most** logical conclusion to draw on the basis of the last paragraph?

   A. When oil prices rise, gas prices increase.
   B. When oil prices rise, gas prices decrease.
   C. The price of oil will continue to rise this year.
   D. The price of gas will continue to rise this year.

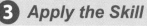

DIRECTIONS: Read the passage, read each question, and choose the **best** answer.

SEPARATE CLASSROOMS FOR BOYS AND GIRLS

1   If schools shortchange girls, why is it surprising when the tests show that they're doing less well? It isn't just the P.S.A.T.'s, where 18,000 boys generally reach the top categories and only 8,000 girls do. While the gap has narrowed, boys also outscore girls on 11 of the 14 College Board Achievement tests, and on the A.C.T. exams and on the S.A.T.'s. It is possible to jimmy selection standards to make sure girls win more scholarships, but equal results don't count for much if those results are forced. Instead of declaring equality, society should be advancing it. The challenge isn't to get more scholarships for baton twirlers but to get more baton twirlers to take up advanced mathematics.

2   One place that happens is in girls' schools and women's colleges. Sometimes separate isn't equal; it's better. Changing the way teachers teach in coed schools, changing the textbooks to make sure they talk about women as well as men, educating parents about raising daughters—all of these things make sense, since most girls will be educated in coed classrooms. But we've been talking about them for a decade, and the problems of gender bias stubbornly persist. In the meantime, for many girls, single-sex education is working. ...

3   The evidence, though scant, is promising. In Ventura, Calif., the public high school has begun offering an all-girls Algebra II course. The girls, one teacher says, think so little of their ability that the teacher spends her time not only teaching math but also building self-confidence, repeatedly telling the girls that they're smart and that they can do it.

From FOR GIRLS' SCHOOLS AND WOMEN'S COLLEGES, SEPARATE IS BETTER by Susan Estrich, © 1994

2.   Which is the **most** logical conclusion to draw from paragraph 3?

A. Separate classrooms have little impact on education.
B. Teachers spend too much time enhancing girls' self-esteem.
C. The evidence shown from the few schools that have offered all-girls' classes is promising.
D. Girls have less self-confidence when entering a coed math or science class after taking an all-girls' class.

3.   How are paragraph 2 and paragraph 3 connected?

A. Paragraph 3 summarizes the information in paragraph 2.
B. Paragraph 3 provides an example of the conclusion based on paragraph 2.
C. Paragraph 3 draws a conclusion about the main reason, stated in paragraph 2, for implementing all-girls' classrooms.
D. Paragraph 3 explains the focus on self-confidence, mentioned in paragraph 2.

4.   According to this passage, which conclusion **best** reflects the author's viewpoint?

A. Math and science are more important for girls than they are for boys.
B. Girls may do better in math and science if they learn in all-girl classrooms.
C. Girls deserve to win more scholarships based on standardized test scores.
D. Girls perform as well as or better than boys on standardized tests in math and science.

5.   What evidence from the passage **best** supports the author's conclusion about separate classrooms?

A. " ... for many girls, single-sex education is working ..."
B. " ... the teacher spends her time not only teaching math but also building self-confidence ... "
C. " ... equal rights don't count for much if those results are forced."
D. " ... changing the textbooks to make sure they talk about women as well as men, educating parents about raising daughters—all of these things make sense ... "

Make Generalizations

READING ASSESSMENT TARGETS: R.2.1, R. 2.7, R.2.8, R.4.3/L.4.3

UNIT 1

1 Learn the Skill

A **generalization** is a broad statement that applies to a group of people, places, or events. Authors often use generalizations to make a point about a group. A generalization may take the form of a hypothesis, a tentative explanation of an idea or observation that is based on facts or details. A generalization without sufficient evidence or support is often a stereotype. Understanding generalizations can help you determine an author's purpose in writing. Making them yourself can help you broaden ideas.

2 Practice the Skill

By practicing the skill of making generalizations, you will improve your study and text-taking abilities, especially as they relate to the GED® Reasoning Through Language Arts Test. Read the passage below. Then answer the question that follows.

MOVING BACK HOME

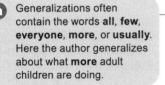

a Generalizations often contain the words **all**, **few**, **everyone**, **more**, or **usually**. Here the author generalizes about what **more** adult children are doing.

b The second paragraph contains a hypothesis about people in their 20s.

<u>A recent survey shows that more adult children are returning home to live with their parents</u>. This pattern has emerged in the past (almost always associated with economic downturns) and this time is no different. As the economy struggles, it becomes more difficult for young people to gain their independence.

Psychologist Jeffrey Arnett suggests that there is a new age classification, emerging adults, which bridges the gap between adolescence and adulthood. According to his theory, people in their 20s go through a time of development that's distinct from other stages of adulthood, and this developmental period explains some of the reluctance of adult children to leave the nest for good.

If this theory is true, though, why should the number of "boomerang" children increase during times of economic hardship? It seems more likely that young people are experiencing failure to launch because of the financial difficulties of living alone during a recession. It's certainly not an easy task. With fewer jobs to choose from and more competition to fill those slots, high school and college graduates have a harder time finding meaningful employment. …

From *Forbes*'s article FAILURE TO LAUNCH: ADULT CHILDREN MOVING BACK HOME by Alan Dunn, © 2012

MAKING ASSUMPTIONS

Do not assume that an author's generalizations are always true. Some may be valid, but others may not be. A valid generalization must be supported by facts and details.

1. What generalization does the author make about "boomerang" children? The author says that

A. they lack the motivation to accept adult responsibilities.
B. the number of children living at home decreases during a recession.
C. the reason for the increase in adult children living at home is a reluctance to leave the nest.
D. more adult children return home to live with their parents when the economy is bad.

DIRECTIONS: Read the passage, read each question, and choose the **best** answer.

FOOD DESERTS

1   This is the real world of eating and nutrition in the rural United States. Forget plucking an apple from a tree, or an egg from under a chicken. "The stereotype is everyone in rural America lives on a farm, which is far from the truth," says Jim Weill, president of the nonprofit Food Research and Action Center (FRAC). New research from the University of South Carolina's Arnold School of Public Health shows just how unhealthy the country life can be. The study, which examined food-shopping options in Orangeburg County (1,106 square miles, population 91,500), found a dearth [lack] of supermarkets and grocery stores. Of the 77 stores that sold food in Orangeburg County in 2004, when the study was done, 57—nearly 75 percent—were convenience stores. Grocery stores, which stock far more fruits and vegetables than convenience stores, are often too far away, says University of South Carolina epidemiologist Angela Liese, lead author of the study, which appeared in last month's Journal of the American Dietetic Association. "Oftentimes a nutritionist will just say, 'Buy more fruits and vegetables,' when, in fact, the buying part is not simple."

2   Like other rural areas (and some inner-city ones), Orangeburg County is an isolated "food desert." "You are pretty much at the mercy of what's in your neighborhood," says Adam Drewnowski, director of the center for obesity research at the University of Washington. Although only 28 percent of all the stores in Orangeburg County carried any of the fruits and vegetables—apples, cucumbers, oranges, tomatoes—that were part of the survey, Liese and her colleagues found plenty of healthy foods in the county's 20 supermarkets and grocery stores. The situation in the convenience stores was decidedly grimmer.

From *Newsweek*'s article JUNK FOOD COUNTY by Karen Springen, © 2007

2. Which generalization about rural America does the author claim is an untrue stereotype?

    A. Rural America has more places to buy food than urban areas have.
    B. All people living in rural America live on farms.
    C. People on farms have apple trees.
    D. People living in rural America are poor.

3. Which generalization does the author make about supermarkets and grocery stores?

    A. They stock more fruits and vegetables than convenience stores do.
    B. They are more common in rural areas of the United States than elsewhere.
    C. Rural supermarkets and grocery stores stock fewer fruits and vegetables than urban stores do.
    D. They are similar to convenience stores in rural areas of the United States.

4. Which fact does the author use to support the generalization that rural areas like Orangeburg County are **food deserts**?

    A. People are limited to the foods and stores available in their neighborhoods.
    B. People's food choices are limited to what they can grow.
    C. People often have to travel great distances to buy any kind of food.
    D. People cannot find food of any kind in their neighborhoods.

5. On the basis of this passage, which is the **most** logical hypothesis to make about food stores in **suburban** areas?

    A. Suburban supermarkets generally stock healthier food than rural supermarkets do.
    B. Convenience stores are less likely to sell food because there are more neighborhood grocery stores.
    C. There are more convenience stores in suburban areas than in rural areas.
    D. Suburban areas have more food stores that stock fruits and vegetables than rural areas have.

Synthesize Information

UNIT 1

1 Learn the Skill

As you learned in Lessons 10 and 11, you can draw conclusions and make generalizations by combining inferences. Combining, or **synthesizing**, information from one source or multiple sources may lead you to an entirely new idea that goes beyond the text and that you can apply to other situations.

2 Practice the Skill

By practicing the skill of synthesizing information, you will improve your study and test-taking abilities, especially as they relate to the GED® Reasoning Through Language Arts Test. Read the passages below. Then answer the question that follows.

FEDERAL WORKERS CAN BE FIRED

In the 2009 fiscal year, 11,275 federal employees were fired for poor performance or misconduct. In addition, a survey of federal managers by the U.S. Merit Systems Protection Board suggests that besides those who are formally terminated, there are a sizable number of employees who voluntarily leave after they are counseled that their performance is unacceptable.

Still, the myth persists that incompetent federal workers cannot be fired.

From *The Washington Post* opinion piece FIVE MYTHS ABOUT FEDERAL WORKERS by Max Stier, © 2010

a The author draws a conclusion about the firing of federal workers. This conclusion helps you understand the author's point of view about federal workers.

GOVERNMENT IS NOT GROWING

Not including the U.S. Postal Service, the federal government employs 2.1 million people. The workforce is now slightly smaller than it was in 1967, at the height of Lyndon Johnson's Great Society, and today there are 100 million more Americans to serve. ...

In the 1990s, Bill Clinton reduced the workforce by nearly 350,000 to 1.8 million. Under George W. Bush, the federal workforce grew predominantly because of post-9/11 homeland security demands and the wars in Iraq and Afghanistan.

From *The Washington Post* opinion piece FIVE MYTHS ABOUT FEDERAL WORKERS by Max Stier, © 2010

b On the basis of the facts and details in this passage, you can make a generalization about the size of the federal government. This generalization can help you understand the author's point of view about whether the government is too large.

MAKING ASSUMPTIONS

When you determine the author's point of view, you can make reasonable assumptions about what the author might think about a subject, even if these thoughts are not stated directly.

1. On the basis of these passages, with which statement would the author **most** likely agree?

   A. The federal government has grown because it is too hard to fire federal workers.
   B. The federal government has grown too large and inefficient to continue as it is.
   C. Firing federal workers is not necessarily the best way to balance the budget.
   D. Federal workers should be fired to help balance the national budget.

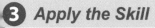

Spotlighted Item: DRAG-AND-DROP

DIRECTIONS: Read the passages and the question. Then use the drag-and-drop option to complete the chart.

RENEWABLE ENERGY IN THE UNITED STATES

1   Unlike fossil fuels, which are exhaustible, renewable energy sources regenerate and can be sustained indefinitely. …

2   In 2012, consumption of renewable sources in the United States totaled … about 9% of all energy used nationally. About 12% of U.S. electricity was generated from renewable sources in 2012. …

3   The use of renewable fuels is expected to continue to grow over the next 30 years, although the Energy Information Administration projects that we will still rely on non-renewable fuels to meet most of our needs.

From the eia.gov article RENEWABLE ENERGY EXPLAINED, accessed 2013

HYDROPOWER

1   Hydropower accounted for about 7% of total U.S. electricity generation and 56% of generation from all renewables in 2012. …

2   Conventional hydroelectric generators … [are] among the oldest of the nation's power plants. … The vast majority … were built before 1980 and recent changes to hydroelectric capacity have been small.

From the eia.gov article HYDROPOWER EXPLAINED AND ENERGY IN BRIEF: WHAT IS THE ROLE OF HYDROELECTRIC POWER IN THE UNITED STATES?, accessed 2013

DO NEW IDEAS SOLVE OLD PROBLEMS?

1   Hydropower, which often involves the use of dams, is a clean, renewable energy source that can be used to produce electricity at about one-third the cost of that produced by fossil fuel or nuclear power plants. Of the 80,000 or so dams in the United States, only a small percentage are hydroelectric dams. Most are non-powered; they are used for flood control or storage of water for drinking and irrigation.

2   Although they have advantages, hydropower plants also have drawbacks that make them unwelcome in many places. Dams block sediment, stopping it from washing over floodplains downstream and depriving farmland of nutrients. Dams affect aquatic ecosystems by changing the depth and temperature in rivers below them. The huge lakes that form behind dams can eliminate beautiful scenery and force people from their homes.

3   Still, engineers hope to expand hydropower. Solutions include adding hydropower plants to existing non-powered dams and increasing capacity at existing hydroelectric dams. A recent study states that expansion of hydropower facilities could result in a 15 percent increase in energy produced by hydropower.

2.   Drag and drop the accurate statements about hydropower into the chart.

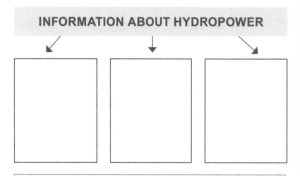

INFORMATION ABOUT HYDROPOWER

Although the use of renewable energy sources is expected to increase, such energy sources have drawbacks and detractors.

Hydropower is an energy source that cannot be sustained indefinitely.

The lack of significant growth in hydropower may be reversed.

More than half of the electricity generated in the United States from renewable energy sources comes from hydropower.

Use Context Clues

READING ASSESSMENT TARGET: R.4.1/L.4.1

1 Learn the Skill

Context clues can help you figure out the meanings of unfamiliar words as you read. *Context* refers to the text that surrounds a word. Context clues, therefore, are hints in the surrounding text. These hints may be synonyms or restatements of the word; they may be details that define the word or explain how it is used. In addition to clues, writers often use words that have **connotations**, or meanings that go beyond their definitions. Connotations may be positive or negative. For example, the word *assertive* has positive connotations, but the word *aggressive* which has a similar meaning, has negative ones.

Combining context clues with your prior knowledge of vocabulary can help you determine the meaning of a word or phrase and thus help you grasp the overall idea of a passage.

2 Practice the Skill

By practicing the skill of using context clues and the skill of answering questions that require you to fill in the blank, you will improve your study and test-taking abilities, especially as they relate to the GED® Reasoning Through Language Arts Test. Read the passage below. Then answer the question that follows.

SIMON WHEELER'S STORY

a The second sentence provides context clues for the word **monotonous** by describing the way in which Simon Wheeler tells his story. He never smiles, frowns, or changes his voice.

... Simon Wheeler backed me into a corner and blockaded me there with his chair, and then sat me down and reeled off the <u>monotonous narrative</u> which follows this paragraph. He <u>never smiled, he never frowned, he never changed his voice from the gentle-flowing key to which he tuned the initial sentence, he never betrayed the slightest suspicion of enthusiasm</u>; but all through the interminable narrative there ran a vein of impressive earnestness and sincerity, which showed me plainly that, so far from his imagining there was any thing ridiculous or funny about his story, he regarded it as a really important matter, and admired its two heroes as men of transcendent genius in finesse. To me the spectacle of a man drifting serenely along through such a <u>queer yarn without ever smiling</u>, was exquisitely absurd.

b The words **without ever smiling** at the end of the paragraph emphasize that Simon Wheeler tells his story without emotion or emphasis.

From THE CELEBRATED JUMPING FROG OF CALAVERAS COUNTY by Mark Twain, © 1867

USING LOGIC

Prior knowledge, in addition to context clues, may help you here. Knowing that the prefix *mono-* means "one" or "single" can lead you to the meaning of **monotonous** and the best answer choice.

1. The narrator says that Simon Wheeler "reeled off the monotonous narrative." The connotations of the terms **reeled off** instead of the neutral word *told*, and **monotonous** instead of the neutral word *steady* suggest that the story will

A. contain many details and be told with much drama.
B. express deep and sincere emotions.
C. be told in a boring and expressionless way.
D. often stray from the main topic.

⭐ Spotlighted Item: **FILL-IN-THE-BLANK**

DIRECTIONS: Read the passage. Then fill in your answers in the boxes below.

HOW BARRY'S FORD GOT ITS NAME

The hamlet of Barry's Ford is situated in a sort of high valley among the mountains. Below it the hills lie in moveless curves like a petrified ocean; above it they rise in green-cresting waves which never break. It is *Barry's* Ford because at one time the Barry family was the most important in the place; and *Ford* because just at the beginning of the hamlet the little turbulent Barry River is fordable. There is, however, now a rude bridge across the river.

From OLD WOMAN MAGOUN by Mary E. Wilkins Freeman, © 1891

2. According to the clues in the passage, a **hamlet** is a [   ].

3. The narrator uses the word **fordable** to describe part of the Barry River. **Fordable** means that the

   river [   ] crossed.

DIRECTIONS: Read the passage. Then fill in your answers in the boxes below.

A BOY'S TRAIN RIDE

I held a florin tightly in my hand as I strode down Buckingham Street towards the station. The sight of the streets thronged with buyers … recalled to me the purpose of my journey. I took my seat in a third-class carriage of a deserted train. After an intolerable delay the train moved out of the station slowly. It crept onward among ruinous houses and over the twinkling river. At Westland Row Station a crowd of people pressed to the carriage doors; but the porters moved them back, saying that it was a special train for the bazaar. I remained alone in the bare carriage. In a few minutes the train drew up beside an improvised wooden platform. I passed out on to the road and saw by the lighted dial of a clock that it was ten minutes to ten.

From ARABY by James Joyce, © 1914

4. The narrator describes the train carriage as **deserted**. What might you find in a **deserted** room?

   [   ]

5. When the narrator says that he "passed out on to the road," he means that he

   [   ] on to the road.

Identify Cause and Effect in Fiction

READING ASSESSMENT TARGETS: R.2.1, R.2.2, R.3.2, R.3.3, R.3.4, R.5.3

UNIT 1

1 Learn the Skill

In Lesson 5, you learned about **cause and effect** in nonfiction writing. In fiction writing, too, authors use cause-and-effect relationships to develop their stories. A **cause** is an element, such as an action, an event, or a situation that makes something happen. An **effect** is what happens as a result of that cause. What one character does in one part of the story can affect the same character or another character in another part of the story. A cause can have more than one effect and an effect more than one cause.

Effects can be both positive and negative. The outcome of stories often depends on whether causes lead to effects that are planned or unplanned.

2 Practice the Skill

By practicing the skill of identifying cause and effect in fiction, you will improve your study and test-taking abilities, especially as they relate to the GED® Reasoning Through Language Arts Test. Read the passage below. Then answer the question that follows.

THE STRANGE HOUSE

a Causes and effects have connections. "Some legal trouble" caused the house to be empty for years.

b The words **so** and **therefore** often signal an effect. Here, **so** means "therefore" and signals that the narrator's action is an effect.

So I will let it alone and talk about the house. …
<u>There was some legal trouble, I believe, something about the heirs and co-heirs; anyhow, the place has been empty for years</u>.

That spoils my ghostliness, I am afraid, but I don't care—there is something strange about the house—I can feel it.

I even said so to John one moonlight evening, but he said what I felt was a draught [draft], and shut the window.

I get unreasonable angry with John sometimes. I'm sure I never used to be so sensitive. I think it is due to this nervous condition.

But John says if I feel so, I shall neglect proper self-control; <u>so</u> I take pains to control myself—before him, at least, and that makes me very tired.

I don't like our room a bit. I wanted one downstairs that opened on the piazza and had roses all over the window, and such pretty old-fashioned chintz hangings! But John would not hear of it.

From THE YELLOW WALLPAPER by Charlotte Perkins Gilman, © 1892

USING LOGIC

Use logic to determine whether a particular cause could have led to an event. Ask yourself, "Why did this happen?" Note, too, that cause-and-effect questions often begin with the word **why**.

1. Why does John shut the window?

   A. The narrator feels a chill from the open window.
   B. The narrator says the house is strange and spooky.
   C. John has a nervous condition and is sensitive to cold.
   D. John does not want to see the moonlight.

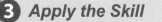

DIRECTIONS: Read the passage, read each question, and choose the **best** answer.

FROM NEBRASKA TO BOSTON

1   I RECEIVED one morning a letter, written in pale ink, on glassy, blue-lined note-paper, and bearing the postmark of a little Nebraska village. This communication, worn and rubbed, looking as though it had been carried for some days in a coat-pocket that was none too clean, was from my Uncle Howard. It informed me that his wife had been left a small legacy by a bachelor relative who had recently died, and that it had become necessary for her to come to Boston to attend to the settling of the estate. He requested me to meet her at the station, and render her whatever services might prove necessary. On examining the date indicated as that of her arrival, I found it no later than to-morrow. He had characteristically delayed writing until, had I been away from home for a day, I must have missed the good woman altogether.

2   The name of my Aunt Georgiana called up not alone her own figure, at once pathetic and grotesque, but opened before my feet a gulf of recollections so wide and deep that, as the letter dropped from my hand, I felt suddenly a stranger to all the present conditions of my existence, wholly ill at ease and out of place amid the surroundings of my study. I became, in short, the gangling farmer-boy my aunt had known, scourged with chilblains and bashfulness, my hands cracked and raw from the corn husking. I felt the knuckles of my thumb tentatively, as though they were raw again. I sat again before her parlor organ, thumbing the scales with my stiff, red hands, while she beside me made canvas mittens for the huskers.

3   The next morning, after preparing my landlady somewhat, I set out for the station. When the train arrived I had some difficulty in finding my aunt. She was the last of the passengers to alight, and when I got her into the carriage she looked not unlike one of those charred, smoked bodies that firemen lift from the débris of a burned building. She had come all the way in a day coach; her linen duster had become black with soot and her black bonnet gray with dust during the journey. When we arrived at my boarding-house the landlady put her to bed at once, and I did not see her again until the next morning.

From A WAGNER MATINEE by Willa Cather, © 1904

2. The narrator's aunt must go to Boston to

    A. visit her nephew.
    B. settle a relative's estate.
    C. get away from her husband.
    D. attend a funeral.

3. Why does the letter from the narrator's uncle arrive so late?

    A. The carrier does not deliver the letter promptly.
    B. The narrator's uncle sent the letter at the last moment.
    C. The narrator's aunt and uncle had little time to prepare for an unexpected trip.
    D. The narrator's uncle had to attend to problems relating to a legacy.

4. How does the thought of Aunt Georgiana affect the narrator?

    A. The narrator fondly remembers his childhood interactions with his aunt.
    B. The narrator resents his uncle for asking him to help his aunt.
    C. The narrator recalls the awkwardness and discomfort of his childhood.
    D. The narrator feels excited to reconnect with his aunt.

5. As a result of her journey in the day coach, Aunt Georgiana

    A. is covered with soot and dust.
    B. arrives in Boston sooner than expected.
    C. is the last passenger to step off the train.
    D. hides from her nephew and his landlady.

6. What is the **most** likely reason Aunt Georgiana goes to bed immediately?

    A. She feels uncomfortable around her nephew.
    B. She is embarrassed about her appearance.
    C. She could not sleep on the train.
    D. She is exhausted from her long journey.

Compare and Contrast in Fiction

READING ASSESSMENT TARGETS: R.2.1, R.2.5, R.2.7, R.3.3, R.3.4, R.4.3/L.4.3, R.5.1, R.5.3

UNIT 1

1 Learn the Skill

Authors use **comparisons** and **contrasts** to describe the people, places, or conflicts in their stories. When authors make comparisons, they show the similarities between two or more elements. When they show contrast, they emphasize the differences. Comparing and contrasting can help you sort out and analyze information. You can group details, events, or people by their similarities and differences.

As you learned in Lesson 6, signal words such as *likewise*, *in the same way*, *similarly*, *like*, and *in like manner* indicate similarities. Signal words such as *on the other hand*, *however*, *whereas*, *unlike*, and *but* indicate differences.

2 Practice the Skill

By practicing the skill of comparing and contrasting in fiction, you will improve your study and test-taking abilities, especially as they relate to the GED® Reasoning Through Language Arts Test. Read the passage below. Then answer the question that follows.

EMILY AND SUSAN

a The narrator contrasts two sisters, Susan and Emily. The narrator first describes Susan and then says that Emily is not the same at all.

Oh there are conflicts between the others too, each one human, needing, demanding, hurting, taking—but only between Emily and Susan, no, Emily toward Susan that corroding resentment. It seems so obvious on the surface, yet it is not obvious. Susan, the second child, Susan, golden- and curly-haired and chubby, quick and articulate and assured, everything in appearance and manner Emily was not; Susan, not able to resist Emily's precious things, losing or sometimes clumsily breaking them; Susan telling jokes and riddles to company for applause while Emily sat silent (to say to me later: that was my riddle, Mother, I told it to Susan); Susan, who for all the five years' difference in age was just a year behind Emily in developing physically.

b The narrator continues to emphasize the differences between Susan and Emily, explaining that Susan is outgoing and amuses her audiences whereas Emily is quiet.

I am glad for that slow physical development that widened the difference between her and her contemporaries, though she suffered over it. She was too vulnerable for that terrible world of youthful competition, of preening and parading, of constant measuring of yourself against every other, of envy. ...

From I STAND HERE IRONING by Tillie Olsen, © 1961

TEST-TAKING TIPS

A Venn diagram is a useful tool for organizing comparison and contrast. A comparison of Emily and Susan might look like this:

Emily — Both — Susan

1. Which statement describes one way in which Emily and Susan are different?

   A. Susan is clumsy and ill at ease in company, but Emily is not.
   B. Susan finds more riddles than Emily does.
   C. Emily enjoys sharing her possessions, but Susan does not.
   D. Emily is slower to develop physically than Susan is.

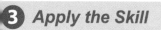

⭐ Spotlighted Item: **FILL-IN-THE-BLANK**

DIRECTIONS: Read the passage. Then fill in your answers in the boxes below.

A DIFFERENCE IN MUSICAL TASTES

1   No one will believe that I like country music. Even my wife scoffs when told such a possibility exists. "Go on!" Gloria tells me. "I can see blues, bebop, maybe even a little buckdancing. But not bluegrass." Gloria says, "Hillbilly stuff is not just music. It's like the New York Stock Exchange. The minute you see a sharp rise in it, you better watch out."

From WHY I LIKE COUNTRY MUSIC by James Alan McPherson, © 1972

2. How do the musical tastes of Gloria and her husband contrast? Only her husband likes

    [   ].

3. Gloria compares "hillbilly" music with the New York Stock Exchange. She implies that after a sharp rise in the stock market, what comes next is a

    [   ].

DIRECTIONS: Read the passage, read each question, and choose the **best** answer.

SOUTHERN AND NORTHERN PERSPECTIVES

1   I tend to argue the point, but quietly, and mostly to myself. Gloria was born and raised in New York; she has come to believe in the stock exchange as the only index of economic health. My perceptions were shaped in South Carolina; and long ago I learned there, as a waiter in private clubs, to gauge economic flux by the tips people gave. We tend to agree on other matters too, but the thing that gives me most frustration is trying to make her understand why I like country music. Perhaps it is because she hates the South and has capitulated emotionally to the horror stories told by refugees from down home. Perhaps it is because Gloria is third generation Northern-born. I do not know. What I do know is that, while the two of us are black, the distance between us is sometimes as great as that between Ibo and Yoruba.

From WHY I LIKE COUNTRY MUSIC by James Alan McPherson, © 1972

4. The narrator says that "Gloria is third generation Northern-born." This information is important because it

    A. contrasts her background with her husband's.
    B. implies that her husband is also from the North.
    C. emphasizes her indifference toward the North.
    D. shows that she and her husband have similar beliefs.

5. The narrator says that his wife hates the South. Her dislike for the South **most** likely indicates that

    A. he too dislikes the South.
    B. they live elsewhere.
    C. they do not always agree.
    D. she has never been there.

Analyze Plot Elements

READING ASSESSMENT TARGETS: R.2.1, R.3.2, R.3.3, R.3.4, R.3.5, R.6.1

UNIT 1

1 Learn the Skill

The **plot** of a story consists of a series of events and how the characters, or people in the story, face these events. Authors use specific **plot elements** to tell the events in a particular order. The author sets the scene at the beginning with the **exposition**, which provides background and introduces some or all of the characters and details.

The story then introduces **complications**, or difficulties, that the characters in the story must confront and overcome. Complications are often the result of conflicts between two or more characters or within one character. The complications are most intense at the story's **climax**, which usually comes near the end. Complications are resolved, happily or unhappily, in the **resolution** at the end of the story.

2 Practice the Skill

By practicing the skill of analyzing plot elements, you will improve your study and test-taking abilities, especially as they relate to the GED® Reasoning Through Language Arts Test. Read the passage below. Then answer the question that follows.

MR. HALE GOES TO THE HOUSE

a In this story's exposition, a witness, Mr. Hale, retells events that set up the story's plot and provide background information.

"Well, Mr. Hale," said the county attorney … "tell just what happened when you came here yesterday morning … "

"I didn't see or hear anything. I knocked at the door. ... I knocked again, louder, and I thought I heard somebody say, 'Come in.' I wasn't sure—I'm not sure yet. But I opened the door—this door," jerking a hand toward the door by which the two women stood, "and there, in that rocker"—pointing to it—"sat Mrs. Wright. …"

b This news and the way in which it is explained present the story's main plot complication.

"I thought of Harry and the team outside, so I said, a little sharp, 'Can't I see John?' 'No,' says she—kind of dull like. 'Ain't he home?' says I. Then she looked at me. 'Yes,' says she, 'he's home.' 'Then why can't I see him?' I asked her, out of patience with her now. 'Cause he's dead,' says she, just as quiet and dull—and fell to pleatin' her apron."

From A JURY OF HER PEERS by Susan Glaspell, © 1917

CONTENT TOPICS

Think of plot as rising and falling action. The action rises to a climax, then it resolves. During the rising action, you may ask what will happen next. During the falling action you may ask how the story will end.

1. What complication does Mr. Hale discover at Mrs. Wright's house?

   A. He sees that Mrs. Wright is ill.
   B. He learns that John is dead.
   C. No one can answer the door.
   D. Mrs. Wright cannot speak.

DIRECTIONS: Read the passage, read each question, and choose the **best** answer.

NEWS COMES TO A GRIEVING WIFE

1   Two young women sat together by the fireside, nursing their mutual and peculiar sorrows. They were the recent brides of two brothers, a sailor and a landsman, and two successive days had brought tidings of the death of each, by the chances of Canadian warfare and the tempestuous Atlantic. They joined their hearts and wept together silently.

2   Time went on, and their usual hour of repose arrived. Then the widowed ones retired to their own rooms. Mary soon sank into temporary forgetfulness, while Margaret became more disturbed and feverish as the night advanced.

3   While Margaret groaned in bitterness, she heard a knock at the street door. Seizing the lamp from the hearth, she hastened to the window that overlooked the street door. A man in a broad-brimmed hat looked upward to discover whom his application had aroused. Margaret knew him as a friendly innkeeper of the town.

4   "What would you have, Goodman Parker?" cried the widow.

5   "Is it you, Mistress Margaret?" replied the innkeeper. "I was afraid it might be your sister Mary; for I hate to see a young woman in trouble, when I have not a word of comfort to whisper her."

6   "For Heaven's sake, what news do you bring?" screamed Margaret.

7   "Why, there has been an express through the town within this half-hour," said Goodman Parker, "travelling from the eastern jurisdiction with letters from the governor and council. He tarried at my house to refresh himself with a drop and a morsel, and I asked him what tidings on the frontiers. He tells me we had the better in the skirmish you heard of, and that thirteen men reported slain are well and sound, and your husband among them. I judged you would not mind being broke of your rest, and so I stepped over to tell you. Good night."

8   So saying, the honest man departed; and his lantern gleamed along the street, bringing to view indistinct shapes of things, and the fragments of a world, like order glimmering through chaos, or memory roaming over the past. But Margaret stayed not to watch these picturesque effects. Joy flashed into her heart, and lighted it up at once; and breathless, she flew to the bedside of her sister. She paused, however, at the door of the chamber, while a thought of pain broke in upon her.

9   "Poor Mary!" said she to herself. "Shall I waken her, to feel her sorrow sharpened by my happiness? No; I will keep it till the morrow."

Adapted from THE WIVES OF THE DEAD by Nathaniel Hawthorne, © 1832

2. Which sentence from the story belongs to the exposition?

    A. "Time went on, and their usual hour of repose arrived."
    B. "While Margaret groaned in bitterness she heard a knock at the street door."
    C. "They were the recent brides of two brothers … and the tempestuous Atlantic."
    D. "A man in a broad-brimmed hat looked upward to discover whom his application had aroused."

3. What complication does Goodman Parker's news to Margaret reveal?

    A. Margaret's husband is actually alive.
    B. Mary's husband is dead.
    C. Thirteen men have been killed.
    D. Margaret's husband has returned to her.

4. Margaret screams at Goodman Parker to find out his news. In terms of plot events, the **most** likely reason for Goodman Parker to delay telling Margaret the news is to

    A. create humor in the story by showing that Goodman Parker is long winded.
    B. add another complication in the plot.
    C. provide additional exposition by giving more insight into Margaret's character.
    D. heighten the suspense of the plot.

5. What new complication is introduced after Goodman Parker shares his news?

    A. Margaret rushes to Mary's bedside.
    B. Margaret waits to tell Mary the news.
    C. Goodman Parker leaves.
    D. Margaret feels a flash of joy.

Analyze Character

READING ASSESSMENT TARGETS: R.2.1, R.3.2, R.3.3, R.3.5, R.4.3/L.4.3

1 Learn the Skill

Characters are the fictional people that authors create in their stories. Authors bring characters to life by describing their appearance, thoughts, words, gestures, actions, and other characters' responses to them. Understanding characters and why they do what they do can help you understand an author's main ideas and themes.

2 Practice the Skill

By practicing the skill of analyzing character, you will improve your study and test-taking abilities, especially as they relate to the GED® Reasoning Through Language Arts Test. Read the passage below. Then answer the question that follows.

a Because the narrator has known Tiny since childhood, his perceptions of her can provide insight as to how she may have changed over the years.

b Lena's concern that Tiny might grow too miserly indicates that Tiny's interest in making money is not related to a desire to spend money.

GOLD RUSH BUSINESSWOMAN

Of all the girls and boys who grew up together in Black Hawk, Tiny Soderball was to lead the most adventurous life and to achieve the most solid worldly success.

… While she was running her lodging-house in Seattle, gold was discovered in Alaska. Miners and sailors came back from the North with wonderful stories and pouches of gold. … That daring, which nobody had ever suspected in her, awoke. She sold her business and set out for Circle City. …

That winter Tiny kept in her hotel a Swede ... [who] … deeded Tiny Soderball his claim on Hunker Creek. Tiny … went off into the wilds and lived on the claim. She bought other claims from discouraged miners, traded or sold them on percentages.

After nearly ten years in the Klondike, Tiny returned, with a considerable fortune, to live in San Francisco. I met her in Salt Lake City in 1908. … She told me about some of the desperate chances she had taken in the gold country, but the thrill of them was quite gone. She said frankly that nothing interested her much now but making money.

… I was in San Francisco two summers ago when both Lena and Tiny Soderball were in town. … Tiny audits Lena's accounts occasionally, and invests her money for her; and Lena, apparently, takes care that Tiny doesn't grow too miserly.

From MY ÁNTONIA by Willa Cather, © 1918

USING LOGIC

The way that one character perceives another character can provide information about either character or both characters. In the passage, the narrator's words tell about Tiny.

1. What does the narrator's description of Tiny reveal about her?

    A. The hope of becoming rich was her only motivation for going to Alaska.
    B. She has been a bold and resourceful explorer since she was a child.
    C. She is obsessed with making money because she gave up her business for the chance to find gold.
    D. Her sense of adventure has given way to a need for security.

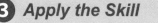

DIRECTIONS: Read the passage, read each question, and choose the **best** answer.

CAREFUL PREPARATIONS

1   It is impossible to say how first the idea entered my brain; but once conceived, it haunted me day and night. Object there was none. Passion there was none. I loved the old man. He had never wronged me. He had never given me insult. For his gold I had no desire. I think it was his eye! yes, it was this! He had the eye of a vulture—a pale blue eye, with a film over it. Whenever it fell upon me, my blood ran cold; and so by degrees—very gradually—I made up my mind to take the life of the old man, and thus rid myself of the eye forever.

2   Now this is the point. You fancy me mad. Madmen know nothing. But you should have seen me. You should have seen how wisely I proceeded—with what caution—with what foresight—with what dissimulation I went to work! I was never kinder to the old man than during the whole week before I killed him. And every night, about midnight, I turned the latch of his door and opened it—oh so gently! And then, when I had made an opening sufficient for my head, I first put in a dark lantern, all closed, closed, so that no light shone out, and then I thrust in my head. Oh, you would have laughed to see how cunningly I thrust it in! I moved it slowly—very, very slowly, so that I might not disturb the old man's sleep. It took me an hour to place my whole head within the opening so far that I could see the old man as he lay upon his bed. Ha!—would a madman have been so wise as this? And then, when my head was well within the room, I undid the lantern cautiously—oh, so cautiously (for the hinges creaked)—I undid it just so much that a single thin ray fell upon the vulture eye. And this I did for seven long nights—and every night just at midnight—but I found the eye always closed; and so it was impossible to do the work; for it was not the old man who vexed me, but his Evil Eye. And every morning, when the day broke, I went boldly into his chamber, and spoke courageously to him, calling him by name in a hearty tone, and inquiring how he had passed the night. So you see he would have been a very profound old man, indeed, to suspect that every night, just at twelve, I looked in upon him while he slept.

From THE TELL-TALE HEART by Edgar Allan Poe, © 1843

2. On the basis of the details in the passage, what relationship does the narrator **most** likely have with the old man?

    A. The old man is the narrator's father.
    B. The narrator takes care of the old man.
    C. The narrator is the old man's employer.
    D. The narrator and the old man are longtime enemies.

3. What is the narrator's motivation for planning to kill the old man?

    A. He resents the old man's wealth.
    B. He seeks revenge for the old man's cruelty toward him.
    C. He is frightened by the old man's pale blue eye.
    D. He wants to end the old man's suffering.

4. The narrator uses words such as **wisely** and **cunningly** to convince readers that he is

    A. rational.
    B. educated.
    C. blameless.
    D. organized.

5. The narrator says that moving his head through the doorway to look into the old man's bedroom took an hour. What does this statement reveal about the narrator?

    A. He is sensibly cautious and methodical.
    B. He respects the old man's need for rest.
    C. His descriptions of his own actions are exaggerated.
    D. His actions are not reasonable.

6. Which words **best** describe the narrator?

    A. dependable and helpful
    B. innocent and trusting
    C. fearless and arrogant
    D. irrational and obsessed

Analyze Setting

READING ASSESSMENT TARGETS: R.3.2, R.3.3, R.3.4, R.3.5, R.4.3/L.4.3

1 Learn the Skill

A story's **setting** is the place and the time in which events happen. Authors may create a setting through details such as scenery, items found in a room, or characters' clothing and ways of speaking. The setting adds depth and complexity to a story, often driving or foreshadowing events. A story that takes place in the middle of the night in an isolated place, for example, is likely to have a different feel to it than a story set in a high-school cafeteria.

2 Practice the Skill

By practicing the skill of analyzing setting, you will improve your study and test-taking abilities, especially as they relate to the GED® Reasoning Through Language Arts Test. Read the passage below. Then answer the question that follows.

A FULL MOON

a Details in the setting affect the feeling of a story. Here the glowing full moon, howling dogs, and crowing roosters create a mood of restlessness, even agitation.

b Details about setting can provide clues about a character. Here, the skeleton of the factory and the glowing full moon describe the setting and help explain the woman's reaction to it.

Up from the skeleton stone walls, up from the rotting floor boards and the solid hand-hewn beams of oak of the pre-war cotton factory, dusk came up. Up from the dusk the full moon came. Glowing like a fired pine-knot it illuminated the great door and soft showered the Negro shanties aligned along the single street of factory town. The full moon in the great door was an omen. Negro women improvised songs against its spell. …

The slow rhythm of her [Louisa's] song grew agitant and restless. Rusty black and tan spotted hounds, lying in the dark corners of porches or prowling around back yards, put their noses in the air and caught its tremor. They began to plaintively yelp and howl. Chickens woke up, and cackled. Intermittently, all over the country-side dogs barked and roosters crowed as if heralding a weird dawn or some ungodly awakening.

"Blood-Burning Moon", from CANE by Jean Toomer. Copyright 1923 by Boni & Liveright, renewed 1951 by Jean Toomer. Used by permission of Liveright Publishing Corporation.

MAKING ASSUMPTIONS

Authors sometimes describe a setting from a character's point of view. In these instances, the setting can help you understand the character's feelings and state of mind.

1. In the second paragraph, Louisa begins singing. The details help clarify her state of mind by suggesting that she believes

   A. singing is a good way to bring sleep.
   B. the cotton factory will burn.
   C. animals grow restless at dusk.
   D. some misfortune is about to occur.

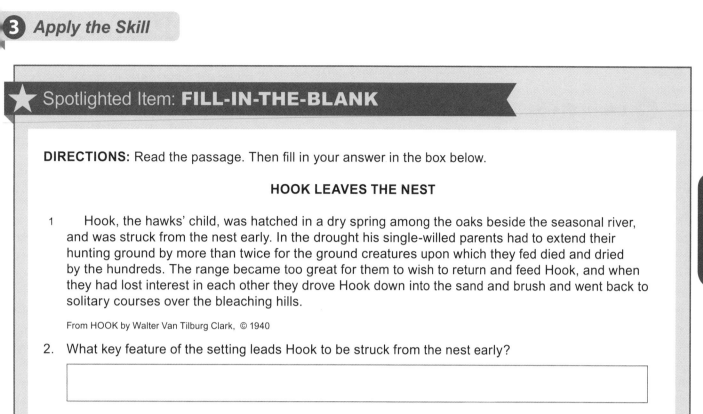

⭐ Spotlighted Item: **FILL-IN-THE-BLANK**

DIRECTIONS: Read the passage. Then fill in your answer in the box below.

HOOK LEAVES THE NEST

1   Hook, the hawks' child, was hatched in a dry spring among the oaks beside the seasonal river, and was struck from the nest early. In the drought his single-willed parents had to extend their hunting ground by more than twice for the ground creatures upon which they fed died and dried by the hundreds. The range became too great for them to wish to return and feed Hook, and when they had lost interest in each other they drove Hook down into the sand and brush and went back to solitary courses over the bleaching hills.

From HOOK by Walter Van Tilburg Clark, © 1940

2. What key feature of the setting leads Hook to be struck from the nest early?

DIRECTIONS: Read the passage, read each question, and choose the **best** answer.

HOOK SURVIVES ALONE

1   Unable to fly yet, Hook crept over the ground, challenging all large movements with recoiled head, erected, rudimentary wings, and the small rasp of his clattering beak. It was during this time of abysmal ignorance and continual fear that his eyes took on the first quality of a hawk, that of being wide, alert and challenging. He dwelt, because of his helplessness, among the rattling brush which grew between the oaks and the river. Even in his thickets and near the water, the white sun was the dominant presence. Except in the dawn, when the land wind stirred, or in the late afternoon, when the sea wind became strong enough to penetrate the half-mile inland to this turn in the river, the sun was the major force, and everything was dry and motionless under it. …

2   The two spacious sounds of his life environed Hook at this time. One was the great rustle of the slopes of yellowed wild wheat, with over it the chattering rustle of the leaves of the California oaks, already as harsh and individually tremulous as in autumn. The other was the distant whisper of the foaming edge of the Pacific, punctuated by the hollow shoring of the waves. But these Hook did not yet hear for he was attuned by fear and hunger to the small, spasmodic rustlings of live things. Dry, shrunken, and nearly starved, and with his plumage delayed, he snatched at beetles, dragging in the

sand to catch them. When swifter and stronger birds and animals did not reach them first, which was seldom, he ate the small, silver fish left in the mud by the failing river.

From HOOK by Walter Van Tilburg Clark, © 1940

3. According to the details in the passage, where does the hawk live?

A. on the beach
B. on an island
C. in the high prairie
D. near the Pacific Ocean

4. The narrator describes the "small, spasmodic rustlings of live things" and the "swifter and stronger birds and animals." The narrator **most** likely mentions these details about the setting to

A. describe the beauty of nature.
B. explain that nature has many sights and sounds.
C. emphasize Hook's keen eyesight and hearing.
D. create a feeling of impending danger to Hook.

Interpret Figurative Language

1 Learn the Skill

Authors use **figurative language** such as **metaphors**, **similes**, and **analogies** to create vivid word pictures and memorable images. A metaphor compares two unlike elements: *the baby's face was a rose*. A simile makes this comparison by using words such as *like, as,* or *similar to: the burned cake was like a brick*. An analogy is a more general term for a comparison that finds a similarity, or parallel, between two unlike elements. Metaphors and similes are specific types of analogies.

Other types of figurative language include **hyperbole**, or extreme exaggeration, and **personification**, giving human qualities to animals or inanimate objects. Words such as *boom* and *splash* reflect the sounds they describe; they are examples of another type of figurative language: **onomatopoeia**.

2 Practice the Skill

By practicing the skill of interpreting figurative language, you will improve your study and test-taking abilities, especially as they relate to the GED® Reasoning Through Language Arts Test. Read the passage below. Then answer the question that follows.

AN AGING WRITER

a A **simile** describes the way the aging writer feels about the end of his career. The narrator says, "it was as violent as a rough hand at his throat."

b The author uses **analogy** in saying that the writer "turned his own leaves." The literal meaning is that the writer turned the pages. Figuratively, these words suggest changing seasons and the writer's age.

The tears filled his mild eyes; something precious had passed away. This was the pang that had been sharpest during the last few years—the sense of ebbing time, of shrinking opportunity; and now he felt not so much that his last chance was going as that it was gone indeed. He had done all that he should ever do, and yet he had not done what he wanted. This was the laceration—that practically his career was over: it was as violent as a rough hand at his throat. He rose from his seat nervously, like a creature hunted by a dread; then he fell back in his weakness and nervously opened his book. It was a single volume; he preferred single volumes and aimed at a rare compression. He began to read, and little by little, in this occupation, he was pacified and reassured. Everything came back to him, but came back with a wonder, came back, above all, with a high and magnificent beauty. He read his own prose, he turned his own leaves, and had, as he sat there with the spring sunshine on the page, an emotion peculiar and intense. His career was over, no doubt, but it was over, after all, with *that*.

From THE MIDDLE YEARS by Henry James, © 1893

TEST-TAKING TIPS

Be careful not to confuse straightforward comparisons with figurative language. If an author says "Angela looks like her sister," the author is comparing two similar elements and is not using figurative language.

1. The narrator says, "This was the laceration—that practically his career was over." Which statement **best** explains this metaphor?

   A. It compares the end of the writer's career with a serious sore throat.
   B. It compares the probable end of the writer's career with a life-threatening wound.
   C. It exaggerates the seriousness of the writer's ending career by comparing it with death.
   D. It describes the writer's feelings by using human qualities to explain the end of his career.

3 *Apply the Skill*

DIRECTIONS: Read the passage, read each question, and choose the **best** answer.

TERROR

1 His room was as black as pitch [tar] with the thick darkness (for the shutters were close fastened, through fear of robbers) and so I knew that he could not see the opening of the door, and I kept pushing it on steadily, steadily.

2 I had my head in, and was about to open the lantern, when my thumb slipped upon the tin fastening, and the old man sprang up in bed, crying out—"Who's there?"

3 I kept quite still and said nothing. For a whole hour I did not move a muscle, and in the meantime I did not hear him lie down. He was still sitting up in the bed listening—just as I have done, night after night, hearkening to the death watches in the wall.

4 Presently I heard a slight groan, and I knew it was the groan of mortal terror. It was not a groan of pain or of grief—oh, no!—it was the low stifled sound that arises from the bottom of the soul when overcharged with awe. I knew the sound well. Many a night, just at midnight, when all the world slept, it has welled up from my own bosom, deepening, with its dreadful echo, the terrors that distracted me. I say I knew it well. I knew what the old man felt, and pitied him, although I chuckled at heart. I knew that he had been lying awake ever since the first slight noise, when he had turned in the bed. His fears had been ever since growing upon him. He had been trying to fancy them causeless, but could not. He had been saying to himself—"It is nothing but the wind in the chimney—it is only a mouse crossing the floor," or "It is merely a cricket which has made a single chirp." Yes, he had been trying to comfort himself with these suppositions: but he had found all in vain. All in vain; because Death, in approaching him had stalked with his black shadow before him, and enveloped the victim. And it was the mournful influence of the unperceived shadow that caused him to feel—although he neither saw nor heard—to feel the presence of my head within the room. …

5 [T]here came to my ears a low, dull, quick sound, such as a watch makes when enveloped in cotton. I knew that sound well, too. It was the beating of the old man's heart. It increased my fury, as the beating of a drum stimulates the soldier into courage.

From THE TELL-TALE HEART by Edgar Allan Poe, © 1843

2. The narrator states in paragraph 3 that he "did not move a muscle." This phrase is an example of hyperbole because it

A. compares the narrator's muscles with motion.
B. is impossible to remain alive without moving muscles.
C. gives human qualities to moving muscles.
D. exaggerates the narrator's fear of the dark room.

3. In paragraph 4, the old man tries to explain the noise in the room as "… merely a cricket which has made a single chirp." How would substituting the word **noise** for the phrase **a single chirp** affect the sentence?

A. The cricket would not be personified because its "song" would not be described.
B. The vague word *noise* would be less vivid and specific both for readers and the old man.
C. The old man would not be convinced that the sound came from a cricket.
D. Readers could share the old man's terror by not knowing the precise sound of a cricket.

4. In paragraph 4, Death is personified as

A. a victim of the narrator's fury.
B. a black shadow outside the window.
C. a stalker in the old man's room.
D. an envelope on the old man's bed.

5. The simile in paragraph 5 comparing a watch wrapped in cotton with the sound of the old man's heart emphasizes the

A. narrator's anger with the old man.
B. late night setting of the story.
C. steady rhythm of the heart.
D. similarity between heartbeats and drums.

6. Figurative language builds suspense in this passage by

A. describing darkness, fear, death, and rage.
B. foreshadowing events that lead to death.
C. personifying abstract feelings of terror.
D. setting the story in a dark room on a dark night.

Determine Narrative Point of View

READING ASSESSMENT TARGETS: R.2.7, R.3.2, R.3.3, R.3.5, R.6.3

UNIT 1

1 Learn the Skill

A story is told from a particular **point of view**. It may be told by an **omniscient**, or all-knowing, narrator who knows the thoughts and feelings of all the characters. Or it may be told by a **first-person** narrator, a character who is part of the story. A first-person narrator does not know the thoughts and feelings of other characters. First-person narrators use *I* as they tell the story. Omniscient narrators use *he, she, they,* or characters' names.

Both kinds of writing can affect how a reader receives information about a story. An omniscient point of view lets the reader know what multiple characters are thinking or feeling. A first-person narrative requires the reader to rely on a single character's perception of events and other characters.

2 Practice the Skill

By practicing the skill of determining narrative point of view, you will improve your study and test-taking abilities, especially as they relate to the GED® Reasoning Through Language Arts Test. Read the passage below. Then answer the question that follows.

A MAN AWAITS EXECUTION

a The pronouns **he** and **his** indicate that this story is told from an omniscient point of view. The narrator informs the reader about the man's situation and thoughts.

b The narrator makes clear that the thoughts and actions are being "set down in words" by the narrator, not by the man in the story.

He closed his eyes in order to fix his last thoughts upon his wife and children. The water, touched to gold by the early sun, the brooding mists under the banks at some distance down the stream, the fort, the soldiers, the piece of drift—all had distracted him. …

He unclosed his eyes and saw again the water below him. "If I could free my hands," he thought, "I might throw off the noose and spring into the stream. By diving I could evade the bullets and, swimming vigorously, reach the bank, take to the woods and get away home. My home, thank God, is as yet outside their lines; my wife and little ones are still beyond the invader's farthest advance."

As these thoughts, which have here to be set down in words, were flashed into the doomed man's brain rather than evolved from it the captain nodded to the sergeant. The sergeant stepped aside.

From AN OCCURRENCE AT OWL CREEK BRIDGE by Ambrose Bierce, © 1890

CONTENT TOPICS

In dialogue, characters other than the narrator may refer to themselves as I or me. This language does **not** show point of view. The pronouns **outside** the quotation reveal how the narrator refers to the characters.

1. In the second paragraph, the narrator includes a quotation. Why is this information quoted?

   A. The quotation indicates that these are the exact thoughts of the man in the story.
   B. The quotation is included because the man in the story is speaking to the captain.
   C. The quotation is included because the narrator has overhead the man say these words.
   D. The quotation shows that the narrator is shifting from the past to the present.

DIRECTIONS: Read the passage, read each question, and choose the **best** answer.

SUNDAYS AND HOLIDAYS

1   During my holidays from school, I was allowed to stay in bed until long after my father had gone to work. He left our house every weekday at the stroke of seven by the Anglican church bell. I would lie in bed awake, and I could hear all the sounds my parents made as they prepared for the day ahead. As my mother made my father his breakfast, my father would shave, using his shaving brush that had an ivory handle and a razor that matched; then he would step outside to the little shed he had built for us as a bathroom, to quickly bathe in water that he had instructed my mother to leave outside overnight in the dew. That way, the water would be very cold, and he believed that cold water strengthened his back. If I had been a boy, I would have gotten the same treatment, but since I was a girl, and on top of that went to school only with other girls, my mother would always add some hot water to my bathwater to take off the chill. On Sunday afternoons, while I was in Sunday school, my father took a hot bath; the tub was half filled with plain water, and then my mother would add a large caldronful of water in which she had just boiled some bark and leaves from a bay-leaf tree. The bark and leaves were there for no reason other than that he liked the smell. He would then spend hours lying in this bath, studying his pool coupons or drawing examples of pieces of furniture he planned to make. When I came home from Sunday school, we would sit down to our Sunday dinner.

From THE CIRCLING HAND by Jamaica Kincaid, © 1985

2. From whose point of view is the passage told?

    A. the parents'
    B. the father's
    C. the mother's
    D. the girl's

3. The narrator says, "I would lie in bed awake, and I could hear all the sounds my parents made as they prepared for the day ahead." What does the pronoun I indicate?

    A. The story is a first-person account.
    B. An omniscient narrator is telling the story.
    C. All the mother's thoughts will be revealed.
    D. Readers will not know the girl's thoughts or feelings.

4. Which statement **best** explains the author's purpose in presenting this point of view?

    A. to provide insight into a family's feelings
    B. to analyze a father's bathing habits
    C. to present the thoughts and feelings of one young girl
    D. to explain what young girls think about their parents

5. The daughter's account of her parents **most** resembles a

    A. journalist's objective account of a current event.
    B. diary writer's explanation of daily events in a family.
    C. poet's expression of personal feelings about family relationships.
    D. mystery writer's presentation of clues about a crime.

Make Inferences in Fiction

UNIT 1

1 Learn the Skill

Like nonfiction writers, fiction writers do not explain all elements directly. As you learned in Lesson 8, readers sometimes must **make inferences**, or educated guesses based on suggestions and clues found in the text. When making an inference, readers combine what they know about a subject with the information found in the text. Then they make a reasonable guess about what the author intended.

2 Practice the Skill

By practicing the skill of making inferences in fiction, you will improve your study and test-taking abilities, especially as they relate to the GED® Reasoning Through Language Arts Test. Read the passage below. Then answer the question that follows.

a The first sentence suggests that the man is detached from his surroundings.

b From the explanation that this is the man's first winter in the area, you can infer that the man may lack experience in cold, rugged climates.

FIFTY DEGREES BELOW ZERO

But all this—the mysterious, far-reaching hairline trail, the absence of sun from the sky, the tremendous cold, and the strangeness and weirdness of it all—made no impression on the man. It was not because he was long used to it. He was a newcomer in the land, a *chechaquo*, and this was his first winter. The trouble with him was that he was without imagination. He was quick and alert in the things of life, but only in the things, and not in the significances. Fifty degrees below zero meant eighty odd degrees of frost. Such fact impressed him as being cold and uncomfortable, and that was all. It did not lead him to meditate upon his frailty as a creature of temperature, and upon man's frailty in general, able only to live within certain narrow limits of heat and cold; and from there on it did not lead him to the conjectural field of immortality and man's place in the universe. Fifty degrees below zero stood for a bite of frost that hurt and that must be guarded against by the use of mittens, ear-flaps, warm moccasins, and thick socks. Fifty degrees below zero was to him just precisely fifty degrees below zero. That there should be anything more to it than that was a thought that never entered his head.

From TO BUILD A FIRE by Jack London, © 1916

USING LOGIC

Note that the passage suggests that the man's lack of imagination causes him trouble. Use the details in the passage and your knowledge of below-freezing temperatures to determine the possible effect of this cause.

1. Why might the man's lack of imagination be a problem?

   A. Because the man considers only facts related to the cold weather, he does not contemplate the extent of the danger it poses.
   B. Because the man is not impressed by the hairline trail and the absence of sun, he risks getting lost in the frozen wilderness.
   C. Because the man does not think about being uncomfortable, he may not have packed the proper gear for his journey.
   D. Because the man does not consider the significances of life, he is not intrigued by the strangeness of the frozen wilderness.

DIRECTIONS: Read the passage, read each question, and choose the **best** answer.

AN INTERRUPTED STANDOFF

1   The two enemies stood glaring at one another for a long silent moment. Each had a rifle in his hand, each had hate in his heart and murder uppermost in his mind. The chance had come to give full play to the passions of a lifetime. But a man who has been brought up under the code of a restraining civilization cannot easily nerve himself to shoot down his neighbor in cold blood and without a word spoken, except for an offense against his hearth and honor. And before the moment of hesitation had given way to action a deed of Nature's own violence overwhelmed them both. A fierce shriek of the storm had been answered by a splitting crash over their heads, and ere they could leap aside a mass of falling beech tree had thundered down on them. Ulrich von Gradwitz found himself stretched on the ground, one arm numb beneath him and the other held almost as helplessly in a tight tangle of forked branches, while both legs were pinned beneath the fallen mass. His heavy shooting boots had saved his feet from being crushed to pieces, but if his fractures were not as serious as they might have been, at least it was evident that he could not move from his present position till someone came to release him. The descending twigs had slashed the skin of his face, and he had to wink away some drops of blood from his eyelashes before he could take in a general view of the disaster. At his side, so near that under ordinary circumstances he could almost have touched him, lay Georg Znaeym, alive and struggling, but obviously as helplessly pinioned down as himself. All around them lay a thick-strewn wreckage of splintered branches and broken twigs.

2   Relief at being alive and exasperation at his captive plight brought a strange medley of pious thank-offerings and sharp curses to Ulrich's lips. Georg, who was nearly blinded with the blood which trickled across his eyes, stopped his struggling for a moment to listen, and then gave a short, snarling laugh.

3   "So you're not killed, as you ought to be, but you're caught, anyway," he cried; "caught fast. Ho, what a jest, Ulrich von Gradwitz snared in his stolen forest. There's real justice for you!"

From THE INTERLOPERS by Saki, © 1919

2. Which is the **most** logical inference to make about the men's unwillingness to shoot each other?

    A. Each man is unwilling to abandon a lifelong passion.
    B. Human laws and traditions curb an inclination toward violence.
    C. The act of murder requires a mental, not a heartfelt, hatred.
    D. Before killing an enemy, an attacker must deliver a statement of wrongs.

3. The narrator states, "Nature's own violence overwhelmed them both." On the basis of this event, the **most** likely inference to make is that Nature

    A. also holds hatred in its heart.
    B. cares nothing for hearth and honor.
    C. is not susceptible to the codes of civilization.
    D. can reinforce the passions of a lifetime.

4. After the accident, Ulrich von Gradwitz cannot move until someone comes to release him, and Georg Znaeym is helplessly pinned down, as well. In this situation, the two men are **most** likely to

    A. shoot each other.
    B. appreciate the importance of their feud.
    C. tend to each other's wounds.
    D. stop being enemies.

5. What does the contrast between the men's potential violence and Nature's actual violence imply?

    A. Nature is more deadly than humans because it lacks feelings.
    B. Humans are more deadly than Nature because they have feelings.
    C. Nature is the deadly enemy of humankind.
    D. Humankind is the deadly enemy of Nature.

6. Which problem does the men's predicament **most** resemble?

    A. carelessness resulting in forest fires
    B. violent crime in urban settings
    C. bullying among schoolchildren
    D. neglect of storm warnings

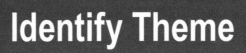

Identify Theme

READING ASSESSMENT TARGETS: R.2.6, R.2.7, R.3.3, R.3.4, R.4.3/L.4.3, R.5.1, R.5.2

UNIT 1

1 Learn the Skill

A story's **theme** is an insight or a general idea about life or human nature that the author shares with readers. A theme does not summarize a story's plot. For example, the plot of the fairy tale "Cinderella" revolves around a poor, mistreated girl who marries a prince. Its theme, however, might be stated as *Keep hoping for better days* or *Kindness is often rewarded, and unfair treatment is punished*. Themes usually are not stated directly, so you must use clues from the text to discover the implied idea.

2 Practice the Skill

By practicing the skill of identifying a story's theme, you will improve your study and test-taking abilities, especially as they relate to the GED® Reasoning Through Language Arts Test. Read the passage below. Then answer the question that follows.

UNEXPECTED GIFTS

a Della and Jim each sell a prized possession—her hair and his watch—to buy a gift for the other. These sacrifices are important in identifying the story's theme.

For there lay The Combs—the set of combs, side and back, that Della had worshipped long in a Broadway window. Beautiful combs, pure tortoise shell, with jeweled rims—just the shade to wear in <u>the beautiful vanished hair</u>. …

But she hugged them to her bosom, and at length she was able to look up with dim eyes and a smile and say, "My hair grows so fast, Jim!"

Jim had not yet seen his beautiful present. …

"Isn't it a dandy, Jim? … Give me your watch. I want to see how it [watch chain] looks on it." …

b Remember that the magi were the wise men who brought gifts to the baby Jesus in the manger. The story's title, "The Gift of the Magi," provides an important clue about the theme.

"Dell," said he, "let's put our Christmas presents away and keep 'em a while. They're too nice to use just at present. I sold the watch to get the money to buy your combs. …"

From THE GIFT OF THE MAGI by O. Henry, © 1905

MAKING ASSUMPTIONS

It is safe to assume that there is a parallel between the magi and Della and Jim. Consider the ways in which Della and Jim show wisdom in the art of gift giving.

1. Which sentence **best** states the theme of this passage?

   A. It is wrong to worship material objects.
   B. Gift giving places hardships on poor families.
   C. Years of poverty and sacrifice can destroy love.
   D. Willingness to sacrifice characterizes true love.

DIRECTIONS: Read the passage, read each question, and choose the **best** answer.

DONALD IS UPSET

1   In a way, Donald's absences are a fine arrangement, even considerate. He is sparing them his darkest moods, when he can't cope with his memories of Vietnam. Vietnam had never seemed such a meaningful fact until a couple of years ago, when he grew depressed and moody. ... He isn't really working regularly at the strip mines. He is mostly just hanging around there, watching the land being scraped away, trees coming down, bushes flung in the air. Sometimes he operates a steam shovel, and when he comes home his clothes are filled with the clay and it is caked on his shoes. The clay is the color of butterscotch pudding.

2   At first, he tried to explain to Jeannette. He said, "If we could have had tanks over there as big as Big Bertha, we wouldn't have lost the war. Strip mining is just like what we were doing over there. We were stripping off the top. The topsoil is like the culture and the people, the best part of the land and the country. America was just stripping off the top, the best. We ruined it. Here, at least the coal companies have to plant vetch and loblolly pines and all kinds of trees and bushes. If we'd done that in Vietnam, maybe we'd have left that country in better shape." ...

3   She didn't want to hear about Vietnam. She thought it was unhealthy to dwell on it so much. He should live in the present. Her mother is afraid Donald will do something violent, because she once read in the newspaper that a veteran in Louisville held his little girl hostage in their apartment until he had a shootout with the police and was killed. But Jeannette can't imagine Donald doing anything so extreme. When she first met him, several years ago, at her parents' ... luncheonette, where she was working then, he had a good job at a lumberyard and he dressed nicely. He took her out to eat at a fancy restaurant. ... Back then, he talked nostalgically about his year in Vietnam, about how beautiful it was, how different the people were. He could never seem to explain what he meant. "They're just different," he said.

From BIG BERTHA STORIES by Bobbie Ann Mason, © 1988

2. Which sentence **best** states the theme of this passage?

    A. Veterans' wives fear violence from their husbands.
    B. The physical injuries from war heal slowly and often incompletely.
    C. War disrupts people deeply.
    D. Strip mining destroys the countryside.

3. How do Donald's depression and moodiness relate to the theme of the passage?

    A. His work at the strip mines makes him uneasy.
    B. His experience in Vietnam still haunts him.
    C. He feels trapped by living with his family.
    D. He cannot explain his feelings to Jeannette.

4. Donald says in paragraph 2 that "We were stripping off the top. The topsoil is like the culture and the people, the best part of the land and the country ..." How does this comparison **best** support the theme of the passage?

    A. Both activities destroy what is valuable in a place.
    B. Both activities are productive for the economy.
    C. Strip mining damages land, but war damages people.
    D. Strip mining damages land, but soldiers tried to help Vietnamese people.

5. Paragraph 3 supports the theme of the passage by

    A. providing background information about Jeannette.
    B. describing Donald as he was when he and Jeannette met.
    C. explaining why Donald feels as he does about strip mining.
    D. comparing Donald with a violent Vietnam veteran.

6. With which theme-related statement would Donald **most** likely agree?

    A. If you break something, you should fix it.
    B. Men should work hard for their families.
    C. Big industry is vital to America's economy.
    D. Families always try to understand soldiers' experiences.

Draw Conclusions in Fiction

READING ASSESSMENT TARGETS: R.2.7, R.2.8, R.3.3, R.3.4, R.3.5

UNIT 1

1 Learn the Skill

As you learned in Lesson 10, **drawing conclusions** is like solving a mystery. As a reader, you gather facts from your reading, combine them with what you know about the topic, and draw a conclusion about the significance of those facts. Conclusions are based on two or more inferences. By drawing conclusions in fiction, you can discover connections between story events and ideas as you read.

2 Practice the Skill

By practicing the skill of drawing conclusions in fiction, you will improve your study and test-taking abilities, especially as they relate to the GED® Reasoning Through Language Arts Test. Read the passage below. Then answer the question that follows.

LAIRD'S ILLNESS

a Laird is in a wheelchair, and he is covered with blankets. Consider what these details indicate.

b The fact that "people who hadn't seen him for a while" are shocked by Laird's appearance indicates that his illness is having a dramatic effect on him.

Her son wanted to talk again, suddenly. <u>During the days, he still brooded, scowling at the swimming pool from the vantage point of his wheelchair, where he sat covered with blankets despite the summer heat.</u> … After he was asleep, Janet would run through the conversations in her mind, and realize what it was she wished she had said. …

A month earlier, after a particularly long and grueling visit with a friend who'd come up on the train from New York, Laird had declared a new policy: no visitors, no telephone calls. She didn't blame him. <u>People who hadn't seen him for a while were often shocked to tears by his appearance</u>, and, rather than have them cheer him up, he felt obliged to comfort them. She'd overheard bits of those conversations. One was no worse than the others, but he was fed up. He had said more than once that he wasn't cut out to be the brave one, the one who would inspire everybody to walk away from a visit with him feeling uplifted, shaking their heads in wonder. He had liked being the most handsome and missed it very much; he was not a good victim.

From IN THE GLOAMING by Alice Elliott Dark, © 1994

TEST-TAKING TIPS

You can conclude from details like "blankets despite the summer heat" and "people … were shocked by his appearance" that Laird is seriously ill, even though the author never states this information.

1. Which statement is the **most** likely conclusion to draw on the basis of the information in the passage?

   A. Laird is being treated for a serious disease.
   B. Laird is indifferent about his medical treatment.
   C. Janet has little background in current medicine.
   D. Janet misses her friends' visits.

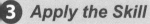

★ Spotlighted Item: **FILL-IN-THE-BLANK**

DIRECTIONS: Read the passage. Then fill in your answers in the boxes below.

A DEADLY COLD

1   All this the man knew. The old-timer on Sulphur Creek had told him about it the previous fall, and now he was appreciating the advice. Already all sensation had gone out of his feet. To build the fire he had been forced to remove his mittens, and the fingers had quickly gone numb. His pace of four miles an hour had kept his heart pumping blood to the surface of his body and to all the extremities. But the instant he stopped, the action of the pump eased down. The cold of space smote [struck] the unprotected tip of the planet, and he, being on that unprotected tip, received the full force of the blow. The blood of his body recoiled before it. The blood was alive, like the dog, and like the dog it wanted to hide away and cover itself up from the fearful cold. So long as he walked four miles an hour, he pumped that blood … to the surface; but now it ebbed away and sank down into the recesses of his body. The extremities were the first to feel its absence. His wet feet froze the faster, and his exposed fingers numbed the faster, though they had not yet begun to freeze. Nose and cheeks were already freezing, while the skin of all his body chilled as it lost its blood. …

2   There was the fire, snapping and crackling and promising life with every dancing flame. He started to untie his moccasins. They were coated with ice. … For a moment he tugged with his numbed fingers, then, realizing the folly of it, he drew his sheath-knife.

3   But before he could cut the strings, it happened. It was his own fault or, rather, his mistake. He should not have built the fire under the spruce tree. He should have built it in the open. ... Now the tree under which he had done this carried a weight of snow on its boughs. No wind had blown for weeks, and each bough was fully freighted. Each time he had pulled a twig he had communicated a slight agitation to the tree—an imperceptible agitation, so far as he was concerned, but an agitation sufficient to bring about the disaster.

From TO BUILD A FIRE by Jack London, © 1916

2. In the first line, the narrator says, "All this the man knew." From the information in the passage, you

can conclude that the man knows he must [   ]

to [   ] his wet, freezing feet.

3. On the basis of the evidence in the passage, you can conclude that the man is suffering from

[   ].

4. From the evidence in paragraph 3, you can conclude that [   ]

drops from the spruce tree and [   ].

Apply Ideas

READING ASSESSMENT TARGETS: R.2.7, R.2.8, R.3.3, R.3.4, R.3.5, R.4.1/L.4.1, R.4.3/L.4.3

UNIT 1

1 Learn the Skill

You have practiced making inferences in fiction (Lesson 21) and used that information to draw conclusions (Lesson 23). By gathering details, thinking of reasonable explanations for inferences and conclusions, and considering their significance, you are **applying ideas**. Applying ideas can help you predict events or outcomes and determine how a character or situation would be similar or different in other circumstances.

For example, when you determine major elements of a character's personality, you can predict how he or she would act in a different situation. Applying ideas to a text can help you understand the text as a whole.

2 Practice the Skill

By practicing the skill of applying ideas, you will improve your study and test-taking abilities, especially as they relate to the GED® Reasoning Through Language Arts Test. Read the passage below. Then answer the question that follows.

THE CONCERT AFFECTS PAUL

a The music has a particular effect on Paul. At first, the music appears to give him a kind of joy that he otherwise does not have.

When the symphony began, Paul sank into one of the rear seats, with a long sigh of relief. It was not that symphonies, as such, meant anything in particular to Paul, but the first sigh of the instruments seemed to free some hilarious and potent spirit within him— something that struggled there like the Geni[e] in the bottle found by the Arab fisherman. He felt a sudden zest of life; the lights danced before his eyes and the concert hall blazed into unimaginable splendor. When the soprano soloist came on, Paul half closed his eyes, and gave himself up to the peculiar stimulus such personages always had for him. The soloist chanced to be a German woman, by no means in her first youth and the mother of many children; but she wore an elaborate gown and a tiara, and above all, she had that indefinable air of achievement, that world-shine upon her, which, in Paul's eyes, made her a veritable queen of romance. ...

b Paul is attracted by performers and glamor that surrounds them. He would like to be part of their world.

Over yonder the Schenley, in its vacant stretch, loomed big and square through the fine rain, the windows of its twelve stories glowing like those of a lighted cardboard house under a Christmas tree. All the actors and singers of the better class stayed there when they were in the city. ... <u>Paul had often hung about the hotel, watching the people go in and out, longing to enter and leave school-masters and dull care behind him forever.</u>

From PAUL'S CASE by Willa Cather, © 1905

INSIDE THE ITEMS

Questions asking you to predict an outcome or a character's behavior in another situation often have a Depth of Knowledge level of 3. Although the question may not be difficult, it requires more steps in the thought process.

1. If Paul were a character living in 2014, he would **most** likely be someone who

   A. follows rock groups.
   B. studies music at school.
   C. shows artistic ability.
   D. has ambitions in the arts.

DIRECTIONS: Read the passage, read each question, and choose the **best** answer.

A PICNIC IN THE COUNTRY

1   People born into the tradition of English country life are accustomed to eccentric owls. Mrs. Leslie and her daughter Belinda accepted the owl with vague acknowledging smiles. Her son-in-law, Leo Cooper, a Londoner whose contacts with nature had been made at the very expensive pleasure resorts patronized by his very rich parents, found midday hoots disconcerting, and almost said so. But did not, as he was just then in a temper and wholly engaged in not showing it.

2   He was in a temper for several reasons, all eminently adequate. For one thing ... impelled by the nervous appetite of frustration he had eaten a traditional country breakfast and it was disagreeing with him; for yet another, he had been hauled out on yet another of his mother-in-law's picnics; finally, there was the picnic basket. The picnic basket was a family piece, dating, as Mrs. Leslie said on its every appearance, from an age of footmen. It was the size of a cabin trunk, built for eternity out of red wicker, equipped with massy cutlery and crockery; time had sharpened its red fangs, and however Leo took hold of it, they lacerated him. Also it caused him embarrassment to be seen carrying this rattling, creaking monstrosity, and today he had carried it farther than usual.

From HEALTHY LANDSCAPE WITH DORMOUSE by Sylvia Townsend Warner, © 1966

2. Leo's exposure to nature has been at "very expensive resorts" (paragraph 1). Which situation does his experience at the picnic **most** resemble?

    A. A person living in the suburbs takes the train to the city to see a show.
    B. A corporate executive does not know how to saddle a horse on a trail ride.
    C. A graphic designer living in the city knows a surprising amount of information about sheep.
    D. A banker living in a big city checks her e-mail while on vacation in the mountains.

3. Leo has been "hauled out on yet another of his mother-in-law's picnics" (paragraph 2). Which is the **most** logical prediction to make on the basis of the connotation of **hauled out** and of the tone of the sentence? Leo probably will

    A. arrange his own picnic.
    B. dislike the picnic.
    C. refuse to carry the basket.
    D. ask to reschedule the event.

4. Each time Mrs. Leslie uses the picnic basket, she tells people that it was first used in "an age of footmen" (paragraph 2). On the basis of Mrs. Leslie's character, which prediction is the **most** accurate? Mrs. Leslie probably will

    A. keep her family's wealth a secret.
    B. make anonymous donations to charity.
    C. find excuses to brag about her family.
    D. be modest about her family's achievements.

5. Given a choice of leisure activities, Leo **most** probably would choose

    A. a weekend at a five-star hotel.
    B. a week of camping in a national park.
    C. forging a new trail in a rain forest.
    D. staying at home watching old movies.

6. On the basis of the events in the passage, Leo's personality, and your prior knowledge of plot in fiction, which prediction about story events is the **most** probable?

    A. Leo will leave his family at the picnic and return to London.
    B. To please her husband, Belinda will convince her mother not to have another picnic.
    C. Leo will pay the price for his bad humor and actions.
    D. While carrying the picnic basket, Leo will get injured.

Unit 1 Review

DIRECTIONS: Read the passage. Then answer the questions that follow.

THE NEW GENERATION OF MOVIEGOER

1   A lot of folks have wondered whether it is too soon, just 10 years after the release of the original film and five years after the third installment, to relaunch Spider-Man. When questioned, a producer of the new picture snapped that anyone who asked that is "too old." He may have been dismissively arrogant, especially to geriatrics over 30, but he may also have been right.

2   Obviously, remakes are nothing new, even if the time between the original and the next version has shrunk dramatically. As Amy Pascal, the co-chairman of Sony Pictures, which distributed the new "Spider-Man," said, "Five years is a lifetime in the movie business," by which she really meant it is a lifetime for the young audiences to which the movie business makes its primary appeal.

3   But the new "Spider-Man" betrays something else—something important about the young audience's relationship to film. Young people, so-called millennials, don't seem to think of movies as art the way so many boomers did. They think of them as fashion, and like fashion, movies have to be new and cool to warrant attention. Living in a world of the here-and-now, obsessed with whatever is current, kids seem no more interested in seeing their parents' movies than they are in wearing their parents' clothes. Indeed, novelty may be the new narcissism. It obliterates the past in the fascination with the present.

4   One has to acknowledge that part of this cinematic ageism is the natural cycle of culture. Every generation not only has its own movies, it has its own aesthetics, and the contemporary aesthetic might be labeled "bigger, faster, louder" because our blockbuster movies are all about sensory overload—quickening the audience's pulse. It is the same force that drives video games. Still, the difference between the attitude of boomers and that of the millennials is that boomer audiences didn't necessarily believe their aesthetics were an advance over those that had preceded them.

5   Indeed, the most ardent movie enthusiasts of the past generation were reverential of old movies. Andrew Sarris, who died last month and who was among the nation's most influential film critics in the '70s and '80s, made his reputation not just by importing the auteur theory from France that celebrated the authorial role of the director but by disinterring many of those old directors from film history. For Sarris and his acolytes, love of movie history was indispensable to a love of the movies generally. One loved both old and new.

6   One might have thought that as film became an acceptable academic subject and film courses burgeoned in universities and high schools, old movies would be protected from obsolescence. And, to be sure, there is still a legion of young movie fanatics who appreciate and even love the films of Hawks, Hitchcock, Ford, Capra, Welles, Truffaut and others.

7   But among many rank-and-file millennials, the attitude doesn't seem to be so generous. They find old movies hopelessly passé—technically primitive, politically incorrect, narratively dull, slowly paced. In short, old-fashioned. Even Tobey Maguire's Spider-Man is a Model T next to Andrew Garfield's rocket ship of a movie. And Model Ts get thrown on the junk heap.

From the *Los Angeles Times*'s article PERSPECTIVE: MILLENNIALS SEEM TO HAVE LITTLE USE FOR OLD MOVIES by Neal Gabler, © 2012

1. In paragraph 1, the author refers to "geriatrics over 30." How would the tone change if the author had written **people** instead of **geriatrics**? The tone would be

   A. more casual.
   B. less ironic and humorous.
   C. more academic.
   D. less professional and detached.

2. How does the author categorize **millennials**?

   A. Millennials are young filmmakers with new ideas about making movies.
   B. Millennials are young people who love old movies.
   C. Millennials are young people who do not love movies as much as earlier generations do.
   D. Millennials are young people with new tastes in movies.

3. In paragraph 4, the author contrasts boomers' and millennials' ideas about movies. The author believes that boomers

   A. think movies from their generation are no better than old movies.
   B. dislike movies that are "big" and "fast."
   C. see movies not as art but as entertainment.
   D. are fanatical about old movies.

4. Which statement **best** summarizes the author's explanation of the importance of Andrew Sarris?

   A. Sarris brought old directors from France to the United States to make important movies.
   B. Sarris believed that understanding film history was an important part of loving movies.
   C. Sarris imported from France the auteur theory that celebrated the role of the director.
   D. Sarris helped establish film studies in universities and high schools.

5. Drag and drop into the boxes the three reasons that millennials do not like old movies.

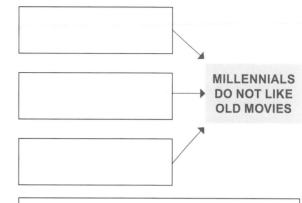

   | Old movies focus on serious issues. |
   | Old movies often demean women. |
   | Old movies are slow paced. |
   | Old movies use few special effects. |

6. Which sentence **best** states the author's point of view about old movies?

   A. The author thinks that old movies are generally better than new movies.
   B. The author believes that old movies are still popular among millenials.
   C. The author likes old movies and regrets that young people do not seem to appreciate them.
   D. The author believes that it is important to protect old movies from obsolescence.

7. From the information in this passage, what can you infer about the author's opinion of teaching film history in school? The author most likely

   the teaching of film history.

8. What does the word **passé** (paragraph 7) mean?

9. Which generalization does the author make about young people today?

   A. They like novelty in the films they see.
   B. They love the films of Hawks and Hitchcock.
   C. They are interested in filmmaking as art.
   D. They like remakes more than previous generations do.

DIRECTIONS: Read the passage. Then answer the questions that follow.

PRESIDENT JOHNSON SIGNS THE HIGHWAY BEAUTIFICATION ACT

1   America likes to think of itself as a strong and stalwart and expanding nation. It identifies itself gladly with the products of its own hands. We frequently point with pride and with confidence to the products of our great free enterprise system—management and labor. These are and these should be a source of pride to every American. They are certainly the source of American strength. They are truly the fountainhead of American wealth. They are actually a part of America's soul.

2   But there is more to America than raw industrial might. …

3   There is a part of America which was here long before we arrived, and will be here, if we preserve it, long after we depart: the forests and the flowers, the open prairies and the slope of the hills, the tall mountains, the granite, the limestone, the caliche, the unmarked trails, the winding little streams—well, this is the America that no amount of science or skill can ever recreate or actually ever duplicate. This America is the source of America's greatness. It is another part of America's soul as well.

4   When I was growing up, the land itself was life. And when the day seemed particularly harsh and bitter, the land was always there just as nature had left it—wild, rugged, beautiful, and changing, always changing. …

5   How do you really put a value on the view of the night that is caught in a boy's eyes while he is stretched out in the thick grass watching the million stars that we never see in these crowded cities, breathing the sounds of the night and the birds and the pure, fresh air while in his ears are the crickets and the wind?

6   Well, in recent years I think America has sadly neglected this part of America's national heritage. We have placed a wall of civilization between us and between the beauty of our land and of our countryside. In our eagerness to expand and to improve, we have relegated nature to a weekend role, and we have banished it from our daily lives. Well, I think that we are a poorer nation because of it, and it is something I am not proud of. And it is something I am going to do something about. Because as long as I am your President, by choice of your people, I do not choose to preside over the destiny of this country and to hide from view what God has gladly given it.

7   And that is why today there is a great deal of real joy within me, and within my family, as we meet here in this historic East Room to sign the Highway Beautification Act of 1965.

8   Now, this bill does more than control advertising and junkyards along the billions of dollars of highways that the people have built with their money—public money, not private money. It does more than give us the tools just to landscape some of those highways.

9   This bill will bring the wonders of nature back into our daily lives. This bill will enrich our spirits and restore a small measure of our national greatness.

10   As I rode the George Washington Memorial Parkway back to the White House only yesterday afternoon, I saw nature at its purest. And I thought of the honor roll of names—a good many of you are sitting here in the front row today—that made this possible. And as I thought of you who had helped and stood up against private greed for public good, I looked at those dogwoods that had turned red, and the maple trees that were scarlet and gold. In a pattern of brown and yellow, God's finery was at its finest. And not one single foot of it was marred by a single, unsightly, man-made construction or obstruction—no advertising signs, no old, dilapidated trucks, no junkyards. Well, doctors could prescribe no better medicine for me …

From REMARKS AT THE SIGNING OF THE HIGHWAY BEAUTIFICATION ACT OF 1965 by Lyndon Baines Johnson, 1965

10. Johnson mentions "the forests and flowers, the open prairies and the slope of the hills ... " Which main idea do these details support?

A. Industrialization has destroyed these aspects of American nature.
B. America is a place of great natural beauty, which is a source of its greatness.
C. When Johnson was a boy, these were the aspects of nature that he saw.
D. The natural landscape is more important than industry and economic wealth.

11. According to Johnson, what has been the effect of America's eagerness to expand and improve? Americans have neglected the importance of

the beauty of nature.

12. Johnson **most** likely includes the description of himself as a boy stretched out in the grass and viewing the night sky in order to

A. emphasize that nature, unspoiled when he was young, is now polluted.
B. provide an example of the kind of experience that the highway bill will make possible.
C. connect with young listeners whose interests would be similar to his when he was younger.
D. personalize his argument with an image that has strong emotional appeal.

13. What does Johnson imply when he refers to highways that are being built by "public money, not private money"?

A. Businesses need to contribute more money to the building of highways.
B. Highways were built with public money and should serve public, not business, interests.
C. The public already has spent too much of its money on highways.
D. The bill will apply only to highways built with public money, not private money.

14. Johnson describes looking out of the car on the parkway and seeing "dogwoods that had turned red, and the maple trees that were scarlet and gold." How do these details relate to the main idea of this speech?

A. They support the idea that Johnson is speaking specifically about the George Washington Memorial Parkway.
B. They confirm that the season is autumn.
C. They provide a contrasting image to unsightly manufactured objects along many highways.
D. They serve as examples of the public good that has resulted from the bill.

15. Which is the **most** likely conclusion to draw about how Johnson would like the nation's highways to look? He would like them

A. to have more trees and flowers and fewer billboards and junkyards.
B. with fewer potholes and good lighting.
C. to have more maple and dogwood trees and fewer evergreens.
D. lined with bustling, successful industries.

16. Johnson **most** likely would have supported a bill to

A. widen roads bordering on forest land.
B. remove advertising from newspapers.
C. plant and maintain public gardens.
D. donate unused farmland to developers.

17. Which type of government bill would be **most** similar to the one described in this speech?

A. a bill to improve air quality in cities
B. a bill to reduce speed limits on highways
C. a bill to increase federal funding for highway repairs
D. a bill to preserve the natural beauty of beaches

DIRECTIONS: Read the story. Then answer the questions that follow.

THE HUNTERS RETURN

1 "My aunt will be down presently, Mr. Nuttel," said a self-possessed young lady of fifteen; "in the meantime you must put up with me."

2 Framton Nuttel endeavoured to say the correct something. Privately he doubted whether formal visits to total strangers would help the nerve cure which he was undergoing.

3 "I know how it will be," his sister had said when he was preparing to migrate to this rural retreat; "you will bury yourself down there and not speak to a soul, and your nerves will be worse than ever from moping. I shall just give you letters of introduction to all the people I know there. Some were quite nice."

4 "Do you know many of the people round here?" asked the niece.

5 "Hardly a soul," said Framton. "My sister stayed at the rectory four years ago, and she gave me letters of introduction to some people here."

6 "Then you know nothing about my aunt?"

7 "Only her name and address," admitted the caller. He was wondering whether Mrs. Sappleton was married or widowed. The room suggested masculine habitation.

8 "Her great tragedy happened three years ago. You may wonder why we keep that window open on an October afternoon," said the niece, indicating a French window that opened on to a lawn.

9 "It is warm for this time of year," said Framton; "but is it related to the tragedy?"

10 "Out through that window, three years ago her husband and her two brothers went off for their day's shooting. They never came back. In crossing the moor they were engulfed in a bog. It had been that dreadful wet summer, and places that were safe gave way suddenly. Their bodies were never recovered. Poor aunt always thinks they will come back someday, they and the little brown spaniel that was lost with them, and walk in at that window just as they used to do. That is why the window is kept open every evening. Poor dear aunt, she has often told me how they went out, her husband with his white waterproof coat over his arm, and Ronnie, her youngest brother, singing. Sometimes on quiet evenings like this, I get a creepy feeling that they will all walk in through that window."

11 She broke off with a shudder. It was a relief when the aunt bustled into the room.

12 "Don't mind the open window," said Mrs. Sappleton; "my husband and brothers will be home directly.

13 She rattled on cheerfully about the shooting and the scarcity of birds. To Framton it was horrible. He made a desperate effort to turn to a less ghastly topic; he was conscious that his hostess was giving him only a fragment of her attention, her eyes straying past him to the open window and the lawn.

14 "The doctors ordered complete rest, no mental excitement, and minimal physical exercise," announced Framton, deluded that strangers and chance acquaintances hunger for details of one's ailments.

15 Then she suddenly brightened to attention, but not to what Framton was saying.

16 "Here they are at last!" she cried. "Just in time for tea."

17 Framton shivered slightly and turned to the niece to convey comprehension. She was staring through the window with dazed horror in her eyes. Framton swung around and looked in the same direction.

18 Three figures were walking across the lawn towards the window, all carried guns under their arms, and one was additionally burdened with a white coat hung over his shoulders. A brown spaniel kept close.

19 Framton grabbed at his stick and hat; the hall door, gravel drive, and front gate were dimly noted stages in his headlong retreat.

20 "Here we are, " said the bearer of the white mackintosh, coming in through the window.

21 "Who was that who bolted as we came up?"

22 "A Mr. Nuttel," said Mrs. Sappleton; "could only talk about his illnesses, and dashed off without a word. You'd think he had seen a ghost."

23 "I expect it was the spaniel," said the niece calmly; "he told me he had a horror of dogs. He was once hunted into a cemetery and had to spend the night in a new grave with wild dogs snarling and foaming just above him."

24 Romance at short notice was her specialty.

Adapted from THE OPEN WINDOW by Saki, © 1914

18. From which point of view is this story told?

   A. the niece's
   B. the aunt's
   C. first-person
   D. third-person

19. Which statement **best** explains how paragraphs 4 and 6 relate to the story?

   A. The niece must find out why Framton has come to the village before her aunt comes downstairs.
   B. The niece hopes that the conversation will encourage Framton to reveal details about his illness.
   C. His acquaintance with the neighbors and aunt is likely to determine whether Framton will believe the niece's story.
   D. These questions are usual topics of polite conversation, which the niece must continue until her aunt takes over.

20. Drag and drop the events into the chart to show the order in which they occur in the story.

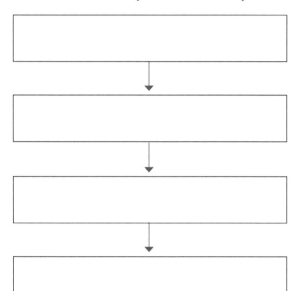

Framton acts as though he has seen a ghost.	Framton's sister stays at the rectory.
The niece explains why the window remains open.	The "tragedy" takes place.

21. Which detail **best** indicates that the story takes place during the early 1900s, not at the present time?

   A. "Here they are at last!" she cried. "Just in time for tea."
   B. "Poor aunt always thinks that they will come back someday … "
   C. "It is quite warm for the time of the year," said Framton.
   D. "I shall just give you letters of introduction to all the people I know there."

22. The aunt ironically describes Framton's departure by saying "One would think he had seen a ghost." This expression usually indicates that someone is

   A. pale.
   B. nervous.
   C. horrified.
   D. invisible.

23. The **most** likely conclusion to draw about the niece is that she is

   A. visiting her aunt to recover from an illness.
   B. selfish and demands constant attention.
   C. highly imaginative and thinks quickly.
   D. well acquainted with Framton's sister.

24. What causes Framton to leave the house suddenly?

   A. He cannot bear to be in a room with open windows because his illness makes him sensitive to chill.
   B. Mrs. Sappleton is rude to him because her attention is elsewhere as he discusses his illness.
   C. The arrival of the dog terrifies him, reminding him of an earlier incident in a cemetery.
   D. He believes the niece's story and thinks he is seeing dead men walk through the door.

25. Which sentence **best** states a theme of this story?

   A. People with nervous conditions will believe whatever they are told.
   B. A convincing story may seem more believable than the truth.
   C. Children who make up tales eventually will be punished.
   D. Telling ghost stories to people in poor health can cause severe damage.

DIRECTIONS: Read the story. Then answer the questions that follow.

AFTER TWENTY YEARS

1   The policeman on the beat moved up the avenue impressively. The impressiveness was habitual and not for show, for spectators were few. The time was barely 10 o'clock at night, but chilly gusts of wind with a taste of rain in them had emptied the streets. He tried doors as he went and twirled his club with intricate movements, turning now and then to cast his watchful eye down the quiet thoroughfare.

2   About midway down a certain block, the policeman suddenly slowed his walk. In the doorway of a darkened hardware store a man leaned, with an unlighted cigar in his mouth. As the policeman walked up to him, the man spoke up quickly. "It's all right, officer," he said, reassuringly. "I'm just waiting for a friend. It's an appointment made twenty years ago. Sounds funny to you, doesn't it? Well, I'll explain if you'd like to make certain it's all straight. About that long ago there used to be a restaurant where this store stands."

3   He struck a match and lit his cigar. The light showed a pale, square-jawed face with keen eyes, and a little white scar near his right eyebrow. His scarfpin was a large diamond, oddly set. "Twenty years ago tonight," said the man, "I dined here with Jimmy Wells, my best chum, and the finest chap in the world. He and I were raised here in New York, just like two brothers. I was eighteen and Jimmy was twenty. The next morning I was to start for the West. You couldn't have dragged Jimmy out of New York; he thought it was the only place on earth. Well, we agreed that we would meet here again exactly twenty years from that date and time, no matter what our conditions might be or from what distance we might have to come. We figured that in twenty years each of us ought to have our destiny worked out and our fortunes made."

4   "Sounds pretty interesting," said the policeman. "Rather long between meets, though. Have you heard from your friend?"

5   "After a year or two, we lost track of each other. I kept hustling around the West. I know Jimmy will meet me here if he's alive, for he always was the truest chap in the world. He'll never forget." The waiting man pulled out a handsome watch set with small diamonds. "Three minutes to ten," he announced.

6   "Did pretty well out West, didn't you?" asked the policeman.

7   "You bet! I hope Jimmy has done half as well. He was a kind of plodder, though, good fellow as he was. I've had to compete with some of the sharpest wits to get my pile. A man gets in a groove in New York. It takes the West to put a razor-edge on him."

8   The policeman twirled his club and took a step. "I'll be on my way. Hope your friend comes around."

9   There was now a fine, cold drizzle falling, and the wind had risen into a steady blow. In the door of the hardware store the man smoked his cigar and waited. After about twenty minutes a tall man in a long overcoat, with collar turned up to his ears, hurried across from the opposite side of the street. "Is that you, Bob?" he asked, doubtfully.

10   "Is that you, Jimmy Wells?" cried the man in the door.

11   "Bless my heart!" exclaimed the new arrival. "It's Bob, sure as fate. I was certain I'd find you here if you were still in existence. How has the West treated you, old man?"

12   "Bully; it has given me everything I asked it for. You've changed lots, Jimmy. I never thought you were so tall by two or three inches."

13   "Oh, I grew a bit after I was twenty."

14   "Doing well in New York, Jimmy?"

15   "Moderately. I have a position in one of the city departments. Come on, Bob; we'll go around to a place I know of and have a good long talk about old times."

16   The two men started up the street, arm in arm. The man from the West, his egotism enlarged by success, was beginning to outline the history of his career. The other, submerged in his overcoat, listened with interest. When they came under the glare of a streetlight, each turned to gaze upon the other's face. The man from the West stopped suddenly. "You're not Jimmy Wells," he snapped. "Twenty years is a long time, but not long enough to change a man's nose from a Roman to a pug."

17   "It sometimes changes a good man into a bad one," said the tall man. "You've been under arrest for ten minutes, 'Silky' Bob. Chicago thinks you may have dropped over our way and wires us she wants to have a chat with you. Now, before we go on to the station here's a note I was asked to hand you. It's from Patrolman Wells."

18   The man from the West unfolded the paper. His hand was steady when he began to read, but it trembled a little by the time he had finished. The note was short: "Bob: I was at the appointed place on time. When you struck the match to light your cigar, I saw it was the face of the man wanted in Chicago. Somehow I couldn't do it myself, so I went around and got a plain clothes man to do the job. JIMMY."

Adapted from AFTER TWENTY YEARS by O. Henry, © 1906

26. The details about the policeman in paragraph 1 show that he **most** likely

   A. is nervous about patrolling at night.
   B. works overtime to earn extra money.
   C. does his job enthusiastically.
   D. likes to impress others.

27. How do the details of the rain and wind in paragraph 9 parallel the story's developments?

   A. The worsening weather indicates that events will be mysterious.
   B. The heavier rain and wind make it impossible for Jimmy to arrive.
   C. The worsening rain and wind make the characters eager to go indoors.
   D. The worsening weather indicates that the appointment may cause sorrow.

28. Drag and drop the descriptions into the correct places in the Venn diagram.

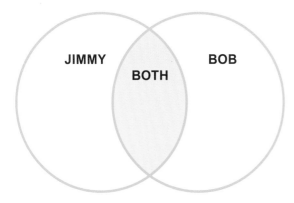

from New York	ambitious
police officer	adventurous
sensitive	honest
criminal	keeps appointment

29. What does Bob's lack of recognition of the policeman reveal about Bob?

   A. He has a poor memory for dates and faces.
   B. He cannot see well in the dark.
   C. He is deceitful and lies about his reason for waiting in the doorway.
   D. He is more interested in bragging about himself than in meeting Jimmy.

30. Which event is the climax of the story?

   A. Bob tells his story to the policeman.
   B. Bob leaves New York.
   C. Bob realizes the tall man is not Jimmy.
   D. Bob reads Jimmy's note.

31. What does the sentence "I saw it was the face of the man wanted in Chicago" reveal?

   A. Jimmy notices that Bob has a scar near his right eyebrow.
   B. Bob is no longer the "Bob" that Jimmy knew twenty years before.
   C. Bob's financial success has changed him beyond recognition.
   D. Bob disappointed Jimmy by not remaining in touch over the years.

32. Which sentence **best** states a theme of the story?

   A. Leaving one's home town does not guarantee happiness.
   B. People may not see themselves as others see them.
   C. It is important to keep in touch with friends and family.
   D. People should not make appointments that they cannot keep.

33. Which situation is **most** like the situation in the story?

   A. A parent must apply the principle of tough love.
   B. A family reunion causes anger among relatives.
   C. Old friends meet and brag about their successes.
   D. Two friends are shocked at how each has aged in 20 years.

Mark Wahlberg

Mark Wahlberg grew up in the Dorchester neighborhood of Boston and had a traumatic and troubled youth. Despite his natural abilities which ultimately led him to his successful career as a musician and actor, he struggled with anger and a life of petty crime. However, he foun inspiration in music and looking back on his early years this is what he has said:

"I've made a lot of mistakes in my life and I've done bad things, but I never blamed my upbringing for that. I never behaved like a victim so that I would have a convenient reason for victimizing others. Everything I did wrong was my own fault. I was taught the difference between right and wrong at an early age. I take full responsibility."

Wahlberg first rose to prominence as the front man for the musical group *Marky Mark and the Funky Bunch*. He managed to parlay that success into a very successful movie career and has had prominent roles in films such as *Three Kings, The Perfect Storm, Ted,* and *The Departed*.

People earn their GED® certificate for many different reasons. For Wahlberg it was largely because of his desire to be a positive ro model for his children. He didn't want them assuming that because he has been successful without completing high school that they should expect the same. "I can't tell my kids to go to school if I don have a diploma," he said when he successfully earned his GED® certificate in 2013.

Earning his GED® certificate was a way for Wahlberg to reinforce the importance of education as a pathway to success with his children.

"You don't want to give your kids everything without giving them the tools to be great people."

CAREER HIGHLIGHTS: *Mark Wahlberg*

- Born June 5, 1971, Boston Massachusetts
- Began recording in the early 1990's
- Enjoyed acclaim and success as a film actor
- Now produces television series such as *Boardwalk Empire*
- Active in youth service programs through his Mark Wahlberg Youth Foundation
- Dedicated and passionate parent

Argument Analysis and Text Comparison

Unit 2: Argument Analysis and Text Comparison

In Unit 2, you will take the skills that you learned in Unit 1 and apply them to persuasive texts and paired passages. In Lessons 1 through 8, you will practice reading and evaluating persuasive texts. You will learn how writers try to persuade readers to accept their arguments by presenting facts and evidence, appealing to emotions, using logic, and providing examples from personal experience. Understanding what makes an effective persuasive text is important to your success as a reader and writer.

In Lessons 9 through 13, you will compare how different authors and different types of texts explore similar subjects. You will learn about the importance of a writer's perspective, purpose, structure, emphasis, and audience. Practicing reading and analyzing a range of paired passages will prepare you for the text comparisons you will be asked to make on the GED® Reasoning Through Language Arts Test.

Table of Contents

UNIT 2

Examples of persuasive writing include marketing brochures, movie reviews, editorials, and work performance evaluations.

Determine Author's Purpose

READING ASSESSMENT TARGETS: R.2.5, R.5.1, R.5.2, R.5.4, R.6.1, R.6.2, R.8.2

1 Learn the Skill

Authors write for different **purposes**, or reasons: to describe, inform, persuade, entertain, or tell a story. In fact, authors often write for more than one purpose. For example, in a persuasive article encouraging regular exercise, an author may tell a funny story about trying to keep up in an aerobics class. The main purpose of this article may be to persuade, but the author does so by entertaining. Sometimes authors directly state their purpose. Other times they have implicit, or unstated, purposes.

Authors keep their readers, or **audience**, in mind. Audiences may be general—anyone who chooses to read the work. Or they may be specific according to age, political view, income, education, technical background, interest, or profession. Authors try to appeal to their audiences and use appropriate language.

2 Practice the Skill

By practicing the skills of determining author's purpose and identifying audience, you will improve your study and test-taking abilities, especially as they relate to the GED® Reasoning Through Language Arts Test. Read the passage below. Then answer the question that follows.

GETTING A FLU SHOT

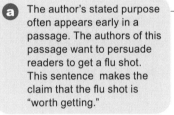

a The author's stated purpose often appears early in a passage. The authors of this passage want to persuade readers to get a flu shot. This sentence makes the claim that the flu shot is "worth getting."

b The CDC is a government agency that studies and advises about health issues. Authors refer to reliable sources to make their arguments more persuasive.

<u>Getting a flu shot often protects you from coming down with the flu.</u> And although the flu shot doesn't always provide total protection, it's worth getting.

This year's annual flu shot will offer protection against H1N1 flu (swine flu) virus, in addition to two other influenza viruses that are expected to be in circulation this fall and winter.

Influenza is a respiratory infection that can cause serious complications, particularly to young children and to older adults. Flu shots are the most effective way to prevent influenza and its complications. The <u>Centers for Disease Control and Prevention</u> (CDC) now recommends that everyone 6 months of age or older be vaccinated annually against influenza.

From the MayoClinic.com article FLU SHOT: YOUR BEST BET FOR AVOIDING INFLUENZA, accessed 2013

MAKING ASSUMPTIONS

Knowing an author's reputation may give you information about the purpose of the passage. The Mayo Clinic is a respected medical facility. You can assume that staff members are reliable sources of medical information.

1. Which statement **best** supports the purpose of persuading readers to get a flu shot?

A. The flu shot does not always provide total protection.
B. The flu shot will offer protection against H1N1 flu (swine flu) virus.
C. Influenza is a respiratory infection.
D. Flu shots are the most effective way to prevent influenza.

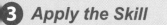

DIRECTIONS: Read the passage, read each question, and choose the **best** answer.

THE IMPACT OF EDUCATION ON POVERTY

1   For decades, America has wrestled with poverty but with little success. In 1964, President Lyndon Johnson famously declared "war on poverty." A 2012 study by the Cato Institute estimates that the United States has spent roughly $15 trillion since then, and yet the poverty rate is close to where it was more than 40 years ago. Cato reports that the United States spends nearly $1 trillion a year between federal and state programs to fight poverty.

2   That amounts to more than $20,000 per poor person and more than $60,000 for a family of three. And yet, the problem has not improved.

3   Both liberals and conservatives recognize this reality. However … some on the left think the problem is that the government has not gone far enough. They call for more government intervention, like living wages and expanded social services. Granted, the government has a role in aiding the poor, particularly the disabled, handicapped and those who are poor largely at no fault of their own.

4   But if history is any indicator, government transactions and services don't seem to be the key drivers of upward mobility. In fact, they can have the opposite effect and insulate lower classes from upward mobility.

5   Instead, conservatives would argue that education, earned success and the all-important mediating institutions—families, churches, communities, private and philanthropic enterprises, associations of coaches, teachers, parents, doctors, civil servants and religious and non-religious volunteers … are the pillars of upward mobility.

6   The evidence seems to support that. In a landmark study, the Brookings Institution found that young adults who finish high school, get a full-time job and wait until age 21 to get married and have children have just a 2% chance of falling into poverty and a 74% chance of ending up in the middle class.

From the cnn.com article REDUCE POVERTY BY PROMOTING SCHOOLS, FAMILIES by William J. Bennett, © 2013

2.   What is the author's main purpose in writing this passage?

   A. to persuade readers to support expanded social services
   B. to inform readers about how much the U.S. government spends to fight poverty
   C. to inform readers about high-school graduation rates
   D. to persuade readers that education is a key factor in overcoming poverty

3.   Which statement **best** explains the author's view about social services and other government programs that aid the poor?

   A. Government programs are not the solution to fighting poverty.
   B. Government programs should be expanded until poverty is largely eliminated.
   C. Graduation rates improve when social services are available.
   D. The government should not spend any more money on social services.

4.   The author assumes that his audience will include liberals as well as conservatives. Which statement **best** supports this assumption?

   A. He says that both liberals and conservatives agree about reality.
   B. He provides facts about the amounts of money spent on fighting poverty.
   C. He presents the liberal viewpoint and counters it with the conservative one.
   D. He mentions historical viewpoints other than those of liberals and conservatives.

5.   How does paragraph 6 relate to the author's purpose?

   A. It explains the details of the Brookings Institution study.
   B. It supports the author's viewpoint stated in paragraph 5.
   C. It confirms the findings of the Cato Institute study mentioned in paragraph 1.
   D. It contradicts the figures the author presents in paragraph 2.

UNIT 2

Analyze Elements of Persuasion

1 Learn the Skill

When an author writes to **persuade**, he or she tries to convince readers to agree with his or her point of view or to do something. **Argument** is a type of persuasion that uses logic and evidence to persuade. Persuasive writing usually starts with a **claim**, or a statement about an issue or a problem. The claim reflects the author's **position**, or point of view. Often, arguments present a **counterclaim**, or response to an opposing view. Counterclaims show that the author has considered both sides of an argument.

Authors use **evidence** to support their claims. Evidence may be facts, opinions, examples, or other reliable information. Authors also try to persuade by appealing to an audience's emotions, such as fear or anger. The writing ends with a **conclusion** that asks readers to do something or think in a particular way.

2 Practice the Skill

By practicing the skill of analyzing elements of persuasion and argument, you will improve your study and test-taking abilities, especially as they relate to the GED® Reasoning Through Language Arts Test. Read the passage below. Then answer the question that follows.

a The terms **public transportation** and **mass transit** refer to buses, trains, subways, and other means of transportation operated for the benefit of the public.

b Here, the author responds to the **opposing viewpoint** that investment in mass transit is not affordable.

SUPPORTING INVESTMENT IN PUBLIC TRANSPORTATION

You might take the subway to work or hop on the bus to run errands. Trains may be part of your daily commute. Yet, even if trains, buses, and subways are not part of your daily experience, you likely benefit from them nonetheless. Investment in public transportation generates jobs and boosts the economy.

Thousands of workers are engaged in building buses, repairing and maintaining rail lines, and so on. These jobs are located not only in the areas served by mass transit but also in regions throughout the country. In Imlay City, Michigan, for example, workers build buses that are used across the United States.

And jobs are not created merely in industries directly related to public transportation. Transportation workers and riders spend money throughout a mass transit network, enabling businesses to expand and hire. Although some think we cannot afford public investment in mass transit, the American Public Transportation Association estimates that for every dollar spent in such investment, approximately six dollars are generated in jobs and public benefits. Support legislation to develop mass transit, and help yourself to a better future.

1. Which sentence **best** states the passage's call to action?

   A. Take public transportation whenever you can.
   B. Encourage government investments in public transportation.
   C. Get a job in mass transit in order to have a secure future.
   D. Invest in mass transit projects only if you will benefit directly.

TEST-TAKING TIPS

Take enough time to read the question and all the answer choices very carefully. Even wrong answers can relate to information in the passage or can include language from the passage.

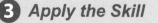

DIRECTIONS: Read the passage, read each question, and choose the **best** answer.

FOSTER YOUTH AND HEALTH CARE

1   What I hope would be neither partisan nor divisive is one small but important provision [of the Patient Protection and Affordable Care Act]: because of the Act, former foster youth may continue to have Medicaid coverage until they turn 26.

2   Why does this matter?

3   These are young people for whom we—and by this I mean all of civil society—have taken responsibility. They have been removed from their homes primarily because they could no longer live there safely. Some are fortunate enough to find a permanent, loving home where they can thrive. But others are not: they grow up in foster care or group homes.

4   Every year, some 26,000 young people who live in foster homes or group homes turn 18 (or in some states, 21) and "age out" of the system. Overnight, crucial support vanishes. Gone is the financial support paid to their foster parents or group homes on their behalf. Gone is any consistent, responsible adult presence or guidance. Gone is their health care coverage.

5   These youth face incredibly long odds if they have to try [to] succeed on their own during their late teens and early 20s. The label "former foster youth" makes it hard for them to get jobs or rent apartments. For them, there is a high risk of becoming homeless. We know these young people have a low rate of college entry, and even if they are admitted to college, many do not complete a degree.

6   It is both compassionate and less expensive for taxpayers to ensure that young adults who grew up in foster care have some basic support during this crucial formative period. One key to this support is health care coverage.

From the huffingtonpost.com article THE AFFORDABLE CARE ACT: GOOD NEWS FOR FORMER FOSTER YOUTH by Michael Piraino, accessed 2013

2. Why does the author pose the question "Why does this matter?"

    A. to introduce supporting evidence and reasons
    B. to express frustration with opposing viewpoints
    C. to invite readers to draw their own conclusions
    D. to create a sense of tension in the passage

3. Which statement **best** expresses the author's main claim?

    A. Society is responsible for supporting former foster youth.
    B. Foster youth face problems when trying to rent apartments.
    C. Extending Medicaid is an important way of helping former foster youth.
    D. Providing employment is the best solution to the problem of homelessness.

4. In paragraph 5, the author explains the challenges former foster youth face. How does this paragraph support the author's claim?

    A. It contrasts the lives of former foster youth with the lives of those in permanent homes.
    B. It explains why former foster youth are more likely to need health care services.
    C. It shows how not having health insurance affects former foster youth.
    D. It emphasizes that extending Medicaid is one way to help former foster youth.

5. The author assumes that readers will feel sympathy and compassion for former foster youth. The author appeals to these feelings by

    A. scolding readers for not doing more to help former foster youth.
    B. detailing the overwhelming lack of support former foster youth face.
    C. providing facts about the expenses of taking care of former foster youth.
    D. calculating the costs of providing Medicaid to former foster youth.

UNIT 2

Identify Evidence

READING ASSESSMENT TARGETS: R.2.2, R.2.5, R.3.5, R.5.1, R.5.4, R.6.1, R.8.1, R.8.2

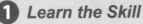

1 Learn the Skill

In persuasive writing, claims are supported by **evidence**—reasons and information that show why readers should believe or agree with the claim. Claims are authors' **opinions** or viewpoints. Evidence is made up of **facts,** information that can be proved true or untrue, and credible or convincing opinions. Authors use different types of evidence, depending on their purpose and audience. Authors also may use appeals to **logic**, appeals to **emotion**, and appeals to **ethics**.

2 Practice the Skill

By practicing the skill of identifying evidence, you will improve your study and test-taking abilities, especially as they relate to the GED® Reasoning Through Language Arts Test. Study the table below. Then answer the question that follows.

▶ Consider how the different types of evidence support this claim: People must take steps to protect the habitats and migration routes of monarch butterflies.

a **Anecdotes** are very short stories. Anecdotes often appear as introductions to persuasive texts or as examples that support or refute claims.

b **Credibility** refers to the reliability or trustworthiness of sources or authors. The appeal relies on knowledge, training, or experience in the subject.

Type of Appeal	Evidence	Example
Logic	facts, data, personal experiences, expert opinions	A study found that the number of monarch butterflies spending the winter in Mexico dropped by a third in a year.
Emotion	anecdotes, visuals, warnings, strong language that stirs feelings	On their migrations, delicate monarch butterflies face many natural challenges. But now they face an even greater danger—destruction of their habitats by humans.
Ethics	author's credibility, source's credibility	The Smithsonian National Zoological Park recommends learning about monarchs so that we can pursue conservation efforts.

USING LOGIC

Appeals to emotion can be an important part of persuasion. However, if an author uses only emotional appeals and no facts to support a claim, think carefully about whether the claim is valid or well supported.

1. Why might a fundraising letter from a conservation group include photographs of trees cut down in a butterfly habitat?

   A. to prove that the number of butterflies is decreasing
   B. to show that the group is a credible source of information
   C. to make readers fearful about the threat to butterflies
   D. to counter claims that butterfly populations are growing

UNIT 2

DIRECTIONS: Read the passage, read each question, and choose the **best** answer.

In 1946, J. A. Krug, Secretary of the Interior, wrote a letter to the Speaker of the House of Representatives asking him to support legislation that would make it easier for Japanese Americans to receive payment for losses they suffered as a result of movement, or "evacuation," to camps during World War II. Part of this letter is paraphrased below.

COMPENSATING JAPANESE AMERICAN EVACUEES

1   In 1942, the War Department ordered that all Japanese Americans be removed from the Pacific Coast of the United States. For approximately two and a half years, more than 100,000 of these American citizens and their alien parents could not return to their homes. In January of 1945, they were allowed to return to their homes to try to resume their lives. It is too early to establish the total financial and property losses the Japanese Americans experienced, but the losses are undoubtedly heavy. Some lost everything they had. Many lost most of what they had.

2   None of these Japanese American evacuees was charged with any crime. Experience has shown that most of them were and are good Americans. The 23,000 Japanese Americans who served in the armed forces in both Europe and the Pacific have an outstanding record. The intelligence agencies have uncovered no instances of sabotage or espionage by Americans of Japanese ancestry during the war.

3   The evacuation orders left people with very little time to get their affairs in order. Merchants had to sell their stocks and businesses at sacrifice prices. Many evacuees sold personal possessions for a fraction of their value. A large number of people had to accept inadequate arrangements for the protection of their property. Some property was abandoned.

4   These losses are the direct result of the evacuation. Now, for the first time in the history of our nation, Japanese Americans are asking for public assistance in substantial numbers. The least that this country can do, in simple justice, is offer some degree of compensation for the incredible losses the evacuees have suffered.

2. Which fact supports the author's claim that Japanese Americans were evacuated without cause?

    A. More than 100,000 Japanese Americans were not allowed to return to their homes.
    B. The intelligence agencies uncovered no espionage by Japanese Americans.
    C. Merchants had to sell their stocks and businesses at sacrifice prices.
    D. Japanese Americans are asking for public assistance in substantial numbers.

3. In paragraph 2, why does the author discuss the service record of Japanese Americans during the war?

    A. to suggest that evacuees made greater sacrifices than other Americans
    B. to express appreciation for what members of the Armed Forces had done
    C. to explain why so few men were among the evacuees
    D. to show that Japanese Americans were patriotic and brave

4. Which statement **best** summarizes the evidence presented in paragraph 3?

    A. The haste of the evacuation resulted in financial losses for Japanese Americans.
    B. More planning could have helped the evacuation run more smoothly.
    C. Japanese Americans had to leave their property with people they did not trust.
    D. Japanese Americans had trouble determining the value of their possessions.

5. Which statement **best** explains the way in which the author uses evidence in this passage?

    A. He relies on his position as Secretary of the Interior to persuade readers.
    B. He states a claim and uses statistics and personal stories to show that it is valid.
    C. He builds to a claim by presenting facts as logical evidence.
    D. He uses emotional language to make readers feel sympathy for Japanese Americans.

Analyze Visuals and Data

READING ASSESSMENT TARGETS: R.2.7, R.7.2, R.8.2

1 Learn the Skill

Authors often use **visuals** to help convey ideas and information. Visuals include photographs, diagrams, drawings, charts, graphs, and tables. Different kinds of visuals support authors' claims in different ways. Photographs and diagrams can give readers a better understanding of what a situation was or is like. Such visuals also may clarify a text or support an author's argument by appealing to readers' emotions, as you learned in Lesson 2 in this unit.

Data, which include numbers, statistics, and other types of similar information, are often easier to read and understand when they appear in charts and tables. Authors often use data to provide logical support for claims, as explained in Lesson 2.

2 Practice the Skill

By practicing the skill of analyzing visuals and data, you will improve your study and test-taking abilities, especially as they relate to the GED® Reasoning Through Language Arts Test. Read the information and study the table below. Then answer the question that follows.

THE TWO TYPES OF FLU VACCINE

▶ Both the flu shot and the nasal spray help protect against influenza. But there are differences to consider before deciding between the two.

a Column headings identify information. The left column has information about the shot, the right column about the nasal spray.

b Authors often use short phrases to convey information quickly. Here, readers can easily review information about two types of flu vaccine.

Flu Shot	Nasal Spray
Administered through a needle—you'll need an injection	Administered through a spray—you won't need an injection
Contains killed viruses—you can't pass the flu along to anyone else	Contains weakened live viruses that won't give you the flu but that can, in rare cases, be transmitted to others
Approved for people 6 months of age and older	Approved for heallty people ages 2 to 49 years
Can be used for people at increased risk of flu-related complications, including pregnant women and those with chronic medical conditions	Given only to nonpregnant, healthy people, not to those with chronic medical conditions, suppressed immune systems, or children and adolescents receiving aspirin therapy

From the MayoClinic.com article FLU SHOT: YOUR BEST BET FOR AVOIDING INFLUENZA, accessed 2013

MAKING ASSUMPTIONS

You can assume that the authors intend to inform readers about the flu vaccine and to persuade them to get vaccinated by providing options for getting the vaccine.

1. Which reader would be **most** likely to choose the nasal spray after studying this table?

   A. a reader with a medical condition
   B. a reader with a fear of needles
   C. a reader who is pregnant
   D. a reader who is sixty years old

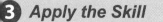

DIRECTIONS: Read the passage, read each question, and choose the **best** answer.

OREGON—LAND OF OPPORTUNITY

1   Oregon is a state of agricultural opportunity. Its broad areas of undeveloped farming land offer matchless advantages to those who will come and till them. Every section of the state wants settlers. To such as have industry and will undertake the development of the idle acres, rich rewards await.

2   Never before has the state of Oregon been so diligent in the development of agriculture, its greatest asset, as now. The state is anxious that every farmer who comes to it shall thrive. Not only the Oregon State Agricultural College, one of the most efficient of all such institutions in the whole country, but every other agency is working for the success of the agricultural interests.

3   Experimental and development farms dot the state. The commercial bodies and the business community are allied to advance the interests of the tiller of the soil, and the business men of the chief cities work for the betterment of the farming districts, knowing that in doing this they are building the surest foundations for the future of Oregon.

4   The whole state bids the farmer welcome. Its fertile soil and genial climate work in partnership with all these interests to make his life pleasant and his work profitable. With the growing markets and the widening demand for his products, the husbandman will find this a region of never-failing, bountiful crops and remunerative rewards.

From the pamphlet THE LAND OF OPPORTUNITY by Oswald West, © 1912

Oregon [State] Agricultural College Campus, 1912

2. How does the picture support the claim that Oregon has "broad areas of undeveloped farming land" and "idle acres"?

   A. The land in the picture looks green and healthy and shows small farms.
   B. The picture of the Oregon Agricultural College proves that past farmers have succeeded.
   C. The college looks well developed, suggesting that it offers many resources for newcomers.
   D. The landscape in the background of the picture seems expansive and unoccupied.

3. Seeing a picture of the Oregon Agricultural College might have reassured readers considering a move to Oregon by showing that

   A. the state was not deserted or lacking community resources.
   B. businesses and farming districts were thriving.
   C. state agencies were committed to helping farmers.
   D. the state offered options for building a successful career.

4. Which statement **best** explains how the passage and picture work together to persuade readers?

   A. The passage provides positive statistics about Oregon, and the picture helps readers imagine what it might be like to live there.
   B. The passage explains the importance of the Oregon State Agricultural College, and the picture provides details about the campus.
   C. The passage explains how agencies and institutions work together to help farmers, and the picture shows one of those institutions.
   D. The passage states how much opportunity and support await farmers in Oregon, and the picture provides an ideal image of the area.

UNIT 2

Identify Faulty Evidence

UNIT 2

1 Learn the Skill

It is important to review arguments to identify claims supported by **faulty reasoning or evidence**. Faulty reasoning involves arguments that are not logical. Faulty evidence may involve inaccurate, insufficient, or irrelevant information, or it may appeal to readers' emotions to support a claim. For example, authors may try to make readers feel afraid or feel as though they belong to or are superior to a particular group.

2 Practice the Skill

By practicing the skill of identifying faulty reasoning and evidence, you will improve your study and test-taking abilities, especially as they relate to the GED® Reasoning Through Language Arts Test. Read the information and study the table below. Then answer the question that follows.

▶ Gluten is a protein found in wheat flour. The examples in this table are intended to support the claim that avoiding gluten increases energy and weight loss.

Faulty Reasoning	Explanation	Example
Inaccurate cause and effect	Suggesting that events have a cause-and-effect relationship because the events occur together	After I removed gluten from my diet, I lost weight.
Irrelevant information	Providing evidence that does not relate to the claim	One in 100 people cannot digest gluten. Like them, you could gain energy by eating gluten-free foods.
Inaccurate either/or situation	Suggesting there are only two options or viewpoints when there are more	If you want to have more energy, you must remove gluten from your diet.
Faulty Evidence	**Explanation**	**Example**
Bandwagon appeal	Arguing in favor of an idea because the idea is popular	Join the thousands of people who have found better health, gluten-free!
Scare tactics	Exaggerating a danger or using threatening language	Do you want to be condemned to a future of obesity and disease?
Testimonial	Supporting an idea by featuring the endorsement of a celebrity	Performer Miley Cyrus believes in the benefits of going gluten-free!

a A generalization with too little information is faulty reasoning. For example, "Three friends have gone gluten-free, and they feel great. Going gluten-free improves your health!"

b Authors also may try to make readers feel patriotic. This emotional appeal is considered part of bandwagon appeal.

USING LOGIC

Some authors exhibit bias—they write about only one side of an issue or ignore information that contradicts their claims. Biased arguments are unreliable. So are arguments without enough support.

1. Why is the fact that one in 100 people cannot digest gluten irrelevant to the claim that gluten-free food increases energy?

A. The fact inaccurately suggests an either/or situation.
B. The fact is intended to persuade readers to give up gluten because many people have removed gluten from their diets.
C. The fact is stated in strong language intended to frighten.
D. The fact does not give any indication of the likely effects of gluten on an individual with his or her own health needs.

⭐ Spotlighted Item: **DRAG-AND-DROP**

DIRECTIONS: Read the passage and the question. Then use the drag-and-drop option to complete the boxes.

GIVE TO THE DUDLEY MEMORIAL SHELTER

1   When animal rescue officers found Lady, the tiny poodle mix was dirty, scrawny, and trembling with fear. Rescuers estimated that she had been cruelly abandoned in the empty house for at least a week. Can you imagine what it must feel like to find yourself in a strange place, without food or water, completely alone?

2   No creature should have to go through what Lady went through, and thanks to the care of the dedicated staff at the Dudley Memorial Animal Shelter, Lady is on the road to recovery. But without your financial support, other animals will not be so lucky. Please consider a donation to save an animal in need.

3   Celebrities such as singer Sarah McLachlan have long been heroes for animal rights, and our own hero, Damian Ferri, says "Supporting helpless animals has given me as much personal satisfaction as it has helped save abused and abandoned animals."

4   You, too, can make a difference for animals in need by donating to support our care, outreach, and education efforts, and you can rest assured that 80 cents of every dollar you donate will go directly to the care of the animals in our charge or to community actions to promote animal welfare.

5   According to the American Pet Products Association, approximately 62 percent of American households own pets. Show the animals in your life that you care by contributing to the Dudley Memorial Animal Shelter. Through the generosity of so many people like you, who care deeply about animals, we are able to help unfortunate creatures that cannot help themselves.

---

2. Drag and drop each detail into the correct box.

Irrelevant Information	Details
	Can you imagine what it must feel like to find yourself in a strange place, without food or water, completely alone?
Inaccurate either/or situation	But without your financial support, other animals will not be so lucky.
	And our own hero, Damian Ferri, says "Supporting helpless animals has given me as much personal satisfaction as it has helped save abused and abandoned animals."
Bandwagon appeal	According to the American Pet Products Association, approximately 62 percent of American households own pets.
Appeal to sympathy	Through the generosity of so many people like you, who care deeply about animals, we are able to help unfortunate creatures that cannot help themselves.
Testimonial	

Classify Valid and Invalid Evidence

READING ASSESSMENT TARGETS: R.8.2, R.8.3, R.8.4, R.8.5

① Learn the Skill

When you classify evidence as valid or invalid, you evaluate the evidence to determine whether it supports a claim effectively. **Valid evidence** is relevant, or directly related to the claim. It must also be reliable. Reliable evidence comes from a trustworthy source, such as an expert in the field. Reliable evidence is fair and complete.

Evidence can be **invalid** (not valid) for several reasons. Evidence that does not come from a reliable source is invalid. Similarly, evidence that does not relate directly to the claim is invalid. If evidence does not fully support a claim or reflects faulty reasoning, it is invalid. Being able to classify evidence will help you decide whether an argument is convincing.

② Practice the Skill

By practicing the skill of classifying valid and invalid evidence, you will improve your study and test-taking abilities, especially as they relate to the GED® Reasoning Through Language Arts Test. Read the passage below. Then answer the question that follows.

SOLAR IS THE SMART WAY TO GO

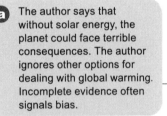

a The author says that without solar energy, the planet could face terrible consequences. The author ignores other options for dealing with global warming. Incomplete evidence often signals bias.

b Most issues have pros and cons. The statement suggests that the author is ignoring opposing viewpoints, and the evidence is likely incomplete.

The sun is an abundant source of energy. Every hour, more energy reaches Earth from the sun than humans use in a year. Harnessing the energy of the sun to power and heat our homes makes sense for our environment and our economy.

Solar energy is a renewable, nonpolluting resource. Unlike burning fossil fuels, changing solar energy into electricity or heat does not produce greenhouse gases that contribute to global warming. If we do not take steps to switch to solar energy, we could soon find ourselves on a planet with unpredictable weather, an unstable food supply, and widespread political upheaval.

Developing solar energy also makes sense from an economic perspective. According to the Solar Foundation's National Solar Jobs Census 2012, the solar industry added 13,872 jobs from September 2011 to September 2012. That figure represents a 13% growth rate in employment in the industry. At a time when employment in other industries is lagging or shrinking, "going solar" is a strategy with no downside!

USING LOGIC

Remember that appeals to emotion or ethics are not necessarily invalid forms of evidence. However, consider whether support would be strengthened if the author included facts or specific information.

1. Which statement is valid evidence in support of the author's argument that solar energy is good for the economy?

   A. "Every hour, more energy reaches Earth from the sun than humans use in a year."
   B. "Developing solar energy also makes sense from an economic perspective."
   C. " ... the solar industry added 13,872 jobs from September 2011 to September 2012."
   D. "At a time when employment in other industries is lagging or shrinking, 'going solar' is a strategy with no downside!"

⭐ Spotlighted Item: **DRAG-AND-DROP**

DIRECTIONS: Read the passage and the question. Then use the drag-and-drop option to complete the chart.

ADOPT A SHELTER MUTT

1   Shelters have all shapes and sizes of lovable mutts, purebreds, all-American cats, shaggy dogs, puppies and kittens, teenagers and oldsters. Your chances of finding a wonderful companion who matches your lifestyle, family, and home are excellent! About 25 percent of these animals are purebreds. However, if you're looking for a truly one-of-a-kind pet unlike anyone else's, animal shelters offer the best selection anywhere of smart, healthy, lovable mixed-breed cats and dogs. According to the Humane Society of the United States, mutts are America's dog of choice, accounting for nearly 60 percent of all pet dogs. What's more, their numbers are increasing for good reasons. As dog trainer and author Brian Kilcommons explains, "mixed breed dogs are often healthier, longer-lived, more intelligent, and of more stable temperament than purebreds because of what geneticists call 'hybrid vigor.' "...

2   A "second-hand" pet in no way means second-rate. On the contrary, shelter workers have often observed that many shelter animals seem to sense what they were up against and become among the most devoted and grateful companions. ...

3   Dogs, cats, and small mammals like guinea pigs, rabbits, and rats end up in shelters because of circumstances beyond their control. They're victims of a death, an illness, a divorce, or a move that didn't include them. Or they were displaced by a new baby. Or their owners just didn't learn how to train them. ...

4   The simple fact is that there are many more animals needing adoption than there are homes for them. So when you adopt from a shelter, you become part of the solution to the overpopulation crisis.

From the apsofdurham.org article WHY ADOPT A SHELTER PET?, accessed 2013

2.   Drag and drop the evidence into the correct location on the chart.

Invalid	Valid

Evidence
According to the Humane Society of the United States, mutts are America's dog of choice, accounting for nearly 60 percent of all pet dogs.
Dog trainer and author Brian Kilcommons explains, "mixed breed dogs are often healthier, longer-lived, more intelligent, and of more stable temperament than purebreds."
Shelter workers have often observed that many shelter animals seem to sense what they were up against and become among the most devoted and grateful companions.
Dogs, cats, and small mammals like guinea pigs, rabbits, and rats end up in shelters because of circumstances beyond their control.

READING ASSESSMENT TARGETS: R.2.5, R.2.8, R.5.2, R.5.4, R.8.1, R.8.6

1 Learn the Skill

Structure refers to the way authors arrange and present, or build, ideas in a text. Authors choose structures to present their ideas in the most effective way possible. As you read, consider how the overall structure of a passage and the structure of each paragraph contribute to the author's argument.

2 Practice the Skill

By practicing the skill of analyzing the structure of arguments, you will improve your study and test-taking abilities, especially as they relate to the GED® Reasoning Through Language Arts Test. Study the table below. Then answer the question that follows.

a This author "sandwiches" evidence between the claim and conclusion. Evidence might include responses to opposing views or support for smaller claims related to the main claim.

b An author might use a pro/con structure to discuss buying a certain computer. There might be pros, such as more memory, and cons, such as high price. In the conclusion, the author might make a recommendation.

Structure	Description
Traditional "sandwich" structure	The author begins with an introduction that usually ends in a claim. The author then provides reasons and evidence to support the claim. The author ends with a conclusion that could include a call to action.
Pro/con structure	The author lists the positives (pros) and negatives (cons) related to a claim. This structure is effective when the author wants to acknowledge the drawbacks of a position or to suggest that a particular solution might not work in every situation or for everyone.
Refutation/proof structure	The author begins by referring to an opposing viewpoint or claim and stating that this claim is false or inaccurate. The author then provides evidence and reasons supporting his or her viewpoint. This structure is especially effective when an author's claim is that another claim is inaccurate.
Order of importance	The author states a claim and then lists evidence in order of effectiveness. The author might start with the strongest evidence and move to the weakest, or vice versa. This structure is most effective when evidence or reasons are not equally convincing.

TEST-TAKING TECH
Before you click to submit an answer, reread the question and all four answer choices. Doing so will help you catch important information you might have missed.

1. If a scientist wanted to argue that another scientist's conclusions were inaccurate, which structure would **best** support his or her ideas?

A. traditional "sandwich" structure
B. pro/con structure
C. refutation/proof structure
D. order of importance

UNIT 2

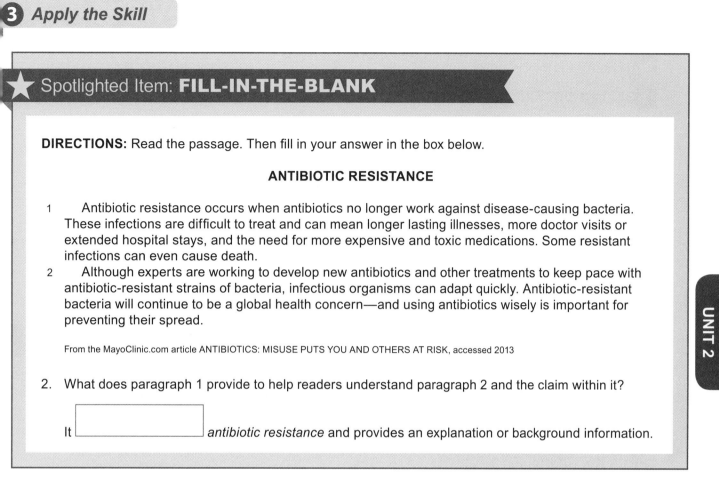

UNIT 2

★ Spotlighted Item: **FILL-IN-THE-BLANK**

DIRECTIONS: Read the passage. Then fill in your answer in the box below.

ANTIBIOTIC RESISTANCE

1   Antibiotic resistance occurs when antibiotics no longer work against disease-causing bacteria. These infections are difficult to treat and can mean longer lasting illnesses, more doctor visits or extended hospital stays, and the need for more expensive and toxic medications. Some resistant infections can even cause death.

2   Although experts are working to develop new antibiotics and other treatments to keep pace with antibiotic-resistant strains of bacteria, infectious organisms can adapt quickly. Antibiotic-resistant bacteria will continue to be a global health concern—and using antibiotics wisely is important for preventing their spread.

From the MayoClinic.com article ANTIBIOTICS: MISUSE PUTS YOU AND OTHERS AT RISK, accessed 2013

2. What does paragraph 1 provide to help readers understand paragraph 2 and the claim within it?

It [_____] *antibiotic resistance* and provides an explanation or background information.

DIRECTIONS: Read the passage, read each question, and choose the **best** answer.

PROBLEMS WITH ANTIBIOTICS

1   If antibiotics are used too often for things they can't treat—like colds, flu or other viral infections—not only are they of no benefit, they become less effective against the bacteria they're intended to treat.

2   Not taking antibiotics exactly as prescribed also leads to problems. For example, if you take an antibiotic for only a few days—instead of the full course—the antibiotic may wipe out some, but not all, of the bacteria. The surviving bacteria become more resistant and can be spread to other people. When bacteria become resistant to first line treatments, the risk of complications and death is increased. …

3   When you misuse antibiotics, you help create resistant microorganisms that can cause new and hard-to-treat infections. That's why the decisions you make about using antibiotics—unlike almost any other medicine you take—have far-reaching consequences. Be responsible in how you use antibiotics to protect your health and that of your family, neighbors and community.

From the MayoClinic.com article ANTIBIOTICS: MISUSE PUTS YOU AND OTHERS AT RISK, accessed 2013

3. Which claim do paragraphs 1 and 2 **best** support?

A. Antibiotic-resistant bacteria are a threat.
B. Antibiotics must be used wisely.
C. Antibiotics may cause serious complications.
D. Antibiotics provide only partial cures.

4. The structure of this passage helps the author build an argument based on the assumption that

A. doctors require more funding to research antibiotic-resistant bacteria.
B. infections are the greatest health crisis the world currently faces.
C. organisms that adapt quickly are generally very dangerous.
D. misuse of antibiotic medications is a significant problem.

Analyze Rhetorical Devices

READING ASSESSMENT TARGETS: R.4.3/L.4.3, R.6.1, R.6.3, R.6.4

1 Learn the Skill

A **rhetorical device** is a particular use of language to achieve an effect—for example, to emphasize a significant point, attract audience attention, or create a feeling. Rhetorical devices are common in all writing, especially in speeches and arguments.

2 Practice the Skill

By practicing the skill of analyzing rhetorical devices, you will improve your study and test-taking abilities, especially as they relate to the GED® Reasoning Through Language Arts Test. Study the table below. Then answer the question that follows.

a Style and tone are not rhetorical devices, but authors use them to create a desired effect. For example, a patriotic tone can make readers feel proud and moved to take action.

b **Parallelism**, the repetition of the structure of a phrase or clause, is a form of repetition. For example, *When we go to the polls, when we go to the protests, when we go to the steps of the Capitol*, our voices ring out.

RHETORICAL DEVICES

Device	Definition	Example
Analogy	An extended comparison to help clarify an idea or make a point more persuasively	Think of stem cells as blank computer chips that we can program to do different tasks.
Enumeration	List of details to create rhythm or emphasize a point	This bill would benefit many in the community—teachers, parents, school workers, and, most importantly, students.
Repetition and parallelism	Restatement of the same or similar phrases or words to create rhythm and emphasis	Preserving the land would protect local wildlife. That is good. It would generate tourism. That is good. And it would save a unique ecosystem for future generations. That is good.
Juxtaposition of opposites (antithesis)	Two opposing concepts placed side by side to emphasize a point	"That's one small step for a man, one giant leap for mankind."—Neil Armstrong
Qualifying statements	A statement that modifies, or changes, a previous statement to emphasize a point	Few people survived the blast—although fewer escaped with no injuries.

TEST-TAKING TIPS

When a question asks you to choose the **best** answer, choose the one that would apply in most or all situations. Some incorrect answer choices may be incomplete, too broad, or not always applicable.

1. If a writer favors tighter restrictions on factory pollution, which rhetorical device would be **most** effective for persuading readers?

A. an analogy explaining how the pollution is produced
B. enumeration of the diseases caused by pollution
C. juxtaposition of two opposite adjectives to describe factories
D. a qualifying statement saying that some pollution is acceptable

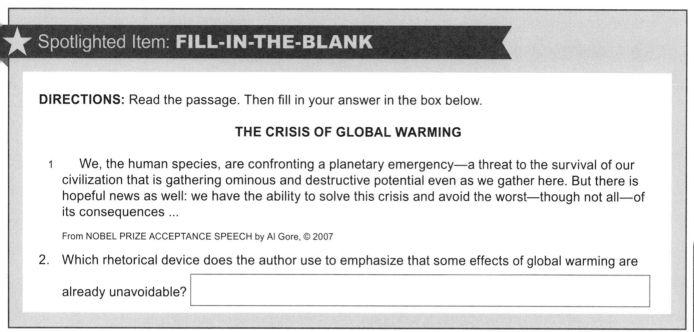

★ Spotlighted Item: **FILL-IN-THE-BLANK**

DIRECTIONS: Read the passage. Then fill in your answer in the box below.

THE CRISIS OF GLOBAL WARMING

1   We, the human species, are confronting a planetary emergency—a threat to the survival of our civilization that is gathering ominous and destructive potential even as we gather here. But there is hopeful news as well: we have the ability to solve this crisis and avoid the worst—though not all—of its consequences ...

From NOBEL PRIZE ACCEPTANCE SPEECH by Al Gore, © 2007

2.   Which rhetorical device does the author use to emphasize that some effects of global warming are already unavoidable?

DIRECTIONS: Read the remainder of passage, read each question, and choose the **best** answer.

2   However, despite a growing number of honorable exceptions, too many of the world's leaders are still best described in the words Winston Churchill applied to those who ignored Adolf Hitler's threat (and I quote): "They go on in strange paradox, decided only to be undecided, resolved to be irresolute, adamant for drift, solid for fluidity, all powerful to be impotent."

3   So today, we dumped another 70 million tons of global-warming pollution into the thin shell of atmosphere surrounding our planet, as if it were an open sewer. And tomorrow, we will dump a slightly larger amount, with the cumulative concentrations now trapping more and more heat from the sun.

4   As a result, the earth has a fever. And the fever is rising. The experts have told us it is not a passing affliction that will heal by itself. We asked for a second opinion. And a third. And a fourth. And the consistent conclusion, restated with increasing distress, is that something basic is wrong.

5   We are what is wrong, and we must make it right. ...

6   In the last few months, it has been harder and harder to misinterpret the signs that our world is spinning out of kilter. Major cities in North and South America, Asia and Australia, are nearly out of water due to massive droughts and melting glaciers. Desperate farmers are losing their livelihoods. Peoples in the frozen Arctic and on low-lying Pacific islands are planning evacuations of places they have long called home ...

From NOBEL PRIZE ACCEPTANCE SPEECH by Al Gore, © 2007

3.   Which statement **best** explains why the quotation from Winston Churchill is effective?

A. It uses repetition to draw readers in and stress the importance of finding a solution.
B. It lists the many ways that leaders acted with bravery during World War II.
C. It uses juxtaposition of opposites to emphasize that leaders find excuses to avoid taking action.
D. It includes a qualifying statement to suggest that quick action can defeat the evil of global warming.

4.   The author uses an analogy in paragraph 4 to

A. make the solution seem as simple as taking a pill to lower a fever.
B. show that he is a reliable source who has expert knowledge.
C. suggest that those who deny global warming are like a disease.
D. emphasize that global warming is as dangerous as a serious disease.

5.   In paragraph 6, the author lists the effects that global warming is already having. The author **most** likely included this enumeration to

A. make readers believe that the problem is urgent.
B. encourage punishment for polluters.
C. reassure readers about the future.
D. make readers aware of how to take action.

Compare and Contrast Texts

READING ASSESSMENT TARGETS: R.4.3/L.4.3, R.7.3, R.9.1/R.7.1

1 Learn the Skill

When you **compare and contrast texts that address similar topics**, you examine all aspects of the texts to find similarities and differences. You can use basic questions to gather information about the content. For example, *What topics are addressed? How does each author approach the topics?* Also, in examining the structure of the texts, you may ask *How does each author organize information and ideas? What structural devices does each author use to achieve his or her purpose?*

Look for clues that show each author's **perspective**, **style**, and **tone**. As you examine the texts, understand that texts that seem similar may have big differences, and texts that seem different may have similarities.

2 Practice the Skill

By practicing the skill of comparing and contrasting texts that address similar topics, you will improve your study and test-taking abilities, especially as they relate to the GED® Reasoning Through Language Arts Test. Read the passages below. Then answer the question that follows.

INDIVIDUALISM AND THE PEACE CORPS

[T]he Peace Corps is an example of free enterprise at work. It is a working model of some of the most basic and fundamental American ideas and beliefs. First, the Peace Corps is based upon the individual—his freedom, his initiative and his responsibility. We take Americans, give them three months' intensive training and set them to work in a foreign land. They do not live in a group or in a barracks. They are sometimes alone; in a strange village. They decide how hard they will work, what projects they will undertake, where they will travel.

From SPEECH BEFORE THE COMMONWEALTH CLUB OF CALIFORNIA by R. Sargent Shriver, 1963

a Shriver emphasizes the importance of individualism and supports this assertion. For example, Peace Corps members often live alone, "in a strange village." His perspective is from an organizer, not a participant.

KIKUYU BINDS

The women cluck at me sympathetically and admonish the children. For all the heart I put into new tasks—building raised beds, gardening—the women know too well the ongoing struggle. Kikuyu requires vigilance. The persistent grass returns to reclaim its hold on the earth as soon as a back is turned. And these women have many babies, fields to plow, boulders to move, corn to shuck and grind into flour, houses of manure and mud to build and floors to sweep. Their heads are often down; their backs often bent.

From KIKUYU BINDS by Michele Graves, Courtesy of the Peace Corps, © 2010

b Graves, a Peace Corps volunteer, writes of her experience from a participant's perspective. The use of first-person pronouns can help you identify that she is writing a personal narrative to express her feelings about the topic.

USING LOGIC

When determining an author's style, look at specific words and sentences. For example, Shriver uses commonplace verbs, such as *live* and *decide*, whereas Graves uses more expressive verbs, such as *cluck* and *admonish*.

1. Which statement **best** reflects the differences in the authors' styles?

   A. Shriver uses descriptive, colorful language, but Graves uses formal, stiff language.
   B. Shriver uses poetic language, but Graves uses straightforward language and simple sentences.
   C. Shriver uses straightforward, simple language, but Graves uses visual details and descriptive language.
   D. Shriver uses informal language, but Graves uses powerful, intimidating language.

⭐ Spotlighted Item: **DRAG-AND-DROP**

DIRECTIONS: Read the remainder of the passages. Then use the drag-and-drop option to complete the chart.

INDIVIDUALISM AND THE PEACE CORPS

1   They receive enough money to live, are sent to do a job for America and are expected to do that job.

2   We operate this way because we have faith in the American individual—his skill and his dedication. We do it because we believe in personal responsibility—not in corporate anonymity or bureaucratic protection. And this faith has been justified.

3   Second, the Peace Corps exemplifies and even generates private enterprise. We have no organization men, no protected corporation jobs, no pensions, no coffee breaks. We place the Volunteer down in a new environment and say to him: See what you can come up with. And we often find that they have become the Wright Brothers or Edisons or Fords of the world in which they are living.

From SPEECH BEFORE THE COMMONWEALTH CLUB OF CALIFORNIA by R. Sargent Shriver, 1963

KIKUYU BINDS

1   Soon I croon to myself as I find a regular rhythm in my digging. I add "Lesotho Fatse La Bontat'a Rona" and "Fiela" to my repertoire. I grow tanner and, somehow, fatter, although I walk f[a]rther for groceries than I ever will in my life: an hour and a half over a mountain alongside barefooted grandmothers who carry 50-pound bags of flour on their heads. My hands crack and weather. I learn to speak the language, Sesotho, beautiful and flowing like wind through corn stalks or the rivers I cross on my travels by foot to seven villages in the valley. I explain my mission to the women in halting phrases, using the words I know. Softness. Life.

2   I mix the soil with air and cow manure and rake it into a fine mesh piled high. The raised bed sits a foot off the earth buoyed by molecules of air and moisture-retaining compost. Sifted light and fluffy as cake

flour, it provides a home for the tender long taproots of carrots, bulbous onions and the fragile roots of tomatoes. On a diet of boiled corn and cabbage, children suffer and die. A small plot of earth the size of a grave with soft soil provides space to grow foods with Vitamin A and C that prevent diseases with consequences as difficult as their names; marasmus, kwashiorkor.

From KIKUYU BINDS by Michele Graves, Courtesy of the Peace Corps, © 2010

2.   Drag and drop the statements into the correct chart.

Shriver

Graves

Drag-and-Drop Answer Options
emphasizes that the Peace Corps represents American ideals and ingenuity
appeals to human sympathy
promotes the Peace Corps by providing an overview of the program
has gained knowledge and experience from the Peace Corps
appeals to American patriotism
describes the Peace Corps by providing aspects of a specific experience

Compare Texts in Different Formats

READING ASSESSMENT TARGETS: R.7.2, R.7.3, R.9.1/R.7.1

1 Learn the Skill

Remember that when you **compare** and **contrast** texts, you look for ways in which they are similar or different. Sometimes, information in written texts can appear in **different formats**, such as tables, charts, graphs, timelines, illustrations, photographs, or maps. When you compare texts in different formats, you look for ways in which they present similar information. Ask yourself these questions: *Which format is more effective in presenting ideas? For what audience or purpose was each written? Which is easier to read?*

2 Practice the Skill

By practicing the skill of comparing and contrasting texts in different formats, you will improve your study and test-taking abilities, especially as they relate to the GED® Reasoning Through Language Arts Test. Read the passages below. Then answer the question that follows.

UNIT 2

ABIGAIL ADAMS LETTER

Washington, 21 November 1800

My Dear Child:
    You must keep all this to yourself, and, when asked how I like it, say that I write you the situation is beautiful, which is true. The house is made habitable, but there is not a single apartment finished ... We have not the least fence, yard, or other convenience [outside], and the great unfinished audience room I made a drying room of, to hang up the clothes in. The principal stairs are not up, and will not be this winter. Six chambers are made comfortable; two are occupied by the President and Mr. Shaw; two lower rooms, one for a common parlor, and one for a levee room. Upstairs there is the oval room … and has the crimson furniture in it. It is a very handsome room now; but, when completed, it will be beautiful.

From LETTER TO HER DAUGHTER FROM THE NEW WHITE HOUSE, by Abigail Adams, © 1800

THE WHITE HOUSE, 1803

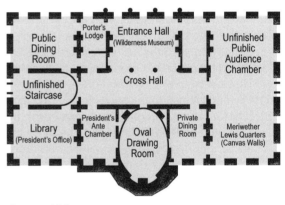

Source: whitehousemuseum.org

a Notice that the first text is in a letter format whereas the second is a floor plan, or diagram. Both contain some similar information.

b The letter and floor plan give information about the White House during different administrations: those of John Adams and Thomas Jefferson.

TEST-TAKING TIPS

Base your answers on information in the passages or images. Other answer choices may be accurate, but correct answers **must** come from what you are asked to read or interpret, rather than from prior knowledge only.

1. Both the letter and the floor plan show that

   A. the White House today is different from the White House in the early 1800s.
   B. the White House was still a work in progress even after the first residents lived in it.
   C. many years of hard work and planning went into building the White House.
   D. building and decorating costs for the original White House were higher than expected.

DIRECTIONS: Read the passage and the timeline, read each question, and choose the **best** answer.

ROSA PARKS, ACTIVIST

1   Before the day Parks refused to give up her bus seat, she had spent twelve years involved with her local NAACP chapter; ... local teachers; and other members of Montgomery's African American community. The summer before, Parks had attended a ten-day training session at Tennessee's labor and civil rights organizing school, the Highlander Center, where she'd met an older generation of civil rights activists, like Septima Clark, and discussed the Supreme Court's recent decision banning "separate but equal" schools. In the process, Parks also became familiar with previous challenges to segregation: Another Montgomery bus boycott, fifty years earlier, had successfully eased some restrictions; and a bus boycott in Baton Rouge had won limited gains two years before.

2   In short, Parks' decision didn't come out of nowhere. ... Rather, she was part of a longstanding effort to create change, when success was far from certain and setbacks were routine. That in no way diminishes the personal courage, moral force, and historical importance of her refusal to surrender her seat. But the full story of Rosa Parks reminds us that her tremendously consequential act, along with everything that followed, depended on all the humble, frustrating work that she and others had undertaken earlier on. ...

From SOUL OF A CITIZEN: LIVING WITH CONVICTION IN CHALLENGING TIMES by Paul Rogat Loeb, © 2010

LIFE OF ROSA PARKS

1943 Parks has first run-in on segregated bus when she enters from front and walks through white section to back. Driver insists she leave bus and re-enter from back door. Joins NAACP (National Association for the Advancement of Colored People). Works to mobilize voter registration.

1944 Works at Maxwell Air Force Base; rides integrated trolley and is inspired by the experience.

1945 After three unsuccessful attempts, Parks registers to vote.

1949 Works at Montgomery NAACP as secretary to local president, Edgar Nixon, and later as advisor to NAACP Youth Council. Parks's husband, Raymond Parks, works to help free defendants in Scottsboro case.

1950 Works as part-time seamstress for liberal white couple who encourage her civil rights efforts.

1954 Supreme Court rules public school segregation unconstitutional. Parks receives scholarship to attend workshop for community leaders working on desegregation.

1955 Arrested on December 1 for refusing to give up seat to white passenger on segregated bus. Fined for violating segregation laws. Montgomery Improvement Association, led by Martin Luther King, Jr., formed on December 5 to protest incident. Montgomery, Alabama, bus boycott begins.

UNIT 2

2. How are the passage and timeline similar in scope?

A. Both present a clear chronological review of Parks's life.
B. Both highlight Parks's importance in the civil rights movement.
C. Both provide information about Parks's activities before 1955.
D. Both offer perspectives on the Supreme Court's 1954 decision banning segregation.

3. Which is the **most** accurate statement about the passage and the timeline?

A. Both indicate that Parks's 1955 arrest was not an isolated incident.
B. Both cover a specific period of 12 years.
C. Both offer opinions about Parks's courage.
D. Both present all of the same information but in different formats.

4. Paragraph 1 of the passage relates to the timeline by

A. contradicting information in the first five years indicated in timeline.
B. mentioning some civil rights activities, which appear in the timeline.
C. summarizing important events in Parks's life.
D. presenting opinions about events in the timeline.

Compare Texts in Similar Genres

READING ASSESSMENT TARGETS: R.9.1/R. 7.1, R.9.2

1 Learn the Skill

When you **compare and contrast texts** in **similar genres**, begin by thinking about each author's perspective and tone. *How are they similar or different?* Then determine what each author is trying to achieve. Analyze how the structure of the text and author's style further his or her purpose. For example, *does the author compare and contrast concepts or use specific rhetorical techniques?* Finally, evaluate the overall impact, or effectiveness, of each text, in regard to each author's purpose. *Does each author achieve his or her purpose, using the identified techniques?*

2 Practice the Skill

By practicing the skill of comparing and contrasting texts in similar genres, you will improve your study and test-taking abilities, especially as they relate to the GED® Reasoning Through Language Arts Test. Read the passages below. Then answer the question that follows.

FRANKLIN D. ROOSEVELT'S NOMINATION ADDRESS

What do the people of America want more than anything else? To my mind, they want two things: work, with all the moral and spiritual values that go with it; and with work, a reasonable measure of security—security for themselves and for their wives and children. Work and security—<u>these are</u> more than words. <u>They are</u> more than facts. <u>They are</u> the spiritual values, the true goal toward which our efforts of reconstruction should lead. <u>These are</u> the values that this program is intended to gain. …

From NOMINATION ADDRESS by Franklin D. Roosevelt, © 1932

a Roosevelt repeats similar, or parallel, sentence structure to emphasize the importance of "work and security" at a time when many were unemployed and had lost their savings.

JOHN F. KENNEDY'S NOMINATION ADDRESS

Woodrow Wilson's New Freedom promised our nation a new political and economic framework. Franklin Roosevelt's New Deal promised security and succor to those in need. But the New Frontier of which I speak is not a set of promises. It is a set of challenges.

It sums up not what I intend to offer to the American people, but what I intend to ask of them. It appeals to their pride—it appeals to our pride, not our security. It holds out the promise of more sacrifice instead of more security.

From NOMINATION ADDRESS by John F. Kennedy, © 1960

b Kennedy contrasts government programs to highlight his approach to governance. He contrasts the word **promise** with the word **challenge** to emphasize that he looks toward the future.

MAKING ASSUMPTIONS

Sometimes you can make assumptions about the importance of what an author does **not** say. If authors do not mention something, they may believe it is insignificant to their audience.

1. Which statement **best** explains the authors' perspectives?

A. Both authors believe that the American people have been unwilling to contribute to the success of the nation.

B. Roosevelt believes that people need jobs and security, but Kennedy assumes that people have these and can move forward.

C. Both authors believe that the American people have to work and contribute more to build a strong, secure society.

D. Roosevelt believes that government should provide security, but Kennedy believes that the American people must work for security.

DIRECTIONS: Read the remainder of the passages. Then use the drag-and-drop option to complete the Venn diagram.

FRANKLIN D. ROOSEVELT'S NOMINATION ADDRESS

1 Yes, when—not if—when we get the chance, the Federal Government will assume bold leadership in distress relief. …

2 I say that while primary responsibility for relief rests with localities now, as ever … the Federal Government has always had and still has a continuing responsibility for the broader public welfare. It will soon fulfill that responsibility. …

3 I pledge you, I pledge myself, to a new deal for the American people. Let us all here assembled constitute ourselves prophets of a new order of competence and of courage. This is more than a political campaign; it is a call to arms. Give me your help, not to win votes alone, but to win in this crusade to restore America to its own people.

From NOMINATION ADDRESS by Franklin D. Roosevelt, © 1932

JOHN F. KENNEDY'S NOMINATION ADDRESS

1 The New Frontier is here whether we seek it or not.

2 Beyond that frontier are uncharted areas of science and space, unsolved problems of peace and war, unconquered problems of ignorance and prejudice, unanswered questions of poverty and surplus. It would be easier to shrink from that new frontier, to look to the safe mediocrity of the past, to be lulled by good intentions and high rhetoric—and those who prefer that course should not vote for me or the Democratic Party.

3 But I believe that the times require imagination and courage and perseverance. I'm asking each of you to be pioneers towards that New Frontier. My call is to the young in heart, regardless of age—to the stout in spirit, regardless of Party, to all who respond to the scriptural call: "Be strong and of a good courage; be not afraid, neither be … dismayed."

From NOMINATION ADDRESS by John F. Kennedy, © 1960

UNIT 2

2. Drag and drop the items on each list into the correct locations in the Venn diagram. Some categories may appear twice in the same location.

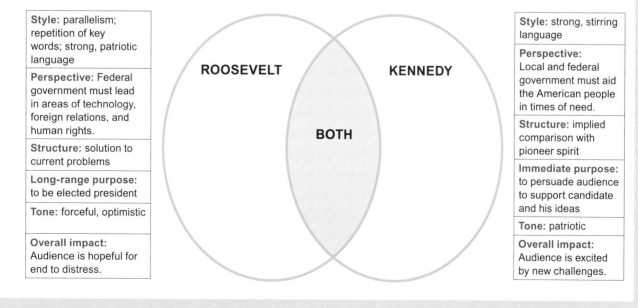

Style: parallelism; repetition of key words; strong, patriotic language

Perspective: Federal government must lead in areas of technology, foreign relations, and human rights.

Structure: solution to current problems

Long-range purpose: to be elected president

Tone: forceful, optimistic

Overall impact: Audience is hopeful for end to distress.

ROOSEVELT   KENNEDY

BOTH

Style: strong, stirring language

Perspective: Local and federal government must aid the American people in times of need.

Structure: implied comparison with pioneer spirit

Immediate purpose: to persuade audience to support candidate and his ideas

Tone: patriotic

Overall impact: Audience is excited by new challenges.

Compare Texts in Different Genres

READING ASSESSMENT TARGETS: R.6.2, R.7.3, R.8.2

1 Learn the Skill

When you **compare and contrast texts in different genres**, or forms of writing, you may find that they cover the same topic but differ in their purpose or overall impact. For example, one text may set out to persuade you to feel or think a certain way about a topic, while the other text may simply inform you about a topic. Each text may address the same audience, but the texts may vary in scope or emphasize different ideas. For example, a news article gives you information, and an editorial gives you an opinion about the information in the article.

2 Practice the Skill

By practicing the skill of comparing and contrasting texts in different genres, you will improve your study and test-taking abilities, especially as they relate to the GED® Reasoning Through Language Arts Test. Read the passages below. Then answer the question that follows.

FIGHT IN PORTLAND

... [T]he fight over fluoridation has erupted in Portland. ...

The debate has prompted something of an existential crisis in this ... city, which votes Tuesday on whether to overturn the city council's 2012 decision to fluoridate. Citizens who pride themselves on tolerance are divided on the ... response to fluoridated water: Is it an intrusion into personal liberty, or a compassionate public health measure?

From *The Wall Street Journal*'s article TOOTH AND NAIL: FLUORIDE FIGHT CRACKS PORTLAND'S LEFT by Joel Millman, © 2013

a The term **scope** refers to the extent to which an author covers a topic. Look for ways in which each author delves into the same topic. Ask yourself, "Does each author refer to specific details or take a more general approach?"

NO TO FLUORIDE

Fluoridation chemicals are unpurified industrial byproducts from fertilizer manufacturing, and are not the same as the fluoride in toothpaste. The Portland Water Bureau said it will add 1.1 million pounds a year of the fluoridation chemical fluorosilicic acid (FSA) to our drinking water if fluoridation is approved. ...

Adding it to our water would expose Portlanders and our kids to another risky chemical at a time when we are already over-exposed to a host of chemicals from plastics to pesticides.

From the cleanwaterportland.org editorial 12 REASONS TO VOTE NO, © 2013

b To determine purpose, style, and overall impact, note the author's language. Dramatic language can indicate an appeal to emotions.

CONTENT TOPICS

The purpose of a news article is to present a factual report of an event in the news. The purpose of an editorial is to present an author's or organization's opinion about a newsworthy event or situation.

1. How do the two passages differ in purpose?

A. The article reports about the fluoride debate, but the editorial argues against fluoridating Portland's water.
B. The article entertains with a story about the fluoridation debate, but the editorial tells who supports fluoridation.
C. The article explains why water fluoridation in Portland is controversial, but the editorial argues why fluoridation is necessary.
D. The article asks readers to support Portland's water fluoridation, but the editorial explains the dangers of fluoridation.

DIRECTIONS: Read the remainder of the passages, read each question, and choose the **best** answer.

FIGHT IN PORTLAND

1   The Centers for Disease Control and Prevention calls water fluoridation "a safe and healthy way to effectively prevent tooth decay" and "one of 10 great public health achievements of the 20th century." But ... [a]nti-fluoride campaigners argue that it poses serious health dangers. ...

2   Until last year, Portland was the largest city in the U.S. not to approve fluoridation. ... Portland city leaders say they were spurred toward fluoride when a citizens' group noted rising tooth decay among low-income and minority children. With support of the Oregon Health Authority, the city council voted to begin fluoridation in 2014.

3   "I concluded fluoridation is a safe, cost-effective and common sense approach to promoting public health," said Nick Fish, Portland's City Council Commissioner. "I did not reach this decision lightly. I have heard from Portlanders who strongly oppose adding fluoride to Portland's water."

From *The Wall Street Journal*'s article TOOTH AND NAIL: FLUORIDE FIGHT CRACKS PORTLAND'S LEFT by Joel Millman, © 2013

NO TO FLUORIDE

1   There is no scientific dispute that fluoridation chemicals would add arsenic, lead, and mercury to our water along with fluoride. The CDC admits that 43% of fluoridation chemicals tested contain arsenic, 2% contain lead and 3% contain copper. Other toxics from mercury to chromium have also been found in fluoridation chemicals.

2   Promoters claim the levels are too low to matter, but The Environmental Protection Agency is clear that toxics like arsenic and lead have no safe level, and even the smallest levels increase cancer and IQ deficit risks. The idea that it is ok to add any of these toxics to our clean drinking water is a remnant from 1940s thinking and doesn't reflect what we know today about the importance of clean water for our health and the health of our kids. ...

3   Recent science supports that fluoridation is more dangerous than previously believed. The National Academy of Sciences 2006 report Fluoride in Drinking Water reviewed hundreds of recent studies linking fluoride levels in drinking water to a broad spectrum of human health ailments from neurological damage and thyroid disorders to excessive fluoride consumption in infants and increased risks of bone cancer.

4   The 500-plus page report found "fluorides have the ability to interfere with the functions of the brain," and "Down's syndrome is a biologically plausible outcome of exposure" to fluoride, and that "fluoride appears to have the potential to initiate or promote cancers, particularly of the bone."

From cleanwaterportland.org's editorial 12 REASONS TO VOTE NO, © 2013

2. How do the two texts differ in audience?

    A. The article is written for a general audience, but the editorial is written for Portland voters.
    B. The article is written for Portland voters, but the editorial is written for a general audience.
    C. The article is written for Portland city leaders, but the editorial is written for scientists.
    D. The article is written for fluoridation supporters, but the editorial is written for fluoride protesters.

3. Which detail in the editorial shows that the author acknowledges an opposing side on the issue?

    A. The CDC admits that fluoridation chemicals contain arsenic, lead, and copper.
    B. Recent scientific studies reveal that fluoridation is more dangerous than once believed.
    C. The Environmental Protection Agency says that no exposure to arsenic, lead, or copper is safe.
    D. Promoters of fluoridation claim that chemical levels in water are too low to matter.

4. Both authors use direct quotations to support their ideas. How do these quotations affect the overall impact of the texts?

    A. Quotations make the texts more interesting, adding to their entertainment value.
    B. Quotations lend credibility, while adding striking commentary.
    C. Quotations emphasize the authors' expertise on the topic, giving weight to their claims.
    D. Quotations motivate the reader to action by presenting experts' opinions.

Gain Information from Multiple Texts

❶ Learn the Skill

When you use more than one text to obtain information, you most likely **synthesize**, **draw conclusions**, and **apply information** to new situations. As you recall from Unit 1, synthesizing means "combining information to reach a new idea." Drawing conclusions means "making a larger inference based on multiple inferences." Applying information to new situations means "taking what you learn from a text and using that knowledge to understand a similar situation or to make a prediction."

❷ Practice the Skill

By practicing the skills of synthesizing, drawing conclusions, and applying information from multiple texts, you will improve your study and test-taking abilities, especially as they relate to the GED® Reasoning Through Language Arts Test. Read the passages below. Then answer the question that follows.

MAKING FOOTBALL SAFER

Observers have proposed a variety of changes that could diminish the number of head injuries and long-term brain conditions suffered by football players. In his "10 Point Plan to Save Football," [Christopher] Nowinski notes that half of the hits to the head take place in practice during dangerous drills, and he proposes making practices safer by eliminating contact drills. Nowinski also recommends that the NFL reevaluate techniques of tackling and blocking, and rules governing the game. …

From the Facts On File and Issues and Controversies On File article NFL HEAD INJURIES, accessed 2013

a Notice that the formats of the texts are different. The first is an article; the second is a 10-point plan appearing as a list.

b As you synthesize ideas from both texts, consider what the authors are not saying directly. Use one text to read between the lines of the other.

PLAN TO SAVE FOOTBALL

Below are 10 paths to a safer game … to reduce brain trauma. …

1. *Reevaluate how the game is practiced* Greater than 50% of hits to the head occur outside of games. NFL teams rarely hit in practice due to risk of injury. Youth teams could only be allowed to have full contact once a week. …

2. *Encourage mandatory brain trauma and concussion education for coaches, athletic trainers, parents, and athletes* Coaches, athletic trainers, and athletes cannot diagnose concussions if they aren't trained to look for them or know how to recognize them. [They] will not voluntarily choose to rest concussions and reduce overall brain trauma if they don't understand why it is good for the athlete's … health.

From the sportslegacy.org letter 10 POINT PLAN TO SAVE FOOTBALL by Christopher Nowinski, © 2009

USING LOGIC

The first text refers to NFL practices, but the second text refers to youth team practices. To synthesize ideas, note how the information in the second text builds on that of the first.

1. Both texts indicate that team practices

    A. would be safer if they eliminated contact drills.
    B. could require the presence of adults trained to deal with head injuries.
    C. lower the incidence of brain trauma and concussions.
    D. must now follow the same game rules.

DIRECTIONS: Read the remainder of the passages, read each question, and choose the **best** answer.

MAKING FOOTBALL SAFER

1   Ira Casson, the former co-chair of the NFL committee on brain injury, has suggested that if scientists were to prove that disorders such as CTE [Chronic Traumatic Encephalopathy] were directly related to football, the league would have to consider imposing a cap on the number of years players can compete in the NFL. Casson notes, however, that such limits were never imposed in boxing despite widespread brain damage in that sport. He asks rhetorically in *The New Yorker*, "Why would a boxer at the height of his career, six or seven years in, stop fighting, just when he's making million-dollar paydays?"

2   Other experts have suggested providing players with better information about concussions. Journalist Jonathan Starkey writes in *The Washington Post*, "[T]he best defense against concussions might just be simple education and prevention. Players should not put such trust in their helmets that they use their heads as battering rams, for example. And if they feel abnormal after a big hit, they should resist the urge to shake it off and keep playing."

From the Facts on File News Services' Issues and Controversies On-line article NFL HEAD INJURIES, accessed 2013

2. According to **both** passages, why do football players often play despite head injuries? Players

A. often do not care about their health.
B. are afraid to seem weak in front of the public.
C. feel pressured by the sport's culture and do not want to hurt their careers or lose their pay.
D. know that by not following coaches' orders or NCAA rules, they will sit out other games.

3. If the authors of these passages saw a young athlete suffer a head injury during a game, they most likely would

A. insist that the athlete shake it off and return to the game.
B. urge the athlete to stop playing and seek medical attention.
C. help the athlete's coach diagnose and treat the injury.
D. threaten to contact the media if the athlete continued to play.

PLAN TO SAVE FOOTBALL

3. *Reevaluate protective equipment* Investigate changes to helmets, shoulder pads, and other … equipment to reduce brain trauma.

4. *Develop better methods of concussion detection and diagnosis* The CDC provides clipboards with concussions diagnosis protocols on the back at no cost. Coaches could be required to carry them. We can invest more in research to find simple, objective ways to diagnose concussion. …

5. *Develop better methods of concussion management* Return to play too soon after concussion can result in more extensive brain damage, and can actually result in death. It is now law in Washington State that players are required to see a medical professional with brain trauma expertise before return to play. Minimum return-to-play standards should be enforced at all levels.

6. *Consider minimum medical resources* Football is a dangerous game. Minimum medical resource standards, like having an athletic trainer or doctor on the sideline, should be considered.

7. *Reevaluate techniques of tackling and blocking* We can teach and enforce different methods of tackling and blocking that minimize contact to the head. …

8. *Reevaluate the rules* Recently the NFL banned the wedge on kickoffs to reduce trauma. Many other rules could be changed. …

9. Reevaluate rule enforcement and the role of referees The NCAA recently began suspending players for intentional helmet-to-helmet hits. Referees could eject players for illegal hits to the head. Referees could be trained to identify concussed players on the field.

10. Reconsider the culture of the game Television announcers could stop glorifying illegal hits. Children could stop being pressured to play through concussions. …

From the sportslegacy.org letter 10 POINT PLAN TO SAVE FOOTBALL by Christopher Nowinski, © 2009

4. According to **both** passages, what do intentional helmet-to-helmet hits indicate about the sport?

A. Players must be large and powerful.
B. Regulations are ignored for the sake of the game.
C. Only referees can call out players for such behavior.
D. Players put too much trust in protective equipment.

DIRECTIONS: Read the passage and study the graph. Then answer the questions that follow.

OCEAN ACIDIFICATION

1 Earth's atmosphere isn't the only victim of burning fossil fuels. About a quarter of all carbon dioxide emissions are absorbed by the earth's oceans, where they're having an impact that's just starting to be understood.

2 Over the last decade, scientists have discovered that this excess CO_2 is actually changing the chemistry of the sea and proving harmful for many forms of marine life. This process is known as ocean acidification.

3 A more acidic ocean could wipe out species, disrupt the food web and impact fishing, tourism and any other human endeavor that relies on the sea.

4 The change is happening fast—and it will take fast action to slow or stop it. Over the last 250 years, oceans have absorbed 530 billion tons of CO_2, triggering a 30 percent increase in ocean acidity.

5 Before people started burning coal and oil, ocean pH had been relatively stable for the previous 20 million years. But researchers predict that if carbon emissions continue at their current rate, ocean acidity will more than double by 2100.

6 The polar regions will be the first to experience changes. Projections show that the Southern Ocean around Antarctica will actually become corrosive by 2050.

7 The new chemical composition of our oceans is expected to harm a wide range of ocean life—particularly creatures with shells. The resulting disruption to the ocean ecosystem could have a widespread ripple effect and further deplete already struggling fisheries worldwide.

8 Increased acidity reduces carbonate—the mineral used to form the shells and skeletons of many shellfish and corals. The effect is similar to osteoporosis, slowing growth and making shells weaker. If pH levels drop enough, the shells will literally dissolve.

9 This process will not only harm some of our favorite seafood, such as lobster and mussels, but will also injure some species of smaller marine organisms—things such as pteropods and coccolithophores.

10 You've probably never heard of them, but they form a vital part of the food web. If those smaller organisms are wiped out, the larger animals that feed on them could suffer, as well.

11 Delicate corals may face an even greater risk than shellfish because they require very high levels of carbonate to build their skeletons.

12 Acidity slows reef-building, which could lower the resiliency of corals and lead to their erosion and eventual extinction. The "tipping point" for coral reefs could happen as soon as 2050.

13 Coral reefs serve as the home for many other forms of ocean life. Their disappearance would be akin to rainforests being wiped out worldwide. Such losses would reverberate throughout the marine environment and have profound social impacts, as well—especially on the fishing and tourism industries. …

14 Ultimately, though, reducing the amount of carbon dioxide absorbed into the oceans may be the only way to halt acidification. The same strategies needed to fight global warming on land can also help in the seas.

15 The acidification of our oceans is the hidden side of the world's carbon crisis, says Lisa Suatoni, [a Natural Resources Defense Council] ocean scientist, and only reinforces that we need to make changes in how we fuel our world—and we need to do it quickly.

From the nrdc.org article OCEAN ACIDIFICATION: THE OTHER CO_2 PROBLEM, accessed 2013

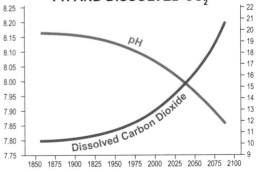

HISTORICAL AND PROJECTED PH AND DISSOLVED CO₂

As the ocean concentration of carbon dioxide increases, so does acidity (causing pH to decline).

From the pmel.noaa.gov article CARBON DIOXIDE AND OUR OCEAN LEGACY, © 2006 accessed 2013

UNIT 2

1. Which sentence **best** explains why the authors provide background information in paragraphs 1, 2, and 3?

   A. The authors wish to contrast carbon absorption in the atmosphere and in the oceans.
   B. The authors assume that many readers are unfamiliar with the problem of ocean acidification.
   C. The authors wish to emphasize the ways in which human activities affect the oceans.
   D. The authors assume that readers will disagree with their claims about ocean acidification.

2. The data in paragraphs 4, 5, and 6

   A. support the claim that changes in ocean acidity are happening fast.
   B. show that efforts to reduce carbon emissions have not been effective.
   C. challenge the claim that the atmosphere is not the only victim of fossil fuels.
   D. illustrate how ocean acidity can harm coral reefs and other sea life.

3. Osteoporosis is a disease in which the bones become weak and fragile. The authors compare osteoporosis with what is happening to shellfish in order to

   A. help readers understand how acidity affects shellfish and coral.
   B. show that human skeletons can be affected by ocean acidity.
   C. explain how the mineral carbonate functions in shell formation.
   D. teach readers about the nutritional needs of shellfish.

4. Which statement **best** explains the relationship between paragraphs 9 and 10?

   A. Paragraph 10 provides more information about what pteropods and coccolithophores are and where they are found.
   B. Paragraph 9 describes small organisms that inhabit coral reefs, and paragraph 10 describes large organisms.
   C. Paragraph 9 identifies small organisms, and paragraph 10 explains how they are affected by acidification.
   D. Paragraph 10 explains why the effects of ocean acidity on pteropods and coccolithophores are significant.

5. Which statement is an **implicit** purpose of the passage?

   A. to interest readers in the life cycles of coral reefs and their inhabitants
   B. to inspire readers to visit the coral reefs before they disappear
   C. to encourage readers to reduce their use of fossil fuels
   D. to alert readers to the challenges the fishing industry faces

6. Drag and drop the sentences into the chart to show which claims are supported by evidence in the passage and which are not.

Supported	Unsupported

Ocean acidity has increased rapidly in the past 250 years.
Human activity is the likely cause of increased CO_2 emissions.
The "tipping point" for coral reefs could happen as soon as 2050.
Humans must act quickly to save the coral reefs and shellfish.

7. Which claim from the passage does the graph support?

   A. Excess CO_2 is actually changing the chemistry of the sea.
   B. Ocean pH had been relatively stable for the previous 20 million years.
   C. The polar regions will be the first to experience changes.
   D. The strategies needed to fight global warming on land also can help in the seas.

THE COMING ENERGY CRISIS

1   Tonight I want to have an unpleasant talk with you about a problem that is unprecedented in our history. With the exception of preventing war, this is the greatest challenge that our country will face during our lifetime.

2   The energy crisis has not yet overwhelmed us, but it will if we do not act quickly. It's a problem that we will not be able to solve in the next few years, and it's likely to get progressively worse through the rest of this century.

3   We must not be selfish or timid if we hope to have a decent world for our children and our grandchildren. We simply must balance our demand for energy with our rapidly shrinking resources. By acting now we can control our future instead of letting the future control us.

4   Two days from now, I will present to the Congress my energy proposals. Its members will be my partners, and they have already given me a great deal of valuable advice.

5   Many of these proposals will be unpopular. Some will cause you to put up with inconveniences and to make sacrifices. The most important thing about these proposals is that the alternative may be a national catastrophe. Further delay can affect our strength and our power as a nation.

6   Our decision about energy will test the character of the American people and the ability of the President and the Congress to govern this nation. This difficult effort will be the "moral equivalent of war," except that we will be uniting our efforts to build and not to destroy.

7   Now, I know that some of you may doubt that we face real energy shortages. The 1973 gas lines are gone, and with this springtime weather, our homes are warm again. But our energy problem is worse tonight than it was in 1973 or a few weeks ago in the dead of winter. It's worse because more waste has occurred and more time has passed by without our planning for the future. And it will get worse every day until we act.

8   The oil and natural gas that we rely on for 75 percent of our energy are simply running out. In spite of increased effort, domestic production has been dropping steadily at about 6 percent a year. Imports have doubled in the last 5 years. Our Nation's economic and political independence is becoming increasingly vulnerable. Unless profound changes are made to lower oil consumption, we now believe that early in the 1980s the world will be demanding more oil than it can produce.

9   The world now uses about 60 million barrels of oil a day, and demand increases each year about 5 percent. This means that just to stay even we need the production of a new Texas every year, an Alaskan North Slope every 9 months, or a new Saudi Arabia every 3 years. Obviously, this cannot continue. …

10   If we fail to act soon, we will face an economic, social, and political crisis that will threaten our free institutions. But we still have another choice. We can begin to prepare right now. We can decide to act while there is still time. That is the concept of the energy policy that we will present on Wednesday.

11   Our national energy plan is based on 10 fundamental principles. The first principle is that we can have an effective and comprehensive energy policy only if the Government takes responsibility for it and if the people understand the seriousness of the challenge and are willing to make sacrifices. …

12   I believe that this can be a positive challenge. There is something especially American in the kinds of changes that we have to make. We've always been proud, through our history, of being efficient people. We've always been proud of our ingenuity, our skill at answering questions. Now we need efficiency and ingenuity more than ever.

13   We've always been proud of our leadership in the world. And now we have a chance again to give the world a positive example.

14   We've always been proud of our vision of the future. We've always wanted to give our children and our grandchildren a world richer in possibilities than we have had ourselves. They are the ones that we must provide for now. They are the ones who will suffer most if we don't act.

From ADDRESS TO THE NATION ON ENERGY by Jimmy Carter, 1977

UNIT 2

8. Which statement **best** explains why paragraph 1 displays faulty logic or reasoning?

A. The author appeals to the audience's sense of patriotism.
B. The author presents a false cause-and-effect relationship.
C. The author provides facts that are irrelevant to the claim.
D. The author uses exaggerated emotional language.

9. In paragraph 5, the author acknowledges that many of his ideas will be unpopular and states that the alternative to his proposals "may be a national catastrophe." Why does he make these statements?

A. to frighten readers about what the future could hold
B. to remind readers of the nation's accomplishments
C. to anticipate and respond to possible conflicting viewpoints
D. to compare and contrast his ideas with past proposals

10. Throughout paragraph 7, which begins "Now, I know that some of you may doubt," the author repeats the word **worse**. This repetition creates a sense of

A. fright and emphasizes the dangers of not taking action.
B. urgency and emphasizes the seriousness of the problem.
C. hopelessness and makes the crisis seem overwhelming.
D. anger and makes the opposition seem weak.

11. Which statement **best** describes the relationship between paragraphs 7 and 8?

A. Paragraph 7 claims that energy shortages are worsening, and paragraph 8 gives evidence to support the claim.
B. Paragraph 7 identifies the worst shortages, and paragraph 8 describes these shortages in greater detail.
C. Paragraph 7 describes the negative aspects of pursuing a new energy policy, and paragraph 8 describes the positive ones.
D. Paragraph 7 introduces the worsening problem of wasted energy, and paragraph 8 details possible solutions.

12. Paragraph 10 begins "If we fail to act soon …" Which statement **best** explains how the structure and purpose of this paragraph are related?

A. In the first sentence, the author describes a crisis. The word **but** in the second sentence signals that in the rest of the paragraph, the author explains a way to avoid the crisis.
B. In the first sentence, the author lists the types of crises the United States could face, and in the rest of the paragraph, he describes these crises in greater detail.
C. In the first half of the paragraph, the author states the opinions of his opponents. In the second half of the paragraph, the author responds to those views.
D. The author uses the word **now** to signal a shift in time between the events described in the first two sentences and the events described in the rest of the paragraph.

13. In the last three paragraphs, the author tries to persuade his audience by using repetition to appeal to the

A. sense of fear.
B. sense of patriotism.
C. desire for popularity.
D. desire for wealth.

14. The author's **implicit** purpose in the passage is to encourage readers to support the

.

15. Drag and drop the words that have emotional connotations, in the context of this passage, into the web.

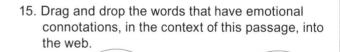

EMOTIONAL WORDS

proposal, selfish, timid, policy, grandchildren, changes, catastrophe

DIRECTIONS: Read the passages. Then answer the questions that follow.

LEDS ARE THE FUTURE

1   GE [General Electric] invented the light-emitting diode in 1962. The first ones to come into wide use—glowing a space-age red—turned up in the clock radios, pocket calculators, and digital watches of the 1970s. Additional colors came along over the next couple of decades.

2   LEDs are manufactured more or less like any other semiconductor. Each diode is cut from a wafer of crystals layered over a base of silicon or sapphire. The crystal layer on early LEDs was gallium arsenide or gallium phosphide, which lent that reddish color. Additional colors and increased brightness required more nuanced control of layer composition and depth. Modern LED makers accomplish this by using precise ratios of indium, gallium, aluminum, and nitrogen for the crystal layer, which results in a bluish color.

3   But on their own, not even advanced LEDs can produce anything suitable for the living room. The blue-tinged illumination is fine for, say, a pen flashlight on a keychain, but it doesn't come close to the warm light the human eye desires.

4   There are two ways LED makers create a more pleasant white. In the 1990s, the favored technique was to combine red, green, and blue LEDs. But they all have differing efficiencies and operating requirements. Heat management, power supply, and drivers—the bulbs' controlling circuit boards—get more complex.

5   So the LEDs found in current household applications are blue diodes daubed with a powdered coating called a phosphor, which includes rare-earth elements that filter blue light. The phosphor is generally yellow, and depending on the composition of the phosphor and the ratio of unconverted blue light, the resulting "white" light can range from the warm glow preferred for home use to cooler tints more suited to, say, retail and outdoor use.

From *Wired*'s article THE FUTURE OF LIGHT IS THE LED by Dan Koeppel, © 2011

FAQ ABOUT ENERGY-SAVING BULBS

1   **Q:** How exactly are these new bulbs better than traditional incandescent bulbs?

2   **A:** … Newer energy-saving bulbs such as ENERGY STAR-qualified CFLs and LEDs, as well as halogen incandescent technologies, can produce the same amount of light (lumens) as a traditional incandescent bulb while using significantly less energy. So when you replace your traditional incandescent bulbs with the energy-savers, you will pay less to get the same amount of light. …

3   Many of the newer bulbs also last significantly longer than traditional bulbs, so you won't need to replace them as often, and will keep saving into the future. ENERGY STAR LEDs use about 25% of the energy and last up to 25 times longer than traditional incandescent bulbs they replace. An ENERGY STAR CFL uses about 25% of the energy and lasts 10 times longer than a comparable traditional incandescent bulb.

4   Switching to energy-saving bulbs will reduce the growth of U.S. energy demand and avoid carbon emissions. Nationwide, lighting accounts for about 14% of all building electricity use (about 10% of home electricity). With the EISA standards, U.S. households could save nearly $6 billion dollars in 2015 alone.

5   **Q:** What is the cost difference between the new lights and my incandescent bulbs? How much money will I save when I switch to these new bulbs?

6   **A:** Upgrading 15 traditional incandescent bulbs in your home with energy-saving bulbs could save you about $50 per year.

7   While the initial price of the newer lightbulbs is typically higher than the inefficient incandescent bulbs you are replacing, you'll spend less each year to operate them. Most CFLs pay for themselves with the energy they save in less than 9 months.

8   Average consumers will spend about $4.80 to operate a traditional incandescent bulb for a year (electricity cost). By comparison, average consumers will spend about $1.00 to operate an ENERGY STAR LED bulb, about $3.50 on a halogen incandescent bulb, and about $1.20 on an ENERGY STAR CFL bulb—each that produces about the same amount of light. …

Source: energy.gov FREQUENTLY ASKED QUESTIONS: LIGHTING CHOICES TO SAVE YOU MONEY, accessed 2013

16. In paragraph 3 of the article, the word

    illumination means .

17. The signal words in paragraph 8 of the FAQ
    indicate that the information in this paragraph

    will [_____] the costs of different bulbs.

18. Which statement **best** explains the overall
    impact of the FAQ?

    A. Inadequately supported arguments leave the
       reader with more questions than answers.
    B. Emotional language encourages the reader to
       take action on the issue.
    C. Convincing and well-supported points
       motivate the reader to follow the author's
       advice.
    D. Failure to incorporate well-researched facts
       forces the reader to question the author's
       credibility.

19. Which statement **best** describes the audience of
    the article and the FAQ?

    A. Both address politicians.
    B. Both address electrical engineers.
    C. The article addresses people with some
       scientific background, but the FAQ address
       consumers.
    D. The article addresses scientists, but the
       FAQ address people who want only to save
       money.

20. How do the article and the FAQ differ in
    purpose?

    A. The article explains the steps in the process
       of making LEDs, but the FAQ explain the
       steps in the process of replacing old bulbs
       with LEDs.
    B. The article explains how LEDs produce
       different colors, but the FAQ persuade
       readers that new bulbs save energy and
       money.
    C. The article persuades readers that LEDs
       produce the best quality of light, but the FAQ
       inform how LEDs work.
    D. The article persuades readers that LEDs
       save energy, but the FAQ entertain with an
       anecdote about LEDs.

21. How do the article and FAQ differ in structure?

    A. The article is a list of steps in a process, but
       the FAQ show cause and effect.
    B. The article shows main ideas and details,
       but the FAQ present ideas listed in order of
       importance.
    C. The article shows sequential order, but the
       FAQ compare and contrast information.
    D. The article is written in straightforward
       paragraph form, but the FAQ are questions
       and answers.

22. Which perspective do the two passages share?

    A. The United States wastes too much energy
       and must avoid carbon emissions.
    B. People must look to save on energy costs.
    C. LED bulbs are the lights of the future.
    D. LED bulbs produce poor lighting that cannot
       compare with the glow of older bulbs.

23. On the basis of the information in the article,
    why might a reader of the FAQ still be reluctant
    to switch to LED bulbs?

    A. LEDs cost more to use than traditional bulbs.
    B. Traditional bulbs are safer to install than
       LEDs.
    C. LEDs do not always give off the "warm glow"
       of traditional bulbs.
    D. Traditional bulbs are easier to manufacture
       than LEDs.

24. Which statement is **most** likely true about the
    authors of both the article and FAQ?

    A. The authors know how to manufacture
       energy-saving bulbs.
    B. The authors have switched from traditional
       bulbs to energy-saving bulbs in their homes.
    C. The authors test the efficiency of light bulbs
       for the Department of Energy.
    D. The authors prefer to work with the cooler,
       brighter tones of LED lights.

DIRECTIONS: Read the passages. Then answer the questions that follow.

HONORING THE FALLEN

1   Mr. President, Mrs. Obama, Secretary Shinseki, General Dempsey, fellow veterans, service members, and distinguished guests. Lilibet and I are greatly honored to be here with all of you today as we observe Memorial Day.

2   Together, we gather to remember America's sons and daughters who sacrificed everything in the defense of our nation. For generations, Americans have set aside this day to honor those who have fought and died to keep our nation safe. A Civil War veteran, Supreme Court Justice Oliver Wendell Holmes once said, "Every year in the full tide of spring, at the height of the symphony of flowers and love and life, there comes a pause and, through the silence, we hear the lonely pipe of death."

3   Every Memorial Day, America is reminded of these selfless individuals, America's quiet heroes. We also think of America's new generation of defenders, protecting the nation's interests in every corner of the globe, preserving our freedoms and our way of life. They work for a more peaceful and hopeful world. As General Douglas MacArthur said, "The soldier above all other people prays for peace, for he must suffer and bear the deepest wounds and scars of war."

4   The memories of America's heroes laid to rest here at Arlington and at American cemeteries around the world are kept alive by families and communities across our great land. This Memorial Day, we honor those families whom our heroes left behind. We honor them in appreciation for the sacrifices they have endured. We also honor the perseverance and the resilience of our military families today, for they are dealing with all of the challenges of life. America thanks you.

5   All of us in positions of trust and responsibility must always make decisions that are worthy of the sacrifices of those who serve our country. On this sacred day, as we recall the words of President Lincoln when he referred to the mystic bonds and chords of memory, we honor America's fallen patriots by striving to be worthy of their great sacrifices as we all work toward making a better future for all mankind.

From MEMORIAL DAY OBSERVANCE by Chuck Hagel, 2013

A SPECIAL SALUTE

1   President Barack Obama gave a special salute Monday to Americans who lost their lives fighting in the Korean War … and asked Americans to remember the troops' work in Afghanistan as that war winds down.

2   "Last Memorial Day, I stood here and spoke about how, for the first time in nine years, Americans were no longer fighting and dying in Iraq. Today, a transition is under way in Afghanistan, and our troops are coming home," the president said after laying a wreath at the Tomb of the Unknowns. "This time next year, we will mark the final Memorial Day of our war in Afghanistan." …

3   Calling Virginia's Arlington National Cemetery "a monument to a common thread in the American character," Obama asked the audience not to forget the "men and women who are willing to give their lives and lay down their lives" for the freedoms the nation enjoys.

4   A serviceman recently wrote the president to say he feared "our work in Afghanistan is fading from memory," Obama said. "And he's right. As we gather here today, at this very moment, more than 60,000 of our fellow Americans still serve far from home in Afghanistan. They're still going out on patrol, still living in spartan forward operating bases, still risking their lives. ...

5   "And when they give their lives, they are still being laid to rest in cemeteries in the quiet corners across our country, including here in Arlington."…

6   "For those of us who bear the solemn responsibility of sending these men and women into harm's way, we know the consequences all too well," Obama said. "I feel it every time I meet a wounded warrior, every time I visit Walter Reed and every time I grieve with a Gold Star family."

7   Chuck Hagel, a former Army sergeant who volunteered for the Vietnam War and is the first enlisted combat veteran to hold the post of defense secretary, told CNN's Barbara Starr that he remembers soldiers who served alongside him, including a captain who was killed 14 days into his tour. Hagel was next to him when he died, he said.

8   "Anybody who has ever been in combat remembers the names, remembers the faces, remembers the fun, remembers the uniqueness of every person," the defense secretary said.

From the cnn.com article OBAMA OFFERS SALUTE TO KOREAN WAR VETS AS AFGHANISTAN WAR WINDS DOWN, © 2013

Unit 2 Review | Argument Analysis and Text Comparis

25. In paragraph 4 of the speech, the word **resilience** refers to a person's ability to cope

with [   ] .

26. The author of the speech quotes Oliver Wendell Holmes to show that

    A. remembering America's fallen soldiers is a time-honored event.
    B. sacrifices often must be made in the name of freedom.
    C. wars must be fought to guarantee peace for future generations.
    D. choosing to send others to war is a serious responsibility.

27. Which three expressions indicate that paragraph 2 of the article is organized according to a time sequence?

[   ]

28. Which idea do both passages emphasize?

    A. Those who have experienced combat always remember the others with whom they fought.
    B. Soldiers most hope for peace because they must sacrifice the most in times of war.
    C. Those responsible for sending others to war are aware of the sacrifices soldiers and their families make.
    D. Members of the armed forces are too often disrespected by the public.

29. Drag and drop the phrases that describe the passages into the correct location on the chart.

Speech	News Article

third-person point of view
specific audience
first-person point of view
general audience

30. How do the speech and the article differ in purpose?

    A. The speech motivates audience members to join the armed forces, but the article informs readers of the sacrifices that soldiers make.
    B. The speech honors those who fought and died, but the article describes a Memorial Day tribute.
    C. The speech persuades others to help support military families, but the article explains how to show this kind of support.
    D. The speech explores various Memorial Day observances, but the article entertains with details about a Memorial Day celebration.

31. What information in the news article contributes to the credibility of the author of the speech? The author of the speech

    A. quotes experienced career soldiers.
    B. volunteered for and saw active combat.
    C. is a member of President Obama's cabinet.
    D. has a son and daughter in the military.

32. On the basis of the information in both texts, which is the **most** logical conclusion to draw about men and women who serve in the military?

    A. They must learn to forget their combat experiences.
    B. Their long absences can cause hardships in their family lives.
    C. They seek fame and glory by going to war.
    D. Their sacrifices are too often taken for granted.

GED® JOURNEYS

Augusten Burroughs

Augusten Burroughs turned trauma into triump**l** In his 2002 book *Running with Scissors,* Burroughs recounte**d** his unconventional childhood. The book remained on *The New York Times* best seller list for four straight years and was made into a film in 2006. Burroughs also has written five other memoirs that have been published in more than 30 countries. As he notes, "**I** really look at my childhood as being one giant rusty tuna can that **I** continue to recycle in many different shapes."

Although Burroughs had no formal education beyond element**a** school, he earned his GED® certificate and began a more than 17-year career in advertising. However, struggles with alcoholism nearly cost him his life. The turning point came as Burroughs near**e** completion of his first novel, *Sellevision.* Burroughs wrote the book in just seven days, during which time he stopped drinking. He has remained sober since.

In addition to authoring books, Burroughs speaks regularly at colleges and universities. The range of topics he explores includes sexual abuse, alcoholism, writing, and humor. He lives in western Massachusetts and New York City with his partner and their dogs.

Despite his lack of formal education, Augusten Burroughs earned his GED® credential and became a best-selling author.

"I really look at my childhood as being one giant rusty tuna can that I continue to recycle in many different shapes."

CAREER HIGHLIGHTS: *Augusten Burroughs*

- Born October 23, 1965, in Pittsburgh, Pennsylvania
- Experienced a turbulent childhood that provided the basis for his 2002 book *Running with Scissors*
- Overcame alcoholism to become a noted author
- Honored twice by *Entertainment Weekly* as one of the 25 funniest people in America

Extended Response

Unit 3: Extended Response

In the last unit, you analyzed and evaluated persuasive texts and compared and contrasted passages in various genres and formats. You will now take what you have learned and apply it to writing an extended response to texts that you will read.

The GED® Reasoning Through Language Arts Test includes one 45-minute extended response that integrates reading and writing into tasks that require you to support your written analysis with evidence drawn from texts. Unit 3 will take you step-by-step through the process of writing a response—from analyzing source texts, through developing a thesis, gathering evidence, planning and developing your ideas, drafting the response, and reviewing your writing. Practicing these skills will help you write an effective and well-developed response on the GED® test.

Table of Contents

UNIT 3

Practicing the steps of the writing process will help prepare you to write your extended response on the GED® test.

Compare Opposing Arguments

1 Learn the Skill

When two authors write about the same debatable topic, they may present opposing claims or points of view. They also may use different evidence or interpret evidence differently. By analyzing each author's argument, you will be able to determine which claim is better supported and write an extended response that demonstrates your written communication skills and your ability to analyze texts.

When **identifying the similarities and differences between two arguments**, first define each author's purpose and main and supporting claims. Then analyze the reasons and evidence, rhetorical strategies, and responses to counterarguments in each passage. Also note how the authors use sentences, paragraphs, and transitions to develop their ideas.

2 Practice the Skill

By practicing the skill of comparing and contrasting opposing arguments, you will improve your study, writing, and test-taking abilities, especially as they relate to the GED® Reasoning Through Language Arts Test. Read the passages below. Then answer the question that follows.

I'LL NEVER TEACH ONLINE AGAIN

I trained for it, I tried it, and I'll never do it again. While online teaching may be the wave of the future (although I ... hope not), it is not for me. Perhaps I'm the old dog that resists new tricks. Maybe I am a technophobe. It might be that I'm plain old-fashioned.

This much I can say with certainty: I have years of experience successfully teaching in [college] classrooms and online teaching doesn't compare.

From the universityworldnews.com article I'LL NEVER TEACH ONLINE AGAIN by Elayne Clift, © 2009 accessed 2013

> **a** Clift tries to persuade readers to agree with her claim by describing her experience. Because she references teacher training, it is likely that her audience includes other teachers.

THE BENEFITS OF ONLINE EDUCATION

Jalen Rollins, who earned his GED® credential two years ago, was employed by a popular restaurant chain. However, he wanted to increase his earnings to support himself and his family. Because he worked in the evenings, he had several available hours during the day to begin an educational program and change his future. He, like many others, took advantage of the benefits of an online degree program over a traditional classroom education.

From THE BENEFITS OF ONLINE EDUCATION by Carl Jones, © 2013

> **b** Jones tries to persuade readers to agree with his claim by explaining the benefits of online learning. Because he describes a student—Jalen Rollins— it is likely that his audience includes students or potential students.

USING LOGIC

Some authors qualify statements by adding information that may explain a claim, but also weaken it. Think about the effect of the introduction and the phrases **old dog** and **old-fashioned** in Clift's claim.

1. How do the authors' points of view differ?

A. A teacher and a student disagree about the demands of online education.
B. Clift is opposed to online teaching, but Jones understands the benefits for students.
C. Clift is opposed to teaching online, but Jones enjoys teaching online.
D. A teacher and a student view online teaching differently.

UNIT 3

DIRECTIONS: Read the remainder of the passages, read each question, and choose the **best** answer.

I'LL NEVER TEACH ONLINE AGAIN

1   So I'll just chalk up my first and only venture to experience and make my way back to the traditional [classroom]. Among the reasons why are these.

2   * "Virtual community" is the ultimate … contradiction in terms—like saying one is "fresh from the tennis court." While some people find anonymity enabling and are able to bond with their [online group] and engage in true confessions, I find it [very] difficult to communicate with people for whom I have no face, … no body language, no in-the-moment exchange …

3   * The quality of education is compromised in online learning. In online teaching, I was only able to introduce students to a limited amount of material outside of the textbook readings; it is simply impossible to replicate a lecture online. Nor could I adequately help them develop better writing and critical thinking skills or to foster original ideas because there simply wasn't enough time or a proper [way to discuss ideas].

4   * Show me the money. I devoted at least three times as many hours and triple the energy to online teaching than was necessary for traditional courses. But I received no additional [pay] for that effort …

5   Try to talk me down. Tell me I didn't give it enough time. Call me old-fashioned and out-of-date. Just don't call me to teach online.

From the universityworldnews.com article I'LL NEVER TEACH ONLINE AGAIN by Elayne Clift, © 2009 accessed 2013

THE BENEFITS OF ONLINE EDUCATION

1   One of the biggest appeals of online education is a flexibility that the standard classroom cannot match. Although there are still deadlines, students may complete assignments at preferred times. A student who works during the evening may complete assignments during the day. Another student may complete the same assignments during the evening. In addition, because students access virtual classrooms electronically, they may attend classes in other states or countries without leaving home and driving to a specific location. Online programs also may offer more course choices than a traditional campus.

2   Another appeal of online education is self-management. Students can choose their own certificate or degree programs, plan the pace at which they want to complete these programs, and access course materials at any time. Rebecca, an online student, recalls, "When I missed a class, I missed the notes. Now I'm able to access the professor's course notes whenever I need them."

3   Lastly, online education offers exciting options for students with different learning styles. In place of the traditional classroom lecture, many courses feature multimedia elements. These may range from video and audio clips to live chats and discussion forums.

4   Today, statistics show that about 32% of college students take at least one online class. It's clear that technology is revolutionizing education and providing new and exciting opportunities for students such as Jalen Rollins.

From THE BENEFITS OF ONLINE EDUCATION by Carl Jones, © 2013

2.   Both authors mention time as evidence. How do they interpret this evidence?

   A. Both authors acknowledge that online education is time consuming.
   B. Clift says that online education is flexible about time, but Jones says that online education is time consuming.
   C. Both authors acknowledge that online education is flexible about time.
   D. Clift says online education is time consuming, but Jones says that online education is flexible about time.

3.   Both authors discuss the differences between in-person lectures and online classes. How are their interpretations of evidence different?

   A. Clift states that she cannot reproduce a lecture online, but Jones emphasizes other learning options.
   B. Both authors agree that a lecture cannot be reproduced online.
   C. Jones states that a lecture cannot be reproduced online, but Clift emphasizes other learning options.
   D. Both authors are excited about other learning options.

Develop a Thesis

READING ASSESSMENT TARGETS: R.8.1, R.8.2, R.8.3, R.9.2, R.9.3
WRITING ASSESSMENT TARGETS: W.1, W.2

1 Learn the Skill

A **thesis** is a key statement or claim that answers the question posed by the extended response prompt. The extended response itself is an argument in which you work to prove your thesis and persuade your audience that your reading and evaluation of the source texts are accurate, complete, and worthy of consideration.

To begin an extended response, read the prompt, and identify the task. During a test, it is best to read the prompt both before and after you read the passages. This practice will help you establish a purpose for reading. It can also provide guidance for taking notes or marking the passages as you read. After you have finished reading, develop your thesis.

2 Practice the Skill

By practicing the skill of developing a claim or thesis, you will improve your study, writing, and test-taking abilities, especially as they relate to the GED® Reasoning Through Language Arts Test. Read the prompt and study the table below. Then answer the question that follows.

EXTENDED RESPONSE PROMPT

While Elayne Clift's article outlines the drawbacks of online education, Carl Jones's article identifies the benefits of online education.

In your extended response, analyze both articles to determine <u>which position is **better** supported</u>. Use relevant and specific evidence from both sources to support your response.

a To respond to this prompt, introduce a claim that states which article is better supported. You will develop your claim by logically organizing your reasons and textual evidence in the form of examples, facts, or details from both texts.

CLAIM OR THESIS

Position 1	Clift supports her argument better than Jones supports his argument because _____ _____ _____.
Position 2	Jones supports his argument better than Clift supports her argument because _____ _____ _____

b To develop a claim or thesis, phrase the prompt as a question: *Which position is better supported?* Then answer the question in a single sentence.

1. Which claim is the **best** thesis statement for the prompt above?

   A. Jones is a supporter of online education.
   B. Jones would make a better online teacher than Clift.
   C. Clift makes a stronger argument than Jones.
   D. Clift is not a supporter of online education.

TEST-TAKING TIPS

When drafting a thesis, set up a series of argumentative frames:
While _____ argues that _____, _____ makes a better argument in favor of/ against _____ because _____.

★ Spotlighted Item: **EXTENDED RESPONSE**

DIRECTIONS: Study and complete the chart. Then read the questions that follow, and write your answers on the lines provided.

What is the author's position?	What reasons does the author give to support the position?	What evidence does the author give to support the position?
Clift's position: Online courses are troublesome and not worth the effort.	1. Anonymity 2. _____ 3. _____	1. Acknowledgment of other point of view/personal admission 2. _____ 3. _____
Jones's position: Online courses have many advantages and benefits.	1. Flexibility 2. _____ 3. _____	1. Description of assignment completion and course choices 2. _____ 3. _____

2. What are the strengths and weaknesses of Clift's argument?

_____

_____

_____

3. What are the strengths and weaknesses of Jones's argument?

_____

_____

_____

4. Which position—Clift's or Jones's—is better supported?

_____

_____

5. Write a claim or thesis statement for your extended response.

_____

_____

_____

Define Points and Gather Evidence

READING ASSESSMENT TARGETS: R.9.1/R.7.1, R.9.2, R.9.3
WRITING ASSESSMENT TARGETS: W.1, W.2

1 Learn the Skill

After you have developed your thesis, the next step is to **define points of comparison or contrast** between the passages and **start gathering textual evidence**. Begin by rereading the passages. As you read, identify the main arguments, or reasons, and supporting evidence given by each author. Note how their reasons and evidence are alike or different. Look also for examples of rhetorical techniques the authors use to support their arguments.

In your extended response, you can use specific points of comparison and contrast between the passages as topics to include in your own argument. Select at least one example from each passage to support every point you identify.

2 Practice the Skill

By practicing the skills of defining points of comparison or contrast and gathering textual evidence, you will improve your study, writing, and test-taking abilities, especially as they relate to the GED® Reasoning Through Language Arts Test. Study the diagram below. Then answer the question that follows.

a The circles indicate points of comparison or contrast between the two articles. Start thinking about how each author uses these points.

b Take note of elements such as word choice and point of view in each text. They can help you determine an author's attitude toward the subject.

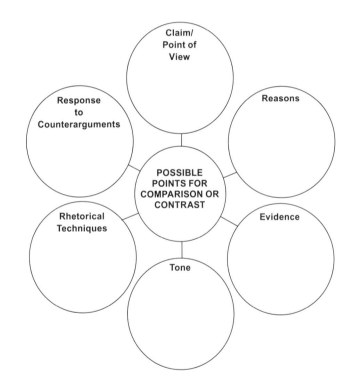

TEST-TAKING TECH

The GED® format allows electronic highlighting and note taking. Use these tools as you identify important points in each text. You will need to refer to the text frequently as you write your extended response.

1. How does the overall tone of the Clift article contrast with that of the Jones article?

    A. The tone of the Clift article is gloomy, but the tone of the Jones article is sarcastic.
    B. The tone of the Clift article is positive, but the tone of the Jones article is neutral.
    C. The tone of the Clift article is negative, but the tone of the Jones article is positive.
    D. The tone of the Clift article is neutral, but the tone of the Jones article is positive.

⭐ Spotlighted Item: **EXTENDED RESPONSE**

DIRECTIONS: Study the chart. Then complete the chart by writing your answers on the lines provided.

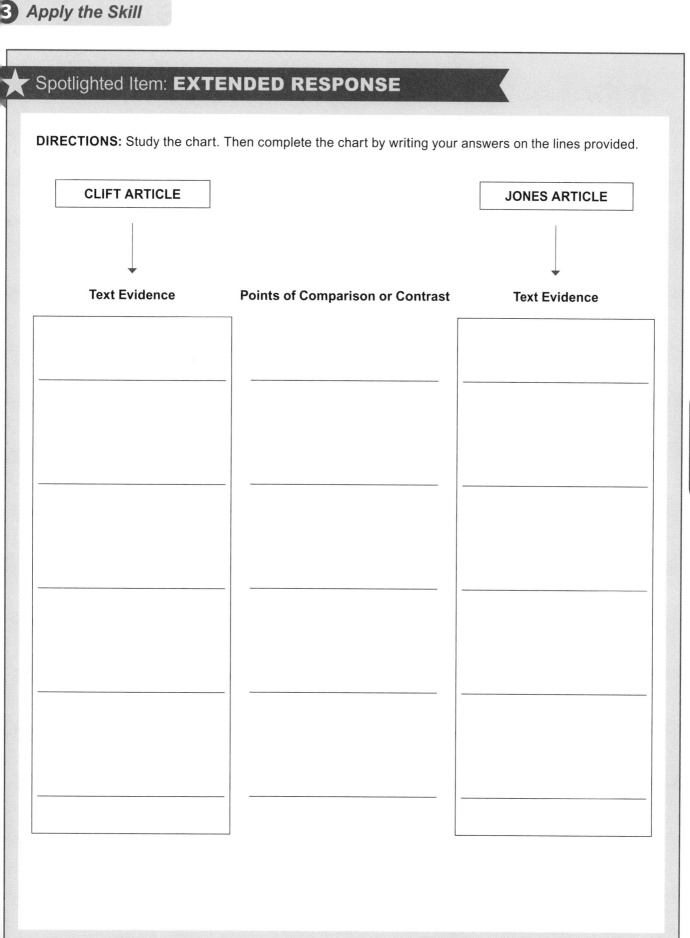

CLIFT ARTICLE

JONES ARTICLE

Text Evidence

Points of Comparison or Contrast

Text Evidence

UNIT 3

Plan the Extended Response

1 Learn the Skill

Before you draft your extended response, **choose an organizational structure**, and prepare an informal outline or graphic organizer with all of your points. For a comparison-and-contrast response, you can use one of two possible organizational structures: **subject by subject** or **point by point**.

When you organize your extended response according to subject, you discuss all points of comparison relating to one subject and then do the same for the second subject. When you organize according to points, you discuss both subjects with regard to one point before moving to the next point. In both cases, decide whether you want to sequence the order of points from **most important to least important, or vice versa**.

2 Practice the Skill

By practicing the skill of planning an extended response, you will improve your study, writing, and test-taking abilities, especially as they relate to the GED® Reasoning Through Language Arts Test. Study the charts below. Then answer the question that follows.

SUBJECT BY SUBJECT

State and explain the first point of comparison.	Provide an example of this point from the first passage.
State and explain the second point of comparison.	Provide an example of this point from the same passage.
State and explain the third point of comparison.	Provide an example of this point from the same passage.

POINT BY POINT

State and explain the first point of comparison.	Provide an example of this point from each passage.
State and explain the second point of comparison.	Provide an example of this point from each passage.
State and explain the third point of comparison.	Provide an example of this point from each passage.

a For a subject-by-subject comparison, you will need to repeat this structure for the second passage. Use this organizational structure with short essays or with essays on complex, less familiar topics.

b Use the point-by-point organizational structure with longer essays or with essays that focus on topics already familiar to you.

TEST-TAKING TIPS

For both structures, each point and its accompanying example(s) will serve as one or two body paragraphs in the actual extended response. Keep this information in mind as you plan the outline for your response.

1. In a point-by-point structure, what should follow an example about the use of tone in the Clift passage?

   A. an example of the use of point of view in the Clift passage
   B. an explanation of what tone is
   C. the introduction of another point
   D. an example of the use of tone in the Jones passage

⭐ Spotlighted Item: **EXTENDED RESPONSE**

DIRECTIONS: Study the charts. Choose an organizational structure for your extended response. Then complete the appropriate chart to plan your response. Place individual ideas in order of importance from most important to least important. You may refer to the evidence chart in Lesson 3 as needed.

SUBJECT BY SUBJECT

What is the first point of comparison or contrast? What explanation will this point require?	Which example from the Clift passage supports this point?
What is the second point of comparison or contrast? What explanation will this point require?	Which example from the Clift passage supports this point?
What is the third point of comparison or contrast? What explanation will this point require?	Which example from the Clift passage supports this point?

Restate the first point of comparison or contrast.	Which example from the Jones passage supports this point?
Restate the second point of comparison or contrast.	Which example from the Jones passage supports this point?
Restate the third point of comparison or contrast.	Which example from the Jones passage supports this point?

POINT BY POINT

What is the first point of comparison or contrast? What explanation will this point require?	Which example from the Clift passage supports this point? Which example from the Jones passage supports this point?
What is the second point of comparison or contrast? What explanation will this point require?	Which example from the Clift passage supports this point? Which example from the Jones passage supports this point?
What is the third point of comparison or contrast? What explanation will this point require?	Which example from the Clift passage supports this point? Which example from the Jones passage supports this point?

Write Introduction and Conclusion

1 Learn the Skill

The body of your extended response, which will include all of your arguments, points of comparison, and examples from the passages, should come between a thoughtful **introduction** and **conclusion**.

The purpose of the introduction, or "lead," is to gain readers' attention and prepare them for the thesis, which is often the final sentence of the introduction. The purpose of the conclusion, on the other hand, is to confirm or prove the thesis by summarizing the main ideas and details of the extended response. The conclusion also should leave readers with a final thought or call to action that will help them think about the topic beyond the extended response.

2 Practice the Skill

By practicing the skill of writing an introduction and a conclusion for your extended response, you will improve your study, writing, and test-taking abilities, especially as they relate to the GED® Reasoning Through Language Arts Test. Review the charts below. Then answer the question that follows.

INTRODUCTION STRATEGIES

Action	Begin with a description of someone doing something, such as posting an assignment in an online class.
Dialogue/ Quotation	Begin with a conversation in the chat room of a virtual classroom or with a quotation from an expert in the subject area.
Reaction	Use thinking verbs such as **consider**, **remember**, or **reflect** as you relate the thoughts of someone such as an online student or teacher.

CONCLUSION STRATEGIES

Anecdote	End with a short story that supports your thesis.
Connection	End by connecting with your audience. How does the argument affect them?
Fact or Statistic	End with a memorable or even shocking fact or statistic to support your thesis.

a After using one of these strategies, transition to the thesis. For example, *The growing popularity of such online classes has stimulated a debate regarding their value. Authors such as Clift and Jones are weighing in with differing opinions.*

b Before using one of these strategies for a final thought, first summarize the thesis, main ideas, and important details by restating them in different words.

TEST-TAKING TIPS

When beginning the conclusion of your extended response, use one of these transitions:
- Eventually,
- All in all,
- In conclusion,
- In the end,
- Therefore, as you can see

1. Which statement is an example of an action lead?

A. Online education is a growing trend at many secondary and post-secondary campuses.
B. Today, many adult students wonder how they will work and go to school at the same time.
C. "How am I supposed to transfer three pages of lecture notes to a few screens?" asked Professor Clift.
D. Jefferson clicked the Submit button and waited for confirmation of his enrollment in the online English course.

⭐ Spotlighted Item: **EXTENDED RESPONSE**

DIRECTIONS: Study and complete the charts. Remember to use the thesis statement you developed in Lesson 2 and revise it as needed.

INTRODUCTION

Circle one lead strategy: Action   Dialogue/   Reaction   Other   Quotation Describe your idea for the lead.
Develop a transition from the lead to the thesis.
Write the thesis.

CONCLUSION

Choose a transition to open the conclusion.
Restate the thesis.
Rephrase important points of comparison and/or supporting examples.
Circle one strategy for a final thought: Anecdote   Connection   Fact/Statistic   Other Describe your idea for the final thought.

UNIT 3

Draft the Extended Response

READING ASSESSMENT TARGET: R.5.3
WRITING ASSESSMENT TARGETS: W.1, W.2, W.3
LANGUAGE ASSESSMENT TARGET: L.1.9

1 Learn the Skill

After analyzing the passages and planning your extended response, you are ready to **write the draft**. As you write, be sure to maintain a consistent focus, keeping in mind both your purpose (to persuade) and your intended audience (in this case, the GED® test scorers).

Remember that each paragraph should connect to the thesis as well as to the surrounding paragraphs. Be sure that the paragraphs follow a logical and appropriate order, and use effective transitions to show the relationships among ideas. You should also be sure that the body paragraphs contain enough text evidence from the passages to support your thesis and the points of comparison or contrast you have chosen.

2 Practice the Skill

By practicing the skill of drafting an extended response, you will improve your study, writing, and test-taking abilities, especially as they relate to the GED® Reasoning Through Language Arts Test. Read the outline and strategies below. Then answer the question that follows.

OUTLINE

I. Introduction and Thesis

II. First Point of Comparison or Contrast
   A. State and explain point.
   B. Provide example from passage 1.
   C. Provide example from passage 2.

III. Second Point of Comparison or Contrast
   A. State and explain point.
   B. Provide example from passage 1.
   C. Provide example from passage 2.

IV. Third Point of Comparison or Contrast
   A. State and explain point.
   B. Provide example from passage 1.
   C. Provide example from passage 2.

V. Conclusion

a This is a point-by-point organizational structure. To organize by subject, add to the outline by repeating Points 1–3 and repositioning the items marked **C**.

b Use transitions to connect ideas within and between paragraphs. Each paragraph should connect back to the thesis statement.

1. Which transition **best** shows the relationship between two examples that fall under the same point of comparison or contrast?

   A. Although Clift favors lecture, Jones favors media.
   B. Clift favors lecture, and, in the same way, Jones favors media.
   C. Clift and Jones favor lecture and media equally.
   D. Similarly, Clift favors lecture, and Jones favors media.

TEST-TAKING TIPS

To show comparison, use transitional phrases like by the same token, similarly, and in the same way. To show contrast, try however, conversely, or in contrast.

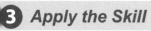

★ Spotlighted Item: **EXTENDED RESPONSE**

DIRECTIONS: Read the information below, and refer to the notes and planning organizers you completed in Lessons 1–5. Then write your extended response on the lines provided. If you chose a subject-by-subject organizational structure, you will need to adjust the frame. If you require additional space, you may continue your response on a separate sheet of paper.

EXTENDED RESPONSE

INTRODUCTION/LEAD

_____

_____

_____

_____

THESIS

_____

_____

_____

_____

POINT 1

_____

_____

_____

_____

PASSAGE 1 EVIDENCE

_____

_____

_____

_____

UNIT 3

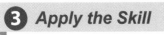
★ Spotlighted Item: **EXTENDED RESPONSE**

PASSAGE 2 EVIDENCE

_____

_____

_____

_____

_____

POINT 2

_____

_____

_____

_____

_____

PASSAGE 1 EVIDENCE

_____

_____

_____

_____

_____

PASSAGE 2 EVIDENCE

_____

_____

_____

_____

_____

POINT 3

_____

_____

_____

_____

PASSAGE 1 EVIDENCE

_____

_____

_____

_____

_____

PASSAGE 2 EVIDENCE

_____

_____

_____

_____

CONCLUSION

_____

_____

_____

_____

_____

_____

Review the Extended Response

WRITING ASSESSMENT TARGETS: W.1, W.2, W.3
LANGUAGE ASSESSMENT TARGETS: L.1.4, L.1.8, L.1.9, L.2.2

1 Learn the Skill

When your extended response draft is complete, use the remaining time to **review and revise** your draft for word choice, sentence structure, and grammatical correctness. Be sure that words are specific, logical, and appropriate. Check that the sentences are complete, concise, varied, and parallel.

Edit your draft to show a command of standard English conventions and mechanics, including subject-verb agreement, frequently confused words, modifier placement, pronoun use, capitalization, possessive apostrophes, and other punctuation, including commas. When you have finished editing, reread your draft one final time to ensure overall clarity and flow of ideas.

2 Practice the Skill

By practicing the skill of reviewing your extended response, you will improve your study, writing, and test-taking abilities, especially as they relate to the GED® Reasoning Through Language Arts Test. Read the chart and strategies below. Then answer the question that follows.

a Eliminate wordiness by using descriptive words in moderation, avoiding needless repetition, and using specific language.

b Whenever possible, edit to make your writing more interesting by incorporating a variety of sentence structures.

Review Category	Original Draft	Revision
Word Choice/ Transitions/ Wordiness	Clift focuses on the amount of stuff she is able to cover through materials and lectures, and Jones focuses on how material is covered through technological means. (Vague/Wordy)	Clift and Jones fundamentally disagree about the importance of quantity versus quality in education. (Clear/Concise)
Sentence Structure	Because Clift is a seasoned classroom teacher. (Fragment)	Because Clift is a seasoned classroom teacher, she is able to speak first-hand of her experiences. (Complete)
Conventions and Mechanics	One wonders why Clift does not present her student's points of view. (Singular vs. Plural Possessive)	One wonders why Clift does not present her students' points of view. (Correct)

TEST-TAKING TECH

The Spell Check tool is useful when editing, but do not rely on it too much. It does not always recognize names or new words and may not catch certain usage errors.

1. "The flexibility of online education demands that <u>people be adaptable to changing circumstances</u>, too." Which is the **best** way to write the underlined portion of the sentence?

   A. people change
   B. students and teachers be flexible
   C. online curriculum developers be flexible
   D. people in education be adaptable to all changing circumstances

UNIT 3

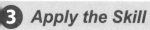

⭐ Spotlighted Item: **EXTENDED RESPONSE**

DIRECTIONS: Study the chart. Choose examples for revision from your draft in Lesson 6, and record them in the chart. Then revise each example as directed. If you require additional space, you may continue your response on a separate sheet of paper. Part of the chart has been filled in to help you get started.

REVIEW CHART

Word Choice/Transition/Wordiness List two phrases or sentences that need to be revised for vague word choice, transitions, informality, or wordiness. 1. *Finally, Clift and Jones both employ rhetorical strategies to convince readers that their ideas are better than the ideas of others, but Clift's qualifying statements work against her.* 2.	Revise the examples here. 1. *Finally, Clift and Jones both employ rhetorical strategies to convince readers of their points of view, but Clift's qualifying statements work against her.* 2.
Sentence Structure List two fragments, comma splices, run-ons, fused sentences, or awkward constructions. 1. 2.	Revise the examples here. 1. 2.
Conventions and Mechanics List two phrases or sentences that need to be revised for conventions or mechanics, such as those skills listed in the Learn the Skill section on the previous page. 1. 2.	Revise the examples here. 1. 2.

UNIT 3

Unit 3 Review

DIRECTIONS: Read the passages. Then answer each question on the next page.

CELL PHONES AND TEXTING ENDANGER DRIVERS

1   In 2008 … Wil Craig … was an Indiana high school senior … riding in his girlfriend's car as she drove and texted at the same time. Distracted, she wrecked the car. … Craig suffered a collapsed lung, four broken ribs, and a [harmful] brain injury. He spent eight weeks in a coma. … While there are many activities that can distract a driver … sending text messages may be the worst.

2   "Texting is among the most dangerous activities for drivers because it involves taking your eyes and attention off the roadway," says Justin McNaull, director of state relations for AAA. … "Even taking your eyes off the road for two seconds doubles your chances of being in a crash."

3   Not convinced? Stats from a Federal Motor Carrier Safety Administration study tell the story:

4   • Compared with 16 other distracting activities, texting had the highest odds of causing a serious crash.

5   • Drivers who were texting were 23.2 times more likely to crash than those drivers who weren't texting.

6   • When texting, drivers took their eyes off the road for an average of 4.6 seconds. …

7   As the risks of texting while driving have become more obvious, lawmakers across the country have begun to take notice—and to take action.

8   • Currently, laws in 30 states and the District of Columbia make it illegal to text … while driving. …

9   • Thirty-one states have separate restrictions for teens, including bans on using phones while driving. …

10   The penalties for breaking those laws range from fines to jail time. On the federal level, … Congress is considering several bills that would encourage all states to pass laws banning texting while driving.

From the *Current Health Teens*'s article DN'T TXT N DRV: WHY YOU SHOULD DISCONNECT WHILE DRIVING by Nancy Mann Jackson, © 2011

USELESS TEXTING LAWS

1   Oprah Winfrey asked you to join her "No Texting Campaign." Transportation Secretary Ray LaHood said he would not "stop pressing forward to make [roads] safer." Yet such efforts to stop people from using their cell phones while driving are useless. They focus only on a small part of the bigger issue of distracted drivers, who are paying attention to everything but driving. While cell phones may certainly capture a driver's attention, there are many other distractions that may lead to crashes. Until the government collects good data about the relationship between crashes and distractions, laws banning cell phone use, whether texting or talking, in cars will not work.

2   In a study done by the Transportation Department's National Highway Traffic Safety Administration, researchers named 13 driving distractions in addition to texting. These distractions included using a cell phone for a reason other than texting, looking at objects in the car, and talking with a passenger. In fact, talking seemed to cause more crashes than all cell phone use combined. In addition, auto makers are adding features to new cars, such as navigation systems and video screens, which may add to the number of distractions.

3   Certainly, cell phone use in the car is a popular media issue right now, but the research doesn't support this focus. Jayne O'Donnell, a consumer reporter, points out that the Insurance Institute for Highway Safety found that "using a cell phone while driving quadruples the risk of a crash." However, "research shows there was no concurrent increase in crashes as the number of cell phones increased throughout the 2000s." O'Donnell also notes that, "there is so little reliable data on how distraction is contributing to crashes."

4   While Secretary LaHood may be correct in calling distracted driving an "epidemic," we will not find a cure until we can identify, as O'Donnell puts it, "which distraction is responsible for a given accident."

From USELESS TEXTING LAWS by Sherie Trapper, © 2013

1. What is Jackson's main claim or point of view?

   A. Texting is the worst driving distraction.
   B. Texting is not the only dangerous driving distraction.
   C. Texting while driving involves taking one's eyes off the road.
   D. Texting causes worse crashes than other distractions.

2. What is Trapper's main claim or point of view?

   A. Texting is the worst driving distraction.
   B. Laws will help stop texting while driving and end texting-related crashes.
   C. Laws to ban cell phone use in cars will not work.
   D. Texting-related crashes have not increased with cell phone increases.

3. How does Jackson's supporting claim differ from Trapper's?

   A. Jackson says laws banning cell phone use in cars will not work, but Trapper believes texting is the worst driving distraction.
   B. Jackson claims that laws in 30 states make texting while driving illegal, but Trapper says automakers add distracting devices to cars.
   C. Jackson claims that laws will help stop crashes related to texting while driving, but Trapper argues that texting is not the only dangerous distraction.
   D. Jackson says laws in 31 states place separate restrictions on teen drivers, but Trapper points out that talking with a passenger causes crashes.

4. Trapper acknowledges and refutes a counterclaim in her article by

   A. pointing out that cell phone use in the car is a popular issue in the media, then citing research showing this focus is unwarranted.
   B. mentioning that texting is often considered the main cause of crashes, then quoting an expert who disagrees.
   C. noting that lawmakers do not believe texting while driving is a problem, then citing statistics showing the relationship between texting and crashes.
   D. acknowledging that there are other driving distractions, then sharing an anecdote about a crash caused by texting.

5. What lead-in strategies do Jackson and Trapper use?

   A. Both authors use action leads.
   B. Both authors use reaction leads.
   C. Jackson uses a quotation lead while Trapper uses a reaction lead.
   D. Jackson uses a reaction lead while Trapper uses an action lead.

6. How do Jackson and Trapper differ in their interpretations of data about cell phone use and car crashes?

   A. Jackson thinks cell phones do not affect the chances of being in a crash, but Trapper believes that cell phones are the main cause of increased crashes.
   B. Jackson states that drivers who do not text are safe from crashes, but Trapper believes that increased cell phone ownership has led to more serious crashes.
   C. Jackson argues that crashes involving texting lead to more serious injuries for passengers, but Trapper praises automakers for making cars safer.
   D. Jackson sees a cause-and-effect relationship between cell phone use and the likelihood of crashing, but Trapper says that the current data about distractions that cause crashes are unreliable.

7. What is one way that Jackson uses enumeration to advance her point of view?

   A. She cites a series of anecdotes about people who have crashed while texting.
   B. She lists statistics showing the relationship between texting and increased crashes.
   C. She gives the names of several experts who warn of the dangers of texting while driving.
   D. She lists the legal penalties for those caught texting while driving.

8. In paragraph 3 of her article, which transition word does Trapper use to signal the introduction of an opposing idea?

   [   ]

CYBER BULLYING HAS A BROADER IMPACT THAN TRADITIONAL BULLYING

1   The suicide of a young girl named Phoebe Prince in January of 2010 received a great deal of media attention. Phoebe was the victim of bullying … by classmates who posted [hurtful] remarks about her on Facebook. A few months ago, digital bullying was again in the news when Tyler Clementi, an 18-year old college student, [killed himself] after his roommate and a friend posted a [private] webcam video of Tyler. …

2   Cyber bullying is defined as electronic … behaviors among peers such as making fun of, telling lies, spreading rumors, threats and sharing private information or pictures without permission to do so. One of the … differences between traditional bullying and cyber bullying is that victims can be bullied anytime and from anywhere because most children have access to digital devices outside of school. As such, it is difficult to escape this type of bullying. … In addition, … a bully can torment a victim in front of a virtual audience of many people. … The Internet also allows anonymity, and a bully can target a victim while shielded behind a computer screen or mobile phone. Finally, … a person who bullies on a screen rather than face to face may not clearly understand how their behavior affects the victim. …

3   A recent study … found that the cyber bullying victims [showed] higher rates of depression. … Another study of U.S. children completed in 2005 found that 13% reported being cyber bullied more than 4–6 times in the past year. …

4   A recent study in Sweden … separated the kinds of cyber bullying into text (email and text) and visual (video and phone). Text based cyber bullying was perceived to have a less severe impact than traditional bullying, but visual felt more severe than traditional bullying.

From the psychologyinaction.org article IS BULLYING GOING DIGITAL? CYBER BULLYING FACTS by Yalda T. Uhls, © 2010

TRADITIONAL BULLYING STILL THE REAL PROBLEM

1   You may remember hearing the unfortunate stories of cyber bullying victims Phoebe Prince and Tyler Clementi on your local news station. Widespread media reports on events like these tend to turn public attention away from standard bullying. Unfortunately, standard bullying is a more common problem in schools, homes, and workplaces. People must, therefore, turn off their televisions and computers and focus on the real problems.

2   To begin, research statistics do not support the media hype about cyber bullying. Susan M. Swearer, a professor of school psychology at the University of Nebraska, writes, "as many as 25 percent of American schoolchildren continue to be bullied in traditional ways." On the other hand, as few as "10 percent claim to have been cyber bullied." The majority of bullying victims are subject to standard bullying, which includes physical abuse (like hitting or kicking), verbal abuse (like gossip or threats), and rejection from social groups.

3   Secondly, there are no clear roles when it comes to standard bullying. A bully in one situation may be the victim in another. An international study from 2007 found that children who are exposed to home violence are more likely to become bullies or bullying victims in situations outside the home.

4   There is also no age limit on standard bullying. *The Journal of Management Studies* claims that almost 50% of U.S. employees have been exposed to bullying at work. Employees have reported instances of physical, verbal, and sexual abuse. In most cases, workplace bullies hold positions of power over their targets.

5   In the end, stopping all types of bullying—cyber and standard—depends on our willingness to act. Bullying prevention programs have proven unsuccessful. However, a 2009 study published in the *Journal of Educational Psychology* shows evidence that programs that focus on reporting bullying behavior and punishing offenders have had more positive results.

From TRADITIONAL BULLYING IS STILL THE REAL PROBLEM by Stephen Farmer, © 2013

DIRECTIONS: Read and respond to the prompt. Use separate sheets of paper for planning. Then write your response on the lines below. If you require additional space, you may continue your response on a separate sheet of paper.

9.

> While Uhls's article outlines the disturbing effects of cyber bullying, Farmer's article identifies the prevalence of traditional bullying.
>
> In your response, analyze both articles to determine which position is **better** supported. Use relevant and specific evidence from both sources to support your response.

_____

_____

_____

_____

_____

_____

_____

_____

_____

_____

_____

_____

_____

_____

_____

_____

_____

_____

_____

_____

_____

DIRECTIONS: Read the passages, and answer the question on the next page.

AMERICA NEEDS SPACE EXPLORATION TO MAINTAIN ITS VISION OF ITSELF

1   Our nation finds itself on a treadmill … burning calories but not exactly sure where it is going. … For our national health, … [limiting] the space program is a bad idea. …

2   Our Founding Fathers established the U.S. as an idea … of liberty and creativity combined, never to be [limited] by the status quo. The vision of George Washington, Thomas Jefferson, Benjamin Franklin, and [others] … was rooted in the [practical matters] of daily life and cast … into the boundless frontier. …

3   This is exactly why the U.S. must explore space. We need a program to reimagine a frontier that will allow us to open up this [fearful] existence. The arguments against it are coldly logical and sometimes all too true. It is too expensive; there is little immediate benefit. The problem with those [ideas] is that they are blind to the human need to address the [big] questions of life: Who are we? How are we unique? Why are we here? How did it all begin?

4   The U.S. has been a place—and should remain one—in which these types of questions are asked. Admittedly, these "big" questions may never be answered satisfactorily but during the search, exploration itself becomes the driving force—our nation in search of the frontier. … To make this happen, we need a sense of place that includes what is known and what is not, what is possible and what lies beyond our [skills]. …

5   The U.S. was founded on the idea of never accepting the status quo and always exploring further. It is our national heritage, and it is not nice to fool with a nation's nature. NASA's manned space program … can help remind each American what it means to look up and open up—to have an idea of "you" that has a little elbow room.

From *USA Today*'s article SAVING OUR SPACE PROGRAM by Bob Deutsch, © 2010

THE US GOVERNMENT SHOULD CUT NASA FUNDING

1   Forget giant leaps for mankind. … While most Americans have moved on, NASA is stuck in the 1960s. That explains the desire to go to Mars. … Bush's project, priced at $400 billion, was inspired by his desire to stay ahead of the Chinese in the new space race. Just as in the 1960s, the ability to make shallow gestures in space is still assumed to be an indicator of a nation's [power]. …

2   Expensive manned missions mean that practical, earth-based science suffers, as does the genuinely valuable satellite research so essential to the way we live today. …

3   Recently, Stephen Hawking has argued that we must colonise other planets to ensure mankind's long-term survival. Much as I admire Hawking, that's nonsense. The Earth is indeed doomed, but where might refugees go? Mars makes Antarctica seem like paradise. …

4   The time has come to pull the plug on meaningless gestures in space. An expensive mission to the moon … seems [crazy] when [earthly] frontiers such as disease, starvation and drought cry out for cash. …

5   Obama … would do well to study what Nixon and Eisenhower had to say about space. Nixon was the first president to catch on to NASA's trick of using past [expenses] to justify future investment. As the agency argues, going to Mars will make what was spent going to the Moon a good investment. That's a clever way of endlessly spending money without ever producing anything.

6   But the final word goes to Eisenhower, who once vetoed Apollo. He reminded Americans that "every rocket fired signifies, in the final sense, a theft from those who hunger and are not fed, those who are cold and are not clothed."

From the telegraph.co.uk editorial THE SPACE RACE IS A POINTLESS WASTE OF MONEY by Gerard DeGroot, © 2009, accessed 2013

DIRECTIONS: Read and respond to the prompt. Use separate sheets of paper for planning. Then write your response on the lines below. If you require additional space, you may continue your response on a separate sheet of paper.

10.

> While Deutsch's article outlines the benefits of space exploration, DeGroot's article identifies its drawbacks.
>
> In your response, analyze both articles to determine which position is **better** supported. Use relevant and specific evidence from both sources to support your response.

_____

_____

_____

_____

_____

_____

_____

_____

_____

_____

_____

_____

_____

_____

_____

_____

_____

_____

_____

_____

_____

_____

RAISING THE MINIMUM WAGE WILL REDUCE POVERTY

1   Recent minimum wage raises are so little, so late that even with the minimum wage increase on July 24, 2009, to $7.25, workers will still make less than they did in 1956, adjusting for the increased cost of living. … We cannot build a strong 21st-century economy on 1950s wages.

2   Workers have taken many steps back for every step forward since 1968. The minimum wage reached its peak value in 1968. It would take a $9.92 minimum wage today to match the buying power of the minimum wage in 1968. …

3   The July 24, 2009, minimum wage of $7.25 comes to just $15,080 a year. …

4   The federal minimum wage was enacted in 1938 through the Fair Labor Standards Act (FLSA), designed to [get rid of] "labor conditions [harmful] to the maintenance of the minimum standard of living necessary for health, efficiency and general well-being of workers."

5   When set too low, the minimum wage does the opposite of what the Fair Labor Standards Act intended. … People are continually juggling which necessities to go without. …

6   • According to the National Low Income Housing Coalition, there is no county in the country where a full-time worker making minimum wage can afford a one-bedroom apartment (without spending more than 30% of their income on housing).

7   • The 2008 Conference of Mayors' Hunger and Homelessness Survey found that 42% of persons requesting emergency food assistance were employed, as were 19% of the homeless. …

8   Workers have not gotten "a fair day's pay for a fair day's work."

9   "As the productivity of workers increases, one would expect worker [pay] to experience similar gains," a 2001 U.S. Department of Labor report observed. Workers used to share in the gains of rising worker productivity. In recent decades, worker productivity went up, but workers' wages went down. Increasingly, the gains have gone to owners and top executives. …

10   Critics routinely oppose minimum wage increases in good times and bad, claiming they will increase unemployment, no matter the real-world record to the contrary. The buying power of the minimum wage reached its peak in 1968. The unemployment rate went from 3.8% in 1967 to 3.6% in 1968 to 3.5% in 1969.

11   The next time the unemployment rate came close to those levels was after the minimum wage raises of 1996 and 1997. Contrary to what critics predicted when the minimum wage was raised, our economy had unusually low unemployment, high growth, low inflation, and declining poverty rates between 1996 and 2000. … As *Business Week* put it in 2001, "Many economists have backed away from the argument that minimum wage [laws] lead to fewer jobs."

12   States that raised their minimum wages above the long stagnant $5.15 federal level [had] better employment and small business trends than states that did not.

13   Recent studies by the Institute for Research on Labor and Employment (Univ. of CA, Berkeley), carefully controlling for non-minimum wage factors, further advance the extensive research, which shows that minimum wage raises do not cause increased unemployment. …

14   Today, there is a great gap between the minimum wage and a minimum living standard. … The official poverty measure has become so out of touch with reality that research shows you need about double the official poverty threshold to get a more realistic measure of what people actually need to afford necessities. …

15   The minimum wage should be raised to $10. … That's a full-time annual wage income of $20,800. Future minimum wage increases should reflect the updated cost of an adequate minimum living standard. We should not repeat the error of the poverty measure and lock in an [outdated] minimum wage by indexing it to inflation from an inadequate base level.

From the letjusticeroll.org article RAISE THE MINIMUM WAGE TO $10 IN 2010 by Holly Sklar, © 2009, accessed 2013

DIRECTIONS: Read and respond to the prompt. Use separate sheets of paper for planning. Then write your response on the lines below. If you require additional space, you may continue your response on a separate sheet of paper.

11.

> Sklar's article outlines the benefits of raising the minimum hourly wage to $10.
>
> In your response, analyze the article to determine how well Sklar supports her position. Use relevant and specific evidence from the article to support your response.

_____

_____

_____

_____

_____

_____

_____

_____

_____

_____

_____

_____

_____

_____

_____

_____

_____

_____

_____

_____

_____

_____

UNIT 3

Chris Rock

Chris Rock dropped out of school to pursue his dreams of being a comedian but later received his GED® certificate.

UNIT 4

Chris Rock took pain and turned it into humor. Rock attended a mostly all-white public school while growir up in Brooklyn, New York. He faced discrimination at an early age. That discrimination, however, influenced the comedic material often on display in his act, on television, and in his movies

As a young comedian, Rock decided to leave school to perform on the New York club circuit. In 1984, fellow comedian Eddie Murphy—by then himself a success on television and in movies— caught Rock's act. Murphy cast Rock in a small role in *Beverly Hills Cop II*, marking the beginning of an entertainment career tha continues to this day. Rock, then only 18, had caught his big break

From 1990 to 1993, Rock starred on *Saturday Night Live*. He later worked on films such as *Dogma, Lethal Weapon 4, Madagascar,* and *Grown Ups*. Rock wrote a book called *Rock This* and created an produced the television series *Everybody Hates Chris*. The show was inspired by Rock's childhood in Brooklyn.

Rock's comedic talents resulted in Grammy awards and Emmy awards. Whatever the form of media, Rock uses his comedy to tacl topics such as race, politics, and parenting. Despite his successes, Rock always strives to improve his craft. As he notes, "If you think you're good, there's only one way to really be good and (that's to) be around the best. And learn. You (need to) learn more."

> "If you think you're good, there's only one way to really be good and (that's to) be around the best. And learn. You (need to) learn more."

CAREER HIGHLIGHTS: *Chris Rock*

- Raised in Brooklyn, New York
- Traveled the New York comedy club circuit extensively as a teenager
- Starred on the sketch comedy show *Saturday Night Live*

- Acted in dozens of films and voiced animated characters in several others
- Created the semi-autobiographical sitcom, *Everybody Hates Chris* in 2005

Editing

Unit 4: Editing

Good writing is not only engaging and persuasive, but it also displays a command of standard English conventions. The GED® Reasoning Through Language Arts Test includes an editing portion that assesses components of grammar, usage, capitalization, and punctuation. In Unit 4, you will practice these skills to improve your writing and test-taking abilities.

Like the GED® test, this unit asks you to edit the types of texts that you encounter or produce in your daily life, including workplace letters and memos, letters to the editor, flyers, and descriptions of policies and activities. Beginning with lessons on the building blocks of usage, such as proper use of verb tenses and subject-verb agreement, you will move on to lessons requiring you to practice techniques that will help you build strong sentences. Most test items in this unit appear as alternatives within drop-down menus, simulating the editing experience you will have on the GED® test.

Table of Contents

UNIT 4

Editing is a critical step in the writing process. Good writers edit their work to ensure proper grammar, usage, capitalization, and punctuation.

Nouns

LANGUAGE ASSESSMENT TARGET: L.2.1
WRITING ASSESSMENT TARGET: W.3

1 Learn the Skill

Nouns are words that name people, places, ideas, or things. Nouns may be singular (one person, place, idea, or thing) or plural (more than one person, place, idea, or thing). Proper nouns are names of specific people, places, titles, or things. Proper nouns are always capitalized (*Dr. Anna Jones*, *Arkansas*, *Bill of Rights*). **Collective nouns** are nouns that name groups, such as *team* or *jury*. They may be singular or plural, depending on whether the group acts as a unit or members of the group act as individuals.

2 Practice the Skill

By practicing the skill of using nouns correctly, you will improve your writing and test-taking abilities, especially as they relate to the GED® Reasoning Through Language Arts Test. Study the explanations and examples below. Then answer the question that follows.

▶ Use these rules to change nouns from singular to plural.

Rule	Singular	Plural
Add –s to most nouns	book, message	books, messages
Add –es to certain nouns ending in o	hero, potato	heroes, potatoes
Add –es to nouns ending in ch, sh, ss, or x	church, class	churches, classes
For nouns ending in y after a consonant, drop the y and add –ies	city, body	cities, bodies
For nouns ending in y after a vowel, add –s	boy, day	boys, days
For nouns ending in f or fe, drop the f(e) and add –ves	shelf, knife	shelves, knives
Some nouns change in form	man, child	men, children
Some nouns do not change at all	deer, fish	deer, fish

COLLECTIVE NOUNS

Singular	Plural
The <u>army fights</u>.	The <u>soldiers</u> in the army <u>fight</u>.
The <u>jury decides</u>.	<u>Members</u> of the jury <u>decide</u>.
The <u>team heads</u> to the field.	The <u>players head</u> to the field.

TEST-TAKING TIPS

Collective nouns are singular more often than plural. For clearer writing, use a word such as **members** to indicate plural. For example, "Some group members attend the yearly meeting."

1. **The company believes that its employies work hard.** Which correction should be made to the sentence?

   A. Change <u>employies</u> to <u>employes</u>.
   B. Change <u>company</u> to <u>companies</u>.
   C. Change <u>employies</u> to <u>employees</u>.
   D. Change <u>company</u> to <u>companys</u>.

★ Spotlighted Item: **DROP-DOWN**

DIRECTIONS: Read the passage. From the drop-down list, choose the answer that **best** completes the sentence.

Dear NBA Commissioner:

I'm sure your office receives many calls and letters asking about the league's various [2. Drop-down 1] regarding player salaries. I am hoping that you can provide some information that will help explain how the league determines the amount each player makes in a year and the amount each team can spend on players.

For many fans like me, the league's salary cap is very confusing. It seems as though some players' salaries don't match the contributions that they make to their teams. The cap also seems to limit unfairly the amount a team can spend on players. For example, why can't my home team, the [2. Drop-down 2], spend what it wants on salaries if it has the money to spend?

I have done some research on the salary cap, and I know that it is negotiated yearly as part of the collective bargaining agreement that provides team owners with rules about how they can negotiate member salaries. I also understand that the salary cap is based on how much revenue the league took in during the previous year. Is team revenue factored in? Are there [2. Drop-down 3] for some teams to spend more money than others?

I know that the [2. Drop-down 4] many factors when determining salary, including how many years a player has been in the league. Can you provide me with a simple explanation of these other factors? I don't understand the complicated rules governing exceptions, restricted and non-restricted free agents, the amnesty clause, and the rules governing rookie salaries.

Any information you could provide would be very helpful!

Sincerely,

Wayne Mack

Drop-Down Answer Options

2.1 A. policy
B. polices
C. policys
D. policies

2.2 A. Miami heat
B. Miami Heat
C. miami Heat
D. miami heat

2.3 A. wayes
B. way
C. ways
D. waies

2.4 A. league weighs
B. league weigh
C. league members weighs
D. leagues weighs

UNIT 4

Pronouns

LANGUAGE ASSESSMENT TARGET: L.1.3

1 Learn the Skill

Pronouns are words that take the place of nouns. The noun that the pronoun replaces is the antecedent. **Pronoun-antecedent agreement** means that pronouns agree in gender (male, female, or neuter) and number (singular or plural) with the nouns (antecedents) they replace. Depending upon their use in the sentence, pronouns may be subjects or objects or may indicate possession.

2 Practice the Skill

By practicing the skill of using pronouns correctly, you will improve your writing and test-taking abilities, especially as they relate to the GED® Reasoning Through Language Arts Test. Read the explanations and examples below. Then answer the question that follows.

▶ The chart lists subject, object, and possessive pronouns. These can be singular or plural.

Pronoun Form	Subject	Object	Possessive
Singular	I, you, he, she, it	me, you, him, her, it	my, mine, your, yours, his, her, hers, its, our, ours, their, theirs
Plural	we, you, they	us, you, them	our, ours, your, yours, their, theirs

a Remember that **me** is never the subject of a sentence. Write, "*Charlie and I are dating,*" not "*Charlie and me are dating.*"

- Charlie and I are dating. ⟶ We are dating.
- That is Zack's car. ⟶ That is his car.
- Janet, Chris, and Richard are flying home. ⟶ They are flying home.
- The victory was mine and Paul's. ⟶ The victory was ours.
- Tell Cara and Frances the story. ⟶ Tell them the story.
- The car's tires are new. ⟶ Its tires are new.

b The possessive pronoun **its** is not written with an apostrophe. *It's* means "it is." For example, "*It's* dinner time."

CONTENT TOPICS

It is easy to misuse the pronoun *they* to avoid mentioning a specific gender. If you do not specify a gender, but your subject is singular, then you must write *he or she.* For example, "Each person can do what he or she wants."

1. **Jonathan and Alison went to dinner after Jonathan and Alison went to the game.** Which is the best way to rewrite this sentence?

A. Jonathan and Alison went to dinner after them went to the game.
B. Jonathan and Alison went to dinner after they went to the game.
C. They went to dinner after Jonathan and Alison went to the game.
D. They went to dinner after she went to the game.

UNIT 4

⭐ Spotlighted Item: **DROP-DOWN**

DIRECTIONS: Read the passage. From the drop-down list, choose the answer that **best** completes the sentence.

First National Bank
200 North Street
Chapel Hill, NC 27514
(919) 555-6237

Mr. Paul Wilford
132 Keppel Street
Dayton, OH 45414

Dear Mr. Wilford:

First, let me express [2. Drop-down 1] appreciation that you have chosen to place a business account with our bank when your company moves to Chapel Hill. I'm sure you will find that First National Bank will be able to meet your business's every need. We offer personalized service and the opportunity for each customer to access [2. Drop-down 2] information 24 hours every day. In addition to corporate checking accounts for both payroll and expenses, we offer short-term loans for qualified customers.

It may be best for you to visit our small-business experts at the bank to ensure a smooth transition for your accounts. Your advisor is Mr. Jamie Parks, who is located at the Elm Street branch. [2. Drop-down 3] secretary will call to set up an appointment. If possible, our president, Emily Rider, and [2. Drop-down 4] would like to take you to lunch. Please accept this gesture as a sign of our southern hospitality.

Please don't hesitate to contact me if you have other questions. We look forward to serving you and Wilford Motors.

Sincerely,
Jean Broadmoor
Accounts Manager

Drop-Down Answer Options

2.1 A. I
B. mine
C. me
D. my

2.2 A. he or she
B. their
C. his or her
D. her

2.3 A. Her
B. Mine
C. His
D. Their

2.4 A. me
B. I
C. her
D. him

UNIT 4

Basic Verb Tenses

1 Learn the Skill

The **basic verb tenses** are **past**, **present**, and **future**. These tenses signal to readers that events occurred in the past, are taking place now, or will happen in the future. To form the past tense of **regular verbs**, add –d or–ed to the end of the verb. Often, to keep a short vowel sound, the final consonant must be doubled. To form the future tense, add the word will before the verb.

Forming tenses can be more challenging with **irregular verbs**. In some cases, you will need to change the spelling of the verb. It is best to memorize the irregular verb forms because they follow no specific rules.

2 Practice the Skill

By practicing the skill of using basic verb tenses correctly, you will improve your writing and test-taking abilities, especially as they relate to the GED® Reasoning Through Language Arts Test. Study the tables below. Then answer the question that follows.

▶ These tables show how verbs appear in different tenses. Note that in the present tense, third-person singular verbs end in s. As in many cases with verbs, if it sounds wrong, it probably is wrong.

REGULAR VERBS

Present	Past	Future
I look, it looks, they look	I looked	I will look
I want, he wants, they want	He wanted	They will want
I play, he plays, they play	They played	He will play
I dance, she dances, they dance	He danced	She will dance
I hope, he hopes, they hope	I hoped	We will hope
I study, she studies, they study	She studied	They will study

IRREGULAR VERBS

Present	Past	Future
I do, it does	I did	I will do
he sees	he saw	he will see
he flies	he flew	he will fly
it eats	it ate	it will eat
she goes	she went	she will go
she drives	she drove	she will drive
they write	they wrote	they will write

USING LOGIC

Look for words that signal the time of the action, such as *tomorrow*, *later*, and *yesterday*. They can provide clues to the correct verb tense by signaling whether the action happened in the past, is happening, or will happen.

1. **At work yesterday, I drop a heavy box on my foot.** Which correction should be made to the sentence?

A. Change drop to dropped.
B. Change drop to dropping.
C. Change drop to will drop.
D. Change drop to drops.

⭐ Spotlighted Item: **DROP-DOWN**

DIRECTIONS: Read the passage. From the drop-down list, choose the answer that **best** completes the sentence.

ABOUT YOUR CYTECH CELL PHONE

Thank you for purchasing your new Cytech cellular phone. We believe that as soon as you start using this phone, you [2. Drop-down 1] it one of the most technologically advanced cell phones on the market today. Your Cytech phone [2. Drop-down 2] all of the standard features discerning customers want, including a state-of-the-art digital camera, video recording and chat, GPS, and high-speed Internet capability.

The Cytech phone represents the cutting edge of cell phone technology today. Scientists and technicians in our San Francisco headquarters [2. Drop-down 3] two years creating the innovative interface. Drawing upon the successful operating system of our popular tablet, we designed the phone's interface to include many of the tablet's key features and unparalleled functionality. The Cytech phone will provide users with the same exceptional performance they have come to expect from our tablet and other products.

Your new phone was designed and manufactured to meet all cellular phone standards set by the U.S. government. These guidelines were based on standards that were developed by scientists. You can be confident that all Cytech phones have been tested to ensure that they meet these guidelines and are safe for our customers.

You [2. Drop-down 4] more information about your new phone in the mail within a few days.

Thank you for your purchase!

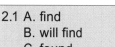

Drop-Down Answer Options

2.1 A. find
B. will find
C. found
D. finded

2.2 A. will have
B. had
C. have
D. has

2.3 A. spend
B. will spend
C. spent
D. spends

2.4 A. will receive
B. receives
C. receive
D. received

UNIT 4

Verbs with Helping Verbs

1 Learn the Skill

Helping verbs combine with main verbs to indicate the time of an action. If an action took place in the past before another past action was completed, use the helping verb *had* with the past participle form of the main verb. If an action began in the past and continues in the present, use the helping verb *has* or *have* with the past participle form of the main verb. If an action will end at a specific point in the future, use the helping verb *will have* with the past participle form of the main verb.

Use a form of the helping verb *to be* (*am, is, are, was,* or *were*) with the present participle form (always ending in *-ing*) of the main verb to indicate action that is ongoing.

2 Practice the Skill

By practicing the skill of using verbs with helping verbs to show tenses, you will improve your writing and test-taking abilities, especially as they relate to the GED® Reasoning Through Language Arts Test. Study the explanations and examples below. Then answer the question that follows.

▶ This information shows when and how to use the helping verb *have*.

Past Perfect Tense	An action took place in the past before another past action was completed.	They <u>had walked</u> more than two miles before they found the turtle. We <u>had heard</u> the senator's speech before we read it in the paper.
Present Perfect Tense	An action began in the past and continues in the present.	I <u>have lived</u> here for a year. She <u>has taken</u> several classes so far.
Future Perfect Tense	An action will be completed at a specific time in the future.	In June, we <u>will have lived here</u> for three years. We <u>will have finished</u> this report by the end of the day.

a Past participles may or may not be the same word as the past tense of a verb. Check a dictionary for **principal parts of verbs**. Entries for all verbs provide the present tense, past tense, and past participle.

b The present participle of a verb always ends in *–ing*. Although spelling rules may apply, present participles are always regular.

▶ This information shows when and how to use the helping verb *be*.

Present Progressive	An action is ongoing at the present time.	I <u>am talking</u> on the phone.
Past Progressive	An action was ongoing in the past.	He <u>was working</u> at the company.
Future Progressive	An action will be ongoing in the future.	They <u>will be making</u> the movie in my town.

TEST-TAKING TIPS

Be sure to read many types of well-written texts. By reading examples of the correct uses of verb tenses, you will know which forms to use in your own writing.

1. **Ravi plans to leave early in the morning, so by lunchtime he <u>was driving</u> for five hours.** Which is the best way to write the underlined portion of this sentence?

    A. had driven
    B. will have driven
    C. has been driving
    D. he has driven

★ Spotlighted Item: **DROP-DOWN**

DIRECTIONS: Read the passage. From the drop-down list, choose the answer that **best** completes the sentence.

CAR BUYING TIPS

There's a simple way to get the best price on a new car. If you follow this three-step system, you can save thousands of dollars on your next car. Step 1 is to find out what the dealer paid for the car before receiving any rebates. Knowing what the dealer paid for a car allows you to know the mark-up that the dealer

| 2. Drop-down 1 | on the car. Typically, more expensive cars have higher mark-ups. You can assume a mark-up in the range of 6–8 percent, although this range can vary by model and dealer. Do your research in advance to find out as much as you can about the dealer's cost.

Step 2 is to find out about the dealer's hidden rebate for the car. By the end of this year, dealers | 2. Drop-down 2 | all kinds of rebates from car makers. They will try to keep these rebates hidden from you during the deal. Although the dealer may not pass along the rebate to you, the existence of a rebate might make the dealer more willing to negotiate on the mark-up. You also should research what rebates the manufacturer | 2. Drop-down 3 | consumers to make sure that you take advantage of all potential rebates currently available.

Step 3 is to avoid paying for extras that you do not want or need. Dealers make much of their money on extras like wheel and tire protection, extended warranties, and rust protection. Before you make your purchase, think about the extras that you need and will use. After you | 2. Drop-down 4 | which extras you definitely want, be sure to look at the total price you will pay for them. Many dealers show only a monthly calculation of the payment, thus hiding the actual cost from you.

Drop-Down Answer Options

2.1 A. will have placed
    B. have placed
    C. has placed
    D. was placing

2.2 A. will have received
    B. had received
    C. are receiving
    D. have received

2.3 A. had offered
    B. is offering
    C. was offering
    D. will have offered

2.4 A. had decided
    B. were deciding
    C. will have decided
    D. have decided

UNIT 4

Apostrophes

LANGUAGE ASSESSMENT TARGETS: L.1.1, L.2.3

1 Learn the Skill

In Lesson 2, you learned one way to show possession—to whom or what something or someone belongs—by using possessive pronouns. Another way to show possession is to use an **apostrophe**. Apostrophes create **possessive** nouns.

You also can use an apostrophe when you combine two words to form a **contraction**. The apostrophe shows where the letters of one or both words have been left out. Contractions allow you to use fewer words when writing informally.

2 Practice the Skill

By practicing the skill of using apostrophes to show possession and contractions, you will improve your writing and test-taking abilities, especially as they relate to the GED® Reasoning Through Language Arts Test. Study the explanations and examples below. Then answer the question that follows.

▶ These examples will help you understand possessives and contractions.

a For plural nouns that do not end in *s*, use an apostrophe and add *s*: for example, *the* **children's** *playground*.

POSSESSIVES

Rule	Example
For singular nouns, use an apostrophe and add –*s*	***child's*** *game*
For most singular nouns ending in *s*, use an apostrophe, and add –*s*	***James's*** *coat*
For plural nouns ending in *s*, use only an apostrophe	***coaches'*** *meeting*

b Remember to avoid confusing the possessive pronouns *your*, *its*, and *their* with contractions that sound the same: **you're**, **it's**, and **they're**.

CONTRACTIONS

I + am = I'm	it + is = it's
will + not = won't	you + are = you're
they + have = they've	should + have = should've

TEST-TAKING TIPS

To test whether an apostrophe is being used for a contraction or a possessive, substitute the full words into the sentence. "*It's* time to go" means "*It is* time to go." Therefore, the apostrophe indicates a contraction, not a possessive.

1. **Not only is camping fun, but it's also a great way to spend time with you're friends or family.** Which correction should be made to the sentence?

   A. Change <u>it's</u> to <u>its</u>.
   B. Change <u>friends</u> to <u>friend's</u>.
   C. Change <u>it's</u> to <u>it was</u>.
   D. Change <u>you're</u> to <u>your</u>.

UNIT 4

★ Spotlighted Item: **DROP-DOWN**

DIRECTIONS: Read the passage. From the drop-down list, choose the answer that **best** completes the sentence.

THE MAPLE HOTEL
Mr. Frank Thomas, CEO
Thomas Building Supplies
864 Fellows Street
Cincinnati, OH 45201

Dear Mr. Thomas:

I am writing to introduce myself to you and your associates. My name is Miranda Snyder, and I am the new Sales Account Manager at The Maple Hotel. I have assumed Pat [2. Drop-down 1] former position. Ms. Charles is now our Director of Sales.

I have learned from Ms. Charles that your company often does business in the Louisville area and frequents our hotel on a regular basis. We thank you so much for your business. I now will be Thomas Building [2. Drop-down 2] main sales correspondent and am looking forward to working with you and your staff on any upcoming business trips.

As part of my introduction to The Maple Hotel's preferred guests, [2. Drop-down 3] my pleasure to offer you 500 extra Maple Points that will be added to your account upon your next stay with us. As you may know, you can use Maple Points toward complimentary rooms, dining in our restaurant, and discounts on [2. Drop-down 4] events here at the hotel.

I look forward to meeting you in person on your next visit. If I can be of assistance in any way, please do not hesitate to call. I have included my business card for your convenience. Thank you again for your continued business.

At your service,

Miranda Snyder

Sales Account Manager

Drop-Down Answer Options

2.1 A. Charles'
    B. Charles's
    C. Charles
    D. Charleses

2.2 A. Supplies'
    B. Supplies
    C. Supplies's
    D. Supplie's

2.3 A. its'
    B. its
    C. it
    D. it's

2.4 A. you're companies's
    B. your company's
    C. your companys'
    D. you're companies'

UNIT 4

Frequently Confused Words

LANGUAGE ASSESSMENT TARGETS: L.1.1, L.1.3

1 Learn the Skill

Words that sound similar but have different spellings and different meanings are called **homonyms**. For example, *ate* and *eight* are homonyms. *Ate* is the past tense of the verb *to eat*, and *eight* is the number 8. Sometimes, words may have the same spelling and sound alike (or different) but have different meanings— for example, the noun *wind* (meaning "air that is blowing") and the verb *wind* (meaning "coil around or curve"). Furthermore, some words that look similar are often confused, such as *lose* and *loose*.

2 Practice the Skill

By practicing the skill of using homonyms and frequently confused words correctly, you will improve your writing and test-taking abilities, especially as they relate to the GED® Reasoning Through Language Arts Test. Study the explanations and examples below. Then answer the question that follows.

▶ These examples will help you understand homonyms and frequently confused words.

a **Then** and **than** are often confused. Remember, **then** refers to time or sequence. **Than** makes a comparison between items.

b The pronouns **its** and **their** are easily confused with the contractions **it's** and **they're**. **Their** is also sometimes confused with **there**, meaning "at that place."

COMMON HOMONYMS AND FREQUENTLY CONFUSED WORDS

by	Be at work <u>by</u> noon tomorrow.	buy	Will you <u>buy</u> me a magazine?
lose	Did they <u>lose</u> the soccer game?	loose	The young girl had a <u>loose</u> tooth.
pale	He wore a <u>pale</u> blue tie.	pail	The child brought a <u>pail</u> and shovel to the beach.
way	You're going the wrong <u>way</u>!	weigh	I <u>weigh</u> less now that I've been on a diet.
hear	Do you <u>hear</u> what I'm saying?	here	The books you need are over <u>here</u>.
then	I mowed the grass and <u>then</u> trimmed the bushes.	than	Steve likes drag racing more <u>than</u> hockey.
new	That <u>new</u> movie looks funny.	knew	She <u>knew</u> the answer right away.
past	The story takes place in the <u>past</u>.	passed	Justine <u>passed</u> the test on her first try.
see	Rico can <u>see</u> better with his glasses.	sea	The cottage overlooks the <u>sea</u>.

TEST-TAKING TIPS

Carefully examine the surrounding text to determine which homonym a writer intends to use. Become more familiar with other homonyms by checking pages 174–175 in this book.

1. **Did you see who just past by driving a new sports car?** Which correction should be made to the sentence?

   A. Change <u>see</u> to <u>sea</u>.
   B. Change <u>past</u> to <u>passed</u>.
   C. Change <u>by</u> to <u>buy</u>.
   D. Change <u>new</u> to <u>knew</u>.

UNIT 4

★ Spotlighted Item: **DROP-DOWN**

DIRECTIONS: Read the passage. From the drop-down list, choose the answer that **best** completes the sentence.

Ms. Eve Nichols
112 Morton Lane
Baltimore, MD 21210

Dear Ms. Nichols:

Thank you for purchasing your policy with Drivers' Car Insurance. As a policyholder with [2. Drop-down 1] types of coverage—property damage and injury liability—you are entitled to many benefits. If you become involved in an accident, this policy will help pay for your medical bills, legal fees, and one year's income. If you cause the accident and other people are injured, this policy will help offset the costs of [2. Drop-down 2] medical treatment. Also, the policy will help pay to repair their vehicles or other property that was damaged in the accident.

Our goal is to provide you with the highest possible level of service. We want your insurance experience to be a positive one. After all, the last thing you want when you've been involved in an accident is to struggle with insurance issues! You can be assured that the response team at Drivers' Car Insurance is [2. Drop-down 3] to serve you.

As a policyholder with Drivers' Car Insurance, you are more [2. Drop-down 4] just another customer. We value our policyholders and take pride in our products and service. When you buy a policy with us, you haven't just purchased a policy, you have bought the peace of mind that comes from knowing that when you need us, we'll be there for you.

We look forward to being there when you need us!

Sincerely,

Anthony Perilla

President

Drop-Down Answer Options

2.1 A. to
B. tow
C. two
D. too

2.2 A. there
B. they're
C. thair
D. their

2.3 A. her
B. here
C. hire
D. hear

2.4 A. then
B. thin
C. than
D. thing

UNIT 4

Basic Subject-Verb Agreement

LANGUAGE ASSESSMENT TARGETS: L.1.2, L.1.7

1 Learn the Skill

Subjects and **verbs** must **agree**—that is, a singular subject takes a singular verb, and a plural subject takes a plural verb. This rule always applies, even when other words come between the subject and verb or when two subjects share the same verb.

2 Practice the Skill

By practicing the skill of using correct subject-verb agreement, you will improve your writing and test-taking abilities, especially as they relate to the GED® Reasoning Through Language Arts Test. Study the explanations and examples below. Then answer the question that follows.

▶ These rules and examples will help you understand subject-verb agreement.

If two subjects are connected by **and**, the resulting compound subject takes a plural verb.

Tom and Jan write. *Think:* They write.

If two subjects are connected by **or**, the verb agrees with the subject closer to the verb:

Tom or Jan writes. *Think*: He or she writes.

	Verb Agreement	Examples
Singular subject	Singular verb	*Right:* Milk spoils easily. *Wrong:* Milk spoil easily.
Plural subject	Plural verb	*Right:* These carrots look fresh. *Wrong:* These carrots looks fresh.
Subjects connected by *and*	Plural verb	*Right:* Fish and meat contain protein. *Wrong:* Fish and meat contains protein.
Singular subjects connected by *or*	Singular verb	*Right:* Jim or Sara prepares breakfast on weekends. *Wrong:* Jim or Sara prepare breakfast on weekends.
Plural subjects connected by *or*	Plural verb	*Right:* Local markets or farm stands feature fresh corn. *Wrong:* Local markets or farm stands features fresh corn.
Singular and plural subjects connected by *or*	Singular or plural verb depending on which subject is closer to verb	*Right:* The dogs or the cat is in the kitchen. *Wrong:* The dogs or the cat are in the kitchen.

CONTENT TOPICS

This chart lists singular and plural forms of the irregular verbs *be, have,* and *do.*

Verb	Singular	Plural
be	am, are, is, was, were	are, were
have	have, has	have
do	do, does	do

1. **Ana play on the company softball team.** Which correction should be made to the sentence?

A. Change play to plays.
B. Change play to playing.
C. Change company to companies.
D. Change team to teams.

★ Spotlighted Item: **DROP-DOWN**

DIRECTIONS: Read the passage. From the drop-down list, choose the answer that **best** completes the sentence.

OFFICE SUPPLY'S REFUND POLICY

At Office Supply, we strive to make your shopping experience as convenient and pleasant as possible. We understand that sometimes you may need to return a purchase. Office Supply's refund policies [2. Drop-down 1] simple. If you paid with cash, Office Supply will refund your purchase with cash if it was bought at the same store. If you paid with a debit card, we will credit your account the same day. If you do not have your receipt, your return is eligible for an in-store credit for the current price of the item you are returning. Office Supply carefully [2. Drop-down 2] returns and, in some cases, may have to refuse returns without a receipt.

Most merchadise can be returned within 30 days of purchase, although some products (such as opened software) can be exchanged for another of the same item. Business machines and furniture [2. Drop-down 3] a return within 14 days to qualify for a refund or exhange. Expired ink or toner cartridges cannot be returned. Unopened and unexpired ink or toner cartridges may be returned at any time for a full refund.

Office Supply associates or the store manager [2. Drop-down 4] available to help if you have a concern about your return. Our staff will work with you to resolve the issue. Our goal is for you to leave our store satisfied and to return to shop with us.

For a detailed description of our return policy, as well as answers to Frequently Asked Questions (FAQ), please go to our Web site at www.OfficeSupply.com/returns.

Thank you for shopping with us!

Drop-Down Answer Options

2.1 A. is
B. are
C. was
D. were

2.2 A. monitor
B. are monitoring
C. monitors
D. were monitoring

2.3 A. require
B. required
C. requires
D. requiring

2.4 A. were
B. are
C. be
D. is

UNIT 4

Standard English

1 Learn the Skill

A good writer avoids using nonstandard or informal language, including slang, except for special purposes. Although the English language is always evolving, at any one moment there exists a widely accepted form of English that is written by educated people and is considered correct. This accepted form is called **Standard English**. It includes rules for spelling, grammar, pronunciation, and vocabulary. Some words and constructions that you might hear in spoken language are not considered Standard English. For example, avoid the word *ain't* in formal speech and writing.

2 Practice the Skill

By practicing the skill of using Standard English, you will improve your writing and test-taking abilities, especially as they relate to the GED® Reasoning Through Language Arts Test. Study the examples and explanations below. Then answer the question that follows.

Examples	Explanation
Ain't	*Ain't* is an improper contraction. Use <u>am not</u>, <u>is not</u>, <u>isn't</u>, <u>are not</u>, or <u>aren't</u> instead.
Could of, should of, would of	The correct construction uses <u>have</u>: I <u>could have</u> done better.
Double negatives	Two negatives do not form a single negation: *She doesn't have no car* should be written instead as *She <u>does not</u> have a car* or *She <u>has no</u> car.*
Dunno	*Dunno* is slang for <u>don't know</u> or <u>do not know</u>.
Pronoun repetition	Avoid unnecessary pronouns. Write *My <u>sister lives</u> in Boston* instead of *My sister she lives in Boston.*
Suppose to	When you mean "should have" or "should," write <u>supposed</u> to with a <u>d</u>. Do not confuse *supposed* and *opposed*. These words also may sound alike in speech.
Try and; go and	You <u>try *to*</u> do something. You don't try *and* do something. You <u>go *to* see</u> someone. You don't *go and* see someone.
Use to	Write <u>used to</u>. The <u>d</u> is often omitted because it is difficult to hear in speech.

TEST-TAKING TIPS

Some constructions sound normal in casual speech but are not correct. Learn some of the most common mistakes, and then proofread your writing carefully to ensure that you have avoided them.

1. **You should try and get some sleep.** Which correction should be made to the sentence?

   A. Change <u>get</u> to <u>got</u>.
   B. Add <u>of</u> before <u>try</u>.
   C. Change <u>and</u> to <u>to</u>.
   D. Add <u>have</u> before <u>try</u>.

★ Spotlighted Item: **DROP-DOWN**

DIRECTIONS: Read the passage. From the drop-down list, choose the answer that **best** completes the sentence.

A CITY EYESORE

Dear Editor:

It is well past time for the city to do something about the apartment building at the corner of Cornell Street and Third Avenue. Or are people simply [2. Drop-down 1] such situations? This building has been nearly vacant for the five years that I have lived on Cornell Street. With each year that goes by, the condition of the property gets worse. It is my understanding that the Montgomery County Bank took over the property in 2003 when the landlord did not make the payments. Since that time, all but two of the tenants have left. Paint is peeling off the outside of the building, weeds are growing in the courtyard, and many windows are broken or boarded up. The problems [2. Drop-down 2] get fixed without the city's intervening.

Many of us in the neighborhood have tried to get the bank to do something, but we have been ignored. This situation isn't right! I thought that the bank would respond to the dozens of calls and letters, but no one there will take responsibility. The bank does not maintain the property and [2. Drop-down 3] in selling it to someone who will.

Does anyone with the city government care? The [2. Drop-down 4] quick to fine folks in my neighborhood who don't maintain the sidewalks in front of their homes, but it takes no notice of this decaying apartment building. When I contact the city, I get the runaround. Please join me in demanding that the city take action!

Daniel Goldman

Drop-Down Answer Options

2.1 A. use to
B. used ta
C. used a
D. used to

2.2 A. are not ever gonna
B. are never not going to
C. ain't never gonna
D. are never going to

2.3 A. takes no interest
B. doesn't take no interest
C. ain't interested
D. don't take no interest

2.4 A. city it is
B. city is
C. city they is
D. city be

UNIT 4

Capitalization

1 Learn the Skill

Capitalization identifies proper nouns and proper adjectives as well as titles or parts of names (such as *Mr., Dr., or Jr.),* holidays, days of the week, and months of the year. The pronoun *I* is always capitalized. Also capitalize the first letter of the first word of a sentence and the main words in titles of newspapers, books, magazines, stories, articles, songs, poems, and plays.

2 Practice the Skill

By practicing the skill of using capitalization correctly, you will improve your writing and test-taking abilities, especially as they relate to the GED® Reasoning Through Language Arts Test. Study the explanations and examples below. Then answer the question that follows.

▶ These definitions and examples will help you understand capitalization.

a A proper noun may contain words that are not always capitalized in other contexts. For example, the word *university* is capitalized when it refers to a specific university, such as the *University of North Carolina.*

Definitions	Examples
A **proper noun** is a name that identifies a particular person, place, or thing. A **proper adjective** is a descriptive word based on a proper noun.	Noun: University of North Carolina Adjective: French bread
A **common noun** or **adjective** is a label that designates a general type of person, place, or thing.	Noun: a university in North Carolina Adjective: white bread

▶ This chart provides examples of common nouns and related proper nouns.

b Proper nouns name specific people, places, or things.

Common Nouns	Proper Nouns
city	Dallas
horse	Secretariat
novel	*The Great Gatsby*
doctor	Dr. Susan Williams
drugstore	Value Plus Drugs
paper towel	Quick Clean Paper Towels
day	Tuesday

TEST-TAKING TIPS

Read passages carefully, and identify any words that should be capitalized. Determining the capitalization errors as you read will help save time when you answer GED® test questions.

1. **I found good recipes for thai dishes in an article called "Simply noodles."** Which corrections should be made to the sentence?

A. Capitalize <u>recipes</u> and <u>thai</u>.
B. Capitalize <u>dishes</u> and <u>noodles</u>.
C. Capitalize <u>thai</u> and <u>article</u>.
D. Capitalize <u>thai</u> and <u>noodles</u>.

UNIT 4

★ Spotlighted Item: **DROP-DOWN**

DIRECTIONS: Read the passage. From the drop-down list, choose the answer that **best** completes the sentence.

MEMO

To: All Agency Employees

Subject: An Explanation of Federal Holidays

As a government agency, we think it is important that our employees understand the history of our country's federal holidays. Below is a brief review.

In 1870, Congress passed a law that officially recognized four federal holidays. [2. Drop-down 1] on January 1, Independence Day on July 4, Thanksgiving on the last Thursday of November, and Christmas on December 25. Over time, Congress has recognized new federal holidays. Today, we celebrate 10 federal holidays each year.

In 1879, Congress established the nation's fifth federal holiday. This holiday is celebrated on the third Monday of February, and most people know it as Presidents' Day. On this day, Americans honor all of the people who have served as [2. Drop-down 2].

On Memorial Day, Americans honor all of the U.S. soldiers who fought and died for their country. This holiday is held on the last [2. Drop-down 3]. Labor Day became the nation's seventh federal holiday in 1894. On this day, Americans honor the workers of the nation. Labor Day is held on the first Monday of September.

Armistice Day was established in 1938. Congress later changed the name to Veterans Day to honor all of the soldiers who served in the United States armed forces. In 1968, Congress recognized Columbus Day to remember Christopher Columbus's voyage to North America. Columbus Day is held on the second Monday of October. Finally, Congress passed a law in 1983 to set aside the third Monday of January to honor the accomplishments of [2. Drop-down 4]

Drop-Down Answer Options

2.1 A. They are New Year's Day
B. they are New Year's day
C. they Are new year's day
D. They Are new Year's Day

2.2 A. President of The United States
B. President of the united states
C. president of the United States
D. president of the United states

2.3 A. monday of may
B. monday of May
C. Monday of may
D. Monday of May

2.4 A. Dr. Martin Luther King, jr.
B. Dr. Martin Luther King, Jr.
C. dr. Martin Luther King, jr.
D. dr. Martin Luther King, Jr.

UNIT 4

Sentence Fragment Correction

LANGUAGE ASSESSMENT TARGETS: L.2.1, L.2.2, L.2.4

1 Learn the Skill

Every complete sentence contains a subject and a verb and must express a complete idea, or make a complete statement. A group of words missing a subject, verb, or complete idea is a sentence fragment, which is usually incorrect. A sentence fragment cannot stand alone because it is incomplete. To **correct a sentence fragment**, you can combine it with a complete sentence by using a comma or a connecting word. You also can add the missing sentence component, such as a subject or verb.

Complete sentences must begin with a capital letter and end with punctuation, such as a period (ends a statement), an exclamation point (emphasizes or expresses excitement), or a question mark (indicates a question).

2 Practice the Skill

By practicing the skills of recognizing sentence components and correcting sentence fragments, you will improve your writing and test-taking abilities, especially as they relate to the GED® Reasoning Through Language Arts Test. Study the explanations and examples below. Then answer the question that follows.

▶ These steps will help you understand sentence components.

a Some imperative sentences (such as *"Hurry!"*) have an implied subject. The subject, **you**, is understood but not stated: *(You) hurry!*

b A sentence that asks a question often begins with **who**, **what**, **when**, **where**, **why**, or **how**. Questions can also begin with **did**, **do**, **should**, **could**, or **would**.

Subject	Verb	Complete Idea
Identifies who or what the sentence is about	Identifies the action performed by the subject	Represents a whole thought; can stand alone

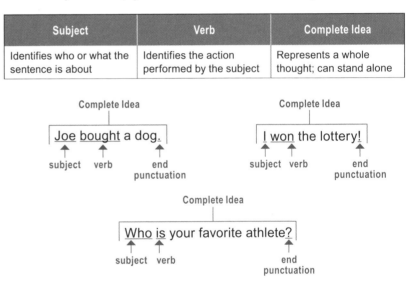

UNIT 4

1. **Went to the gym on Thursday.** Which correction should be made to the sentence?

   A. Replace the period with a question mark.
   B. Insert a verb.
   C. Insert a subject.
   D. Replace the period with an exclamation point.

★ Spotlighted Item: **DROP-DOWN**

DIRECTIONS: Read the passage. From the drop-down list, choose the answer that **best** completes the sentence.

WHAT'S YOUR CREDIT SCORE?

Have you applied for a credit card or a bank loan

| 2. Drop-down 1 | that information regarding your credit score factored into the result. A credit score is a number between 300 and 850 that assesses the likelihood that you will pay back a creditor. A low score is a problem. You are considered a credit risk because you are not likely to pay your debts. If your score is high, you are considered a good risk because you are likely to pay your debts.

| 2. Drop-down 2 | one's credit history. This history includes payment patterns, longevity, and current debt. If your score is above 700, you are likely to get good lending rates. If your score is below 600, you are likely to get high lending rates. In fact, many creditors use 620 as the determining number for credit approval. If your score is extremely low, you may be rejected for credit.

One's credit score is not a stable | 2. Drop-down 3 | If you miss or make a late payment, your score will go down. It is possible to raise a low credit score by using the following tips. Pay your bills on time. Do not maintain high balances on your credit cards. Do not open credit accounts that you don't plan to use.

To have a good credit score, you must show that you are able to manage your credit. Although you need some credit cards and loans, you must manage these accounts effectively. Finally, you should know that a closed account does not

| 2. Drop-down 4 | your credit score.

Drop-Down Answer Options

2.1 A. recently. Chances good
   B. recently? Chances are good
   C. recently. Chances are good
   D. recently! Chances are good

2.2 A. Based on
   B. A person's credit score based on
   C. A credit score is based on
   D. A credit score based on

2.3 A. number. Can go up or down!
   B. number. It go up or down.
   C. number. it can go up or down.
   D. number. It can go up or down.

2.4 A. disappear? That account may still affect
   B. disappear. That account may still affect
   C. disappear. May still affect
   D. disappear. That account still affect

UNIT 4

Commas

1 Learn the Skill

A **comma** separates a sentence into meaningful units. For example, use a comma to form a series or to set off introductory and interrupting (or descriptive) phrases. Use a comma with a conjunction when you combine sentences and when you use two or more adjectives to describe the same noun. Also, use commas with dialogue to set off the tag line (the words that identify the speaker) from the dialogue.

2 Practice the Skill

By practicing the skill of using commas correctly, you will improve your writing and test-taking abilities, especially as they relate to the GED® Reasoning Through Language Arts Test. Study the examples below. Then answer the question that follows.

▶ These examples will help you understand and use commas effectively.

a A **phrase** is a group of related words that cannot stand alone as a sentence. A **clause** is a group of related words with a subject and verb but may be incomplete on its own.

b An interrupting phrase *(a blue sedan)* or clause *(who is turning 50 this year)* in the example sentences provides extra information. If this phrase or clause were removed, the sentence would maintain its meaning.

COMMAS

Usage	Example
Items in a series	*I bought apples, rolls, and milk at the grocery store.*
Introductory phrase	*To stay in shape, football players must work out every day.*
Interrupting or descriptive phrase or clause	*Alex's car, a blue sedan, is in the parking lot.* *My dad, who is turning 50 this year, just went skydiving.*
Combining sentences	*We drove to the lake, but the fishing pier was closed.*
Two or more adjectives	*It was a long, dreary day.*
With quotations and dialogue	*Sophia said, "I'm going to take the dog to the park."*

TEST-TAKING TECH

When using the computer keyboard, be careful not to mistake the apostrophe for the comma. The comma key is directly to the right of the m key. The symbols look similar.

1. **My two brothers Mike and Tom came with me to the baseball game last weekend.** Which is the best way to write the underlined portion of the sentence?

A. brothers, Mike, and Tom,
B. brothers, Mike and Tom,
C. brothers Mike, and Tom
D. brothers, Mike and, Tom

★ Spotlighted Item: **DROP-DOWN**

DIRECTIONS: Read the passage. From the drop-down list, choose the answer that **best** completes the sentence.

To Whom It May Concern:

As a frequent user of the City [2. Drop-down 1] disappointed with the proposal to discontinue Bus Route 97, which provides direct service from Midtown to the Warehouse District. The proposal does not take into account the needs of Midtown's citizens. Like many people in Midtown, I depend on Bus Route 97 to get to and from my job in the Warehouse District. If this route is discontinued, I will have to transfer four times just to get to work.

The City Transit System's proposal also does not take into account Midtown's elderly citizens, such as my mother. My mother does not own a car and relies on Bus Route 97 to get to the city park, the supermarket, and the hospital. It is the [2. Drop-down 2] for her to travel to these places. If the proposal is approved, my mother will have to walk several miles each way to buy [2. Drop-down 3] see her doctor.

As if it weren't enough to discontinue such an important transportation route, the City Transit System also has proposed to increase bus fares. Now it will take longer for many people in Midtown to get to their [2. Drop-down 4] will cost more money for them to do so. The City Transit System claims that cutting bus service and raising fares will help it survive these tough times. However, I believe that these proposals will make the City Transit System's survival in Midtown even tougher.

Sincerely,
James Meyer

Drop-Down Answer Options

2.1 A. Transit System, I, am
B. Transit, System I am
C. Transit System I am
D. Transit System, I am

2.2 A. quickest easiest way
B. quickest, easiest, way
C. quickest, easiest way
D. quickest easiest way,

2.3 A. groceries, pick up
medication or,
B. groceries, pick up
medication, or
C. groceries pick up
medication, or
D. groceries, pick up
medication, or,

2.4 A. jobs, and it
B. jobs and, it
C. jobs, and, it
D. jobs and it

UNIT 4

Sentence Combining

LANGUAGE ASSESSMENT TARGETS: L.1.6, L.1.8, L.1.9 L.2.4

1 Learn the Skill

Writing can sound choppy if it contains too many short sentences. Often short, related sentences can be combined to make longer, more fluid sentences. You can **combine sentences** in several ways: use connecting words, use connecting words and commas, combine repeated elements by using compound subjects or verbs, use a semicolon, use a semicolon with a signal word and comma, or combine sentences to show the relationship of one idea to another.

2 Practice the Skill

By practicing the skill of combining sentences correctly, you will improve your writing and test-taking abilities, especially as they relate to the GED® Reasoning Through Language Arts Test. Study the explanations and examples below. Then answer the question that follows.

▶ Use these techniques to combine sentences.

Eliminate wordiness by using connecting words and connecting words with commas to combine repeated elements.	For better flow, make compound sentences by using connecting words, commas, semicolons, and signal words.	Combine sentences to show the relationship of one idea to another or to subordinate one idea to another idea.
I went to the store. I went to the bank. *becomes* I went to the store and the bank.	I called Todd. He didn't answer. *becomes* I called Todd, but he didn't answer.	I practice. I improve. *becomes* When I practice, I improve.
I bought a dog. I bought a leash. I bought some dog food. *becomes* I bought a dog, a leash, and some dog food.	Tina was exhausted. She could not fall asleep. *becomes* Tina was exhausted; however, she could not fall asleep.	Jake does not like meat. Jake ate it yesterday. *becomes* Although Jake does not like meat, he ate it yesterday.

TEST-TAKING TIPS

You may need to add or delete some words when combining sentences. You can add words to clarify a sentence's meaning or delete repetitive words. Check whether a subject or verb is repeated in back-to-back sentences.

1. **We went to dinner. We went to the movies. We went out for coffee.** Which is the **most** effective revision of the sentences?

A. We went to dinner and then to other places.
B. We went to dinner and we went to the movies and we went out for coffee.
C. My girlfriend and I went out.
D. We went to dinner, to the movies, and out for coffee.

⭐ Spotlighted Item: **DROP-DOWN**

DIRECTIONS: Read the passage. From the drop-down list, choose the answer that **best** completes the sentence.

NOTICE FOR EMERGENCY AWARENESS

Having a plan for what to do in an emergency is important to ensure the safety of your family. An emergency may include a [2. Drop-down 1] a hurricane. Every family should make a family safety plan that outlines what to do in different types of emergencies.

To create a family safety plan, follow these tips:

- Establish an escape route from each room of your home. Every member of the family should know how to get out of the home without assistance. Having a clear escape route is [2. Drop-down 2] could help save your life.

- Select meeting locations in case family members become separated. One location should be in your neighborhood; the other should be outside your neighborhood. You might not have access to a car, so all locations should be within walking distance.

- Choose a person outside the city to contact in the event of an emergency. Be sure that every family member has the telephone number and e-mail address of this person.

- Collect the phone numbers and addresses of the places at which each family member spends the most time, such as a workplace or school. Eventually, you will share this information with all family [2. Drop-down 3] in a safe place.

- Prepare an emergency card for each family member to carry with him or her. The card should have information about emergency contacts, medical conditions, [2. Drop-down 4] the names of family members.

Drop-Down Answer Options

2.1 A. fire or an earthquake. An emergency may include
B. fire, an earthquake, or
C. fire; it may include an earthquake or
D. fire; in addition, it could include an earthquake or

2.2 A. important and having an escape route
B. important. Having an escape route
C. important; however, having an escape route
D. important because it

2.3 A. members. Keep this information you will share
B. members; therefore, keep it
C. members. Keeping it
D. members. And keeping this information

2.4 A. medication,
B. medication, and
C. medication; it should have
D. medication; also include

UNIT 4

Run-on Sentence Correction

LANGUAGE ASSESSMENT TARGETS: L.2.2, L.2.4

1 Learn the Skill

When you combine sentences without using the correct punctuation or connecting word, the result may be a **run-on sentence**. Run-on sentences are usually either comma splices or fused sentences. A comma splice occurs when only a comma connects two sentences. A fused sentence occurs when no conjunction or proper punctuation is used to connect two sentences.

Depending on the type of error, you can correct run-on sentences by adding a comma and connecting word, adding a semicolon, or creating separate sentences.

2 Practice the Skill

By practicing the skill of correcting run-on sentences, you will improve your writing and test-taking abilities, especially as they relate to the GED® Reasoning Through Language Arts Test. Study the explanations and examples below. Then answer the question that follows.

▶ This table will help you identify and correct run-on sentences.

a If the sentence contains two ideas, the best option may be to create two sentences.

Add a semicolon or semicolon, connecting word, and comma.	Add a comma and a connecting word.	Create two sentences.
Wrong: Mario does not enjoy cooking, however he made dinner for the family. *Right*: Mario does not enjoy cooking; however, he made dinner for the family.	*Wrong*: The band played songs from an old album they sounded different. *Right*: The band played songs from an old album, but they sounded different.	*Wrong*: Lakshmi offered to drive she has a new car. *Right*: Lakshmi offered to drive. She has a new car.

b If you create two sentences to avoid a run-on, be sure that neither is a fragment. Remember, a sentence contains three components: a subject, a verb, and a complete idea.

▶ Sentence length does not indicate whether or not a run-on exists. Even a short sentence can be a run-on.

Wrong: I ate dinner, he read a book.

Right: I ate dinner; he read a book.

TEST-TAKING TIPS

If a word like **however** or **therefore** is surrounded by two complete thoughts, use a semicolon before it and a comma after it. If it is not surrounded by two complete thoughts, use a comma before and after it.

1. **Everyone had a great time at the show we're going to see the band play again next month.** Which correction should be made to the sentence?

   A. Replace we're with and.
   B. Insert a comma after show.
   C. Insert , and after show.
   D. Insert but after show.

UNIT 4

★ Spotlighted Item: **DROP-DOWN**

DIRECTIONS: Read the passage. From the drop-down list, choose the answer that **best** completes the sentence.

EMPLOYEE MANUAL
WORK-RELATED INJURIES

MINOR INJURIES

- Do not [**2. Drop-down 1**] all minor injuries to the department manager and the Human Resources Department.

- The Human Resources Department is responsible for the following actions: reporting the claim to the insurance company, referring the employee to an appropriate health-care provider, and working with a department manager to secure any needed recovery time.

- Employees must receive permission from their health-care provider before they return to work. At that point, they can resume work-related or other [**2. Drop-down 2**] must restrict activity so that it does not endanger their recovery.

MAJOR INJURIES

- Without delay, place calls to 911 and the Security Department.

- The Security Department will contact the appropriate employees in the Human Resources [**2. Drop-down 3**] provide a copy of the injury report.

- Seek immediate medical treatment at the nearest emergency facility.

- As soon as possible, contact the Human Resources Department to complete an incident [**2. Drop-down 4**] will provide further counsel.

Drop-Down Answer Options

2.1 A. delay, report
   B. delay, however
   C. delay. Report
   D. delay report

2.2 A. duties; however, they
   B. duties however they
   C. duties however; they
   D. duties, however, they

2.3 A. Department they will
   B. Department, they will
   C. Department, but they will
   D. Department, and they will

2.4 A. report, staff members
   B. report staff members
   C. report. Staff members
   D. report. Staff members,

UNIT 4

Modifiers

LANGUAGE ASSESSMENT TARGET: L.1.5

1 Learn the Skill

Modifiers describe, clarify, and give more detail about another word or word group. Adjectives and adverbs are examples of modifiers. An adjective is a word that modifies a noun (a **large** dog). An adverb is a word that modifies a verb (He walks **quickly**.), an adjective (I'm **quite** busy.), or another adverb (He walks **very** quickly). A prepositional phrase is another type of modifier. A prepositional phrase can modify a noun, a verb, or a group of words (the boy **with brown hair**).

A **misplaced modifier** misleads readers by describing the wrong item in a sentence. A **dangling modifier** describes a subject that is missing from a sentence or is in the wrong position. A modifier belongs as close as possible to the word it modifies.

2 Practice the Skill

By practicing the skill of using modifiers correctly, you will improve your writing and test-taking abilities, especially as they relate to the GED® Reasoning Through Language Arts Test. Study the explanations and examples below. Then answer the question that follows.

▶ This information will help you learn more about modifiers.

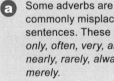

a Some adverbs are commonly misplaced in sentences. These include only, often, very, almost, nearly, rarely, always, and merely.

b Pay careful attention to the placement of prepositional phrases. In the example, on his team modifies players, not advice.

Misplaced Modifiers	Dangling Modifiers
I only ate one slice of pizza. [So you only *ate* the pizza and did not also *throw* it on the floor?] → Instead, try: *I ate only one slice of pizza.*	Having adopted a new dog, the leash was purchased. [*Who purchased* the leash, the dog?] → Instead, try: *Having adopted a new dog, Jane purchased a leash.*
Wrong: When Lucas invites friends to dinner, he tries new recipes often. *Right:* When Lucas invites friends to dinner, he often tries new recipes. *Wrong:* The coach gave the athletes advice on his team. *Right:* The coach gave the athletes on his team advice.	*Wrong:* Before moving to Texas, Florida was my home. *Right:* Before I moved to Texas, Florida was my home.

TEST-TAKING TIPS

Misplaced modifiers can be tricky to identify when you are reading quickly. Underline or highlight any descriptive words or phrases, and then think about what those details are meant to describe.

1. **Although nearly over, we left the game early because the Colts were losing.** Which is the most effective revision of the sentence?

   A. Although we were nearly over, we left early because the Colts were losing the game.
   B. Although nearly over the game, we left early because the Colts were losing.
   C. Although the Colts were losing, we were nearly over and left the game early.
   D. Although the game was nearly over, we left early because the Colts were losing.

★ Spotlighted Item: **DROP-DOWN**

DIRECTIONS: Read the passage. From the drop-down list, choose the answer that **best** completes the sentence.

HOW TO MAKE LASAGNA

Lasagna is a popular pasta dish that is relatively easy to make at home, even for inexperienced cooks. In fact, it is the perfect dish to make when serving a crowd because you can prepare lasagna in advance, and just about everyone loves it. The recipe also is incredibly flexible. Like many other classic [2. Drop-down 1] different variations. For example, you can try out different ingredients to make either meat or vegetarian lasagna.

To make basic lasagna, you will need about one pound of lasagna noodles for a 13" x 9" pan. Basic lasagna also includes three cheeses: ricotta, mozzarella, and Parmesan. For the filling, [2. Drop-down 2] and ground meat. However, if you are feeling adventurous, substitute roasted eggplant, spinach, or other vegetables for the meat.

Now you are ready to cook. [2. Drop-down 3] they are barely softened. A good time-saving tip at this point is to start cooking the tomato sauce, meat, and vegetables while the noodles boil. You should have your cheeses ready so that you can proceed quickly when the noodles and filling are ready.

To prepare the lasagna for baking, [2. Drop-down 4] into the pan in the following manner: noodles, sauce, and a mixture of the three cheeses. Now the lasagna is ready for the oven. Place the pan in the oven, and bake at 350 degrees for about 45 minutes. You will know that the lasagna is done when you see it bubbling and browned.

Drop-Down Answer Options

2.1 A. dishes, you can make lasagna in
B. dishes, lasagna lends itself to
C. dishes, people make lasagna in
D. dishes, there are

2.2 A. often people use tomato sauce
B. people often use tomato sauce
C. people use often tomato sauce
D. people use tomato sauce often

2.3 A. First, boil the noodles in a large pot until
B. Boil the noodles in a large pot first until
C. Boil first the noodles in a large pot until
D. Boil the noodles in a large pot until first

2.4 A. ingredients must be layered
B. layer ingredients
C. layers of ingredients go
D. ingredients are placed in layers

UNIT 4

1 Learn the Skill

As you learned in Lesson 2, **subject pronouns** (*I*, *you*, *he*, *she*, *it*, *we*, *they*) perform an action or are described. **Object pronouns** receive actions. For example, in the sentence *He saw it*, *he* performs the action and *it* receives the action. Object pronouns *me*, *you*, *him*, *her*, *them*, *us*, and *it* usually follow verbs or words such as *above*, *at*, *before*, *between*, *from*, *near*, *of*, and *to*. Be careful when pronouns are compound. Each pronoun in a compound should be in the correct case.

The pronoun *who* indicates an unknown person or persons or introduces a part of a sentence that gives more information about a person or individuals. *Who* changes to *whom* when it is an object. Remember, too, that the pronouns *this*, *that*, and *which* must have antecedents.

2 Practice the Skill

By practicing the skill of using pronouns correctly, you will improve your writing and test-taking abilities, especially as they relate to the GED® Reasoning Through Language Arts Test. Read the examples and explanations below. Then answer the question that follows.

a Use **who**, **whom**, **whoever**, and **whomever** for people. Use **that** or **which** for objects and ideas. For example, *The car that I bought is six years old. The dealer who sold it to me is now out of business.*

b Sometimes words come between a pronoun and the verb. For example, *Choose someone who you know will do a good job*. The pronoun **who** indicates the person who will do the action. The words *you know* come between *who* and the verb *will do*.

Examples	Explanation
Who is asking these questions?	Who is the subject pronoun.
Whom is Sonia inviting?	Whom is the object pronoun, or the person(s) Sonia (the subject) is inviting.
The man **who** asked the question is my brother.	The subject pronoun who indicates a person doing the action of asking the question.
The man **whom** Sonia called was not at home.	Whom represents the person receiving the action. Sonia called the man.
Whoever wins the contest will receive the prize.	Whoever means "whatever person." The person's identity is unknown.
Ella can hire **whomever** she chooses.	Whomever represents the person or individuals who receive the action of Ella's hiring.
Kay and I met Lola at the mall.	I is part of the subject of the sentence.
Lola met **Kay and me** at the mall.	Me is part of the object of *met*.
We have no news. **This situation** is a concern. (We are concerned because we have no news.)	Using this alone gives the pronoun no antecedent. A noun can be added or the sentence can be rewritten.
Everyone knows **his or her** task.	Everyone always takes singular pronouns.
He cooked **himself** a gourmet dinner.	He and himself are the same person. Use pronouns like *myself* or *yourself* only when the subject and object are the same.

TEST-TAKING TIPS

The pronoun **who** is similar to the pronouns *he* and *she*. *Whom* is similar to *him* and *her*. If you are uncertain whether to use **who** or **whom**, try substituting one of the other pronouns.

1. **I wonder whom is calling me again?** Which correction should be made to the sentence?

   A. Change <u>whom</u> to <u>whomever</u>.
   B. Change <u>whom</u> to <u>whoever</u>.
   C. Change <u>whom</u> to <u>her</u>.
   D. Change <u>whom</u> to <u>who</u>.

Spotlighted Item: **DROP-DOWN**

DIRECTIONS: Read the passage. From the drop-down list, choose the answer that **best** completes the sentence.

Dear Mr. Fisk:

I am writing to apply for the Sous-Chef position at Taste, as advertised in *Chicago Restaurants Weekly*. I believe my training and experience qualify me for the position.

My culinary interest began in high school, where I took courses in basic knife skills and restaurant management at the student-run restaurant. Upon graduation, [2. Drop-down 1] received a certificate of excellence for the high grades and commitment we demonstrated throughout the culinary program.

After high school, I attended the Fairfield Culinary Institute, where I completed the Culinary Arts program. I served as an intern for three months in a local restaurant. [2. Drop-down 2] gave me experience in assisting the grill chef and various line cooks. From my entire graduating class, the faculty selected five [2. Drop-down 3] for showing superior kitchen skills and knowledge. We received six-month fellowships at upscale area restaurants. I served as a line cook at Restaurant La France.

After my fellowship, I thought to broaden my experience with other cuisines. I worked for six months as the pantry chef at a Vietnamese and French fusion restaurant. Then I was promoted to grill chef, a position I currently hold.

I would love to take on more responsibility in a kitchen, and Taste is a restaurant whose innovative approach I have long admired. I believe my skills, enthusiasm, and reliability would be a great match for your restaurant. I have several former teachers and supervisors [2. Drop-down 4] can provide references upon request.

Thank you for your consideration.

Emily Carston

Drop-Down Answer Options

2.1 A. several students and me
 B. several students and I
 C. several of we students
 D. me and several students

2.2 A. This
 B. Which internship
 C. This internship
 D. Which

2.3 A. students, including me,
 B. students, including I,
 C. of we students, including me,
 D. of us students, including I,

2.4 A. whom
 B. who
 C. whoever
 D. they

UNIT 4

Advanced Subject-Verb Agreement

LANGUAGE ASSESSMENT TARGET: L.1.7

1 Learn the Skill

As you learned in Lesson 7, **subject-verb agreement** is usually clear when a verb immediately follows the subject. However, verbs do not always follow subjects. Mismatched subjects and verbs often occur in sentences with compound subjects, subjects that sound plural (such as *everyone*), subjects that include indefinite pronouns that can be singular or plural (like *all*), sentences beginning with *there is* or *there are* or with other constructions in which the verb does not follow the subject, compound subjects separated by *nor*, and subjects that include prepositional phrases between the subject and verb.

2 Practice the Skill

By practicing the skill of using advanced subject-verb agreement correctly, you will improve your writing and test-taking abilities, especially as they relate to the GED® Reasoning Through Language Arts Test. Read the explanations and examples below. Then answer the question that follows.

Rule	Example
A **compound subject** connected with *and* takes a **plural verb**, regardless of how far apart the subjects appear in the sentence.	The <u>woman and that snarling dog in the silly pink raincoat we saw last night at dinner</u> are walking down the street.
When **compound subjects** are joined by *nor*, the **verb agrees with the subject that is closer**.	Neither money <u>nor many vacation days</u> make this job appealing.
Asides, or interruptions that come between subject and verb, do not make a singular subject plural.	Janice's brother, <u>in addition to her parents</u>, is moving next week.
When a **prepositional phrase** comes between a subject and verb, agreement is not affected.	The stream <u>behind the barn and the sheds</u> runs quickly.
Each, one of and **every** take a **singular verb**.	<u>One of</u> the soccer players kicks the ball.
A number takes a **plural verb**; **the number** takes a **singular verb**.	<u>A number</u> of people ride the bus to work. <u>The number</u> of potholes in the road is dangerous.
All, none, any, some, more, and **most** can be singular or plural depending on their use.	<u>All the trees</u> are blooming. <u>All the water</u> is missing from the fish tank.
The subject follows the verb in **there is** or **there are** constructions. *Is* or *are* must agree with the subject.	<u>There are a pot and pan</u> missing from the kitchen.
Collective nouns like *jury*, and *navy* take singular verbs (and pronouns) when the group acts as a whole.	The <u>jury</u> delivers its verdict.

USING LOGIC

Sentences that ask questions may cause subject-verb agreement problems because part of the verb comes before the subject. For example, *Does Ken or Amy want to attend?* Remember the agreement rules.

1. **In his pocket was a pencil, a piece of cheese, and a phone.**
   Which correction should be made to the sentence?

   A. Change <u>pocket</u> to <u>pockets</u>.
   B. Change <u>was</u> to <u>were</u>.
   C. Change <u>was</u> to <u>is</u>.
   D. Change <u>a phone</u> to <u>two phones</u>.

★ Spotlighted Item: **DROP-DOWN**

DIRECTIONS: Read the passage. From the drop-down list, choose the answer that **best** completes the sentence.

Walters Architectural Group
612 Sixth Avenue, Suite 420
New York, NY 10012

To Whom It May Concern:

It is with great pleasure that I write this letter of recommendation for Ricardo Sanchez. Mr. Sanchez interned for Walters Architectural Group for the last two summers. He was an integral part of our team. Neither his fellow interns nor his direct supervisor [2. Drop-down 1] anything but positive things to say about him.

Mr. Sanchez's work ethic, his willingness to put in long hours when necessary, and his can-do attitude [2. Drop-down 2] him such a special employee. When a project was due on a tight deadline, he pitched in to ensure that all the work was done on time and done well. Whether a simple task or high-level design assignment with complex specifications was given to him, he was always enthusiastic and conscientious and completed the job. He was happy to help out and make copies or coffee when needed, and he was also able to make significant contributions to our design work.

Mr. Sanchez is a quick-learner who needs very little supervision. Our new suite of drafting software programs [2. Drop-down 3] no match for Mr. Sanchez's technical skill! He mastered the software in only a few weeks. At our firm, we encourage all employees to enhance their technical skills, but only a few have shown the interest and aptitude displayed by Mr. Sanchez.

I strongly recommend Mr. Sanchez. I, as well as my colleagues here, [2. Drop-down 4] confident that he will be a fine addition to your firm.

Sincerely,
Lisa Walters-Gupta, Senior Partner

Drop-Down Answer Options

2.1 A. have
B. have had
C. did has
D. has

2.2 A. has made
B. have made
C. makes
D. is what will make

2.3 A. were
B. are
C. was
D. have been

2.4 A. are
B. is
C. am
D. were

UNIT 4

Parallelism

1 Learn the Skill

When a sentence reflects **parallelism**, also called parallel structure, it uses the same pattern, or grammatical structure, to show that two or more ideas have equal importance. Often, parallelism extends beyond a single sentence. You can create a pattern by using the same word forms or sentence structures to emphasize that ideas are connected.

Writers deliberately use repetition when employing parallel structure. The repetition of certain words creates a pattern that draws attention to important points. Parallel structure is a way to make writing clearer and avoid wordiness or awkwardness.

2 Practice the Skill

By practicing the skill of recognizing and creating parallelism, you will improve your writing and test-taking abilities, especially as they relate to the GED® Reasoning Through Language Arts Test. Study the explanations and examples below. Then answer the question that follows.

▶ This information will help you understand parallelism. Notice that strategic repetition creates emphasis.

Awkward	Improved
I like running, to swim, and biking.	I like running, swimming, and biking.
My friend's son and the daughter of my boss are both in the military.	My friend's son and my boss's daughter are both in the military.
Using only a hot plate and she has a microwave, my girlfriend makes fabulous meals.	Using only a hot plate and a microwave, my girlfriend makes fabulous meals.
Each Tuesday, I go to the gym, and excercising for an hour.	Each Tuesday, I go to the gym and exercise for an hour.
To err is human. Something that is divine, though, is forgiving.	To err is human. To forgive is divine.

a The use of **and**, **but**, or **or** to connect items in a series should alert you to examine the sentence for parallel structure.

b Usually, you eliminate wordiness by avoiding unnecessary repetition, as shown in the "wrong" sentence. However, if you deliberately repeat words for emphasis, be sure to maintain parallel structure.

▶ *Wrong:* I loved you yesterday, today I love you, too, and will tomorrow as well as today and yesterday.

Right: I loved you yesterday, I love you today, and I will love you tomorrow.

UNIT 4

TEST-TAKING TIPS

In your writing, you probably will use parallel structure when including specific details and examples. Be sure to present such items equally, using the correct word forms.

1. **Garage bands often write their own songs and performing them as well.** Which is the **most** effective revision of the sentence?

A. Garage bands often write and perform their own songs.
B. Garage bands often write their own songs, as well as often performing them.
C. Garage bands often write their own songs, as well as performing them.
D. Often writing their own songs, garage bands perform their own songs as well.

DIRECTIONS: Read the passage, read the questions, and choose the **best** answer.

TIPS FOR SAVING ENERGY

The trouble with asking people to save energy is that the task sounds daunting. Sure, most people would like saving energy and to have more money in their pockets. However, they're busy working as well as families. What people need to get the ball rolling are a few simple tips that they can use immediately.

- Take a walk through your home right now. Turn off appliances and electrical gadgets that no one is using. Be sure that you are turning off lights, computer equipment, turn off television sets, DVD players, and other items. Guess what? You just saved energy! To make this task simpler the next time you do it, add power strips to your home so that you can turn off multiple machines with a single switch.

- While you're taking an energy tour of your home, adjust the thermostat. You don't need to be uncomfortable, but choose a temperature that is moderate. Also, don't forget to turn down the thermostat on the water heater to about 120 degrees. You don't need to spend money heating water that's too hot for anyone to use.

- Showering can also be more efficient than taking a bath. Showering uses less water, particularly if you have a low-flow showerhead.

- Run your dishwasher only when it is fully loaded with dishes. If you have a small load of dishes, washing them by hand is more efficient than to wash them in the dishwasher. When you do run the dishwasher, use the air dry cycle instead of the dishwasher's drying cycle.

- Similarly, consider air-drying clothes. A clothes dryer uses a great deal of energy. Hanging clothes to dry saves energy and can reduce unwanted heat in your home during summer months.

2. Which is the best way to rewrite the underlined portion of the sentence? **Sure, most people would like saving energy and to have more money in their pockets.**

   A. saving energy and have
   B. saving energy and liking
   C. saving energy and having
   D. to save energy and

3. Which is the best way to rewrite the sentence? **However, they're busy working as well as families.**

   A. However, they're busy working and families.
   B. However, they're busy with working as well as busy with their families.
   C. However, they're busy with their work and busy families.
   D. However, they're busy with their work and their families.

4. Which is the most effective revision of these sentences? **Turn off appliances and electrical gadgets that no one is using. Be sure that you are turning off lights, computer equipment, turn off television sets, DVD players, and other items.**

   A. Turn off appliances, electrical gadgets, lights, computer equipment, television sets, DVD players, and other items that no one is using.
   B. Turn off appliances and electrical gadgets. Turn off lights, turn off computer equipment, turn off the television sets, turn off the DVD players, and so on that no one is using.
   C. Turn off the appliances and the electrical gadgets that no one is using. Turn off lights, computer equipment, turning off television sets, DVD players, and other items that no one is using.
   D. Turn off the appliances that no one is using and the electrical gadgets, the lights, computer equipment, turn off the television sets, the DVD players, and so on.

5. Which is the best way to write the underlined portion of the sentence? **If you have a small load of dishes, washing them by hand is more efficient than to wash them in the dishwasher.**

   A. to wash them by hand is a more efficient way than the way
   B. washing the dishes by hand is more efficent than to wash the dishes
   C. washing them by hand is more efficient than washing them
   D. washing the dishes by hand is more efficient than to wash the dishes

Transitions

LANGUAGE ASSESSMENT TARGET: L.1.9

1 Learn the Skill

A good writer uses **transitions**, or words and phrases that show connections between ideas, to create a coherent work. Transitions connect ideas within paragraphs and also lead readers logically from one paragraph or section to the next.

2 Practice the Skill

By practicing the skill of using transitions, you will improve your writing and test-taking abilities, especially as they relate to the GED® Reasoning Through Language Arts Test. Study the explanations and examples below. Then answer the question that follows.

▶ These words and phrases often signal a transition.

Time		Similarity		Contrast	
first	subsequently	likewise	furthermore	although	on the other hand
next	earlier	also	similarly	but	nevertheless
then	later	in addition	in the same way	despite	nonetheless
finally	yesterday	what's more	equally	however	yet
after that	today	moreover	just as	in contrast	conversely

a A transitional word or phrase often appears at the beginning of a sentence. In this position, it is usually followed by a comma: **Nevertheless,** I was still very tired.

b Some transitional words join ideas within a sentence: I was tired **although** I had slept for nine hours.

▶ Study the sentences below for examples of how to use transitions.

First, I bought groceries. *Then,* I did laundry and washed the car.

He was nervous. *However,* he didn't let his emotion show.

I called several times and got no answer. *Finally,* I was able to reach him.

1. **Juanita loves music and is a talented pianist. <u>Consequently, her twin sister</u> is not interested in music and cannot play the piano.** Which revision should be made to the underlined portion of the second sentence?

   A. Similarly, her twin sister
   B. In contrast, her twin sister
   C. Therefore, her twin sister
   D. Later, her twin sister

Spotlighted Item: **DROP-DOWN**

DIRECTIONS: Read the passage. From the drop-down list, choose the answer that **best** completes the sentence.

DRESS FOR SUCCESS

When you are going on a job interview, your appearance matters. The saying is true: "You never get a second chance to make a first impression." The next time you are unsure about what to wear, consider these tips:

- Wear clothes that are simple and conservative. You want to match the environment of the workplace.
[2. Drop-down 1] will be wearing suits, then you should wear a suit. If others will be wearing dress shoes, then wear dress shoes. A clean, neat appearance tells people that you care about yourself and others around you.

- Your hair and fingernails should be clean and neat. Choose a simple hairstyle that is flattering to your face. Clean, well-groomed hands suggest attention to detail. Women should choose something simple and subtle that does not attract negative attention. [2. Drop-down 2] they should avoid bright or unusual nail polish colors.

- When you choose accessories, understatement is the key. Do not wear too much jewelry, cologne, or perfume. Too much jewelry can look gaudy. [2. Drop-down 3] cologne or perfume may cause discomfort to those around you. Do not chew gum or suck on mints, but make sure that your mouth is clean and your breath fresh. A winning smile will attract others to you.

Although you want to be yourself and dress in a way that suits your personality and style, remember that your goal is to be noticed for your skills and abilities. Your appearance should make a nice [2. Drop-down 4] it should not distract the interviewer.

Drop-Down Answer Options

2.1 A. For example, if others
    B. Afterward, if others
    C. In addition, if others
    D. Otherwise, if others

2.2 A. First,
    B. Finally,
    C. Therefore,
    D. Similarly,

2.3 A. On the other hand, too much
    B. However, too much
    C. In contrast, too much
    D. Likewise, too much

2.4 A. impression, just as
    B. impression, but
    C. impression; similarly,
    D. impression. In addition,

UNIT 4

Paragraph Organization

WRITING ASSESSMENT TARGET: W.2
LANGUAGE ASSESSMENT TARGET: L.1.9

1 Learn the Skill

A paragraph features a **topic sentence** and **supporting details**. A topic sentence may be implied or stated. When stated, it is often the first or second sentence. Other sentences provide details that support the topic sentence. A paragraph should be organized so that the details follow or lead to the topic sentence in a logical and orderly fashion.

2 Practice the Skill

By practicing the skill of organizing paragraphs, you will improve your writing and test-taking abilities, especially as they relate to the GED® Reasoning Through Language Arts Test. Study the table, and read the paragraph below. Then answer the question that follows.

▶ Use this information to help you organize a paragraph.

a A topic sentence provides a broad idea that the rest of the paragraph develops and supports.

Topic Sentence	Supporting Details
This sentence explains the main idea of the paragraph. Often, it is the first sentence, but it may appear anywhere else in the paragraph.	These sentences support the topic sentence in a logical way. They may be organized by order of importance, time, sequence, or other logical patterns.

b As you read a paragraph, think about the logical sequence of ideas and how one idea leads to another. Transition words help connect ideas.

▶ (1) Archeological evidence suggests that tattoos have existed since prehistoric times. (2) Cultures throughout history have used tattoos and other types of body markings for a variety of purposes. (3) Body markings were used to indicate religious beliefs or to show that a person belonged to a particular group or tribe. (4) Over time, tattoo art developed among several different cultures. (5) Sailors returning from other areas of the world eventually brought tattoos to Europe. (6) For example, the use of color in tattoo design first appeared in Japan.

USING LOGIC

Read the paragraph as written. Determine which sentence or event seems out of place. Then place that sentence in different locations until the paragraph as a whole makes sense. You may have to delete the sentence if it does not fit.

1. Which is the **best** place for sentence 6? **For example, the use of color in tattoo design first appeared in Japan.**

   A. Move sentence 6 to follow sentence 1.
   B. Move sentence 6 to follow sentence 4.
   C. Remove sentence 6.
   D. Move sentence 6 to follow sentence 3.

UNIT 4

DIRECTIONS: Read the passage, read the questions, and choose the **best** answer.

TELEPHONE USE

A

(1) We often look to e-mail as being the easiest and fastest way to communicate with others. (2) But is it the best way? (3) For people in the business world, one of the most important skills is the ability to communicate effectively with associates and clients. (4) While personal computers enable people to respond quickly and efficiently through e-mail, the telephone is still a businessperson's most effective marketing tool. (5) A person's voice offers expression that an e-mail cannot convey. (6) There is nothing that compares to the personal connection that associates and clients get when they hear someone's voice at the other end of the telephone.

B

(7) The telephone allows family members to communicate information with each other, such as what time one will arrive at home. (8) It enables relatives to share stories, ask questions, or voice concerns when they are not physically together. (9) Telephones also enhance communication among family members. (10) However, cell phone use by children should be closely monitored. (11) Cell phones are common, even for children. (12) Today's parents feel secure knowing that their children can contact them from any location.

C

(13) Finally, telephones enable instant access to emergency services. (14) In these ways, telephones make people safer by giving them immediate access to help. (15) Emergency service providers, such as police officers, firefighters, and doctors, are all just a telephone number away. (16) Distressed callers can reach these providers directly or contact them through the 911 system. (17) With new cell phone technology, some of these services can be reached by the simple touch of a button.

2. Which is the best place for sentence 5? **A person's voice offers expression that an e-mail cannot convey.**

   A. Move sentence 5 to follow sentence 1.
   B. Move sentence 5 to follow sentence 6.
   C. Move sentence 5 to follow sentence 2.
   D. Move sentence 5 to follow sentence 3.

3. Which is the best place for sentence 9? **Telephones also enhance communication among family members.**

   A. Move sentence 9 to the beginning of paragraph B.
   B. Move sentence 9 to follow sentence 11.
   C. Move sentence 9 to follow sentence 7.
   D. Move sentence 9 to follow sentence 12.

4. Which is the best place for sentence 10? **However, cell phone use by children should be closely monitored.**

   A. Move sentence 10 to follow sentence 11.
   B. Move sentence 10 to follow sentence 12.
   C. Remove sentence 10.
   D. Move sentence 10 to follow sentence 7.

5. Which is the best place for sentence 14? **In these ways, telephones make people safer by giving them immediate access to help.**

   A. Move sentence 14 to the beginning of paragraph C.
   B. Remove sentence 14.
   C. Move sentence 14 to follow sentence 16.
   D. Move sentence 14 to follow sentence 17.

UNIT 4

Other Punctuation

LANGUAGE ASSESSMENT TARGETS: L.2.2, L.2.4

① Learn the Skill

Punctuation makes written text easier to read. You already have learned about end marks and commas, but there are other types of punctuation important to reading and writing text. These marks include hyphens, parentheses, quotation marks, colons, and semicolons.

② Practice the Skill

By practicing the skill of using punctuation correctly, you will improve your writing and test-taking abilities, especially as they relate to the GED® Reasoning Through Language Arts Test. Study the explanations and examples below. Then answer the question that follows.

▶ These guidelines will help you understand different types of punctuation.

ⓐ Hyphens are used to combine two modifiers when the two words have a combined meaning, such as **low-budget** movie.

ⓑ Remember that when you have a first parenthesis or quotation mark, you need a second one to close the quotation or parenthetical statement.

Punctuation	Symbol	Use	Example
hyphen	-	to combine two modifiers	Dr. Mays is a well-liked teacher.
parentheses	( )	to separate information added to text	We ate at Las Palmas (on Franklin Road).
quotation marks	" "	to indicate exact speech	"You should have watched the game last night," he said.
colon	:	to introduce examples or lists; must follow a complete idea	I have three sisters: Tina, Mary, and Lisa.
semicolon	;	to separate two complete ideas	He lost his car keys; his sister didn't have a spare set.

USING LOGIC

Punctuation can change the meaning of a sentence: for example, *Let's leave, Sam* or *Let's leave Sam*. Examine each sentence's structure carefully to be sure all punctuation is correct.

1. **Janet and Manny were present at the meeting Logan and Allison were out of town and could not attend.** Which correction should be made to the sentence?

   A. Insert a colon after <u>Manny</u>.
   B. Insert a semicolon after <u>meeting</u>.
   C. Insert parentheses around <u>Logan and Allison</u>.
   D. Insert a hyphen between <u>could</u> and <u>not</u>.

UNIT 4

★ Spotlighted Item: **DROP-DOWN**

DIRECTIONS: Read the passage. From the drop-down list, choose the answer that **best** completes the sentence.

Dear Mr. Harvey:

At Eastern Airways, we pride ourselves on being a
[2. Drop-down 1] We take the feedback of our
passengers very seriously, and we make every effort to
improve our service according to the feedback we receive. Our
Customer Satisfaction Department has received your letter
describing your lost baggage experience on your June 11 flight
from Newark to Jacksonville. We are deeply sorry that your
luggage [2. Drop-down 2] did not arrive in time for
the beginning of your vacation in Florida. We understand that
this incident caused you a significant inconvenience.

In your letter to us, you [2. Drop-down 3] $100
to buy a few items of clothing was no compensation for not
having my clothing and fishing gear for three days and having
to purchase and rent replacements with my own money." We
agree with your assessment. We understand that you incurred
significant expenses for clothing and fishing gear rentals while
you waited for your luggage to arrive. We would like to provide
you with the following [2. Drop-down 4] for the
clothing you had to purchase, reimbursement for your fishing
gear rental charges, and a voucher worth $400 toward the
purchase of a future flight on Eastern Airways.

Once again, we apologize. We value your continued business
and hope that this offer provides some compensation to you for
your unfortunate experience.

Sincerely,

Lauren H. Boros

Manager, Customer Satisfaction Department
Eastern Airways

Drop-Down Answer Options

2.1 A. customer focused-airline.
B. customer focused airline.
C. "customer focused"
airline.
D. customer-focused airline.

2.2 A. (including your fishing
gear
B. (including your fishing
gear)
C. including: your fishing
gear
D. including; your fishing
gear

2.3 A. wrote, "Giving me
B. wrote, Giving me
C. wrote, giving me
D. wrote: giving me

2.4 A. compensation
(reimbursement
B. compensation,
reimbursement
C. compensation:
reimbursement
D. compensation;
reimbursement

UNIT 4

Unit 4 Review

DIRECTIONS: Read the passage. From the drop-down list, choose the answer that **best** completes the sentence.

OUR STRAY CAT PROBLEM

To Whom It May Concern,

As an animal lover, I am sad to see how many stray and abandoned cats are living in my neighborhood. Some of them may have had homes in the past, but no one is taking care of these poor cats anymore. [2. Drop-down 1] about to have kittens, while others seem to be wild. Cats are living even in abandoned houses. These unfortunate animals have no one to care for them. They [2. Drop-down 2] that they can find in the neighborhood. If they can't find enough food, they go hungry or starve.

I care about cats, but [2. Drop-down 3] big of a problem. I can't feed and take care of all of the stray cats in the neighborhood. They need loving homes where they will get the food and shelter they deserve. They also need access to proper medical care. Recently, I asked the local animal officer to come to my neighborhood. She looked at a pregnant cat and made sure it was seen by a veterinarian.

This problem is not confined just to my neighborhood, either. There are many abandoned cats in every neighborhood in the city. Every pet owner needs to be responsible and not let [2. Drop-down 4] outside if they are not spayed or neutered. If stray cats become pregnant, the problem gets worse. I ask all of my neighbors to join me in helping resolve the problem of abandoned and stray animals.

Sincerely,

Jenny Briggs

Drop-Down Answer Options

1.1 A. There's many
    B. There's a number of them
    C. There are many
    D. A number of them is

1.2 A. eat the only food
    B. only eat the food
    C. eat the food only
    D. eat only the food

1.3 A. these strays are to
    B. these strays are too
    C. them strays are to
    D. these strays are two

1.4 A. his or her animals go
    B. their animal go
    C. there animals go
    D. he or she's animals go

DIRECTIONS: Read the passage. From the drop-down list, choose the answer that **best** completes the sentence.

Dear Mr. Gold:

We at Ann Arbor Bank wish to take this opportunity to thank you for your continued business over the [2. Drop-down 1] difficult economic times. We appreciate the opportunity to serve your banking and credit needs.

So that we can offer our loyal customers continued access to credit, we must make some important changes to our current credit card agreements. For your account ending in 0478, the annual percentage rate (APR) will increase from 9.99% to 29.99%. You may opt out of the new program if you wish. To do so, you must notify the bank within 60 days of the date of this letter. You may then continue to pay the balance at the existing rate, and the card will be deactivated at the next annual renewal date. Should you choose to continue using your Ann Arbor Bank credit [2. Drop-down 2] 31, 2013, your new APR will take effect upon the following billing cycle.

Further, we regret to announce that soon we will be raising the late-payment fee for all of our credit card account holders. The current fee of $15 will increase to $35. This change will also take effect in your next billing cycle.

We at Ann Arbor Bank are optimistic that these changes will better position us to serve the needs of our customers in the years ahead. Along with the changes described above, we are also offering select credit card account holders the option of raising their existing credit limits. Please contact our Credit Card Services department today to see if you qualify. In just a few minutes, our customer service [2. Drop-down 3] can approve your request and estimate your new credit limit. We thank you for your [2. Drop-down 4] to serving you in the future.

Regards,

Michael Brezina

President, Ann Arbor Bank

Drop-Down Answer Options

2.1 A. years, these are
    B. years because these are
    C. years these are
    D. years. These are

2.2 A. Card beyond December
    B. card beyond december
    C. card beyond December
    D. Card beyond december

2.3 A. representatives who are
       available on Saturdays,
    B. representatives, who are
       available on Saturdays,
    C. representatives, who are
       available on saturdays,
    D. representatives who are
       available, on saturdays,

2.4 A. business. We also look
       forward, too,
    B. business and look forward
    C. business; and also look
       forward
    D. business; subsequently,
       we look forward

DIRECTIONS: Read the passage. From the drop-down list, choose the answer that **best** completes the sentence.

INSTRUCTIONS FOR READING NUTRITION LABELS

The nutrition label on a food product is easy to find and [3. Drop-down 1] understanding the label can be challenging. First, note the serving size at the top of the label. The information that follows relates to the serving [3. Drop-down 2] in one serving, 200 calories in two servings, 300 calories in three servings, and so on. When you are comparing calories in different foods, be sure to compare the serving size. Sometimes, similar foods will show different serving sizes. This labeling information may cause some difficulty when you compare calories.

Next, note the differences between the "good" ingredients and the "bad" ingredients. The "bad" ingredients, such as fat, cholesterol, and sodium are listed first. You'll want to limit your intake of these items. The % (percent) daily value number will help you accomplish this goal. Use this rule of thumb when interpreting % daily value numbers: 5% is low, and 20% is high. Some pre-prepared foods that might seem like healthy choices can actually be very high in % value of "bad" ingredients. For example, a can of tomato soup might have as much as 30% of your daily % value of sodium.

The "good" ingredients, [3. Drop-down 3] are listed last. You want to increase your intake of these items. Again, the % value number will help you accomplish this goal. For example, 45% vitamin C is a good high number.

Good foods do not necessarily have high % values in all "good" areas on the label. Depending on the type of item, the food may be high in some good nutritional areas (calcium, for example) and low in [3. Drop-down 4]. Similarly, foods may be high in some good areas and also high in some bad areas. For example, fruit juices can be high in several vitamins but also high in sugars and calories.

Not everything you eat fills every nutritional need, but reading nutritional labels can help you make informed decisions about what you buy.

Drop-Down Answer Options

3.1 A. read however;
    B. reed, however,
    C. reed howerver
    D. read; however,

3.2 A. size: 100 calories
    B. size; 100 calories
    C. size, 100 calories
    D. size 100 calories

3.3 A. such as: vitamins, calcium and iron,
    B. such as vitamins, calcium, and iron,
    C. such as vitamins calcium and iron
    D. such as vitamins, calcium, and iron

3.4 A. others (vitamin C, for example)
    B. others vitamin C, for example
    C. others; vitamin C, for example
    D. others, vitamin C, for example

DIRECTIONS: Read the passage. From the drop-down list, choose the answer that **best** completes the sentence.

Dear Editor:

Recently, the city placed red light cameras at several major intersections. City leaders argue that the purpose of these cameras is to improve traffic safety in the community. They suggest that red light cameras can reduce the number of accidents that occur when drivers run red lights. However, I believe that the effectiveness and purpose of these cameras deserve further review before the city [4. Drop-down 1] taxpayers' money.

Despite the [4. Drop-down 2] have shown that red light cameras do not necessarily reduce the risk of accidents in the intersections at which they are placed. In fact, these studies suggest that the presence of red light cameras at an intersection will cause more drivers to slam on their brakes for yellow lights. As a result, the number of accidents at an on-camera intersection may actually increase because of a surge in rear-end collisions.

Further examination of the tickets generated by local red light cameras reveals a troubling trend. Over the past six months, the large majority of these tickets have been written for right-turn violations. Only a very small minority of the tickets penalized drivers who had run a red light. Because accidents caused by an improper right turn [4. Drop-down 3] injuries or fatalities, claims that the cameras have been installed primarily for safety seem suspect.

Given the various problems and questions associated with red light cameras, the city's stated motivation for installing these devices seems dubious. If truly concerned with improving safety, [4. Drop-down 4]. As it stands, city leaders appear more concerned with bolstering our community's dwindling revenues through increased ticketing.

Drop-Down Answer Options

4.1 A. tries and spends more of it's
B. tries to spend more of its'
C. tries to spend more of its
D. try to spend more of it

4.2 A. cities' claims, studies
B. city's claims, studies'
C. city's claims, studys
D. city's claims, studies

4.3 A. rarely results in serious
B. rarely result in serious
C. results rarely in serious
D. result in rarely serious

4.4 A. the city could apply other practices
B. other practices could be applied
C. applying other practices would be helpful
D. the ballot box should show the need to apply other practices

UNIT 4

DIRECTIONS: Read the passage. From the drop-down list, choose the answer that **best** completes the sentence.

MEMO

To: Birmingham City Planning Department Staff

From: Chandra Gonzalez, Director

Subject: Highlights from Annual Southeast Groundwater Conference

I realize that many of you have been waiting for some notes from Assistant Director [5. Drop-down 1] summarizing our recent trip to the 10th Annual Southeast Groundwater Conference. Here they are.

Over 200 city managers and regional planners met in Atlanta, Georgia, for the conference. The goal of the conference was to highlight examples of successful regional planning in which urban areas worked together to reduce their water use or cope with water shortages.

Representatives from the United States Environmental Protection Agency and the Southeast Watershed Association reviewed trends in water usage. The data they provided showed the lasting effects of last year's drought, indicating that water levels were only just beginning to return to their pre-drought levels. [5. Drop-down 2] also showed the success of different states' water reduction guidelines in reducing the amount of water spent for landscaping and business use.

The keynote speech of the conference was provided by environmentalist Susan Jeffrey, [5. Drop-down 3] on the possible danger that natural gas drilling poses to groundwater. Her speech raised as many questions as it answered about how groundwater might be affected by natural gas "fracking." Neither the pro-drilling faction nor the anti-fracking faction [5. Drop-down 4] satisfied with her conclusions.

Workshops in the conference developed strategies for helping counties and municipalities work together to develop comprehensive plans, for working closely with state and federal agencies to utilize their watershed resources, and for creating local groups to assist in meeting water quality and usage reduction goals.

Drop-Down Answer Options

5.1 A. Ron Taylor and I
B. Ron Taylor and myself
C. Ron Taylor and me
D. me and Ron Taylor

5.2 A. This
B. Which data
C. That
D. Their data

5.3 A. whom spoke
B. who spoke
C. that spoke
D. which spoke

5.4 A. was entirely
B. entirely was
C. were entirely
D. entirely were

DIRECTIONS: Read the passage. From the drop-down list, choose the answer that **best** completes the sentence.

First Bank of Georgia
1 Commerce Street
Atlanta, GA 30301

Dear Valued Customer:

Banking is no longer the same as it [6. Drop-down 1] .
These days, online banking has changed the ways the system works. Online service is now available to all customers. Our new and free online service allows customers to control [6. Drop-down 2] money easily, 24 hours a day, 7 days a week. Our service is simple, fast, and easy to use!

The main reason that people like online banking is convenience. You can bank from your home or office without having to travel to traditional, fixed-location bank branches. With the simple click of a mouse button, you can view your accounts, check balances, transfer money, and pay bills.

Furthermore, by signing up for our electronic bill-paying system, you can reap the benefits of having our patented E-Bill Notification remind you about upcoming due dates. Each of these features [6. Drop-down 3] easily accessed and tracked via an online checkbook, which also gives you access to your archived bank records.

We feature secure log-in and user authentification, SSL encryption to protect confidential information, and secure firewalls to prevent compromise from the Internet. In addition, our online banking system is backed by an industry-leading security program. Our expert team ensures that our system meets the highest possible security standards.

Do you want to learn more or get [6. Drop-down 4] to our Web site and click "Online Banking" at the top of our home page. You will find more details about this service, as well as an application form. Once we have received and approved your application, we will send your user name and a temporary password via e-mail within 24 hours. With this information, you will be ready to begin your online banking experience!

Drop-Down Answer Options

6.1 A. use to be
    B. been
    C. were being
    D. used to be

6.2 A. there
    B. their
    C. they're
    D. they's

6.3 A. is
    B. was
    C. are
    D. were

6.4 A. started. Go
    B. started, go
    C. started go
    D. started? Go

UNIT 4

DIRECTIONS: Read the passage. From the drop-down list, choose the answer that **best** completes the sentence.

MEMO

To: Sales Team
From: Information Technology Department
Subject: New Laptops

After receiving management approval, [7. Drop-down 1] for the sales team to take on sales calls. The rules regarding the computers are as follows:

Register with Tim Brown from the Information Technology Department, and he will distribute your laptop as needed. Because there are only four new laptops, they need to be available for all team members as much as possible. You can check out a laptop no earlier than one day before a sales call and must return it no later than one day following your call.

Leave a record of your username and password with Joel Goodman, Administrative Assistant for Information Technology. This information will allow management to have access to your files if needed.

The new laptops may leave company premises only when you are away on a sales call. They are not intended for [7. Drop-down 2] telecommuting.

Although the laptops are company property, we expect employees to treat them as they would treat [7. Drop-down 3] checks out a laptop is responsible for the security of confidential company information on the laptop and for the laptop's safekeeping. We ask that you do not leave your laptop unattended in any public area.

We are confident that these new computers will help you with your [7. Drop-down 4] to access company information from remote sites. If you have any questions, contact your supervisor or the Information Technology Department.

Drop-Down Answer Options

7.1 A. four new laptops have been bought by Purchasing
B. Purchasing has bought four new laptops
C. four new laptops were bought
D. the truck arrived with four new laptops

7.2 A. no use at home or no
B. no home use or no
C. use at home or
D. use at home or not for

7.3 A. their own property. Whomever
B. there own property. Whoever
C. their own property. Who
D. their own property. Whoever

7.4 A. sales; however, you will be able
B. sales as you will be able
C. sales, you will be able
D. sales; subsequently, you will be able

HOW TO BUY A DIGITAL CAMERA

A

(1) Although many people use their smart phones to take pictures, you may get higher quality photographs from a digital camera that isn't part of a phone. (2) If you haven't purchased a digital camera before, the prospect of buying one may seem confusing. (3) You may find yourself wondering, *What's a megapixel, and how many do I need?* (4) We have compiled the following information to bring the task of purchasing a digital camera into focus.

B

(5) More megapixels mean higher-quality images. (6) If you want to print the same clear images that you get from a photo lab, you need four or five megapixels. (7) If you plan to exchange photographs with others electronically, one or two megapixels is enough. (8) Two megapixels are enough if you are exchanging electronically.

C

(9) With this feature, you can get clear images without sacrificing high-quality prints. (10) If you like to take close shots, you will want to get a camera with an optical zoom. (11) Even more zoom features are possible with cameras that allow you to change the lens.

D

(12) A camera with a lot of memory can hold more pictures at one time. (13) Once the memory card is full, transferring or the deletion of pictures is necessary before you can take more. (14) Note, however, that you can buy and add memory cards to most cameras to increase capacity.

8. Which word or phrase would be **most** effective if inserted at the beginning of sentence 4? **We have compiled the following information to bring the task of purchasing a digital camera into focus.**

   A. Finally,
   B. Similarly,
   C. Therefore,
   D. On the other hand,

9. Which is the **best** place for sentence 8? **Two megapixels are enough if you are exchanging electronically.**

   A. Move sentence 8 to the beginning of paragraph B.
   B. Move sentence 8 to follow sentence 6.
   C. Combine sentence 8 with sentence 7 to eliminate wordiness.
   D. Remove sentence 8.

10. Which is the **best** place for sentence 10? **If you like to take close shots, you will want to get a camera with an optical zoom.**

    A. Move sentence 10 to the beginning of paragraph C.
    B. Move sentence 10 to follow sentence 11.
    C. Remove sentence 10.
    D. Move sentence 10 to follow sentence 8.

11. Which is the **most** effective revision of sentence 13? **Once the memory card is full, transferring or the deletion of pictures is necessary before you can take more.**

    A. Once the memory card is full, transfer or the deleting of pictures is necessary before you can take more pictures.
    B. Once the memory card is full, you must transfer or deleting pictures before you can take more.
    C. Once the memory card is full, it is necessary that you transfer or necessary that you delete the pictures before you can take more pictures.
    D. Once the memory card is full, you must transfer or delete pictures before you can take more.

Appendix

Appendix Table of Contents

APPENDIX

Glossary

Adjective: modifies or describes a noun or a pronoun: *fast, pretty, new, old*

Adverb: modifies a verb, an adjective, or another adverb: *A deliciously ripe apple fell quickly from the tree.*

Apostrophe: (') used to indicate possession: *Chandra's jeans;* also used to form a contraction: *They're hungry.*

Cause and effect: are an action (cause) that makes another event (effect) happen

Colon: (:) used to separate phrases and to introduce lists or examples: *We knew what would happen next: the band would play an encore. I asked three people to come over: John, Melissa, and Mike.*

Collective nouns: name a group of people, animals, or things: class, herd, pack.

Compare and contrast: determine similarities and differences

Connecting words: used to connect words or combine sentences: *and, or, but, nor, for, so, yet*

Contractions: used in informal writing to combine words: *will + not = won't, you + are = you're*

Homonyms: sound alike or nearly alike but are spelled differently and have different meanings: *acts are deeds; an ax is a tool;* also include words that sound and are spelled alike but have different meanings: *a bat is both a flying animal and a stick for hitting a ball*

Main idea: the most important idea in a passage

Nouns: name people, places, or things, such as *mother, home, Asia, book, car, Frisbee*

Object: receives or completes the subject's action in a sentence: *Dan drove the truck.*

Paragraph: group of sentences that form a complete idea

Plot: consists of a series of events in a story and how the characters, or people in the story, face these events

Plural: indicates more than one thing or person: *five books, two sodas, they*

Point of view: the perspective and/or purpose with which an author writes a particular piece

Possessive: indicates ownership: *It was Dan's truck.*

Punctuation marks: provide structure within written text, such as periods (.), commas (,), question marks (?), and exclamation marks (!)

Quotation marks: (" . . . ") appear immediately before and after something that someone has said: *"Don't forget your cell phone," she said.*

Semicolon: (;) used between two complete ideas: *I was running late; I missed the bus to work.*

Singular: indicates just one thing or person: *one book, one girl, it, she*

Style: is the way in which an author communicates thoughts or feelings

Subject: person or thing doing the action in a sentence: *Dan drove the truck.*

Supporting details: support the topic sentence in a logical way

Tone: shows the author's attitude toward a topic

Topic sentence: explains the main idea of a paragraph; usually the first sentence in a paragraph

Transitions: show connections between ideas: *First, I brush my teeth. Next, I take a shower.*

Verb: states an action or state of being: *Dan drove the truck.*

Grammar Rules

Capitalization: Proper nouns and proper adjectives, including titles, holidays, days of the week, and months of the year, are capitalized.

> **proper noun:** a name that identifies a particular person, place, or thing
>   • the Cleveland Cavaliers

> **proper adjective:** a description based on a proper name
>   • German sausages

Comma: A comma separates a sentence into meaningful units. It is used to represent a pause or to connect clauses or phrases.

> **to form a series:** I made roast chicken, mashed potatoes, and a salad for dinner.

> **after an introductory phrase:** To get to the restaurant, she had to take the bus.

> **to set off an interrupting or descriptive phrase:** My sister, who is in the Air Force, came home for Christmas.

> **to combine sentences:** We went to the game, and we stopped for burgers on the way home.

> **when using two or more adjectives:** She ran a long, hard race.

Combine sentences: Short, related sentences can be combined to make writing more cohesive.

> **use connecting words:** I drove to the gas station. I drove to the mall.
>   • I drove to the gas station *and* the mall.

> **create a list:** My son likes baseball. My son likes cars. My son likes ice cream.
>   • My son likes baseball, cars, and ice cream.

> **use a semicolon:** They went to see a movie. It was a scary one.
>   • They went to see a movie; it was a scary one.

Complete sentence: A complete sentence must contain a subject, a verb, and appropriate end punctuation. A complete sentence will present a complete idea.

> Nick loved to skateboard.

Contraction: A contraction occurs when two words are shortened to one word by replacing a letter or letters with an apostrophe. Contractions are used in informal writing.

> Examples: they + have = they've, it + is = it's

Helping verbs: Helping verbs indicate that actions have occurred at various points in time.

> **past perfect tense:** used to indicate that an action took place in the past before another past action was completed. The word *had* appears before the main verb.
>   • We *had driven* for more than three hours before we arrived at my aunt's house.

> **present perfect tense:** used to indicate that an action began in the past and continues into the present. The word *has* or *have* appears before the main verb.
>   • He *has worked* there for more than a year.

> **future perfect tense:** used to indicate that an action will be completed at a specific time in the future. The words *will have* appear in front of the main verb.
>   • By the end of the month, we *will have saved* enough money for a DVD player.

Modifiers: A modifier describes, clarifies, or provides details about other words in a sentence. Avoid a **misplaced modifier,** which misleads readers by describing the wrong word in the sentence, or a **dangling modifier,** which does not apply logically to any word in the sentence.

> **misplaced modifier:** I only ran one mile. **correct:** I ran only one mile.

> **dangling modifier:** Running down the street, my long scarf blew across my face. **correct:** While I was running down the street, my long scarf blew across my face.

Parallel structure: A sentence with parallel structure displays the same pattern to indicate that two or more ideas are of equal importance.

> **wrong:** Both my boyfriend's mom and the cousin of my friend work at the mall.

> **correct:** Both my boyfriend's mom and my friend's cousin work at the mall.

Parentheses: Parentheses are used to separate text and often contain nonessential information—the sentence is intact without the parenthetical material.

> After work, Ryan drove to the gym (the one on Jefferson Road).

Plural nouns: Often, nouns are made plural simply by the addition of *-s* or *-es*.

- ➤ add *-s* to most nouns: bottles, books
- ➤ add *-es* to nouns ending in *o*: tomatoes (tomato), heroes (hero)
- ➤ add *-es* to nouns ending in *ch, sh, ss, z,* or *x*: taxes (tax), churches (church)
- ➤ for nouns that end in *y* after a consonant, drop the *y* and add *-ies*: puppies (puppy), cities (city)
- ➤ for nouns that end in *f* or *fe*, drop the *f(e)* and add *-ves*: wives (wife), thieves (thief)
- ➤ some nouns change form: women (woman), teeth (tooth)
- ➤ some nouns don't change at all: fish, sheep

Possession: Possession, indicated by the use of an apostrophe and *s* (*'s*) or by an *s* followed by an apostrophe (*s'*), shows ownership.

- ➤ for singular nouns, use an apostrophe and add *s*: **dog's** bone
- ➤ for most singular nouns ending in *s*, use an apostrophe and add *s*: **Mars's** moon
- ➤ for plural nouns ending in *s*, use only an apostrophe: **players'** meeting

Pronouns: Pronouns are words that take the place of nouns. Pronouns must agree in gender and number with the nouns they replace.

- ➤ Sharon drove Keith home after work. **Replace nouns with pronouns:** *She* drove *him* home after work.
- ➤ **Examples:** *you, he, she, it, they, we, them, him, her, myself, whoever, whomever, each, somebody*

Regular and irregular verbs: Regular verbs indicate past, present, and future tenses when *-ed, -s,* or *-ing* is added to the base verb. Irregular verbs are less consistent; the spelling of such verbs often changes to indicate a particular tense.

Run-on sentence: A run-on sentence occurs when two or more sentences are joined incorrectly. A run-on sentence can be corrected by adding a connecting word, adding a comma and a connecting word, or creating two separate sentences.

- ➤ **wrong:** I met a friend at the movies we had a good time.
- ➤ **correct:** I met a friend at the movies, and we had a good time.

Sentence fragment: A sentence fragment does not express a complete idea.

- ➤ **Example:** Two days after it rained

Subject-verb agreement: In a sentence, subjects and verbs must agree in person and number.

- ➤ **wrong:** Amber and I am going out to eat Friday.
- ➤ **right:** Amber and I *are* going out to eat Friday.

Verb tenses: The three basic verb tenses are *past, present,* and *future*. Using the correct tense of the verb lets your readers know whether events have occurred in the past, are happening now, or will happen in the future. In the **past tense,** regular verbs end in *-d* or *-ed* (*walk* becomes *walked*). Irregular verbs often indicate the past tense by a spelling change (*eat* becomes *ate*). In the **present tense,** a regular verb maintains its root form (*make, walk, come*) or adds an *-s* (*makes, walks, comes*). In **future tense,** the helping verb *will* appears in front of the main verb (*move* becomes *will move*).

Frequently Confused Words

Some frequently confused words are homonyms. These are words that sound the same or nearly the same but are spelled differently and have different meanings. Sometimes the two words may be spelled alike but have different meanings. Below is a list of frequently confused words. Learn these words and you will be sure of using the right word every time.

accept: *to receive; to endure; to approve*
except: *to exclude; excluding*

affect: *to influence*
effect: *a result*

ate: *past tense of eat*
eight: *the number 8*

be: *to exist*
bee: *an insect*

beat: *to strike or hit*
beet: *a type of root vegetable*

board: *a piece of wood*
bored: *uninterested*

brake: *to stop*
break: *to damage or destroy; a rest period*

buy: *to get by paying money*
by: *near; according to*

capital: *city that is the seat of government; money to invest; very important*
capitol: *building in which the legislature meets*

cell: *a small room, as in a prison*
sell: *to offer for sale*

cent: *a penny*
scent: *to smell*
sent: *caused to go; transmitted*

close: *to shut; to finish; near*
clothes: *something to wear on the body, usually made of cloth*

complement: *to go with; to make whole*
compliment: *flattering words*

coarse: *rough or harsh*
course: *a path or track; part of a meal*

dear: *much loved; sweet*
deer: *an animal*

desert: *a dry, barren, sandy region*
dessert: *the final, usually sweet, course of a meal*

feat: *an accomplishment*
feet: *plural of foot*

flour: *ground grain used in making bread*
flower: *the bloom or blossom on a plant*

for: *to be used as; meant to belong to*
four: *the number 4*

grate: *to shred*
great: *very good*

hear: *to listen*
here: *in this place*

hole: *opening*
whole: *entire*

hour: *60 minutes*
our: *belonging to us*

its: *possessive of it*
it's: *contraction of it is*

knew: *was certain of*
new: *modern; recent*

know: *to have information*
no: *not at all; opposite of yes*

lessen: *to decrease*
lesson: *something that is taught*

leave: *to go away*
let: *to allow*

loose: *not tight*
lose: *to fail to keep or win*

made: *created*
maid: *a person who cleans*

mail: *letters or packages delivered by the post office*
male: *man or boy; the opposite of female*

main: *most important*
mane: *the hair of a horse or lion*

meat: *animal flesh that is eaten*
meet: *to get together*

one: *the number 1*
won: *past tense of win*

pail: *a bucket or tub*
pale: *light in color*

pain: *soreness, aching*
pane: *the glass in a window*

passed: *went by*
past: *a time before; opposite of future*

patience: *ability to wait*
patients: *plural of patient*

peace: *freedom from war; harmony; calm*
piece: *a part of something*

plain: *ordinary; simple*
plane: *airplane; a flat surface*

pole: *a long piece of wood or metal*
poll: *a listing of people; a vote*

principal: *first in rank; the head of a school*
principle: *a rule or belief*

quiet: *silent; still*
quite: *completely; really; positively*

right: *correct; opposite of left*
write: *to form visible words*

road: *a path or street*
rode: *past tense of the verb ride*

role: *a part played*
roll: *to turn over; a type of bread*

scene: *a view; part of a play or movie*
seen: *past participle of see*

sea: *the ocean*
see: *to look at*

set: *to put or lay something in a place*
sit: *to rest oneself on a chair or perch*

sight: *the ability to see*
site: *a place or location*

some: *a few*
sum: *the total amount*

stake: *a pointed piece of metal or wood for driving into the ground*
steak: *a slice of beef or fish for cooking*

steal: *to take dishonestly or unlawfully*
steel: *a hard, tough metal*

than: *a conjunction used to compare two things, as in larger than or more than*
then: *an adverb meaning at that time, next, or after*

their: *belonging to them*
there: *at or in that place*
they're: *a contraction of the words they are*

threw: *past tense of throw*
through: *in one side and out the other side*

to: *in the direction of*
too: *in addition; very*
two: *the number 2*

wait: *to stay until something happens; to serve food at a meal*
weight: *how heavy something is*

weak: *opposite of strong*
week: *seven days*

wear: *to have clothing on the body*
where: *referring to a place*

weather: *the climate*
whether: *in case; in either case*

who's: *contraction of who is or who has*
whose: *possessive of who*

wood: *what trees are made of*
would: *helping verb; also, the past tense of will*

you're: *contraction of you are*
your: *belonging to you*

Frequently Misspelled Words

Although most word processing programs include a spell-checker, you won't be able to count on that feature when you write your essay for the GED® Reasoning Through Language Arts Test. Below is a list of some commonly misspelled words for you to study.

A
a lot
absence
accept
accident
achieve (*When in doubt, think* i *before* e, *except after* c, *and words that say "hey!" as in* n<u>eigh</u>bor *and* w<u>eigh</u>.)
accommodate
address
again
against
agree
all right
almost
already
although
always
appear
approach
argue
attention
August
author
awful
awkward

B
balloon
beautiful
because
beginning
being
believe
benefit
between
bicycle
borrow
business

C
calendar
captain
career
cereal
chief

coffee
college
congratulate
curiosity

D
daily
daughter
definitely
delicious
describe
difference
different
discover
disease
distance
dollar
doubt

E
easy
education
effect
eight
either
embarrass
emergency
English (The *E* is always capitalized.)
enough
environment
equipment
especially
excellent
except
exercise
extreme

F
familiar
February
financial
forehead
foreign
former
fourteen
fourth

friend
further

G
gallon
general
genius
government
governor
grammar
grateful
great
grocery
guard
guess

H
half
happiness
healthy
heard
heavy
height
heroes
holiday
hopeless
hospital
hurrying

I
immediately
increase
independence
independent
innocence
instead
interrupt
invitation
island

J
January
jealous

K
kitchen
knowledge

L

language
laugh
library
license
light
likely
losing
loyal

M

maintenance
marriage
mathematics
measure
medicine
million
muscle
mystery

N

natural
necessary
neighbor
neither
niece
night

O

o'clock
occasion
ocean
often
operate
opinion

P

parallel
particular
patience
people
perfect
perform
perhaps
permanent
personal
personality
picture
piece
poison

political
positive
possess
potatoes
prepare
prescription
probably
produce
professional
profit
promise
pronounce

Q

quality
quiet
quite

R

raise
realize
reason
receipt
receive
recipe
recognize
recommend
relieve
responsible
restaurant
rhythm
ridiculous
right
roommate

S

sandwich
scene
schedule
science
season
secretary
sense
separate
service
sight
signal
similar
since
soldier

sophomore
soul
source
special
stomach
strength
stretch
succeed
successful
supposedly
surprise
sweat
sympathy

T

technical
though
through
together
tomorrow
tongue
toward
tragedy
tries
twelfth
twelve

U

unnecessary
unusual
usual

V

vacuum
valuable
variety
vegetable
view
voice
volume

W

weather
Wednesday
weird
whether
which
while

Verb Conjugation Tables

to be	past	present	future	past perfect	present perfect	future perfect
I	was	am	will be	had been	have been	will have been
you	were	are	will be	had been	have been	will have been
he/she/it	was	is	will be	had been	has been	will have been
we	were	are	will be	had been	have been	will have been
they	were	are	will be	had been	have been	will have been

to say	past	present	future	past perfect	present perfect	future perfect
I	said	say	will say	had said	have said	will have said
you	said	say	will say	had said	have said	will have said
he/she/it	said	says	will say	had said	has said	will have said
we	said	say	will say	had said	have said	will have said
they	said	say	will say	had said	have said	will have said

to make	past	present	future	past perfect	present perfect	future perfect
I	made	make	will make	had made	have made	will have made
you	made	make	will make	had made	have made	will have made
he/she/it	made	makes	will make	had made	has made	will have made
we	made	make	will make	had made	have made	will have made
they	made	make	will make	had made	have made	will have made

to become	past	present	future	past perfect	present perfect	future perfect
I	became	become	will become	had become	have become	will have become
you	became	become	will become	had become	have become	will have become
he/she/it	became	becomes	will become	had become	has become	will have become
we	became	become	will become	had become	have become	will have become
they	became	become	will become	had become	have become	will have become

to come	past	present	future	past perfect	present perfect	future perfect
I	came	come	will come	had come	have come	will have come
you	came	come	will come	had come	have come	will have come
he/she/it	came	comes	will come	had come	has come	will have come
we	came	come	will come	had come	have come	will have come
they	came	come	will come	had come	have come	will have come

to live	past	present	future	past perfect	present perfect	future perfect
I	lived	live	will live	had lived	have lived	will have lived
you	lived	live	will live	had lived	have lived	will have lived
he/she/it	lived	lives	will live	had lived	has lived	will have lived
we	lived	live	will live	had lived	have lived	will have lived
they	lived	live	will live	had lived	have lived	will have lived

to have	past	present	future	past perfect	present perfect	future perfect
I	had	have	will have	had had	have had	will have had
you	had	have	will have	had had	have had	will have had
he/she/it	had	has	will have	had had	has had	will have had
we	had	have	will have	had had	have had	will have had
they	had	have	will have	had had	have had	will have had

to read	past	present	future	past perfect	present perfect	future perfect
I	read	read	will read	had read	have read	will have read
you	read	read	will read	had read	have read	will have read
he/she/it	read	reads	will read	had read	has read	will have read
we	read	read	will read	had read	have read	will have read
they	read	read	will read	had read	have read	will have read

to bring	past	present	future	past perfect	present perfect	future perfect
I	brought	bring	will bring	had brought	have brought	will have brought
you	brought	bring	will bring	had brought	have brought	will have brought
he/she/it	brought	brings	will bring	had brought	has brought	will have brought
we	brought	bring	will bring	had brought	have brought	will have brought
they	brought	bring	will bring	had brought	have brought	will have brought

to write	past	present	future	past perfect	present perfect	future perfect
I	wrote	write	will write	had written	have written	will have written
you	wrote	write	will write	had written	have written	will have written
he/she/it	wrote	writes	will write	had written	has written	will have written
we	wrote	write	will write	had written	have written	will have written
they	wrote	write	will write	had written	have written	will have written

Verb Conjugation Tables

to begin	past	present	future	past perfect	present perfect	future perfect
I	began	begin	will begin	had begun	have begun	will have begun
you	began	begin	will begin	had begun	have begun	will have begun
he/she/it	began	begins	will begin	had begun	has begun	will have begun
we	began	begin	will begin	had begun	have begun	will have begun
they	began	begin	will begin	had begun	have begun	will have begun

to take	past	present	future	past perfect	present perfect	future perfect
I	took	take	will take	had taken	have taken	will have taken
you	took	take	will take	had taken	have taken	will have taken
he/she/it	took	takes	will take	had taken	has taken	will have taken
we	took	take	will take	had taken	have taken	will have taken
they	took	take	will take	had taken	have taken	will have taken

to lay	past	present	future	past perfect	present perfect	future perfect
I	laid	lay	will lay	had laid	have laid	will have laid
you	laid	lay	will lay	had laid	have laid	will have laid
he/she/it	laid	lays	will lay	had laid	has laid	will have laid
we	laid	lay	will lay	had laid	have laid	will have laid
they	laid	lay	will lay	had laid	have laid	will have laid

to sell	past	present	future	past perfect	present perfect	future perfect
I	sold	sell	will sell	had sold	have sold	will have sold
you	sold	sell	will sell	had sold	have sold	will have sold
he/she/it	sold	sells	will sell	had sold	has sold	will have sold
we	sold	sell	will sell	had sold	have sold	will have sold
they	sold	sell	will sell	had sold	have sold	will have sold

to leave	past	present	future	past perfect	present perfect	future perfect
I	left	leave	will leave	had left	have left	will have left
you	left	leave	will leave	had left	have left	will have left
he/she/it	left	leaves	will leave	had left	has left	will have left
we	left	leave	will leave	had left	have left	will have left
they	left	leave	will leave	had left	have left	will have left

to run	past	present	future	past perfect	present perfect	future perfect
I	ran	run	will run	had run	have run	will have run
you	ran	run	will run	had run	have run	will have run
he/she/it	ran	runs	will run	had run	has run	will have run
we	ran	run	will run	had run	have run	will have run
they	ran	run	will run	had run	have run	will have run

to sit	past	present	future	past perfect	present perfect	future perfect
I	sat	sit	will sit	had sat	have sat	will have sat
you	sat	sit	will sit	had sat	have sat	will have sat
he/she/it	sat	sits	will sit	had sat	has sat	will have sat
we	sat	sit	will sit	had sat	have sat	will have sat
they	sat	sit	will sit	had sat	have sat	will have sat

to lose	past	present	future	past perfect	present perfect	future perfect
I	lost	lose	will lose	had lost	have lost	will have lost
you	lost	lose	will lose	had lost	have lost	will have lost
he/she/it	lost	loses	will lose	had lost	has lost	will have lost
we	lost	lose	will lose	had lost	have lost	will have lost
they	lost	lose	will lose	had lost	have lost	will have lost

to know	past	present	future	past perfect	present perfect	future perfect
I	knew	know	will know	had known	have known	will have known
you	knew	know	will know	had known	have known	will have known
he/she/it	knew	knows	will know	had known	has known	will have known
we	knew	know	will know	had known	have known	will have known
they	knew	know	will know	had known	have known	will have known

Extended Response Scoring Rubrics

Score	Description
Trait 1: Creation of Arguments and Use of Evidence	
2	Generates text-based argument(s) and establishes a purpose that is connected to the prompt
	Cites relevant and specific evidence from source text(s) to support argument (may include few irrelevant pieces of evidence or unsupported claims)
	Analyzes the issue and/or evaluates the validity of the argumentation within the source texts (e.g., distinguishes between supported and unsupported claims, makes reasonable inferences about underlying premises or assumptions, identifies fallacious reasoning, evaluates the credibility of sources, etc.)
1	Generates an argument and demonstrates some connection to the prompt
	Cites some evidence from source text(s) to support argument (may include a mix of relevant and irrelevant citations or a mix of textual and non-textual references)
	Partially analyzes the issue and/or evaluates the validity of the argumentation within the source texts; may be simplistic, limited, or inaccurate
0	May attempt to create an argument or lacks purpose or connection to the prompt or does neither
	Cites minimal or no evidence from source text(s) (sections of text may be copied from source)
	Minimally analyzes the issue and/or evaluates the validity of the argumentation within the source texts; may completely lack analysis or demonstrate minimal or no understanding of the given argument(s)

Non-scorable Responses (Score of 0/Condition Codes)
- Response exclusively contains text copied from source text(s) or prompt
- Response shows no evidence that test-taker has read the prompt or is off-topic
- Response is incomprehensible
- Response is not in English
- Response has not been attempted (blank)

Courtesy of the GED® Testing Service

Score	Description
	Trait 2: Development of Ideas and Organizational Structure
2	Contains ideas that are well developed and generally logical; most ideas are elaborated upon
	Contains a sensible progression of ideas with clear connections between details and main points
	Establishes an organizational structure that conveys the message and purpose of the response; applies transitional devices appropriately
	Establishes and maintains a formal style and appropriate tone that demonstrate awareness of the audience and purpose of the task
	Chooses specific words to express ideas clearly
1	Contains ideas that are inconsistently developed and/or may reflect simplistic or vague reasoning; some ideas are elaborated upon
	Demonstrates some evidence of a progression of ideas, but details may be disjointed or lacking connection to main ideas
	Establishes an organization structure that may inconsistently group ideas or is partially effective at conveying the message of the task; uses transitional devices inconsistently
	May inconsistently maintain a formal style and appropriate tone to demonstrate an awareness of the audience and purpose of the task
	May occasionally misuse words and/or choose words that express ideas in vague terms
0	Contains ideas that are insufficiently or illogically developed, with minimal or no elaboration on main ideas
	Contains an unclear or no progression of ideas; details may be absent or irrelevant to the main ideas
	Establishes an ineffective or no discernable organizational structure; does not apply transitional devices, or does so inappropriately
	Uses an informal style and/or inappropriate tone that demonstrates limited or no awareness of audience and purpose
	May frequently misuse words, overuse slang or express ideas in a vague or repetitious manner

Non-scorable Responses (Score of 0/Condition Codes)
- Response exclusively contains text copied from source text(s) or prompt
- Response shows no evidence that test-taker has read the prompt or is off-topic
- Response is incomprehensible
- Response is not in English
- Response has not been attempted (blank)

Courtesy of the GED® Testing Service

Score	Description
	Trait 3: Clarity and Command of Standard English Conventions
2	Demonstrates largely correct sentence structure and a general fluency that enhances clarity with specific regard to the following skills: 1) varied sentence structure within a paragraph or paragraphs 2) correct subordination, coordination and parallelism 3) avoidance of wordiness and awkward sentence structures 4) usage of transitional words, conjunctive adverbs and other words that support logic and clarity 5) avoidance of run-on sentences, fused sentences, or sentence fragments Demonstrates competent application of conventions with specific regard to the following skills: 1) frequently confused words and homonyms, including contractions 2) subject-verb agreement 3) pronoun usage, including pronoun antecedent agreement, unclear pronoun references, and pronoun case 4) placement of modifiers and correct word order 5) capitalization (e.g., proper nouns, titles, and beginnings of sentences) 6) use of apostrophes with possessive nouns 7) use of punctuation (e.g., commas in a series or in appositives and other non-essential elements, end marks, and appropriate punctuation for clause separation) May contain some errors in mechanics and conventions, but they do not interfere with comprehension; overall, standard usage is at a level appropriate for on-demand draft writing.
1	Demonstrates inconsistent sentence structure; may contain some repetitive, choppy, rambling, or awkward sentences that may detract from clarity; demonstrates inconsistent control over skills 1–5 as listed in the first bullet under trait 3, score point 2 above Demonstrates inconsistent control of basic conventions with specific regard to skills 1–7 as listed in the second bullet under trait 3, score point 2 above May contain frequent errors in mechanics and conventions that occasionally interfere with comprehension; standard usage is at a minimally acceptable level of appropriateness for on-demand draft writing.
0	Demonstrates consistently flawed sentence structure such that meaning may be obscured; demonstrates minimal control over skills 1–5 as listed in the first bullet under Trait 3, Score point 2 above Demonstrates minimal control of basic conventions with specific regard to skills 1–7 as listed in the second bullet under Trait 3, Score point 2 above Contains severe and frequent errors in mechanics and conventions that interfere with comprehension; overall, standard usage is at an unacceptable level for on-demand draft writing OR Response is insufficient to demonstrate level of mastery over conventions and usage

*Because test-takers will be given only 45 minutes to complete Extended Response tasks, there is no expectation that a response should be completely free of conventions or usage errors to receive a score of 2.

Non-scorable Responses (Score of 0/Condition Codes)
- Response exclusively contains text copied from source text(s) or prompt
- Response shows no evidence that test-taker has read the prompt or is off-topic
- Response is incomprehensible
- Response is not in English
- Response has not been attempted (blank)

Courtesy of the GED® Testing Service

APPENDIX

Answer Key

UNIT 1 READING COMPREHENSION

LESSON 1, *pp. 2–3*
1. B; DOK Level: 2; **Reading Assessment Targets:** R.2.1, R.2.5. In the final sentence of the first paragraph, the author provides examples of the negative effects that disrupting the circadian rhythm can have on a person's health. He says, "a misaligned body clock can … increase risk of developing diabetes, depression, obesity and even some forms of cancer." The other answer options do not provide examples of health problems resulting from the disruption of the circadian rhythm. Rather, they describe the disruptions that many people experience in their circadian rhythms due to their lifestyles and experiences.

2. C; DOK Level: 2; **Reading Assessment Targets:** R.2.1, R.2.5. The author's main idea is that more people are using wind turbine power. The other answer options do not provide a main idea. The author's statements about ancient mariners and farmers (answers A and B) lead to the main idea but are not main ideas on their own. The fact that wind provides only a fraction of the world's energy is a detail; this idea is not developed in the passage.

3. D; DOK Level: 2; **Reading Assessment Target:** R.2.4. The best restatement of the implied main idea is that wind energy is good for the environment and relatively inexpensive. This statement is broad enough to encompass all the ideas in the paragraph. The other answer options are details about the positive aspects of wind energy but are not broad enough to provide a main idea for the whole paragraph.

4. C; DOK Level: 2; **Reading Assessment Targets:** R.2.4, R.2.5. The author acknowledges the negative aspects of wind power in this paragraph (answer C). Answer A is a detail that supports this main idea. Answer B is incorrect because the author does not mention how turbines could avoid killing birds or bats, nor does it cover the information in the paragraph. Answer D is incorrect as well; although the passage explains that wind power is becoming more popular, its negative aspects do not make it popular. In addition, the question asks about the paragraph, not the passage as a whole.

5. A; DOK Level: 2; **Reading Assessment Targets:** R.2.1, R.5.2, R.5.3. The word *nevertheless* is a clear indicator of contradiction. Answers B and C indicate no contradiction and, therefore, cannot be correct. Nor do they answer the question. In addition, answer C does not address the relationship between the two paragraphs. Although answer D does indicate contradiction, it is incorrect because the contradiction applies to the information in the previous paragraph, not to the same paragraph. The correct answer must include both paragraphs.

LESSON 2, *pp. 4–5*
1. C; DOK Level: 2; **Reading Assessment Target:** R.2.2. Although the passage does state that vivid imagination and the power of suggestion create false memories, this information is not new and not part of the new study. Therefore, answer A is incorrect. Answer B simply restates the fact that the new study has ended but does not indicate what was concluded. It is clear that the study focused on how watching a video of someone doing a small action can result in a false memory, so answer C is correct. The study may be an extension of earlier work, but this fact is not the main idea of the passage as answer D indicates it is.

2. D; DOK Level: 2; **Reading Assessment Targets:** R.2.2, R.6.1. Answer A is close, but Nixon wanted to explain the charges, not question them. He states that the political thing to do is "to either ignore them or to deny them." Because Nixon does not want to do this, answer B is incorrect. Although Nixon makes a passing remark about wrongdoing in the current administration, it is not his main point here to accuse a particular group or individual. Because Nixon is defending himself against charges, answer D is correct. The author's purpose (or reason for writing) is often the main idea of a passage.

3. B; DOK Level: 2; **Reading Assessment Target:** R.2.2. Although Nixon may be implying that he should be elected, a summary would not include this implication because it is not stated. Answers A and C, therefore, are incorrect. Answer B best summarizes the author's statement because it includes the fact that Nixon thinks the office is important and should be held by someone whom the people trust. Answer D contains correct information but is incomplete.

4. A; DOK Level: 2; **Reading Assessment Target:** R.2.2. In paragraph 4, Nixon lists the conditions of what would make taking the money morally wrong. Answer A is the most comprehensive summary of those conditions. Answers B and C reflect a misreading of the passage, although both contributors and taxpayers are mentioned in other contexts. Answer C states what the money actually was used for. Although declaring a contribution on one's taxes might appear logical, there is no reference made to this action in the passage.

5. D; DOK Level: 2; **Reading Assessment Target:** R.2.2. Answer D clearly summarizes Nixon's explanation of why he took the money, which is first offered in paragraph 5 ("it was used to pay for political expenses"), then elaborated in paragraph 6. Nixon does not claim any misunderstanding about why he took the money, nor does he say he used it for personal expenses as indicated in answers A and B. Answer C restates that taking the money was not morally wrong, but this statement does not summarize his reasoning.

LESSON 3, *pp. 6–7*
1. B; DOK Level: 1; **Reading Assessment Target:** R.3.1. The first paragraph clearly lists the steps of the scientific method: " making an observation, forming a hypothesis ... conducting a test, and making a conclusion." Therefore, "making an observation" comes before "forming a hypothesis." Answer D is not part of the scientific method, as indicated in the first paragraph, although it seems either a logical extension of it or directly involved with each step.

Answer Key

UNIT 1 (continued)

2. DOK Level: 1; **Reading Assessment Targets:** R.3.1, R.5.3. This is the correct sequence of events:
1) **Rehearsals for the Christmas play begin.**
2) **The author is shifted to a different fourth-grade class.** 3) **The author reads poetry to his students.**
4) **The author is fired.** Students should understand that these events form a chronology. In addition, there is a causal relationship between the third and fourth events.

LESSON 4, pp. 8–9
1. B; DOK Level: 2; **Reading Assessment Target:** R.2.1. The author states that voters ages 18 to 29 are the "most disengaged," directly suggesting that they are less likely to vote than other age groups. Answer A is the direct opposite; this age group is the "most disengaged," meaning that they are the least interested. The author does not mention that this group is a growing population or refer to it in relation to swing states.

2. D; DOK Level: 2; **Reading Assessment Targets:** R.2.1, R.2.3. The author describes the four basic tastes (sweet, salty, sour, and bitter) and says that umami does not fit into these tastes. Therefore, it is dubbed the fifth taste. It is not an artificially created taste because it exists in many natural foods, such as mushrooms. Umami is not necessarily a healthful category, although many foods may be. Although first described by the Japanese, it is not a specifically Japanese category of taste.

3. C; DOK Level: 1; **Reading Assessment Target:** R.2.1. In paragraph 2, the author says that umami is "usually defined as a meaty, savory" taste. Although chicken soup falls within that category, "savory" is a better general classification for taste. Umami is not low-sodium. It does not fall within the salty category because that category is one of the four basic categories.

4. A; DOK Level: 2; **Reading Assessment Targets:** R.2.5, R.5.1, R.5.2, R.5.4. The author helps the reader understand the taste of umami by describing a number of foods and dishes with the umami taste. The author provides a list, but it does not include every food that falls within the umami category. The author does not repeat how delicious the foods taste, nor would such repetition help the reader understand the taste. The author mentions pepperoni-and-mushroom pizza as an example of umami, not as a recommendation. In fact, it would seem that other varieties of pizza would contain the umami taste as well.

5. B; DOK Level: 1; **Reading Assessment Target:** R.2.1. Answer B is correct: in the final paragraph, the author says that a Japanese scientist found that foods with the umami taste have a high level of glutamate. Some foods with the umami taste may contain MSG, but MSG is a substance added to foods; it is not a natural element. Because food companies are involved in ramping up the umami flavor in their foods, umami foods would have to be packaged or processed in some way. Some foods in the umami category may be Japanese, but others are not. No dish is indicated as specifically Japanese.

LESSON 5, pp. 10–11
1. D; DOK Level: 2; **Reading Assessment Targets:** R.2.1, R.3.4, R.5.1. Answer A is partially correct. Greenhouse gas emissions indirectly may cause flooding (through global warming), but nothing in the passage indicates that the emissions cause more or heavier rain. In fact, they make dry climates drier. Answer B seems like a logical choice; however, it is not the best answer because elements other than global warming and greenhouse gas emissions may endanger species or prevent their survival. Answer C is a misreading of the text. Losing ground refers to the scientists whose strong wording was weakened in the report. Answer D is correct; global warming causes the conditions mentioned in the first two paragraphs, and the implication is that curbing greenhouse gas emissions will reduce global warming. This response is an example of a causal chain, in which one event leads to another which leads to another (emissions → global warming → flooding, hunger, disease, etc.).

2. B; DOK Level: 2; **Reading Assessment Targets:** R.2.3, R.3.4. Nothing is mentioned about the nutritional value of either sweetener. Nor is the means of obtaining either sweetener discussed. Although fructose is present in fruits, nothing is mentioned or implied that it has been used because it is natural. That it has more calories would not be a reason to use the sweetener, as the author confirms in the rest of the passage. The fact that it is sweeter and cheaper seems the most likely reason for its use, as stated in paragraph 1.

3. C; DOK Level: 2; **Reading Assessment Targets:** R.2.1, R.2.2. Answer C summarizes the process of lipogenesis, the conversion of sugar into fat, explained in paragraph 3. The rapid conversion is the effect of high-fructose corn syrup in drinks that study group members consumed. Overweight people were not part of the study, so answer A is incorrect. Nothing is mentioned about actual weight gain nor about ease of digestion of either sweetener.

4. A; DOK Level: 2; **Reading Assessment Targets:** R.5.1, R.5.2. The author mentions that Dr. Parks noted that the study was limited to lean and healthy people and that the results may be amplified in overweight people. Answer B contradicts what Dr. Parks says: the results likely would be amplified, not the same. No other studies are mentioned, so answer C is incorrect. Answer D is incorrect because natural fruit is not mentioned in paragraph 6.

5. A; DOK Level: 1; **Reading Assessment Target:** R.2.1. The text indicates that dieters should continue to eat fruit because it contains beneficial nutrients. The passage states that dieters should limit processed foods with high-fructose corn syrup, not limit natural fruits. Answer C is a direct contradiction of the text. Processed foods are to be avoided. Answer D is incorrect because it misstates information in the passage, which suggests that dieters should cut calories and eat fruit, even though it contains fructose.

LESSON 6, pp. 12–13

1. **D; DOK Level: 2; Reading Assessment Targets:** R.2.4, R.3.2, R.3.3, R.3.4. The passage provides information about strategies that each general thought should be used to win the war, indicating that although they had different ideas about how to obtain victory, each wanted victory for his side. Both generals may have had the desire to destroy the spirit of the opposition, but the passage attributes this goal only to Sherman. The passage also states that Sherman, not Lee, employed the strategy of taking food and livestock from farmers. Controlling new territories would have been an ongoing goal of both military leaders, but the ultimate goal for each was overall victory in the war.

2. **A; DOK Level: 2; Reading Assessment Target:** R.3.4. Because they have the same genes, when identical twins are raised apart, scientists can study the extent to which upbringing and genes affect traits. Only one key variable is different: upbringing is different, but genes are the same. The effect of genes on upbringing is not a logical conclusion nor does it consider twins. Answer D is incorrect as well; comparing identical twins raised apart with fraternal twins raised together would not provide a useful comparison because it could not isolate for genes or upbringing.

3. **D; DOK Level: 2; Reading Assessment Target:** R.2.1. In paragraph 2, the author is clear that the significant finding of the study was that genes, not parenting, had the bigger effect on traits. Comparing different traits in the twins raised apart found this commonality. The effects of nature and nurture were not the same for different traits. The author does not make a claim that genes had a greater effect on health than on any other trait.

4. **A; DOK Level: 2; Reading Assessment Targets:** R.2.1, R.5.3. The author uses the signal words *but not* to contrast the effect of genes on personality traits with the effect of upbringing on those traits. Genes have a big effect; parenting does not. Answers B and D are statements made by the author but are not the contrast being set up here. The author does not suggest that genes have a greater effect on ambition than on aggression.

5. **C; DOK Level: 2; Reading Assessment Target:** R.2.1. Many scientists expected that "socialization" would have a bigger effect than genes on how religious each twin was. However, the comparison in the study showed that genes had the major effect. Upbringing was not the major factor, although it did affect the religions that the twins chose.

LESSON 7, pp. 14–15

1. **D; DOK Level: 2; Reading Assessment Target:** R.6.1. The author expresses the point of view that federal employees are not overpaid in comparison with private-sector workers. Although the author might believe that federal employees should be paid the same as or (sometimes) more than private-sector workers, this idea is less developed in the passage and thus does not reflect the author's point of view as strongly as answer D does. The author refutes the "accepted truth" that federal workers earn more and cites government analyses of federal pay to support this position; the author does not criticize its accuracy.

2. **A; DOK Level: 2; Reading Assessment Targets:** R.4.1/L.4.1, R.4.3/L.4.3, R.6.1. The use of the word *stingy* suggests that the appropriations have been unfairly small. The word implies a judgment of mean-spiritedness beyond simply saying that the appropriations have been "too small." The author does not suggest that the appropriations have been delayed or misused, rather that they deserve to be larger. Later in the paragraph, the author refers to the potential new management policies as "potentially harmful," not the appropriations.

3. **B; DOK Level: 2; Reading Assessment Target:** R.6.1. The passage's initial focus is on the National Park Service Centennial Initiative and the money it would cost to enact it. At the end of the passage, the author encourages the legislature to provide the money for this initiative. Answer B best states the author's point of view. Answer A is incorrect because the author mentions voting during the election year, not after the election. Answer C is incorrect because the House Democratic leadership needs to schedule a vote; the committee has already approved the initiative, so another committee meeting is unnecessary. Although the author likely would support campaigning for conservation, this idea is not the focus of the passage.

4. **B; DOK Level: 2; Reading Assessment Target:** R.6.1. The author's point of view is that the Centennial Initiative deserves support. Answers A and D are incorrect because the author does not believe that representatives are doing all they can, nor is the National Park Service budget adequate. Answer C is incorrect because Dirk Kempthorne has already rewritten the National Park Service's management policy.

5. **C; DOK Level: 3; Reading Assessment Targets:** R.2.7, R.6.1. The author clearly believes the National Park Service needs more support from the federal government. Answer A is incorrect because the federal government seems to be working slowly rather than quickly to provide support for the national parks. Answer B is a misreading of the sentence "... the Democratic leadership should schedule a vote." Answer D is incorrect because the author believes that the federal government together with private donors should support the parks.

LESSON 8 pp. 16–17

1. **A; DOK Level: 2; Reading Assessment Targets:** R.2.3, R.2.4, R.4.1/L.4.1, R.4.3/L.4.3. A scuba diver is able, very slowly, to explore the deep underwater world. The author is saying that he used to be able to take time to process information and to research more deeply, or thoroughly. Rather than moving quickly through words, the author moved slowly and with more concentration before the Internet. He has not lost sight of how information should be obtained, but he obtains it differently and more superficially. Nothing in the passage mentions specific research about a topic; the analogy of scuba diving and jet skiing is to show the change in the way people think, do research, and learn.

Answer Key

UNIT 1 *(continued)*

2. DOK Level: 2; **Reading Assessment Targets:**
R.2.3, R.2.4. The web should contain **lack purpose and motivation**, **watch too much television**, and **have few interests**. The author implies that couch potatoes have evolved from "The Silent Majority," known for not voicing opinions or standing up for beliefs. Although the word *too* is not mentioned specifically, the "Viewing Public" refers to people who watch a great deal of television. The author asks what couch potatoes are seeking other than more television. Therefore, she implies that their interests are few other than television.

3. D; DOK Level: 2; **Reading Assessment Targets:** R.2.3, R.2.4. Answers A, B, and C are incorrect because the passage goes more deeply into the inability to understand why people watch so much television. The author does not mention old movies in the passage. Nor does she mention watching sporting events. She does mention her husband's and son's watching television, but no implication is made about not getting along. All evidence in the passage shows disappointment with the inactivity and isolation that come from watching television.

4. A; DOK Level: 2; **Reading Assessment Targets:** R.2.3, R.2.4. The author states that she and her family see less of their neighbors and indicates that people seem less involved in civic, athletic, and social activities. Answer B is incorrect because families may go out less, but the time spent seems more isolated than families together doing things at home. Mention of fewer car accidents and meeting strangers is stated and thus not implied; the examples are meant to be ironic.

LESSON 9, *pp. 18–19*

1. D; DOK Level: 2; **Reading Assessment Target:**
R.4.3/L.4.3. The language in answer D touches readers' feelings of patriotism: "deeply rooted in a set of beliefs firmly etched in the national conscience." Answers A, B, and C contain straightforward language that conveys information. Although answer C hints at or introduces an opinion, the language is nonetheless direct and does not reflect the author's attitude.

2. C; DOK Level: 2; **Reading Assessment Target:**
R.4.2/L.4.2. The word *upset* is less critical than the phrase *sick to my stomach* and lacks the strong connotation of vomiting. Therefore, the highly critical tone would be softened (answer C). The tone remains critical, so answers A and B are incorrect. Although the tone remains critical, it is not sarcastic, so answer D is incorrect.

3. A; DOK Level: 2; **Reading Assessment Targets:**
R.4.3/L.4.3, R.6.1. Answer A is correct because of the highly connotative words (*ridiculous, flagrant*) and even more exaggerated expressions, such as *sick to my stomach* and *kindergarten basketball*. The author does not use jargon in this paragraph, but even if he did, his intention is to show disdain and disgust with the caution of playoff officials. He compares the playoffs with kindergarten basketball to express his view that the playoffs contain less aggressive action than he would like. The tone is not academic, given his exaggerations and vivid language; the research it reflects is his familiarity with playoffs in the previous century.

4. B; DOK Level: 2; **Reading Assessment Targets:**
R.4.3/L.4.3, R.5.1, R.5.4. The short paragraph provides extra emphasis, and the use of *bogus* underscores the author's critical attitude toward NBA officiating (answer B). The short paragraph gives it greater impact on the passage, calling attention to it, so answer A is incorrect. The use of *bogus* relates to the author's opinion of NBA officiating, so answer C is incorrect. The short paragraph emphasizes the tone of the passage rather than subdues it, so answer D is incorrect.

5. D; DOK Level: 2; **Reading Assessment Targets:**
R.4.3/L.4.3, R.5.1, R.6.4. In paragraph 7, the author's repetition of the words *could never* and the sentence beginning *And, it's a shame* emphasize his admiration for NBA playing style and players of previous decades. Therefore, answer D is correct. The author admires the rough style of play, so answers A and B are incorrect. When the author says "it's a shame," he is addressing the inability of today's players to play as players did in previous decades; he is not indicating shame about the way players used to play. Therefore, answer C is incorrect.

LESSON 10, *pp. 20–21*

1. A; DOK Level: 2; **Reading Assessment Targets:**
R.2.8, R.5.4. The author's use of the phrase "suggesting that more increases ... are coming" lets you know of a link between increased oil prices and the likelihood of increased gas prices. Answer B reflects a misreading of the text. The information in answers C and D may or may not happen, and no conclusion can be drawn on the basis of information in the passage.

2. C; DOK Level: 2; **Reading Assessment Targets:** R.2.1, R.2.8. Although the evidence showing girls' improved performance is scant, the author believes it is promising. The rest of the paragraph supports this idea. Answer A does not reflect the positive results of even the few samples and is thus incorrect. The statement in answer B is taken from the passage, but it is a detail about what teachers must do, not the outcomes of all-girls' classes. Nothing is mentioned in the passage about what happens after girls have taken all-girls' classes.

3. B; DOK Level: 2; **Reading Assessment Target:**
R.5.2. The author begins focusing on all-girls' schools and classrooms in paragraph 2. Paragraph 3 provides a narrower example of a school that has instituted an all-girls' math class. Answer A is incorrect because paragraph 3 does not summarize paragraph 2. Answer C does not explain the reason for implementing the all-girls' classroom. The reasons are explained earlier, in general; they are not specific to the school mentioned in this paragraph. Answer D is incorrect because self-esteem is not mentioned in paragraph 2.

4. B; DOK Level: 2; Reading Assessment Targets: R.2.1, R.2.8. The author's conclusion is that girls do better in math and science when they are taught in all-girl classrooms. Answer A is a misinterpretation of the text. There is no implication that math or science is more important to boys or to girls. Answer C is incorrect because the author states that girls' test scores do not match boys' and that girls should be encouraged to study math and science, not given scholarships simply because they are female. Answer D misstates the text; girls do not do as well as boys on these tests.

5. A; DOK Level: 2; Reading Assessment Targets: R.2.5, R.2.8, R.3.4. Answer A is the only possible evidence that supports the author's conclusion. Answer B is something that occurs in all-girls' classrooms. Answers C and D state ideas about which the author has strong feelings, but these opinions do not directly support her conclusion about classroom education.

LESSON 11, *pp. 22–23*

1. D; DOK Level: 2; Reading Assessment Target: R.2.7. In the final paragraph, the author claims that when the economy is bad, more adult children return home to live with their parents. The economy is given as the reason for the increase. A reluctance to leave the nest is cited by the psychologist as a reason that some adult children live at home. It does not explain the increase. The author does not suggest that these adult children lack motivation; in fact the contrary is implied.

2. B; DOK Level: 1; Reading Assessment Target: R.2.1. The author says that not all people living in rural America live on farms. The author does not discuss whether people living in rural America are poor or whether people who do live on farms have apple trees. The passage suggests that rural areas in the United States have fewer places at which to buy food, not more.

3. A; DOK Level: 2; Reading Assessment Targets: R.2.1, R.2.7. The author says that supermarkets and grocery stores stock more fruits and vegetables than do other types of food stores, such as convenience stores. The author does not say that rural supermarkets and grocery stores are different from those in other places, nor does the author say they are similar to convenience stores. The passage suggests that supermarkets and grocery stores are less common in rural areas because these areas are less populated.

4. A; DOK Level: 2; Reading Assessment Targets: R.2.7, R.4.3/L.4.3. Rural areas are called "food deserts" because there are fewer nearby places to buy food, and people are limited to the foods available in their neighborhoods. People may have to travel great distances to buy healthful foods but not to buy any kind of food. People are not limited to what they can grow. They are limited by the types of nearby food stores.

5. D; DOK Level: 3; Reading Assessment Targets: R.2.7, R.2.8. The only hypothesis that follows logically from the passage is that suburban areas are likely to have more food stores that stock fruits and vegetables. This is an implied comparison in the passage. Rural areas have fewer grocery stores. As a result, rural areas have fewer food stores that stock fruits and vegetables. Answers A, B, and C could be true, but the statements are not explicitly supported or implied in the passage.

LESSON 12, *pp. 24–25*

1. C; DOK Level: 3, Reading Assessment Targets: R.2.7, R.2.8, R.6.1. The author would most likely agree with the statement that firing federal workers is not the best way to balance the national budget. Both excerpts express the author's support for federal workers. In the first passage, he says it is a myth that federal workers cannot be fired. You can conclude that the author does not believe that many federal workers are incompetent and should be fired. In the second excerpt, the author makes it clear that the government is not getting larger. By implication, the government is not too large, and there is no need to reduce the number of federal workers.

2. DOK Level: 3; Reading Assessment Targets: R.2.7, R.2.8, R.9.1/R.7.1, R.9.2. The completed chart should include these statements: **Although the use of renewable energy sources is expected to increase, such energy sources have drawbacks and detractors. The lack of significant growth in hydropower may be reversed. More than half of the electricity generated in the United States from renewable energy sources comes from hydropower.** The first statement is based on the following information: The "Renewable Energy in the United States" passage says that the use of renewable energy sources is expected to grow over the next 30 years, but the "Do New Ideas Solve Old Problems?" passage indicates that the renewable energy source hydropower has unwelcome drawbacks. The second statement is based on the following information: The "Hydropower" passage says that the vast majority of hydropower plants were built before 1980 and that recent changes to hydroelectric capacity have been small, but the "Do New Ideas Solve Old Problems?" passage indicates that engineers are looking for solutions that might increase hydropower output by about 15 percent. The third statement is based on the following information: The "Hydropower" passage states that hydropower accounted for about 7 percent of total U.S. electricity generation in 2012, and the "Renewable Energy in the United States" passage states that about 12 percent of U.S. electricity was generated from renewable sources in 2012; 7 percent is more than half of 12 percent. The statement that hydropower is an energy source that cannot be sustained indefinitely is false, according to the following information: The "Renewable Energy in the United States" passage states that renewable energy sources can be sustained indefinitely, and the "Do New Ideas Solve Old Problems?" passage states that hydropower is a renewable energy source.

LESSON 13, *pp. 26–27*

1. C; DOK Level: 2; Reading Assessment Target: R.4.1/L.4.1. The clues describe Simon Wheeler's telling of the story with no variation in his voice or expression. This sameness, combined with the prefix *mono-*, indicates that *monotonous* means "one" or "the same" voice. A story's many details may make it boring or interesting. That it will be *reeled off* suggests no drama. Although the narrator may show sincerity and earnestness, nothing in the text indicates deep emotion; in fact the lack of expression and the "reeling off" of the story indicate little emotion. A lack of expression may bore a listener, but it has nothing to do with the focus of the story.

UNIT 1 *(continued)*

2. **DOK Level: 2; Reading Assessment Target:**
R.4.1/L.4.1. A **hamlet** is a **small village** or **small town**.
The context clues indicate that it is a "place" in which the
Barry family was important and that it is "located in a valley
beside a part of the Barry River that is fordable." Families
are generally important (or not) in the places where they
live; therefore, the *hamlet* must be that place. You might
recall from prior knowledge that villages often spring up at
fordable points along rivers. This knowledge may help you
answer the next question as well.

3. **DOK Level: 2; Reading Assessment Target:**
R.4.1/L.4.1. *Fordable* means that the river **can be** crossed.
The context clue is that now a bridge spans the river. You
may have prior knowledge that villages often spring up at
fordable points along rivers.

4. **DOK Level: 2; Reading Assessment Target:**
R.4.1/L.4.1. A deserted room would contain **nothing; it
would be empty**. The context clue "alone in the bare
carriage" later in the passage is a restatement of "third-
class carriage in a deserted train."

5. **DOK Level: 2; Reading Assessment Target:**
R.4.1/L.4.1. In this context, *passed out* means **moved**,
walked, or **stepped**. It does not mean "fainted" or "handed
out," as the context supports neither definition. The narrator
could not have fainted because he notices the lighted dial of
the clock, nor does he hand anything to anyone.

LESSON 14, *pp. 28–29*
1. **B; DOK Level: 2; Reading Assessment Target:** R.3.4.
Answer B is correct; the narrator's comment about the
strangeness of the house causes John to think she feels a
draft. Therefore, he shuts the window. Her feeling is caused
by her reaction to the house, not to the cold. Answer A is
incorrect; although the narrator's reaction to her house may
cause her to feel a chill, she simply says that the house is
strange, and John infers that she has a chill. The narrator,
not John, has a nervous condition, but nothing is mentioned
about sensitivity to cold. Therefore, answer C is incorrect.
Answer D is incorrect because nothing is mentioned about
either character's desire to see the moonlight.

2. **B; DOK Level: 1; Reading Assessment Target:**
R.2.1 Answer B is correct; the information is stated in
paragraph 1. Although she visits her nephew, the visit is
not the purpose of her trip. Nothing is mentioned about her
relationship with her husband, so there is no indication that
she wishes to distance herself from him. Answer D is a
misreading of the text; she is not attending a funeral.

3. **B; DOK Level: 2; Reading Assessment Targets:** R.3.3,
R.3.4. In paragraph 1, the narrator indicates that his uncle
"characteristically delayed writing" the letter, causing it to
arrive late. The narrator implies that his uncle might have
kept the letter in his pocket for several days before mailing
it. Answer A is, therefore, incorrect because the uncle is
responsible for the lateness. The word **carrier** refers to the
person who carried the letter in his pocket, not the person
delivering mail. Therefore, answer A is incorrect. Although
readers can infer that the trip was unexpected, the narrator
does not indicate that a limited amount of preparation time
caused his uncle to send the letter late; therefore, answer
C is incorrect. Answer D is a misreading of the text; the
narrator's aunt, not his uncle, had to attend to the legacy.

4. **C; DOK Level: 2; Reading Assessment Targets:** R.2.2,
R.3.2, R.3.3, R.3.4. In paragraph 2, the narrator thinks of
his aunt, recalling how awkward and uncomfortable he felt
as a child. When reminiscing, the narrator does not indicate
that he enjoyed his interactions with his aunt or that he looks
forward to reconnecting with her, so answers A and D are
incorrect. Although the narrator notes that his uncle tends
to procrastinate, he does not display resentment toward his
uncle; therefore, answer B is incorrect.

5. **A; DOK Level: 2; Reading Assessment Target:** R.3.4.
In paragraph 3, the narrator says that his aunt rode in a
day coach, or train with no sleeping facilities, and within the
same sentence provides details about her dirtied clothing,
indicating a causal relationship. Answer B is incorrect
because the narrator does not indicate that his aunt arrives
in Boston sooner than expected. Although the narrator
mentions that his aunt is the last passenger to step off the
train, he does not indicate that her ride in the day coach
caused her delayed exit (answer C). Answer D is incorrect
because after the landlady puts Aunt Georgiana to bed,
her nephew does not see her until the next day. She is very
tired and is not hiding from anyone.

6. **D; DOK Level: 2; Reading Assessment Targets:**
R.3.2, R.3.4, R.3.5. Answer D is correct; on the basis of
details in paragraph 3, you can infer that exhaustion from
the trip causes Aunt Georgiana to go to bed immediately.
She has had a long journey from Nebraska to Boston and
is sooty and disheveled when she arrives. Answers A and
B are incorrect because the narrator makes no mention of
discomfort or embarrassment. Although the day coach is
not equipped with sleeping compartments, Aunt Georgiana
might or might not have slept for a while. Answer C,
therefore, is not the best choice.

LESSON 15, *pp. 30–31*
1. **D; DOK Level: 1; Reading Assessment Target:** R.2.5.
Answer D is the only possible one. The passage states that
Emily and Susan are five years apart but that Emily is only
one year ahead of Susan in terms of physical development.
Answer A is incorrect because Susan is not ill at ease in
company, as evidenced by her willingness to perform and
be rewarded with applause. Answer B is incorrect because
Emily finds the riddles, but Susan tells them and receives
the attention. Answer C is incorrect because Emily most
likely does not enjoy sharing her possessions with Susan,
who sometimes loses or breaks them. Nothing is mentioned
about Susan's willingness to share.

2. DOK Level: 2; **Reading Assessment Target:** R.2.1. Only the husband likes **country music**, also called "hillbilly" music and "bluegrass" in the passage. Gloria probably likes blues, bebop, and a little buckdancing, but not "bluegrass," which is a form of country music.

3. DOK Level: 3; **Reading Assessment Targets:** R.3.4, R.4.3/L.4.3, R.5.1. Gloria's comparison implies that after a sharp rise in the New York Stock Exchange, watch out for a **fall** or **sharp fall** or **crash**, implying that the prices that just soared will drop dramatically. The comparison between country music and the stock exchange suggests that the sharp rises and falls of country melodies are as uneven, and unnerving, as those of stock prices.

4. A; DOK Level: 2; **Reading Assessment Targets:** R.3.3, R.3.4, R.5.1. The narrator contrasts his wife's northern background with his southern background. Answer B is incorrect because the narrator specifically states that he was raised in South Carolina. Answer C is incorrect because the text specifically states that Gloria hates the South; her attitude toward the North is not stated, but the implication is that she favors it over the South. Therefore, indifference would not be the best choice. Answer D is incorrect because contrast is meant to show difference, not similarity.

5. C; DOK Level: 2; **Reading Assessment Targets:** R.2.7, R.3.3, R.3.4. Answer A is incorrect because he does not necessarily agree or disagree with everything his wife likes or dislikes. Therefore, answer C is correct. They do live elsewhere; however Gloria's dislike of the South does not necessarily or entirely explain why they live where they do. Nothing suggests that she has never been to the South.

LESSON 16, *pp. 32–33*

1. B; DOK Level: 2; **Reading Assessment Targets:** R.2.1, R.3.2. Answer B is correct because Mrs. Wright states that John is dead. This is the first complication in the passage. The other answers contradict the information in the story.

2. C; DOK Level: 2; **Reading Assessment Target:** R.3.2. "They were the recent brides of two brothers … the tempestuous Atlantic" is part of the exposition. The sentence gives the critical background information that sets up the action of the story. Answers A, B, and D describe actions in the story, not exposition.

3. A; DOK Level: 2; **Reading Assessment Target:** R.3.2. Goodman Parker reveals that Margaret's husband, who has been presumed dead, is actually alive. Answer B is incorrect because Mary's husband is not among those presumed dead, according to Goodman Parker's information. Answer C is incorrect because 13 men were thought dead, but this information was untrue. Answer D is incorrect; Margaret's husband has not yet returned to her, but it is assumed that he will.

4. D; DOK Level: 3; **Reading Assessment Targets:** R.3.2, R.3.3, R.3.5, R.6.1. Delaying the announcement increases the tension of the plot and thus adds suspense. Readers are likely to want the news as badly as Margaret does. The delay is not a complication nor is it intended to provide more exposition about Margaret. Goodman Parker is represented as honest and serious. It is not likely that the delay is intended to add humor.

5. B; DOK Level: 2; **Reading Assessment Targets:** R.3.2, R.3.3, R.3.4. Margaret decides not to tell Mary the news that Margaret's husband is alive for fear that it will make Mary even sadder to hear Margaret's happy news. This decision sets up a potential complication because Margaret now has a secret. The reader does not know whether this secret will become important as the story continues. The other answer options do not introduce complications because they do not suggest unexpected outcomes or plot twists.

LESSON 17, *pp. 34–35*

1. D; DOK Level: 2; **Reading Assessment Targets:** R.3.2, R.3.4, R.3.5. The narrator relates that at one time, Tiny set off for Alaska after hearing miners' "wonderful stories" and lived in the wilds but now is interested only in making money. Moreover, he relates that another character helps keep her from becoming too miserly, indicating that she has a tendency to hold on to her money. These details lead to the inference that her sense of adventure has given way to a need for security. Tiny went to Alaska in part because of the gold she saw but also because of the stories told by the people who had been there, so the prospect of becoming rich was not her only reason for going. The narrator says that Tiny sold her business and went to Alaska as a result of a daring that nobody had ever suspected in her; this statement suggests that she was not known as a bold and resourceful explorer when she was a child. Tiny was successful in turning a gold claim into a considerable fortune, so her need to make money does not result from giving up her business for the chance to find gold.

2. B; DOK Level: 2; **Reading Assessment Targets:** R.3.2, R.3.3. The narrator describes going into the old man's bedroom each morning to ask how he got along during the night, so it is logical to infer that he takes care of the old man. No details from the passage suggest that the old man is the narrator's father or employee; rather, it seems that the narrator works for, or at least helps, the old man. It is clear that the narrator and old man are not enemies because the narrator states in the first paragraph of the passage that he loved the old man and that the old man had never wronged him.

3. C; DOK Level: 1; **Reading Assessment Target:** R.2.1. In the first paragraph, the narrator explains that he decided to kill the old man so that he no longer would have to see the old man's eye, which frightened the narrator. The narrator also makes it clear that he has no desire to have the old man's money and that the old man has never done anything to harm him, so he does not resent the old man's wealth or think that the old man has been cruel to him. Although it may be inferred that the old man is not well, the narrator gives no indication of wanting to end the old man's suffering.

4. A; DOK Level: 2; **Reading Assessment Targets:** R.3.2, R.3.5, R.4.3/L.4.3. In paragraph 2, the narrator acknowledges that readers will judge him to be mad and then argues against this judgment. He uses words such as *wisely* and *cunningly* to show that his actions result from wisdom and intelligence, not mental illness. His choice of words relates to proving only that he is rational; he seems unconcerned about whether readers think him educated, blameless, or organized.

Answer Key

UNIT 1 *(continued)*

5. D; DOK Level: 2; **Reading Assessment Targets:**
R.3.2, R.3.5. Common sense suggests that taking an
hour to thrust one's head through a doorway to look into a
room is not an action that a reasonable person would take.
Therefore, the narrator's actions are not reasonable or
sensible; rather, he is irrationally cautious and methodical
as he makes preparations to kill the old man. Because
the narrator is taking steps to kill the old man, it is unlikely
that he is concerned about the old man's need for rest.
No evidence in the passage suggests that the narrator is
exaggerating his own actions.

6. D; DOK Level: 2; **Reading Assessment Target:** R.3.2.
The narrator believes that the old man's eye is a threat,
and he is obsessed with killing the old man when the eye is
open. Although the narrator may have been a dependable
and helpful caregiver for the old man at one time, he now
merely feigns concern for the old man to keep his plan of
murder a secret. The secretive and elaborately practiced
steps the narrator is taking to kill the old man, based on
his fear of the old man's eye, prove that the narrator is not
innocent, trusting, fearless, or arrogant.

LESSON 18, *pp. 36–37*

1. D; DOK Level: 2; **Reading Assessment Targets:** R.3.2,
R.3.3, R.3.5, R.4.3/L.4.3. Details such as "skeleton stone
walls," "rotting floor boards," "weird dawn," and "ungodly
awakening" suggest that some misfortune is about to occur.
Answer A is incorrect because the woman sings to ward
off an omen, not to bring sleep. In fact, the agitation and
restlessness imply wakefulness. Answer B is incorrect
because the moon, not the factory, glows "like a fired
pine-knot." Answer C is incorrect because the animals are
restless in response to setting details just as the woman
is; nothing is implied or stated about animals' becoming
restless at dusk.

2. DOK Level: 2; **Reading Assessment Targets:** R.3.2,
R.3.3, R.3.4. The **drought** is the key feature that leads to
Hook's being struck from the nest early. His parents have
to fly longer distances for food and do not wish to return to
feed him. They choose to strike him from the nest and let
him fend for himself.

3. D; DOK Level: 2; **Reading Assessment Targets:** R.3.2,
R.3.3. Because Hook can hear the Pacific Ocean, he most
likely lives near it. If it were distant, he could not hear it.
Answer A is incorrect because the sound is in the distance,
not close enough to be at the beach. Answer B is incorrect
as there is no indication of his living on an island. Answer C
is incorrect because California is not home to high prairies.

4. D; DOK Level: 3; **Reading Assessment Targets:**
R.3.2, R.3.3, R.4.3/L.4.3. The description creates a feeling
of impending danger to Hook. The world around him is full
of animals that could prey on him, and he has to be on his
guard. The description of these details does not emphasize
the beauty of nature. Although Hook may have keen
eyesight and hearing, and nature may be full of the sights
and sounds of living things, the major effect of these details
is to emphasize a feeling of danger.

LESSON 19, *pp. 38–39*

1. B; DOK Level: 2; **Reading Assessment Target:**
R.4.3/L.4.3. The hurt that the writer feels about the
possibility that his career is over is compared with a deep
wound, or laceration. The implication is that it cuts off
his breathing and, by extension, his life. Answer A does
not go far enough, nor is illness implied in explaining the
writer's feelings about the likelihood that his career is over.
Hyperbole, or exaggeration, is not used here, despite the
depth of the character's emotions. So, although plausible,
answer C is not the best choice because the comparison
is specifically about a laceration to the throat. Answer D
reflects a misunderstanding of personification.

2. B: DOK Level: 2; **Reading Assessment Target:**
R.4.3/L.4.3. Answer B is correct because muscles are
involved in functions that keep a person alive, such as
breathing. Answers A and C indicate misinterpretations
of figurative language. No comparison is made between
muscles and motions; no human qualities, indicating
personification, are attributed to muscles. Answer D
addresses the idea of hyperbole, but the explanation is
incorrect. The old man, not the narrator, is afraid of the
dark, and the hyperbole refers to the narrator's lack of
motion, not fear.

3. B; DOK Level: 2; **Reading Assessment Targets:**
R.4.2/L.4.2, R.4.3/L.4.3. Answer B is correct because the
onomatopoeia imitates the cricket's sound. Answer A shows
confusion between personification and onomatopoeia. The
cricket is not given human characteristics. Answer C is
incorrect because the old man is trying to explain the sound;
he is not certain that it is a cricket, even if he does use the
word *chirp*. Answer D is inconclusive because not knowing
the sound of the cricket may or may not add to the sense of
terror.

4. C; DOK Level: 2; **Reading Assessment Target:**
R.4.3/L.4.3. Although some of these words appear in
paragraph 4, answer C is the only correct choice: Death
stalked the old man. Answers A, B, and D are misreadings
of the passage. In paragraph 5, the narrator compares
his increasing fury with a beating drum that encourages
soldiers. The word *victim* appears in paragraph 4 but refers
to the old man. The black shadow is Death's shadow, but
it is in the room, not outside. The word *enveloped* is a verb
meaning "engulfed"; it is not the noun *envelope*.

5. C; DOK Level: 2; **Reading Assessment Target:**
R.4.3/L.4.3. Answer C is correct. In addition to describing
the muffled sound of a heartbeat, the steady ticking of a
watch reflects the steady rhythm of the heart. Answers A, B,
and D are misreadings of the passage. Although midnight is
mentioned earlier in the passage, nothing in the comparison
specifies time; therefore, answer B is not as good a choice
as answer A. Answer C is incorrect because the narrator's
anger is part of the next simile, not this one. Answer D is
incorrect because it mixes the elements of the two similes in
the paragraph.

6. A; DOK Level: 3; **Reading Assessment Targets:**
R.4.3/L.4.3, R.5.4. Answer A is correct because the images
help clarify these abstract ideas. Answer B is incorrect
because nothing leading to death is foreshadowed except,
perhaps, death itself. Answer C is plausible, but the answer
is too narrow; in the passage, personification applies only to
death. Answer D addresses setting, not figurative language,
and, therefore, is incorrect.

LESSON 20, pp. 40–41

1. **A; DOK Level:** 2; **Reading Assessment Targets:** R.3.2, R.3.3. The quotation shows that these are the exact thoughts of the man. The man is not speaking his thoughts aloud. The quotation is in the present tense because the narrator tells the thoughts as if they were spoken. However, the excerpt is told in the past tense. The man "thought" this—the thinking occurred in the past.

2. **D; DOK Level:** 2; **Reading Assessment Targets:** R.3.2, R.3.5. The narrator says that she is still in school and lives with her parents. Answers A, B, and C reflect a misunderstand of the concept of narrator. Answer D is the only possible answer.

3. **A; DOK Level:** 2; **Reading Assessment Targets:** R.3.2, R.3.5 . Answer A correctly distinguishes the main characteristic of first-person narration. Answer B is incorrect because *I* indicates a first-person narrator, not an omniscient one. Answer C is incorrect because the mother is not the narrator; the girl does not know her mother's thoughts. Answer D misinterprets point of view. The narrator's thoughts and feelings are revealed.

4. **C; DOK Level:** 2; **Reading Assessment Target:** R.6.3. By presenting first-person point of view, the author reveals the thoughts and feelings of the young girl telling the story. Answer A might seem logical if the story were told from another pint of view but is incorrect in this context. Answer B is incorrect; the girl observes her father's habits, but the author's purpose in first-person narration is not to analyze the father or his habits. Answer D is too broad; the passage is about one girl. It is not about other girls and is broader than her attitude toward her parents.

5. **B; DOK Level:** 3; **Reading Assessment Target:** R.2.7. Answer B is the best answer because someone writing a diary would be writing about events as he or she sees them and probably would include personal thoughts and feelings. Answer A is incorrect because a first-person narrator, unlike the journalist, does not have to be objective. Although answer C could be close, a poem does not necessarily record daily events and is usually based more on imagination. It is not a recording of events. Answer D is incorrect because the analogy does not fit; neither mysteries nor clues are part of this narrative.

LESSON 21, pp. 42–43

1. **A; DOK Level:** 2; **Reading Assessment Targets:** R.2.4, R.3.2, R.3.3, R.3.4. The final sentence of the passage and details leading to that final sentence suggest that the man does not think about the significance of the reality that it is fifty degrees below zero—that humans are especially frail and even vulnerable to death in such extreme conditions. The man may not be impressed by the trail and the lack of sun, but he is aware of where the trail is and where the sun should be, so there is no indication that he may get lost. Also, the man is aware of how uncomfortable a person can be in cold weather and understands that special gear is required to guard against such discomfort and protect oneself from frostbite. The fact that the man is not intrigued by the strangeness of the frozen wilderness is not necessarily a problem.

2. **B; DOK Level:** 2; **Reading Assessment Targets:** R.3.2, R.3.3, R.3.4, R.3.5. The two men do not shoot each other because they have been "brought up under the code of a restraining civilization," meaning that they have been taught to act against base instincts. In each man's case, murder would be the fulfillment, not the abandonment, of a lifelong passion. The act of murder requires a disregard for the restraining code of civilization, not necessarily hatred of any kind or a statement of wrongs.

3. **C; DOK Level:** 2; **Reading Assessment Targets:** R.3.2, R.3.3, R.3.4, R.3.5. While the men restrain themselves because they adhere to human codes of conduct, Nature has no such limitations. Nature does not have feelings, so it does not feel hatred or care about honor, for example. Although nature may reinforce—or, for that matter, diminish—someone's passion, the statement that Nature's violence overwhelmed both men is intended to emphasize the physical results of Nature's violence.

4. **D; DOK Level:** 2; **Reading Assessment Targets:** R.3.2, R.3.3, R.3.4, R.3.5. The situation is likely to change the relationship between the men. They must help each other or die. They are not likely to shoot each other now that they need each other. In fact, they are likely to realize the foolishness of their feud, not elevate its significance. Although they may wish to tend to each other's wounds, it is unlikely that either man will be able to do so, given that both are held captive under the tree.

5. **A; DOK Level:** 2; **Reading Assessment Targets:** R.3.2, R.3.3, R.3.4. The men do not kill each other because they care about a code of propriety. Nature cares nothing for such codes; it simply acts without regard for feelings or consequences, making it more deadly than humans. Nature and humankind are deadly enemies, but they rely on each other for survival, as well.

6. **D; DOK Level:** 3; **Reading Assessment Targets:** R.2.7, R.3.3. The men are single-mindedly focused on their feud, so they ignore the storm, which endangers them. This situation is similar to the problem of people putting themselves and others in danger by ignoring storm warnings in favor of their own interests. The men are not in their current situation because of careless actions or a violent crime; they are the victims of a natural phenomenon. Although one man has more land than the other, the men seem to regard each other as equal partners in their feud; one is not bullying the other.

LESSON 22, pp. 44–45

1. **D; DOK Level:** 2; **Reading Assessment Targets:** R.2.6, R.2.7, R.3.3, R.3.4. Della and Jim each sacrifice a prized possession to buy a Christmas present, as a token of love, for the other. Answer A is incorrect; although Della may "worship" the combs, she chooses to sacrifice her hair to buy the watch chain for her husband. Answer B is incorrect because nothing suggests that Della and Jim's poverty brings hardship to the family. Answer C is incorrect because their sacrifices reveal that their love is strong despite poverty.

Answer Key

2. **C; DOK Level:** 2; **Reading Assessment Target:** R.2.6. Answer A may be accurate in some real situations, but Jeannette is not afraid of Donald in this passage, even though her mother might be. Answer B, too, may be true in real life, but nothing is mentioned in this passage about healing. Answer D can support the theme and is used as a comparison, but it is not the theme of the passage. Answer C is the correct answer because the war has affected Jeannette's family deeply.

3. **B; DOK Level:** 2; **Reading Assessment Targets:** R. 2.6, R.3.3. Answer A is incorrect because the theme is not about strip mining. Donald's feelings about his living arrangements are not mentioned, and his living arrangements are not the theme of the passage; even though he stays away from home occasionally, he may or may not feel trapped by living at home. Although he may feel as though he cannot explain his feelings to Jeannette, his inability to do so is not the theme of the passage. Answers A, C, and D all support the theme, but Donald's moodiness and depression stem directly from his experience in Vietnam, not from the other situations in his life, for which his war experiences are also responsible.

4. **A; DOK Level:** 3; **Reading Assessment Targets:** R.2.6, R.3.3, R.4.3/L.4.3, R.5.1. Answer A best supports the theme that war destroys what is valuable. Donald compares strip mining with American action in Vietnam to explain that both destroy what is best in the land and the human spirit. Although strip mining and war may be productive for the industries involved, answer B is incorrect because it does not address the destruction that both activities cause. Answer C misinterprets the comparison; there was no strip mining in Vietnam. Answer D, too, misinterprets the comparison, which is between strip mining and war, not about soldiers trying to help.

5. **B; DOK Level:** 3; **Reading Assessment Targets:** R.2.6, R.3.3, R.3.4, R.5.1, R.5.2. Answer B is correct because it contrasts Donald in better times and helps describe the changes in him. Answer A is incorrect because Jeanette's past is not related to the theme. Answer C is incorrect because paragraph 3 does not mention strip mining, nor is it part of the theme. Answer D is incorrect because the theme in this passage is not about violence. Although the incorrect answer choices may support the theme in some way, they are not the best responses to this question because they provide partial support rather than address the bigger picture.

6. **A; DOK Level:** 3; **Reading Assessment Targets:** R.2.6, R.2.7. At the end of paragraph 2, Donald is satisfied that the coal companies have to plant trees and bushes to replace what they have taken from the land and wonders if they could have left Vietnam "in better shape." Nothing in the passage supports Donald's agreement or disagreement with the other statements.

LESSON 23, *pp. 46–47*

1. **A; DOK Level:** 2; **Reading Assessment Target:** R.2.8. Answer A is the only logical conclusion to draw on the basis of the details in the passage. Despite the summer heat, Laird needs blankets, people are shocked by his appearance, and they are saddened by his condition. Answers B and C are incorrect because no reference is made to Laird's attitude toward his treatment nor to Janet's knowledge of current medicine. Answer D is incorrect because, although plausible, no references are made as to Janet's feelings about her friends' visits.

2. **DOK Level:** 2; **Reading Assessment Target:** R.2.8. In the first two lines of the passage *this* and *it* refer to details mentioned later in the passage: "to build a fire" and "His wet feet froze the faster." Therefore, the man must **build a fire** to **warm** his wet feet or eventually he will freeze to death.

3. **DOK Level:** 3; **Reading Assessment Targets:** R.2.7, R.2.8, R.3.3, R.3.4, R.3.5. The man's blood flow is slowing down: "it ebbed away and sank down into the recesses of his body." The slowing blood flow results in numbness and insensitivity in the man's extremities. These conditions are symptoms of **hypothermia**, or a condition of abnormally low body temperature. It is sufficient to indicate that the character is suffering from **extreme and dangerous exposure to cold**.

4. **DOK Level:** 2; **Reading Assessment Targets:** R.2.7, R.2.8, R.3.4, R.3.5. The man's moccasins are coated with ice as is the spruce tree under which he builds his fire. The warmth of his fire and his pulling twigs off the tree lead to the **snow**'s falling from the tree and **putting out the fire.**

LESSON 24, *pp. 48–49*

1. **A; DOK Level:** 3; **Reading Assessment Targets:** R.2.7, R.2.8, R.3.5. On the basis of the information in the passage, answer A is the most logical choice. Paul is awestruck by the singer; he sees her not as a middle-aged mother but as a romantic heroine. He spends hours at the hotel in which singers and actors stay. The passage indicates that he is not interested in the music or in school, so answer B is not the best choice. Answer C is incorrect because nothing is mentioned about Paul's abilities, even though he enjoys the atmosphere of a concert hall or theater. Nor is anything mentioned about Paul's ambitions.

2. **B; DOK Level:** 3; **Reading Assessment Targets:** R.2.7, R.3.4. Answer B is correct because the executive, like Leo, is probably thought of as knowledgable and sophisticated, yet he or she does not know how to do what the others do easily. Both are out of place in rural surroundings. Answer A is incorrect because the areas are reversed (the person is going to the city not away from it) and is doing so for pleasure. Answer C is incorrect because the city person knows something about farm animals; Leo is not shown as knowing anything about the country. Answer D is incorrect because Leo is not doing work while on vacation.

3. **B; DOK Level: 3; Reading Assessment Targets:** R.2.7, R.3.4, R.4.1/L.4.1, R.4.3/L.4.3. Answer B is correct because the tone implies that Leo has disliked other picnics and will continue to dislike them, especially because of having to carry the basket. The connotation of *hauled out* implies that Leo is going against his will and would rather do something else. Answers A and D are incorrect because nothing in the passage indicates that Leo will arrange his own picnic or ask to reschedule the event. Answer C may seem plausible, but it is not the best choice on the basis of the tone of the passage. Leo is complaining and criticizing; he is neither planning to refuse nor thinking about refusing to carry the basket.

4. **C; DOK Level: 3; Reading Assessment Targets:** R.2.7, R.3.3, R.3.5. Answer C is correct because Mrs. Leslie is someone who seems to brag about her possessions to raise her status in the eyes of her son-in-law. Extending this information leads to answer C. Answers A, B, and D contradict the information in the passage because Mrs. Leslie is not likely to be secretive, modest, or anonymous if the subject is money or status.

5. **A; DOK Level: 3; Reading Assessment Targets:** R.2.7, R.3.3, R.3.5. Answer A is the most probable choice because Leo likes luxury and city comforts rather than "roughing it." Given his mother-in-law's character, Leo probably would prefer being away from family. Answers B and C involve the outdoors and conditions that are opposite of those of city life and luxury. Answer D is not the best choice because nothing in the passage indicates that Leo would enjoy or not enjoy staying home and watching old movies.

6. **C; DOK Level: 3; Reading Assessment Targets:** R.2.7, R.3.3. Although all answer choices are possible, answer C represents the best choice because it addresses plot in general rather than events in this story. Many answer choices require you to be as specific as possible, but here the broader answer is a better choice because it encompasses the other answers. Answers A, B, and D represent guesswork, but answer C includes any event, in keeping with Leo's disagreeable thoughts, that might happen to him.

UNIT 1 REVIEW, pp. 50–57

1. **B; DOK Level: 2; Reading Assessment Target:** R.4.2/L.4.2. The phrase contributes to a sarcastic, humorous tone. People over 30 are far from being geriatrics. The author jokes that young people have a skewed view of age. This tone continues throughout the passage. If the author had used the word *people* instead, the tone would become less ironic and more detached. The tone would not become more casual even though *people* is a more frequently used word. The humor throughout the passage keeps the tone from being formal and academic or professional and detached.

2. **D; DOK Level: 2; Reading Assessment Targets:** R.2.1, R.2.5. The author categorizes millennials as young people with new tastes in movies. Although millennials are not precisely defined by age, readers can assume that millennials are approximately 30 years old or younger. Their tastes in movies are described as different from those of older "boomer" audiences. Millennials prefer innovation and novelty, not old movies. Although they may not like older movies, they do like new movies, particularly those that are "bigger, faster, louder." The author discusses viewers, not filmmakers.

3. **A; DOK Level: 2; Reading Assessment Targets:** R.2.1, R.2.5, R.3.4. The author says that millennials think new movies are better than older movies, whereas boomers do not think movies made in their generation are necessarily better than older movies. Many boomers see movies as art and as entertainment. Although some boomers are fanatical about old movies, the author does not say that all boomers are fanatical. The author says that millennials like movies that are big and fast, but he does not say that boomers do not like these movies.

4. **B; DOK Level: 2; Reading Assessment Target:** R.2.2. The author describes Andrew Sarris as someone who believed that understanding movie history was an important part of loving movies, both old and new. Answer A is a misreading—Sarris did not bring directors from France to the United States; he brought their films. Although the author mentions that Sarris imported the auteur theory from France, this information is not the author's main point; it is a detail. The author does not directly suggest that Sarris helped establish film studies.

5. **DOK Level: 3; Reading Assessment Targets:** R.2.4, R.2.5, R.3.4. The completed chart should read: **Old movies often demean women, Old movies are slow paced,** and **Old movies use few special effects.** These are reasons the author either states or implies to explain why young people do not like old movies and find them passé. The indication that old movies are politically incorrect includes the implication that women are treated as they were during the time the films were made. One reason for considering old movies primitive is that they use few special effects. They are slow paced because of this lack as well as their intentions to show drama and human conflict rather than "action."

6. **C; DOK Level: 2; Reading Assessment Targets:** R.6.1, R.6.3. It is clear that the author likes old movies and regrets that young people do not appreciate them. It is not clear that he thinks old movies are better than new movies, and he does not believe that old movies are popular with millennials. Although the author may want old movies to be protected from obsolescence, this statement is too narrow to explain the author's point of view.

7. **DOK Level: 3; Reading Assessment Targets:** R.2.3, R.2.7. The author most likely **supports** the teaching of film history. He most likely believes that teaching film history exposes people to old movies.

8. **DOK Level: 2; Reading Assessment Target:** R.4.1/L.4.1. The word is defined as **old-fashioned, outdated** in the text that follows its appearance: "technically primitive, politically incorrect, narratively dull, slowly paced: in short, old-fashioned."

9. **A; DOK Level: 2; Reading Assessment Target:** R.2.7. The author generalizes that young people today like novelty. He claims that young people have a fascination with the present and want movies that are new and cool. Although some young people may love the films of Hawks and Hitchcock, answer B is incorrect because the author does not claim that all young people love them. In fact, he implies that most do not. Answer C is incorrect because the author states that millennials "don't seem to think of movies as art ... " Although he discusses the remaking of *Spider-Man*, he does not claim that young people like remakes more than previous generations like them; therefore answer D is incorrect.

Answer Key

UNIT 1 (continued)

10. **B; DOK Level: 2; Reading Assessment Targets:** R.2.1, R.2.5. These details support the idea that the United States is a place of great natural beauty and that this beauty is a source of its greatness. These aspects of the country are as important as industry and economic wealth, but Johnson does not say that they are more important. Although industrialization may have hurt these aspects of the United States, Johnson does not claim that they have been destroyed. These details are not used to compare the current landscape with how it looked when Johnson was a boy.

11. **DOK Level: 2; Reading Assessment Target:** R.3.4. People living in the United States have neglected the importance of **preserving** the beauty of nature. Johnson says that people have placed a "wall of civilization" between themselves and the beauty of the land; Americans have "relegated nature to a weekend role."

12. **D; DOK Level: 3; Reading Assessment Targets:** R.4.3/L.4.3, R.5.1, R.6.3. Johnson most likely includes the image of himself stretched out on the grass and viewing the stars as a way to make his speech more personal and to create an image with a strong emotional appeal to listeners. Many listeners have experienced something similar when young, and the image has a sentimental appeal. The highway bill will not specifically make this type of experience possible, but it will contribute to a broader appreciation of nature's beauty. Mentioning his experience as a young boy is less about appealing to young people than about appealing to listeners who remember similar experiences from their youth. In fact, few, if any, young people would be in the audience at the occasion of a bill signing. His point is not that nature used to be unspoiled. Rather, it is about keeping it unspoiled and ensuring that it is appreciated.

13. **B; DOK Level: 2; Reading Assessment Targets:** R.2.3, R.2.4, R.5.1, R.6.3. Johnson implies that because highways were built with public money, they should serve the interests of the public, not of businesses. The government spent public money collected from taxpayers to build the highways. He does not suggest that businesses need to contribute more to the building of highways, nor does he suggest that the public has spent too much money on highways. All highways are built with public money, so answer D is not logical.

14. **C; DOK Level: 3; Reading Assessment Targets:** R.2.3, R.2.5, R.5.1, R.5.2, R.6.3. These details of what Johnson sees contrast with the unsightly manufactured objects that line many other highways. Johnson describes the type of scene that he wishes to see along highways. Although the image may imply an autumn scene, pointing out the season is not Johnson's purpose in describing the trees. Johnson is less concerned with describing the specific highway than with providing an image of the type of scene he hopes will be created by the new highway bill after it is implemented. Answer D incorrectly indicates that the bill has been implemented.

15. **A; DOK Level: 2; Reading Assessment Targets:** R.2.2, R.2.8. Johnson would like America's highways to have more trees and flowers and fewer billboards and junkyards. He does not promote the idea of planting a specific type of tree, nor does he address the issue of potholes and lighting. Johnson likely supports American industries, but his goal is to encourage more nature near highways, not more industries lining them.

16. **C; DOK Level: 3; Reading Assessment Targets:** R.2.7, R.2.8. Johnson would likely have supported a bill to plant and maintain public gardens. This concept is closest to the highway bill in that it preserves nature. Answers A and D are incorrect because both would require nature to be destroyed. Answer B is incorrect because Johnson is opposed to advertising on highways, not in newspapers.

17. **D; DOK Level: 3; Reading Assessment Targets:** R.2.7, R.2.8. A bill to preserve the natural beauty of beaches would be most similar to the one described in the speech. This bill would address preserving the beauty of nature so that people could enjoy the experience. Improving air quality in cities would address environmental issues, but this option is less closely related to the appearance of nature. Reducing speed limits on highways and increasing funding for highway repairs might improve highway conditions but would not address the issue of preserving the beauty of nature.

18. **D; DOK Level: 2; Reading Assessment Targets:** R.3.3, R.6.1. Answer D is correct because the narrator uses third-person pronouns to tell the story. Answers A and B are incorrect because both characters are referred to in third-person pronouns, by name, or by relationship. Answer C is incorrect because the narrator is not a character in the story.

19. **C; DOK Level: 3; Reading Assessment Targets:** R.3.3, R.3.4, R.5.1, R.5.4. Answer C is the best choice. If Framton knew the aunt or many people in the town, he would know that the story the niece is about to tell him could not be true. Answers A and B are incorrect because nothing in the story indicates that the niece or the aunt is curious about his reasons for being there, and no one is interested in the details of his illness, as indicated in paragraph 14. Answer D is more plausible, but because the conversation does not continue with small talk, it is not as good a choice as answer C.

20. **DOK Level: 1: Reading Assessment Target:** R.3.1. The sequence of events is as follows, as indicated in the text: **Framton's sister stays at the rectory. The "tragedy" takes place. The niece explains why the window remains open. Framton acts as though he has seen a ghost.**

21. **D; DOK Level: 2; Reading Assessment Targets:** R.3.2, R.3.5. Answer D is the best choice because it refers to letters of introduction, which were written as a way to introduce people, particularly when one moved to a new location. In this case, Framton's sister provides him with such letters so that he will meet people while he rests and be invited to social events. At the time the story takes place, telephones were not in wide use, particularly in rural areas. Answer A is incorrect because tea may be served at various times during the day (especially in England) and does not indicate an outdated custom. Answer B makes no reference to anything relevant to time, nor does the weather in answer C.

22. C; DOK Level: 2; Reading Assessment Targets: R.4.1/L.4.1, R.4.3/L.4.3. Answer C is correct because the expression describes the shock and fear that someone would experience upon seeing something unbelievable. Although someone might turn pale, the pallor would come as a result of shock; furthermore, the expression "pale as a ghost" should not be confused with the similar expression Mrs. Sappleton uses. Answer B is incorrect because "seeing a ghost" does not indicate nervousness. In fact, Framton is nervous throughout the story and is in the village because of his nerves. His abrupt exit indicates far more than nervousness. Although ghosts may be thought of as invisible, the expression refers to Framton, who is not invisible.

23. C; DOK Level: 2; Reading Assessment Targets: R.2.8, R.3.2. Answer C is correct. She has just frightened an adult guest with a highly detailed and believable story and continues, at the end, to improvise another tale explaining Framton's departure. Answer A is a misreading of the passage; Framton is the character recovering from an illness. Answer B is not as good a choice as answer C because nothing about the niece's behavior indicates that she is selfish or seeks attention. If answer C were correct, she likely would talk about herself or make demands on others. Answer D is not supported in the text; most likely she is not acquainted with Framton's sister who spent time in the village four years earlier when the niece would have been 11 years old.

24. D; DOK Level: 2; Reading Assessment Targets: R.2.8, R.3.3, R.3.4. Answer D best explains Framton's reasons for leaving as he does. The niece's story is vivid and accurately detailed; when Framton sees the men arrive, they are exactly as the niece has described them. In his fragile state of mind, Framton is likely to be frightened easily. Answers A and C are less likely to cause someone to bolt out of the door so suddenly. A cold room or an inattentive hostess might cause visitors to leave but not as if they had seen a ghost. Answer B is a misreading of the story. The niece invents the tale in paragraph 22 to explain Framton's sudden departure and perhaps to avoid explaining her role in causing it.

25. B; DOK Level: 2; Reading Assessment Target: R.2.6. Answer B is correct because the accuracy and detail of the niece's story, as well as her self-possession, convince Framton that the men actually disappeared. He has no reason to doubt her and continues to believe her even when the men return. In fact, he believes her tale more than he believes what he sees. Answer A is incorrect because no evidence in the story indicates that this generalization is accurate. Although Framton seems gullible, readers do not know whether he does believe everything he is told, nor can they infer that his gullibility results from his condition. Answer C is incorrect because nothing in the story suggests that the niece will be punished. No one seems upset by Framton's departure, nor is there any indication that the aunt and uncles are angry with the niece for frightening him with her story; in fact, they do not know that she has told it. Answer D, too, is incorrect. The story causes Framton to believe he has seen ghosts and to flee the house in a panic. Although the incident creates mental excitement, which Framton's doctor has ordered him to avoid, nothing suggests worsening of his condition or severe damage.

26. C; DOK Level: 2; Reading Assessment Targets: R.3.2, R.3.5. From the "impressiveness" with which the policeman patrols his beat and the fact that no one is watching him, readers can infer that the policeman does his work with enthusiasm. He is not showing off or exerting "power." Rather he seems to take his job seriously and seems anything but nervous. Nothing is mentioned about overtime or earning extra money. Answer D is a contradiction of information in the story; no one is watching him, and there is no one to impress.

27. D; DOK Level: 3; Reading Assessment Targets: R.3.2, R.3.5. Answer A is possible, but it is not the best answer once the story has been read; the story is not a mystery, although the ending may come as a surprise. Answer B contradicts the narrative: Jimmy does arrive for the meeting. Answer C may be plausible, but answer D is more accurate. Although this meeting was arranged years ago, both characters end up greatly disappointed and saddened by the turn of events. The weather parallels their emotions.

28. DOK Level: 2; Reading Assessment Targets: R.2.2, R.3.2, R.3.4. Jimmy—**police officer, sensitive, honest**. Bob—**criminal, ambitious, adventurous**. Both—**from New York, keeps appointment**. Jimmy is honest because he must—and does—arrest his friend and is sensitive because he cannot do it himself, thinking that such an act would be inconsiderate, at best. The text indicates that Bob is a criminal known as "Silky Bob." He is ambitious and adventurous because he left New York to make his fortune, traveling to unknown destinations where opportunity invited. The narrative mentions that both grew up as brothers in New York; obviously, both keep the appointment, although not as expected.

29. D; DOK Level: 2; Reading Assessment Targets: R.3.2, R.3.3, R.3.4. Bob is too occupied talking and does not notice that the police officer is his friend. Although nothing is mentioned about Bob's having a poor memory for faces, he certainly remembers the date. Therefore, answer A is incorrect. Answer B is incorrect as well because nothing is mentioned about his vision. Neither character sees in the dark, but Jimmy sees Bob's face when Bob lights the match. Although Bob may be dishonest, he does not lie about his reasons for waiting in the doorway.

30. C; DOK Level: 2; Reading Assessment Targets: R.3.1, R.3.2. The climax of a story is its turning point. Events lead to this point and then resolve themselves. The story events have led to the arranged appointment, made 20 years ago. The climax is Bob's realization that the man is not Jimmy. Answers A and B are part of the exposition and background. Answer D is part of the resolution, or falling action. Although the ending is a surprise, it is not the turning point of the story; rather, it explains the events and why they happened as they did.

31. B; DOK Level: 2; Reading Assessment Targets: R.3.2, R.4.3/L.4.3, R.5.1. Bob has become a criminal and not the man Jimmy knew when they parted. Although he cares for his friend, Jimmy cannot accept that Bob has chosen a life of crime, and the portrait of the wanted man has more significance than the memory of the man Jimmy knew. Jimmy notices the scar, which seems to aid, not hinder, recognition. Bob's financial success may have altered his character, but it has not altered his face. That Bob disappointed Jimmy has nothing to do with Jimmy's recognizing his face.

Answer Key

UNIT 1 (continued)

32. B; DOK Level: 2; **Reading Assessment Target:**
R.2.6. Answer B is correct because each man sees himself and the other differently—both accurately and not. Bob sees himself as financially successful and sees Jimmy as a plodder, whereas Jimmy sees himself as honest and content with his life and sees Bob for what he is. Answer A might be applicable, but nothing indicates that Bob was unhappy about leaving home. Although the friends did not keep in touch for reasons that Bob explains, the separation itself is not part of the story's theme. Answer D is incorrect because the friends do keep the appointment.

33. A; DOK Level: 3; **Reading Assessment Targets:**
R. 2.7, R.2.8. Answer A is the best choice because Jimmy must make the difficult decision to arrest his friend, who was like a brother. This decision is similar to a parent who must do something that will cause unpleasantness or misery to a child for the best interests of that child or others. Answer B is incorrect because no anger is mentioned in the story. Answer C is incorrect because only Bob brags. Answer D is incorrect because nothing is mentioned about aging or shock at the other's appearance.

UNIT 2 ARGUMENT ANALYSIS AND TEXT COMPARISON

LESSON 1, pp. 60–61

1. D; DOK Level: 2; **Reading Assessment Targets:** R.2.5, R.6.1, R.8.2. All of the answers relate to the flu or flu shots, but answer D states in the clearest and strongest terms why readers should get a flu shot—"Flu shots are the most effective way to prevent influenza." Answer A states the flu shot is not always effective, which does not convincingly support the idea that readers should get flu shots. Answer B does support the argument in favor of getting a flu shot by telling readers about what the flu shot protects against, but it is not as strong a statement as answer D. Answer C provides information about influenza but no information about the value of the flu shot.

2. D; DOK Level: 2; **Reading Assessment Target:**
R.6.1. The author argues that education and other social institutions, such as churches and families, are the most important factors in determining whether a person will rise out of poverty. The author begins by noting how much the government spends fighting poverty through social services. However, he goes on to write that these programs alone do not succeed in lifting people out of poverty, so answer A is incorrect. The author includes facts about how much the government spends to fight poverty, but these facts are only one part of an argument, so answer B is incorrect. The author includes the information about graduation rates to support the argument that education is a key factor in determining movement into the middle class, so answer C is also incorrect. Answer D accurately summarizes the author's viewpoint.

3. A; DOK Level: 2; **Reading Assessment Target:** R.6.1. The author argues that education is a key factor in determining whether a person will overcome poverty. He argues that social services and government programs have not succeeded in reducing or eliminating poverty. Answer A best summarizes this opinion. Answer B states the opposing viewpoint that social programs should be expanded to fight poverty. Answer C mentions graduation rates, but the author includes the facts about graduation rates to show that education, not the number of services a person receives, is the factor that most affects whether a person will overcome poverty. Answer D takes the author's position too far. Although he does not think that government programs are the answer to poverty, the author does believe that the government should help "those who are poor largely at no fault of their own."

4. C; DOK Level: 2; **Reading Assessment Targets:** R.6.1, R.6.2. Although the author states that liberals and conservatives recognize poverty as a problem, answer A misstates the author's words. The author does mention amounts of money spent fighting poverty, but these figures do not address the fact that both liberals and conservatives comprise his audience. Therefore, answer B is incorrect. Answer C is correct because the author acknowledges the liberal viewpoint and then presents his own logical counterargument. Answer D is incorrect because although he refers to past attempts to fight poverty, he does not mention political viewpoints other than conservative and liberal.

5. B; DOK Level: 3; **Reading Assessment Targets:** R.5.1, R.5.2, R.5.4. Although the paragraph does indicate some findings of the study, answer A is incorrect because the purpose of the last paragraph is broader than the mention of this information. Answer B is correct because it supports the author's viewpoint, explained in the previous paragraph: that education, employment, and mediating institutions are keys to upward mobility. Answer C is incorrect because the Brookings study and the Cato study mentioned in the first paragraph are not related. Answer D is incorrect because these percentages do not refer to the dollar amounts mentioned earlier.

LESSON 2, pp. 62–63

1. B; DOK Level: 2; **Reading Assessment Targets:** R.5.1, R.6.1, R.8.1. The author ends the passage by encouraging readers to support legislation for developing mass transit. Answer B best states this call to action. The passage does not encourage readers to take public transportation whenever possible (answer A), nor does it suggest that getting a job in mass transit will lead to a secure future (answer C). The passage argues that mass transit benefits even those who do not live in areas that have mass transit, so answer D is incorrect.

2. A; DOK Level: 2; **Reading Assessment Targets:** R.5.1, R.5.2, R.6.4, R.8.1. In the question "Why does this matter?" the word *this* refers to the extension of Medicaid. After this question, the author begins exploring the reasons and evidence that support his argument about the importance of extending Medicaid coverage for former foster youth. Answer A is correct. Answers B, C, and D do not make sense in the context of the passage.

3. C; DOK Level: 2; Reading Assessment Targets: R.5.1, R.8.1, R.8.2. The main claim is that extending Medicaid is one necessary provision to help former foster youth until they reach the age of 26. Answer C, therefore, is the best choice. Answer A is incorrect because it is too broad a statement; the claim itself could be part of that statement. Answer B is incorrect because it is a piece of evidence supporting the problems that former foster youth face. Answer D is incorrect because the passage is not about homelessness; homelessness is another of the problems that former foster youth may face.

4. D; DOK Level: 2; Reading Assessment Targets: R.5.1, R.5.4, R.6.1, R.8.1. In this passage, the author tries to persuade readers that Medicaid coverage should be extended to former foster youth until they are 26 years old. Paragraph 5 explains the challenges former foster youth face in order to emphasize that having health insurance is one way to make their lives easier (answer D). The paragraph does not contrast the lives of former foster youth with the lives of those in permanent homes (answer A), nor does it state that former foster youth are more likely to need health services (answer B). Although the author is arguing that former foster youth should have health insurance, the paragraph does not explain how the lack of coverage affects them (answer C).

5. B; DOK Level: 2; Reading Assessment Targets: R.8.1, R.8.6. Throughout the passage, the author presents details showing how difficult the lives of foster youth can be, especially after they grow out of the foster system. Answer B is correct. Answer A is incorrect because although the author states that it is society's responsibility to take care of foster youth, he does not scold readers. Answers C and D are incorrect because the author does not provide facts about the expenses of caring for foster youth or the costs of extending Medicaid. Furthermore, this evidence would be more logical than emotional.

LESSON 3, pp. 64–65

1. C; DOK Level: 2; Reading Assessment Targets: R.6.1, R.8.2. Photographs often appeal to readers' emotions. A photograph of trees cut down in a butterfly habitat would likely arouse readers' senses of fear and urgency, so answer C is correct. A photo would not prove that the number of butterflies is decreasing (answer A) or that the conservation group is a credible source of information (answer B). In addition, a photo would not give information that would counter claims that butterfly populations are growing (answer D).

2. B; DOK Level: 2; Reading Assessment Targets: R.2.5, R.3.5, R.5.1, R.8.1, R.8.2. The fact that intelligence agencies never uncovered disloyal activities, such as espionage, by Japanese Americans shows that Japanese Americans did nothing to deserve evacuation and thus were evacuated without cause. The other answer choices reflect facts the author provides in the letter, but none of these facts supports the idea that Japanese Americans were evacuated without cause. Answer A notes how many Japanese Americans were evacuated. Answers C and D explain consequences of the evacuation.

3. D; DOK Level: 2; Reading Assessment Targets: R.3.5, R.5.1, R.8.1, R.8.2. The author discusses the outstanding service of Japanese Americans to show that Japanese American troops were brave and patriotic. Although the passage implies that evacuees may have made greater sacrifices than other Americans, this implication does not relate to Japanese Americans' record of service (answer A). Although the author appreciates what the Armed Forces did, he does not mention Japanese Americans' service to express appreciation (answer B). Answer C is incorrect because the passage does not mention the number of men among the evacuees.

4. A; DOK Level: 2; Reading Assessment Targets: R.2.2, R.8.1, R.8.2. The evidence in paragraph 3 shows that the evacuation was hasty, and, as a result, Japanese Americans suffered financial losses (answer A). The evidence does not suggest that more planning would have helped the evacuation run more smoothly (answer B) or that Japanese Americans had trouble determining the value of their possessions (answer D). Although one sentence suggests that evacuees might have been forced to leave their property with people they did not trust, accepting "inadequate arrangements" is only one fact among the evidence presented, so answer C is incorrect.

5. C; DOK Level: 2; Reading Assessment Targets: R.5.4, R.8.1, R.8.2. The author presents facts that build to the claim that the United States should "offer some degree of compensation for the losses the evacuees suffered." Answer C, therefore, is correct. The author does not mention his position as Secretary of the Interior to persuade readers (answer A). Answer B is incorrect because he does not begin by stating a claim or use personal stories. The author uses facts, so answer D is incorrect.

LESSON 4, pp. 66–67

1. B; DOK Level: 3; Reading Assessment Targets: R.2.7, R.7.2. After reading this passage, a reader with a fear of needles would learn that he or she could receive the flu vaccine without getting an injection. The other answer choices represent people who, according to the table, should receive the injection rather than the nasal spray.

2. D; DOK Level: 3; Reading Assessment Targets: R.7.2, R.8.2. The author claims that Oregon has "broad areas of undeveloped farming land" and "idle acres." The background shows unoccupied land that looks as though it could be farmed, so answer D best explains how the picture supports the claim. Although the land in the picture looks green and healthy, a key part of the claim is that the land is also undeveloped, so answer A is not the best choice. The picture of the Oregon Agricultural College suggests a successful farming history in Oregon (answer B), but this suggestion does not relate to the claim about the land itself. Similarly, the well-established college suggests that newcomers would have support and resources (answer C), but this suggestion does not relate to the claim.

Answer Key

UNIT 2 (continued)

3. **A; DOK Level:** 3; **Reading Assessment Targets:** R.2.7, R.7.2. Readers considering a move to Oregon might have been reassured to see a well-established college there. The information suggests that the state had a significant population and community resources. The image of the college does not provide information about whether businesses are thriving throughout the state, so answer B is incorrect. The picture does not offer information about whether state agencies are committed to helping farmers (answer C), nor does it provide information about career options in Oregon other than farming (answer D).

4. **D; DOK Level:** 3; **Reading Assessment Target:** R.7.2. The passage encourages farmers to move to Oregon because of all the opportunity and support that await them in the state. The picture supports this message by providing an image that shows a well-established agricultural college surrounded by a healthy, green landscape. Answer D best expresses this relationship. Answer A is incorrect because the passage does not provide statistics about Oregon. Answer B is incorrect because the passage mentions the agricultural college only once and because the picture does not provide specific details about the campus. Answer C is incorrect because although the passage states that agencies are working to support agricultural interests, it does not explain how institutions and agencies work together.

LESSON 5, pp. 68–69

1. **D; DOK Level:** 2; **Reading Assessment Targets:** R.8.2, R.8.3, R.8.4, R.8.5. Answer D is correct because the number of people who cannot digest gluten properly does not relate to whether individuals will have more energy if they stop eating foods that contain gluten. The author does not use the fact to suggest an either/or situation (answer A), nor is it part of a bandwagon appeal (answer B). The author does not use strong language intended to frighten readers (answer C).

2. **DOK Level:** 2; **Reading Assessment Targets:** R.8.2, R.8.3, R.8.5. Irrelevant Information: **According to the American Pet Products Association, approximately 62 percent of American households own pets.** This sentence has nothing to do with supporting the shelter. Inaccurate either/or situation: **But without your financial support, other animals will not be so lucky.** The statement does not address alternatives to financial support. Bandwagon appeal: **Through the generosity of so many people like you, who care deeply about animals, we are able to help unfortunate creatures that cannot help themselves.** The sentence implies that the reader will want to be considered among the many people who care deeply about animals. Appeal to sympathy: **Can you imagine what it must feel like to find yourself in a strange place, without food or water, completely alone?** Readers will feel bad about the dog's situation and identify themselves or their pets in such conditions. Testimonial: **And our own hero, Damian Ferri, says "Supporting helpless animals has given me as much personal satisfaction as it has helped save abused and abandoned animals."** A local celebrity is saying that he donates, and readers may want to do what he does.

LESSON 6, pp. 70–71

1. **C; DOK Level:** 2; **Reading Assessment Targets:** R.8.2, R.8.3, R.8.4, R.8.5. The fact that the solar industry added 13,872 jobs supports the author's claim that developing solar energy is good for the economy. The statement in answer A is invalid evidence because it is not relevant. Answer B states part of the author's claim, so it is not evidence. The statement in answer D is invalid evidence because it does not offer data to show that employment in other industries is lagging or shrinking. In addition, at the end of the sentence, the author makes a broad generalization that does not acknowledge or consider opposing viewpoints.

2. **DOK Level:** 2; **Reading Assessment Targets:** R.8.3, R.8.4, R.8.5. Valid. **Dog trainer and author Brian Kilcommons explains, "mixed breed dogs are often healthier, longer-lived, more intelligent, and of more stable temperament than purebreds." Shelter workers have often observed that many shelter animals seem to sense what they were up against and become among the most devoted and grateful companions.** The two valid details directly support the claim and come from reliable sources—a dog trainer and author, who is an expert, and shelter workers who have experience in dealing with shelter animals. In addition, the quotation from Brian Kilcommons explains some of the reasons mixed-breed dogs can make better pets than purebred dogs. The experience of shelter workers also shows why shelter animals make good pets—they tend to be very devoted.

Invalid. **According to the Humane Society of the United States, mutts are America's dog of choice, accounting for nearly 60 percent of all pet dogs. Dogs, cats, and small mammals like guinea pigs, rabbits, and rats end up in shelters because of circumstances beyond their control.** The invalid details reflect faulty reasoning. Although the Humane Society of the United States is a reliable source, the fact that mutts are "America's dog of choice" is faulty reasoning. This fact is meant to appeal to readers by showing that mutts are popular (bandwagon appeal). The second detail is invalid because it is not relevant to the claim. The reasons animals end up in shelters do not relate to why a person should adopt a shelter pet.

LESSON 7, pp. 72–73

1. **C; DOK Level:** 2; **Reading Assessment Targets:** R.2.8, R.5.4, R.8.1. The refutation/proof structure would be the most effective way for the scientist to construct this argument because his or her claim states that another claim is inaccurate. In the argument, the scientist would state the inaccurate claim, state his or her objection to it, and then explain the reasons for believing the claim is inaccurate. Although the author could use one of the structures mentioned in answers A, B, and D, the refutation/proof structure still would be the most effective way to present the author's ideas.

2. **DOK Level:** 2; **Reading Assessment Targets:** R.5.2, R.8.1. Paragraph 1 **defines** *antibiotic resistance* and explains why it is dangerous. This background is necessary to understand the claim stated at the end of paragraph 2.

3. **B; DOK Level:** 2; **Reading Assessment Targets:**
R.2.5, R.5.2, R.5.4, R.8.1. The two paragraphs provide
evidence to support the claim that antibiotics need to be
used wisely. Answer B is correct. Answer A is incorrect;
although the statement does reflect the author's broad point
of view, the two paragraphs focus directly on misuse of
antibiotics. Answers C and D are possible results of misuse
of antibiotics; they do not state the author's main claim.

4. **D; DOK Level:** 3; **Reading Assessment Targets:** R.5.4,
R.8.1, R.8.6. The claim states that antibiotics need to be
used wisely; the evidence explains the dangers of misusing
antibiotics, and the call to action at the end of the passage
urges readers to use antibiotics responsibly. The elements
of the argument indicate that the author believes the misuse
of antibiotics is a serious problem that must be addressed.
Answer D is correct. The author does not discuss research
costs or anything related to funding, so answer A is
incorrect. The author does not make generalizations that
support the idea that infections are the greatest health
crisis the world currently faces, so answer B is incorrect.
Similarly, the author does not provide evidence showing
that, in general, organisms that adapt quickly are generally
extremely dangerous; therefore, answer C is incorrect.

LESSON 8, *pp. 74–75*
1. **B; DOK Level:** 2; **Reading Assessment Target:**
R.6.4. Of the devices listed in the answers, the one most
likely to persuade readers is enumeration of the diseases
caused by pollution (answer B). Answer A is incorrect
because an analogy explaining how pollution is produced
might help readers understand the process, but it would
not necessarily persuade them. Whether juxtaposition of
adjectives (answer C) would persuade readers depends on
the adjectives, so enumeration of the effects of pollution
would likely be a more effective means. Answer D is
incorrect because a qualifying statement saying that some
pollution is acceptable is unlikely to persuade readers.

2. **DOK Level:** 2; **Reading Assessment Targets:** R.6.1,
R.6.4. The author notes that "we have the ability to solve
this crisis and avoid the worst—though not all—of its
consequences." The phrase *though not all* is a **qualifying
statement**. The author wishes to emphasize that although
some of the consequences of global warming are avoidable,
some are not.

3. **C; DOK Level:** 3; **Reading Assessment Target:**
R.6.4. The quotation from Winston Churchill juxtaposes
opposites—"decided only to be undecided, resolved to be
irresolute, adamant for drift, solid for fluidity, all powerful
to be impotent"—to emphasize that leaders are not taking
action. Answer C is correct. Though the quotation does
repeat parallel phrases, repetition is not what makes it
effective, so answer A is not the best answer. Answer B
is incorrect because the author does not list the ways that
leaders acted with bravery during World War II. Answer D
is incorrect because the quotation does not include a
qualifying statement.

4. **D; DOK Level:** 2; **Reading Assessment Targets:**
R.4.3/L.4.3, R.6.4. By comparing global warming with a
fever, the author makes global warming sound like a serious
disease. Answer D is correct. Answer A is incorrect; the
analogy might be close, but the context does not suggest
that the solution is simple. Answer B is incorrect because
the analogy gives no information about whether the author
is a reliable source. Answer C is incorrect because the
analogy compares global warming with a fever; it does not
refer to those who deny global warming.

5. **A; DOK Level:** 2; **Reading Assessment Targets:** R.6.3,
R.6.4. Readers are likely to read the list of impacts of global
warming and believe that the problem is urgent. Answer A is
correct. Answer B is incorrect because the enumeration does
not refer to the causes of pollution but rather to the negative
effects of global warming. Answer C is incorrect because
the list of negative impacts is unlikely to reassure readers.
Answer D is incorrect because the enumeration is more likely
to make readers believe that the problem is urgent. Most
readers will not have any more or less of an idea of what to
do about global warming after reading the enumeration.

LESSON 9, *pp. 76–77*
1. **C; DOK Level:** 3; **Reading Assessment Targets:**
R.4.3/L.4.3, R.7.3, R.9.1/R.7.1. Shriver uses straightforward,
simple language, such as "ideas and beliefs" and "freedom,"
while Graves uses specific details of her experience and
descriptive language, such as "boulders to move" and
"floors to sweep" (answer C). Shriver's language cannot be
described as colorful, and Graves's account is personal and
moving, so her language is not stiff and formal. Therefore,
answer A is incorrect. Shriver's language is straightforward,
rather than poetic, and most of Graves's sentences are
not simple, so answer B is incorrect. Shriver's language is
not informal or chatty, and Graves's language is subdued,
rather than powerful and intimidating, so answer D is
incorrect.

2. **DOK Level:** 2; **Reading Assessment Targets:** R.7.3,
R.9.1/R.7.1. Shriver **appeals to American patriotism** by
emphasizing American ingenuity and enterprise and by
referring to individuality and personal responsibility. Other
statements reflect the appeal to patriotism as well. He
**emphasizes that the Peace Corps represents American
ideals and ingenuity** by emphasizing "American ideas and
beliefs" and "the American individual." Shriver **promotes
the Peace Corps by providing an overview of the
program.** He provides an explanation of a Peace Corps
worker's path and uses this explanation to promote his
view that the Peace Corps is "the working model of some
of the most basic and fundamental American ideas and
beliefs." Graves **describes the Peace Corps by providing
aspects of a specific experience.** She provides vivid
details of her experience as a Peace Corps volunteer, such
as how she "mix(es) the soil with air and cow manure." She
**has gained knowledge and experience from the Peace
Corps.** She provides images to help readers see and hear
another place with which she became familiar. Throughout
the passage, she mentions some of what she saw, did,
and learned, including the language. The imagery, such as
"barefooted grandmothers who carry 50-pound bags of flour
on their heads" allows readers to visualize the environment
in which Graves lived and worked. Graves **appeals to
human sympathy** by describing some of the conditions
surrounding her, such as disease and the plight of children.

Answer Key

UNIT 2 (continued)

LESSON 10, pp. 78–79

1. **B; DOK Level:** 3; **Reading Assessment Targets:** R.7.2, R.7.3, R.9.1/R.7.1. Both the letter and the floor plan show that the White House was unfinished when President Adams moved into it and still unfinished when President Jefferson moved in later. Answer A is incorrect because neither text mentions the present White House. Choosing answer A depends on prior knowledge because the letter and diagram make no reference to the present White House, nor does the question ask about it. Answer C is incorrect because the floor plan offers no specific details about the work that went into the White House. Answer D is incorrect because neither the letter nor the illustration mentions actual costs.

2. **C; DOK Level:** 3; **Reading Assessment Targets:** R.7.2, R.7.3, R.9.1/R.7.1. Answer C is correct because paragraph 1 of the passage summarizes Parks's activities, and most of the timeline lists her activities leading to the famous incident in 1955. Neither passage includes information spanning the entirety of Rosa Parks's life, nor does the passage present events in chronological order. Therefore, answer A is incorrect. Although answer B may seem plausible, the scope of the timeline is chronological information for a certain time span; the timeline does not include opinions about the person or events. Although both mention the Supreme Court decision, the decision is only a part of the scope in both.

3. **A; DOK Level:** 3; **Reading Assessment Targets:** R.7.2, R.7.3, R.9.1/R.7.1. Answer A is correct because both the passage and timeline focus on what Parks did before the famous incident on the bus in 1955. The passage emphasizes that the event was not spontaneous. The timeline confirms this information by listing Parks's actions for 12 years before the event. Answer B is not the best choice; although the passage indicates that Parks was involved in civil rights activities for 12 years before 1955, those years are mentioned to support the idea that the 1955 event was not spontaneous. Answer C is incorrect because the timeline offers no opinions. Answer D is incorrect because only some of the information—not all of it—is the same. This answer choice may be partially correct, but answer A is the better choice.

4. **B; DOK Level:** 3; **Reading Assessment Targets:** R.7.3, R.9.1/R.7.1. Paragraph 1 mentions some of the same information listed in the timeline, so answer B is correct. Although paragraph 1 mentions some other events, the information does not contradict the information in the timeline; rather it adds to it. Therefore, answer A is incorrect. Answer C is incorrect because neither lists or omits all events in Parks's life. Answer D is incorrect because the author does not present his opinions in paragraph 1.

LESSON 11, pp. 80–81

1. **B; DOK Level:** 3; **Reading Assessment Targets:** R.9.1/R.7.1, R.9.2. Roosevelt focuses on the need for work and security (which the government would help provide), and Kennedy focuses on new challenges, so answer B is the best choice. Prior knowledge may help somewhat here if you know that Roosevelt was elected during the Great Depression when many people lost their life savings and were unemployed. Neither author implies that the American people have been unwilling to contribute to the success of the nation, so answer A is incorrect. Answer C is incorrect because strength is not a focus, nor does Kennedy focus on security. Answer D is incorrect because Kennedy asks his audience to go beyond security.

2. **DOK Level:** 3; **Reading Assessment Targets:** R.9.1/7.1, R.9.2. Kennedy—Perspective: **Federal government must lead in areas of technology, foreign relations, and human rights**; Structure: **implied comparison with pioneer spirit**; Overall impact: **Audience is excited by new challenges**. Roosevelt—Perspective: **Local and federal government must aid the American people in times of need**; Structure: **solution to current problems**; Overall impact: **Audience is hopeful for end to distress**. Both—Style: **parallelism**; **repetition of key words**; **strong, patriotic language**; Style: **strong, stirring language**; Tone: **forceful, optimistic, patriotic**; Immediate purpose: **to persuade audience to support candidate and his ideas**; Long-range purpose: **to be elected president**

LESSON 12 pp. 82–83

1. **A; DOK Level:** 3; **Reading Assessment Target:** R.7.3. The author of the news article reports on the fluoride debate in Portland, Oregon, so the purpose of the news article is to explain the reason for the debate and its effects on voters. The author of the editorial explains why the fluoridation of Portland's water is dangerous, so the purpose of the editorial is to present an argument against fluoridation. Answer B is incorrect because neither statement in the answer choice reflects the information in the passages. Answer C is incorrect because the editorial does not mention the necessity of fluoridation, merely its dangers. Answer D is incorrect because the article does not attempt to persuade.

2. **A; DOK Level:** 3; **Reading Assessment Target:** R.7.3. The article does not directly address a specific audience, nor do the author's comments seem to be aimed at any specific group. It is written for a general audience who would read *The Wall Street Journal*. However, the editorial is written to persuade voters to vote against the fluoridation of Portland's water, so the intended audience is Portland voters. Answer B reverses the options in answer A and is, therefore, incorrect. Answer C is incorrect even though the audiences mentioned might read the passages. The target groups are too narrow. Answer D is incorrect because nothing in the article indicates an attempt at persuasion, and the editorial is written for voters; in fact, those who oppose fluoridation do not need to be persuaded.

3. D; DOK Level: 2; Reading Assessment Target: R.6.2. Most of the editorial addresses reasons not to fluoridate Portland's water; however, answer D mentions promoters of fluoridation. This detail in the passage shows that the author acknowledges those who support water fluoridation. Answers A, B, and C do not address an opposing viewpoint.

4. B; DOK Level: 3; Reading Assessment Targets: R.7.3, R.8.2. The authors of both texts use direct quotations to support their ideas. The quotations add to the credibility of the authors' ideas by showing that the authors have researched the issues. The quotations also add to the force of the authors' messages, providing striking commentary. Answer A is incorrect because the purpose of these passages is not to entertain. Although answer C is plausible, the authors are not necessarily experts on the topic of fluoridation; the quoted sources are. For this reason, answer B is a better choice. Answer D may or may not result from the included quotations; although they are expert opinions, readers may or may not be motivated. The purpose of the article is to inform, not to persuade.

LESSON 13, pp. 84–85

1. A; DOK Level: 3; Reading Assessment Targets: R.7.4, R.9.1/R.7.1. Both texts indicate that half of the hits to the head take place during football practice, which could be made safer by eliminating contact drills. The second text goes further to explain that to avoid head injury, NFL teams rarely hit in practice. The second text, by suggesting that youth teams do the same, implies that youth teams are not taking the same safety measures as NFL teams. Answer B reflects information implied only in the second passage. Answers C and D show a misreading of the texts.

2. C; DOK Level: 3; Reading Assessment Targets: R.7.4, R.9.1/R.7.1. In the first passage, the comment about boxers' not wanting to give up their careers and their high pay over head injuries suggests that NFL players feel the same way. Point 10 in the second passage also implies that football players are pressured by the sport's culture to play through their injuries. Nothing in either text suggests answer choice A, B, or D.

3. B; DOK Level: 3; Reading Assessment Targets: R.7.4, R.9.1/R.7.1. Both authors reveal that they believe athletes should not play through their injuries and should seek immediate medical attention to avoid brain damage. Answer A reflects the opposite perspective of the authors. Answer C is incorrect because nothing in either passage suggests that the authors are qualified medical practitioners. Likewise, contacting the media seems extreme and less important than getting immediate medical attention.

4. D; DOK Level: 3; Reading Assessment Targets: R.7.4, R.9.1/R.7.1. The first text, in paragraph 2, warns that players should not put such trust in their helmets so that they use their heads as battering rams. Point 3 of the second text suggests that protective equipment must be reevaluated and changed to reduce brain trauma. Both suggestions can lead to the conclusion that football players perform intentional helmet-to-helmet hits because they put too much faith in their equipment, taking unnecessary risks on the field. Answers A, B, and C reflect a misreading of the texts.

UNIT 2 REVIEW, pp. 86–93

1. B; DOK Level: 2; Reading Assessment Targets: R.5.1, R.6.1, R.8.1, R.8.6. The authors begin by providing background information because they assume that readers will be unfamiliar with the problem of ocean acidification. Answer B is correct. Answer A is incorrect because although the authors refer to carbon absorption in the atmosphere, the first three paragraphs do not compare and contrast carbon absorption in the atmosphere and in the ocean. Answer C is incorrect because the authors do not discuss the different ways in which human activities affect the oceans. The authors do not provide background information because they assume that readers will disagree with their claims, so answer D is incorrect.

2. A; DOK Level: 2; Reading Assessment Targets: R.5.1, R.5.2, R.7.2, R.8.2. The data in paragraphs 4, 5, and 6 help show that the changes in ocean acidity are happening quickly (answer A). The data do not relate to any efforts to reduce carbon emissions, so answer B is incorrect. The data do not challenge the claim that the atmosphere is not the only victim of fossil fuels (answer C) or show how acidity can harm coral reefs and other sea life (answer D).

3. A; DOK Level: 3; Reading Assessment Targets: R.4.3/L.4.3, R.6.4. The authors use the comparison with osteoporosis to help explain how acidity affects shellfish and coral. Answer A is correct. Answer B is incorrect because human skeletons are not affected by ocean acidity. Answer C is incorrect because the authors do not explain how shells are formed. Answer D is incorrect because the authors provide no information about the nutritional needs of shellfish.

4. D; DOK Level: 2; Reading Assessment Targets: R.5.2, R.8.1. Answer D is correct because paragraph 10 explains why the small organisms are important to the larger ocean food web. Paragraph 10 does not explain what pteropods and coccolithophores are or where they are found. Answer B is incorrect because paragraph 10 does not describe large organisms. Answer C is incorrect because paragraph 10 does not explain how acidification affects smaller organisms but does explain how their disappearance will affect the ocean food web.

5. C; DOK Level: 2; Reading Assessment Target: R.6.3. One implicit purpose of the passage is to encourage readers to reduce their use of fossil fuels, which contribute to the acidification of the oceans. The passage does not provide details about the life cycles of corals, so answer A is incorrect. The purpose of the passage is not to inspire readers to visit the coral reefs, so answer B is incorrect. Answer D is incorrect because the passage does not provide details about challenges the fishing industry faces.

Answer Key

6. **DOK Level: 3; Reading Assessment Targets:** R.8.3, R.8.4. Although the authors state that the "tipping point" for coral reefs could happen as soon as 2050, they do not provide further details or evidence to explain why 2050 could be the tipping point. This claim is not supported by evidence in the passage. The other claims are supported by evidence.

Supported	Unsupported
Ocean acidity has increased rapidly in the past 250 years.	The "tipping point" for coral reefs could happen as soon as 2050.
Human activity is the likely cause of increased CO_2 emissions.	
Humans must act quickly to save the coral reefs and shellfish.	

7. **A; DOK Level: 2; Reading Assessment Targets:** R.7.2, R.8.2. The graph provides information about how rising levels of CO_2 affect ocean acidification. Acidity is part of ocean chemistry. Answer A is correct. Answer B is incorrect because the graph does not show the ocean acidity 20 million years ago. Answer C is incorrect because the graph does not show where and when acidification is taking place. Answer D is incorrect because the graph does not indicate the strategies needed to fight global warming or ocean acidification.

8. **D; DOK Level: 2; Reading Assessment Target:** R.8.5. The author uses exaggerated, emotional language such as "unprecedented in our history" and "greatest challenge that our country will face" to frighten readers. Answer D is correct. The author does not appeal directly to the audience's sense of patriotism in the first paragraph, so answer A is incorrect. The author does not present a cause-and-effect relationship, so answer B is incorrect. The author does not present facts, so answer C is incorrect.

9. **C; DOK Level: 2; Reading Assessment Targets:** R.6.2, R.6.3, R.6.4, R.8.1. In paragraph 5, the author states that many of his ideas will be unpopular and that the alternative to his proposals "may be a national catastrophe" because he is anticipating arguments against his proposals. Despite the inaccurate either/or situation, answer C is correct. Although the statements may be exaggerated and frightening, his purpose is more to acknowledge opposition and imply that sacrifice is better than catastrophe. He does not make these statements merely to frighten readers (answer A), nor are they reminders of the nation's accomplishments (answer B). The author does not compare and contrast his ideas with any other proposals, so answer D is incorrect.

10. **B; DOK Level: 2; Reading Assessment Targets:** R.4.3/L.4.3, R.6.4. The repetition of the word *worse* in paragraph 7 creates a tone of urgency and emphasizes the seriousness of the problem. Answer B is correct. The paragraph does not discuss dangers of not taking action, so answer A is incorrect. The tone of the paragraph is not hopeless, so answer C is incorrect. The tone of the paragraph is not angry, and the paragraph does not discuss the opposition, so answer D is incorrect.

11. **A; DOK Level: 3; Reading Assessment Targets:** R.5.2, R.8.1, R.8.3. In paragraph 7, the author makes the claim that energy shortages are worsening, and in paragraph 8, he provides facts to support that claim. Answer A is correct. Answer B is incorrect because paragraph 8 does not describe past shortages but gives facts about why future shortages are likely. Answer C is incorrect because the paragraphs do not provide the positive and negative aspects of pursuing a new energy policy. Answer D is incorrect because paragraph 8 does not detail solutions to the problem of wasting energy.

12. **A; DOK Level: 3; Reading Assessment Targets:** R.5.3, R.5.4, R.8.1. Answer A is correct. In the first sentence of the paragraph, the author identifies the crisis the country could face. In the second sentence, the word *but* signals that the author is explaining a way to avoid the crisis. Answer B is incorrect because the author does not describe the possible crises in great detail. Answer C is incorrect because the author does not describe and respond to the opinions of opponents in this paragraph. Answer D is incorrect because the author does not use the word *now* to signal a shift in time. Rather, the word emphasizes the need to act quickly.

13. **B; DOK Level: 2; Reading Assessment Targets:** R.5.2, R.5.4, R.6.4, R.8.1, R.8.5. In the last three paragraphs, the author uses repetition to emphasize American pride and positive American traits, thus appealing to his audience's sense of patriotism. Answer B is correct. The language of the last three paragraphs does not appeal to his audience's sense of fear (answer A), desire for popularity (answer C), or desire for wealth (answer D).

14. **DOK Level: 2; Reading Assessment Target:** R.6.3. The author tells readers that he will be proposing a new energy policy, but he does not explicitly ask readers to support it. He explains why the policy will be crucial and tries to gain support for the sacrifices that lie ahead. The implicit purpose of the passage, therefore, is to encourage readers to support the new **energy policy**.

15. **DOK Level: 2; Reading Assessment Targets:** R.4.1/L.4.1, R.4.3/L.4.3, R.6.4, R.8.5. **selfish, timid, grandchildren, catastrophe** The adjectives *selfish* and *timid* describe human character traits and strike an emotional chord. *Catastrophe* is a word that can arouse fear, and the word *grandchildren* is likely to touch on the emotions of love and the desire to protect.

16. **DOK Level: 2; Reading Assessment Target:** R.4.1/L.4.1. The word means **light**, as explained in the sentence through the example of a pen flashlight and the contrast with the "warm light the human eye desires."

17. **DOK Level: 2; Reading Assessment Targets:** R.5.1, R.5.3. In paragraph 8 of the FAQ, the phrase *by comparison* indicates that the author will **compare** the costs of different lightbulbs, thus completing the answer to the FAQ about costs.

18. **C; DOK Level: 3; Reading Assessment Targets:** R.5.4, R.8.3, R.8.4. The FAQ make convincing and well-supported points to persuade energy consumers to switch from traditional bulbs to the new bulbs to save energy and money. Answers A and D are incorrect because the FAQ incorporate researched evidence and strongly supported arguments. Answer B is incorrect because the FAQ do not use emotionally charged language; they use researched evidence to motivate readers.

19. **C; DOK Level:** 3; **Reading Assessment Target:** R.7.3. Answer C is correct because authors assume that readers of *Wired*, the source of the article, have some knowledge about electricity. The author uses technical terms and scientific language. The FAQ, however, focus more on a general audience; as a government Web site, it is available and comprehensible for anyone seeking consumer-level information about lightbulbs. Answer A is incorrect because neither excerpt addresses politicians. Answer B is incorrect because the audience of the article has more technical knowledge than that for the FAQ. Answer D may include those populations but may well include others; therefore, the audience is too limited.

20. **B; DOK Level:** 3; **Reading Assessment Targets:** R.7.3, R.9.1/R.7.1. The purpose of the article is to inform readers how LEDs produce different colors, but the purpose of the FAQ is to explain how new bulbs save energy and money. Neither passage details the steps in a process. Answer C is incorrect because the article makes no argument. Answer D is incorrect because the article does not explain how LEDs save energy, nor do the FAQ entertain with an anecdote.

21. **D; DOK Level:** 3; **Reading Assessment Targets:** R.7.3, R.9.1/R.7.1. The article appears in paragraph form, but the FAQ appear as questions and answers. Answers A, B, and C reveal a lack of familiarity with different text structures.

22. **C; DOK Level:** 3; **Reading Assessment Targets:** R.7.3, R.9.1/R.7.1. Both the article and the FAQ show that LED bulbs are the lights of the future because LEDs save energy and money. Only the FAQ reveal that the United States wastes too much energy and emits too much carbon or that people must look to save on energy costs. Only the article discusses the poor-quality light of some LEDs.

23. **C; DOK Level:** 3; **Reading Assessment Targets:** R.7.4, R.9.1/R.7.1. Although the points made in the FAQ about switching to new energy-saving bulbs are convincing, the reader might still be reluctant to switch to the new bulbs because, according to the article, the new bulbs might not give off the "warm glow" of the old incandescent bulbs. Answers A, B, and D are incorrect because the article does not discuss the cost of running LEDs nor whether traditional bulbs are easier to install or manufacture.

24. **B; DOK Level:** 3; **Reading Assessment Targets:** R.7.4, R.9.1/R.7.1. The authors of the passages most likely support the idea of switching from traditional bulbs to energy-saving bulbs in their homes because the new bulbs save money and energy. Answers A, C, and D reflect a misreading of the passages.

25. **DOK Level:** 2; **Reading Assessment Target:** R.4.1/L.4.1. The word *resilience* refers to a person's ability to cope with **stress**, **misfortune**, or **difficulty**.

26. **A; DOK Level:** 2; **Reading Assessment Targets:** R.5.1, R.6.3, R.6.4. The author quotes Holmes to show that celebrating Memorial Day is a time-honored event. The quotation is about the time of year and the purpose of Memorial Day. Although the other answer choices are plausible in the context of the speech, the actual text of the quotation applies only to answer A.

27. **DOK Level:** 2; **Reading Assessment Targets:** R.3.1, R.5.1, R.5.3. In the article, the phrases "last Memorial Day," "today," and "this time next year" signal shifts in time sequence, or chronology. Their meanings are obvious in context as the author refers to a day one year ago, to the current day, and to a day one year later.

28. **C; DOK Level:** 3; **Reading Assessment Targets:** R.7.3, R.9.1/R.7.1. Both passages show that those responsible for sending others off to war are aware of the sacrifices made by soldiers and their families. Only the article explains that those with combat experience never forget those with whom they fought. Only the speech explains that it is the soldier who hopes most for peace. Neither passage indicates that men and women who serve in the military are not respected.

29. **DOK Level:** 3; **Reading Assessment Targets:** R.7.3, R.9.1/R.7.1. Speech: **specific audience, first-person point of view** News Article: **general audience, third-person point of view** The first passage is a speech delivered by Secretary of Defense Chuck Hagel, in which he directly addresses members of the audience attending the Memorial Day ceremony and speaks in the first person (*we*). The second passage is a CNN news article written for a general news-reading online audience and uses the third-person point of view.

30. **B; DOK Level:** 3; **Reading Assessment Targets:** R.7.3, R.9.1/R.7.1. The purpose of the speech is to honor fallen soldiers who fought for American freedom, but the purpose of the news article is to report what was said and what took place at a Memorial Day tribute. Therefore, answer B is correct. Answer A might motivate some audience members, but the purpose of the speech is not to recruit. Nothing is said about the benefits of joining. Answer C is incorrect because it is not about how to support military families. Answer D reflects a misreading of the text.

31. **B; DOK Level:** 3; **Reading Assessment Targets:** R.7.4, R.9.1/R.7.1. Answer B is correct because this information is mentioned in paragraph 7 of the article. Answers A and D are incorrect because they do not address information in the article or the speech. Whether they are true or plausible is irrelevant because they do not answer the question. Answer C is mentioned in the article; however, Hagel's position as a cabinet member is less significant here than his active combat service. Memorial Day honors those who died while serving their country. Hagel refers to his wartime experience, which connects him more with his audience than his cabinet position does. Both passages are about honoring those who died in combat, not about politics.

32. **D; DOK Level:** 3; **Reading Assessment Targets:** R.7.4, R.9.1/R.7.1. Both passages suggest that the sacrifices of American military men and women are often taken for granted, thus the need to remind the public of these sacrifices. Nothing in either passage suggests that members of the military need to forget combat experiences or are seeking fame or glory. The passages do mention the sacrifices of military families but do not mention specifically that military families suffer because of long separations.

Answer Key

LESSON 1, pp. 96–97

1. **B; DOK Level:** 3; **Reading Assessment Targets:**
R.9.2, R.9.3. Clift opposes online teaching, saying that she
will never teach online again, while Jones focuses on the
benefits of online learning for students; therefore, answer
B is correct. Clift and Jones do not focus on the demands
of online education as much as its advantages and
disadvantages, so answer A is incorrect. In addition, Jones
never describes himself as either a teacher or a student, so
answers C and D are also incorrect.

2. **D; DOK Level:** 3; **Reading Assessment Targets:**
R.9.2, R.9.3. Clift and Jones differ in their interpretations
of time. Clift complains about the tripling of her teaching
time, whereas Jones focuses on time flexibility for students,
so answer D is correct. Answer A is incorrect because
only Clift believes that online education is time consuming.
Answer B is incorrect because it is Clift who believes online
education is time consuming, while Jones focuses on its
flexibility. Answer C is incorrect because only Jones says
that online education is flexible.

3. **A; DOK Level:** 3; **Reading Assessment Targets:**
R.9.2, R.9.3. Clift and Jones differ about the importance
of lectures in online learning. Clift laments that a lecture
cannot be reproduced online, while Jones celebrates the
alternatives to the lecture that online education provides;
therefore, answer A is correct. Answer B is incorrect
because only Clift says that a lecture cannot be reproduced
online. Answer C is incorrect because it is Clift who
says lectures cannot be reproduced online, while Jones
emphasizes other learning options. Answer D is incorrect
because only Jones is excited about the alternative learning
options offered by online education.

LESSON 2, pp. 98–99

1. **C; DOK Level:** 2; **Reading Assessment Targets:** R.9.2,
R.9.3; **Writing Assessment Targets:** W.1, W.2. Answer C
is the best response because it provides an answer to the
prompt's question of which argument is better supported.
For the purposes of this question, it does not matter
whether this position is the one you agree with, as you will
have a chance to develop your own thesis statement on the
next page. The prompt does not ask for the argument of
each author, so answers A and D would be more suitable
as supporting evidence than thesis statements. The prompt
also does not ask which author would make a better online
instructor, so answer B is incorrect.

Chart; DOK Level: 2; **Reading Assessment Targets:**
R.8.1, R.8.2; **Writing Assessment Targets:** W.1, W.2.
Reasons in support of Clift's position:
2. Quality of Materials
3. Time Required
Evidence in support of Clift's position:
2. Anecdote based on personal experience
3. Statistic based on personal experience
Reasons in support of Jones's position:
2. Self-management
3. Learning Options

Evidence in support of Jones's position:
2. Quotation from online student
3. Comparison between classroom lecture and multimedia
elements

2. **DOK Level:** 3; **Reading Assessment Target:** R.8.3.
Clift presents her argument from a teacher's point of view;
her evidence is based on personal experience, but her style
and tone are appealing to a reader.

3. **DOK Level:** 3; **Reading Assessment Target:** R.8.3.
Jones presents his argument by focusing exclusively on the
student experience, but he offers a variety of evidence.

4. **DOK Level:** 3; **Reading Assessment Target:** R.9.3.
Either Clift's position or Jones's position, depending on
which one you choose to support.

5. **DOK Level:** 3; **Writing Assessment Targets:** W.1,
W.2. Possible thesis statement: **While Clift compellingly
argues that online education is inferior to the
classroom, Jones makes a stronger argument in favor
of online education because he offers a greater variety
of evidence.**

LESSON 3, pp. 100–101

1. **C; DOK Level:** 3; **Reading Assessment Target:** R.9.2;
Writing Assessment Targets: W.1, W.2. In the Clift article,
words such as *old dog*, *resists*, and *technophobe* suggest
that Clift holds a negative attitude toward her subject. Her
tone is neither excited (answer B) nor neutral (answer D).
On the other hand, Jones uses words like *benefits*, *appeal*,
and *exciting* to create a tone that is positive and upbeat, not
sarcastic (answer A). The correct response is answer C.

Chart; DOK Level: 3; **Reading Assessment Targets:**
R.9.2, R.9.3; **Writing Assessment Targets:** W.1, W.2.
The chart should contain three points of comparison and
contrast from the web diagram on the previous page or
others of your choosing. You should provide appropriate
and logical text evidence from each article for each point
listed. For example, you may choose **Claim/Point of View**,
Reasons, and **Tone** for your three points of comparison/
contrast. Under **Claim/Point of View**, you may note that
the Clift article focuses on the author's frustration with her
experiences as an online teacher, while the Jones article
focuses on the positive experiences of others with online
learning. Under **Reasons**, you may note that Clift gives
reasons such as quality of materials and insufficient pay,
while Jones gives reasons such as flexibility and self-
management. Under **Tone**, you may note that the Clift
article has a negative, frustrated tone, while the Jones
article is upbeat and optimistic.

LESSON 4, pp. 102–103

1. **D; DOK Level:** 2; **Writing Assessment Targets:** W.1,
W.2. In a point-by-point organizational structure, an
example about the use of tone in the Clift passage should
be followed by a corresponding example about the use
of tone in the Jones passage, so answer D is correct.
An explanation of what tone is would come before the
passage examples, not after, so answer B is incorrect. The
introduction of and examples about another point, such as
point of view, should not come until after the examples of
tone from both passages, so answers A and C are incorrect

Chart; DOK Level: 3; **Writing Assessment Targets:** W.1,
W.2. You should complete one of the two planning charts

by transferring and sequencing the points of comparison or contrast and text evidence from the evidence chart you completed in Lesson 3. However, if needed, you may make logical changes between the two charts for the development of your claims. If you are having trouble choosing a structure, complete both charts, and then choose the one that works best for your thesis statement.

An example of the subject-by-subject chart would be

Subject 1: Clift

First Point of Comparison/Contrast: Claim/Point of View (may require an explanation of how an author's claim or point of view makes up the central argument); Clift's point of view is that online teaching is frustrating and not worthwhile for teachers like her. **Second Point of Comparison/ Contrast:** Reasons (may require explanation of how reasons are the arguments given by each author in support of his or her main claim); Clift gives reasons such as quality of materials and insufficient pay. **Third Point of Comparison/ Contrast:** Tone (may require an explanation of what tone is and how it can influence the persuasiveness of an essay); the Clift passage has a negative, frustrated tone.

Subject 2: Jones

First Point of Comparison/Contrast: Claim/Point of View; Jones's point of view is that online learning offers many advantages for students. **Second Point of Comparison/ Contrast:** Reasons; Jones gives reasons such as flexibility and self-management. **Third Point of Comparison/ Contrast:** Tone; the Jones passage is optimistic and positive.

An example of the point-by-point chart would be

First Point of Comparison/Contrast: Claim/Point of View (may require an explanation of how an author's claim or point of view can be used in persuasive essays to influence readers); Clift's point of view is that online teaching is frustrating and not worthwhile for teachers like her; Jones's point of view is that online learning offers many advantages for students. **Second Point of Comparison/Contrast:** Reasons (may require an explanation of how reasons are the arguments given by each author in support of his or her main claim); Clift gives reasons such as quality of materials and insufficient pay; Jones gives reasons such as flexibility and self-management. **Third Point of Comparison/ Contrast:** Tone (may require an explanation of what tone is and how it can influence the persuasiveness of an essay); the Clift passage has a negative, frustrated tone; the Jones passage is optimistic and positive.

LESSON 5, *pp. 104–105*

1. **D; DOK Level:** 2; **Writing Assessment Targets:** W.1, W.2. An action lead gains the attention of the audience and introduces the topic with a description of someone doing something. In this case, answer D is an action lead because it describes how a student "clicked the Submit button" to enroll in an online course. Answer A is an example of a direct lead that opens by diving into the topic and talking about the growing trend of online education. Answer B is an example of a reactive lead, in which students "wonder" how they will balance work and education. Answer C is an example of a dialogue/quotation lead because it opens with an imagined quotation from Professor Clift.

Chart; DOK Level: 3; **Writing Assessment Targets:** W.1, W.2, W.3; **Language Assessment Target:** L.1.9 Complete the Introduction chart by using the thesis statement you developed in Lesson 2 and the introduction strategies discussed on the previous page.

Chart; DOK Level: 3; **Writing Assessment Targets:** W.1, W.2, W.3; **Language Assessment Target:** L.1.9 Complete the Conclusion chart using the thesis statement you developed in Lesson 2 and the conclusion strategies discussed on the previous page.

LESSON 6, *pp. 106–109*

1. **A; DOK Level:** 2; **Reading Assessment Target:** R.5.3; **Writing Assessment Targets:** W.2, W.3; **Language Assessment Target:** L.1.9. Although both ideas relate to the same point (in this case, teaching tools), the ideas themselves are contrasting, so the use of the transition *although* (answer A) is the most logical. Answers B, C, and D are incorrect because the transitions show similarity between the two ideas, rather than contrast.

Frame; DOK Level: 3; **Writing Assessment Targets:** W.1, W.2, W.3; **Language Assessment Target:** L.1.9. Use the GED® Reasoning Through Language Arts Extended Response Scoring Rubric for Trait 1 (Creation of Arguments and Use of Evidence) and Trait 2 (Development of Ideas and Organizational Structure) to review your draft. You can find these rubrics on pages 182–183. You also may consult the annotated sample extended response on the following page.

LESSON 7, *pp. 110–111*

1. **B; DOK Level:** 2; **Writing Assessment Targets:** W.1, W.2, W.3; **Language Assessment Target:** L.1.8. Answer B is correct because *students and teachers* is more specific than *people*; the phrase *be flexible* is shorter than the original and creates parallelism within the sentence. Answer A is incorrect because the words in the answer choice, although fewer, are far less specific than *be adaptable to changing circumstances* and change the meaning of the sentence. The phrase *online curriculum developers* (answer C) is incorrect because it does not include other groups of people, such as students and teachers, who also need to be flexible when dealing with online education. The phrase *people in education* (answer D) is incorrect because it is not much more specific than *people*, and the action phrase is still too wordy.

Chart; DOK Level: 2; **Writing Assessment Targets:** W.2, W.3; **Language Assessment Targets:** L.1.4, L.1.8, L.1.9, L.2.2. Use the GED® Reasoning Through Language Arts Extended Response Scoring Rubric for Trait 2 (Development of Ideas and Organizational Structure) and Trait 3 (Clarity and Command of Standard English Conventions) to assess your chart. You can find these rubrics on pages 183–184. You may also consult the annotated sample extended response on the following page.

Answer Key

1 Jefferson clicks the Submit button and waits for confirmation of his enrollment in the online English course. This option will allow Jefferson to continue his college education and keep his full-time job. He is not unlike many other students who are taking advantage of the educational options of a technological age. However, the growing popularity of such online classes has stimulated a debate regarding their quality. **2** In this debate, Elayne Clift and Carl Jones are weighing in with differing opinions. **3** While Clift voices concerns about the limitations of online education, Jones more effectively focuses on the possibilities of online education.

4 Clift and Jones offer differing points of view regarding the focus of online education. Clift focuses on her experiences as a teacher. She wants to interact with students in person, she cannot reproduce her lectures online, and she spends more time teaching online without an increase in salary. However, Clift misses a **5** crucial point in her argument: as the teacher, her role is to serve the students, not herself. On the other hand, Jones correctly focuses on the students when he discusses the benefits of online education, which include flexibility, self-management, and the appeal to various learning styles.

6 While Clift and Jones both offer evidence to support their points of view, Jones's evidence is more credible than Clift's. **7** All of Clift's evidence is based on personal experience: "I devoted at least three times as many hours and triple the energy to online teaching than was necessary for traditional courses." **8** She fails to cite evidence from other educators and does not address whether the time and energy commitments remain constant once an instructor gains experience in the medium. On the other hand, Jones offers a variety of convincing evidence. In addition to description and a quotation from a student, he offers the statistic that "32% of college students take at least one online class."

9 Finally, Clift and Jones both employ rhetorical strategies to convince readers of their points of view, but Clift's qualifying statements work against her. **10** She admits, "Perhaps I'm the old dog that resists new tricks. Maybe I am a technophobe. It might be that I'm plain old-fashioned." These statements cause readers to agree that her concerns about online education do, in fact, stem from outdated thinking. Conversely, Jones enumerates his reasons clearly and succinctly with transitional devices: "One of the biggest appeals," "Another appeal," and "Lastly." His straightforward approach is clean and efficient, much like the technology he celebrates.

In conclusion, Jones's argument is focused and well supported, while Clift's comes across as selfish and whining. Jones discusses benefits of online education for students through varied evidence, including quotations and statistics, and clear organization. Clift's article deteriorates into a pity party. **11** In fact, Clift's attitude demonstrates a fundamental problem in education, both in class and online. The purpose of education is not to make a teacher's job easy or quick; it is to prepare students for the complexities of life in the global village.

1 The writer uses an action strategy to grab readers' attention and introduce the thesis statement.

3 The writer's thesis makes a text-based argument, establishes a purpose that is connected to the prompt, and shows an awareness of the audience.

6 The writer demonstrates varied sentence structure with this complex sentence. This variety creates fluency throughout the response.

9 The writer shows a logical progression and development of ideas closely tied to the thesis.

10 The writer integrates text evidence with fluidity.

2 The writer correctly applies standard English conventions by demonstrating subject-verb agreement: the compound subject takes a plural verb.

4 The writer establishes a point-by-point organizational structure and uses transitional devices within the paragraph to show the logical relationships among ideas.

5 The writer shows purposeful word choice and advanced vocabulary.

7 The writer cites relevant, specific, and sufficient evidence to support the thesis and points.

8 The writer assesses the validity of a passage.

11 After summarizing the main ideas, the writer leaves readers with a final thought.

1. A; DOK Level: 2; **Reading Assessment Target:** R.6.1.
In paragraph 1, Jackson says, "While there are many activities that can distract a driver … sending text messages may be the worst." Her main claim is that texting is the worst driving distraction (answer A). Answer B is incorrect because the assertion that texting is not the only driving distraction is Trapper's, not Jackson's. Answer C is incorrect because the idea that texting while driving involves taking one's eyes off the road is a simple fact, not a claim. Answer D is incorrect because Jackson does not claim that texting-caused crashes are more serious than other crashes.

2. C; DOK Level: 2; **Reading Assessment Target:**
R.6.1. At the end of paragraph 1, Trapper states her main claim: "Until the government collects good data about the relationship between crashes and distractions, laws banning cell phone use in cars will not work" (answer C). Answer A is incorrect because Trapper focuses on evidence showing that texting is not the worst driving distraction. Answer B is incorrect because it is Jackson, not Trapper, who believes that laws to stop texting while driving will end texting-related crashes. Answer D is incorrect because the fact that texting-related crashes have not increased with cell phone use is evidence cited by Trapper to support her claims.

3. C; DOK Level: 3; **Reading Assessment Targets:**
R.8.1, R.9.2, R.9.3. Answer C is correct because Jackson's supporting claim is that laws that stop texting will help end these crashes, whereas Trapper's supporting claim is that texting is not the only dangerous distraction. Jackson supports her claim by pointing out several recent laws that show lawmakers taking notice of and reacting to the problem of texting while driving. Trapper, on the other hand, supports her claim by discussing several crash-inducing distractions that are not related to cell phones. Answer A is incorrect because it is Trapper who believes that cell phone bans will not stop crashes, while Jackson believes texting is the worst distraction. Answers B and D are incorrect because they contain specific pieces of evidence that support the authors' claims, but they are not claims themselves.

4. A; DOK Level: 2; **Reading Assessment Targets:** R.6.2, R.8.2. Answer A is correct because Trapper states in her article that "cell phone use in the car is a popular media issue right now, but the research doesn't support this focus." She cites research showing that "there was no concurrent increase in crashes as the number of cell phones increased throughout the 2000s." Answer B is incorrect because Trapper cites an expert who focuses only on the lack of reliable crash data and does not argue that texting is not the main cause of crashes. Answer C is incorrect because Trapper does not state that lawmakers do not believe texting is a problem. Additionally, it is Jackson, not Trapper, who cites statistics showing the relationship between texting and crashes. Answer D is incorrect because it is Jackson, not Trapper, who includes an anecdote about a crash caused by texting.

5. A; DOK Level: 3; **Reading Assessment Targets:** R.5.4, R.9.3; **Writing Assessment Targets:** W.1, W.2
Jackson's article leads with a story about an Indiana teen who was injured while riding in a car. Trapper's article begins with a statement that Oprah Winfrey has asked people to join her "No Texting Campaign." Both are action leads (answer A). Answer B is incorrect because neither article leads with a reaction. Answer C is incorrect because Jackson's article does not lead with a quotation, and Trapper's does not lead with a reaction. Answer D is incorrect because both articles lead with an action.

6. D; DOK Level: 3; **Reading Assessment Targets:**
R.2.8, R.9.3. Answer D is correct because Jackson cites statistics showing that drivers who text and use cell phones are more likely to be in crashes, implying that she sees a cause-and-effect relationship between cell phone use and the likelihood of a crash. Trapper, on the other hand, mentions that "Until the government collects good data … laws banning cell phone use in cars will not work." She also points out inconsistencies in research, implying that she thinks current data are insufficient and unreliable. Answer A is incorrect because Jackson does believe cell phones affect the chances of being in a crash, while Trapper does not think that cell phones are the main cause of increased crashes. Answer B is incorrect because Jackson does not provide evidence that drivers who do not text are safe from crashes, nor does Trapper provide evidence linking cell phone use to crash severity. Answer C is incorrect because Jackson does not provide evidence linking cell phone use to crash severity, while Trapper actually criticizes automakers for adding distracting devices to cars that make crashes more likely.

7. B; DOK Level: 2; **Reading Assessment Target:** R.6.4
Jackson uses the rhetorical technique of enumeration to list statistics from a study showing how texting is related to the increased likelihood of crashing (answer B). Answer A is incorrect because she includes only one anecdote about a texting-related crash at the beginning of the passage. Answer C is incorrect because she quotes only one expert who warns about the dangers of texting while driving. Answer D is incorrect because although she briefly mentions two legal penalties of texting while driving at the end of the article, she does not list them.

8. DOK Level: 2; **Reading Assessment Target:** R.5.3
In paragraph 3, Trapper uses the transition **however** to signal the introduction of an opposing idea: "Jayne O'Donnell, a consumer reporter, points out that the Insurance Institute for Highway Safety found that 'using a cell phone while driving quadruples the risk of a crash.' **However**, 'research shows there was no concurrent increase in crashes as the number of cell phones increased throughout the 2000s.'" The transition shows the opposition between the statistic about cell phones quadrupling the risk of a crash and the lack of evidence linking the rise in cell phone use to increased crashes.

Answer Key

9. Frame; DOK Level: 3; **Writing Assessment Targets:** W.1, W.2, W.3; **Language Assessment Targets:** L.1.2, L.1.6, L.1.9
Use the GED® Reasoning Through Language Arts Extended Response Scoring Rubric for Trait 1 (Creation of Arguments and Use of Evidence), Trait 2 (Development of Ideas and Organizational Structure), and Trait 3 (Clarity and Command of Standard English Conventions) to review your draft. You can find these rubrics on pages 182–184. You also may consult the annotated sample extended response below.

1 The writer uses an action strategy to grab the attention of readers and introduce the thesis statement.

4 The writer applies standard English conventions by using correct subject-verb agreement.

6 The writer establishes a point-by-point organizational structure and uses transitional devices to show the logical relationships among ideas.

8 The writer shows a logical progression and development of ideas tied to the thesis.

10 The writer demonstrates varied sentence structure with this compound sentence. This variety creates fluency throughout the response.

1 During the thirteen years that America's children are required to spend in school, many, if not most, have witnessed some form of bullying. For example, John is always selected last for a softball team. Mary is teased about wearing the same clothes for three days in a row. Jane does not come to school for a week after an embarrassing picture of her is posted on a social media site. **2** School officials, parents, students, and social scientists know that bullying is a complicated topic without an easy solution. **3** Given this difficult situation, Stephen Farmer's article does a better job than Yalda Uhls's of explaining the issue's complexity and offering a solution.

4 Uhls and Farmer use differing text structures and rhetorical techniques to make their points. Uhls compares and contrasts traditional bullying with cyber bullying. **5** Yet this comparison is not supported by convincing evidence that cyber bullying has a broader impact than traditional bullying. On the other hand, Farmer uses a list format to explore the many problems that make bullying a difficult practice to end. He discusses a variety of factors that contribute to the complexity of the issue, including media hype, shifting roles among bullies and victims, and the wide age range of bullies.

6 While Uhls and Farmer both offer evidence to support their points of view, Farmer's evidence is more credible than Uhls's. **7** Uhls states that a small number of American students (13%) claim to have been cyber bullied, while Farmer puts this number even lower (10%). Regardless, Farmer also shows that twice as many students (25%) experience traditional bullying. Farmer makes clear that nearly a third of students experience bullying of some kind and that the distinction between cyber bullying and traditional bullying does not further efforts to end such behavior.

8 Finally, the scope of Farmer's article is broader than Uhls's. **9** While Uhls focuses only on children, Farmer extends his argument to adults, half of whom have been exposed to bullying in the workplace. This number shows that bullying behavior increases, rather than decreases, with age. This information alone may clarify why bullying is such a difficult behavior to end.

In conclusion, Farmer's article does the better job of helping readers understand the complexity of bullying. **10** Farmer also does more than bemoan the problem; he offers some insight into a possible solution. He cites a journal study showing that identification and punishment do more to end bullying than prevention programs. **11** This conclusion may not appeal to all readers, but perhaps for those who act like children, regardless of age, the traditional methods of behavior modification are best.

2 The writer shows purposeful word choice and advanced vocabulary.

3 The writer's thesis makes a text-based argument, establishes a purpose that is connected to the prompt, and shows an awareness of the audience.

5 The writer assesses the validity of a passage.

7 The writer integrates text evidence with fluidity.

9 The writer cites relevant, specific, and sufficient evidence to support the thesis and points.

11 After summarizing the main ideas, the writer leaves readers with a final thought.

10. **Frame; DOK Level:** 3; **Writing Assessment Targets:** W.1, W.2, W.3; **Language Assessment Targets:** L.1.6, L.1.9

Use the GED® Reasoning Through Language Arts Extended Response Scoring Rubric for Trait 1 (Creation of Arguments and Use of Evidence), Trait 2 (Development of Ideas and Organizational Structure), and Trait 3 (Clarity and Command of Standard English Conventions) to review your draft. You can find these rubrics on pages 182–184. You also may consult the annotated sample extended response below.

1 The writer uses a reaction strategy to grab the attention of readers and introduce the thesis statement.

3 The writer shows purposeful word choice and advanced vocabulary.

5 The writer shows a logical progression and development of ideas closely tied to the thesis.

8 The writer establishes a point-by-point organizational structure and uses transitions to show the logical relationships among ideas.

10 The writer correctly uses parallelism.

1 While there is something truly American about the exploration of an unknown frontier, this romantic notion requires a new definition of the term *frontier*. When it comes to exploring unknown territory, space may be the final frontier, but it is by no means a practical one. **2** In a time of economic struggles, Gerard DeGroot's article against space spending is a more practical and well-reasoned argument than Bob Deutsch's idealistic support of such spending.

3 While both authors use the rhetorical technique of alluding to proud moments in American history to support their arguments, their tones vary. Deutsch reverently cites the vision of the Founding Fathers as liberating, creative, and boundless. **4** On the other hand, DeGroot's practical tone dismisses the first walk on the moon by simply saying, "Forget giant leaps for mankind." While readers may wax nostalgic over Deutsch's trip down Memory Lane, DeGroot's voice of reason and practicality snaps them back to the present.

5 Both authors respond to counterarguments, but DeGroot does so more effectively. Deutsch acknowledges but criticizes the logic of the counterarguments about expense and the lack of benefits. **6** Yet his response lacks substance. In essence, he says, "Forget logic; let's focus on philosophy." **7** DeGroot acknowledges and agrees with the argument of Hawking and others that "Earth is indeed doomed." However, his response is more practical. If Americans are unwilling to populate Antarctica, what makes them think they can live on Mars?

8 Finally, each author employs evidence to support his point of view. **9** However, Deutsch's evidence is psychological, whereas DeGroot's is practical. Deutsch argues that Americans should spend billions of dollars, at the expense of practical needs, to maintain their mental health. DeGroot rightly points out that Americans do not have the money to foot the bill for luxury "space therapy" when they face such real problems as disease, starvation, and drought.

In conclusion, **10** DeGroot offers a solution to the seeming union of opposites: psychology and practicality. **11** He suggests that the modern frontier is not a place but a problem that does not yet have a solution. Instead of a physical trip to Mars, Americans might consider looking for the solution to disease or poverty. These are the modern frontiers.

2 The writer's thesis makes a text-based argument, establishes a purpose that is connected to the prompt, and shows an awareness of the audience.

4 The writer integrates text evidence with fluidity.

6 The writer assesses the validity of a passage.

7 The writer cites relevant, specific, and sufficient evidence to support the thesis and points.

9 The writer demonstrates varied sentence structure with this complex sentence. This variety creates fluency throughout the response.

11 After summarizing the main ideas, the writer leaves readers with a final thought.

Answer Key

UNIT 3 *(continued)*

11. **Frame; DOK Level:** 3; **Writing Assessment Targets:** W.1, W.2, W.3; **Language Assessment Targets:** L.1.6, L.1.9, L.2.4

Use the GED® Reasoning Through Language Arts Extended Response Scoring Rubric for Trait 1 (Creation of Arguments and Use of Evidence), Trait 2 (Development of Ideas and Organizational Structure), and Trait 3 (Clarity and Command of Standard English Conventions) to review your draft. You can find these rubrics on pages 182–184. You also may consult the annotated sample extended response below.

1 The writer uses an action strategy to grab the attention of readers and introduce the thesis statement.

3 The writer's thesis makes a text-based argument, establishes a purpose that is connected to the prompt, and shows an awareness of the audience.

5 The writer cites relevant, specific, and sufficient evidence to support the thesis and points.

8 The writer shows purposeful word choice and advanced vocabulary.

10 The writer assesses the validity of a passage.

1 If you work full time for the federal minimum wage of $7.25 per hour, you will earn $290 before taxes this week. This wage equates to $15,080 dollars per year before taxes. **2** If you examine your regular monthly expenses, including housing, food, healthcare, and transportation, you quickly will discover that this salary is not likely to support your family. Is it a morally fair and economically sound practice that U.S. citizens can work full time and still live in poverty? **3** In her editorial, Holly Sklar effectively supports her position that the minimum wage should be raised to $10.00 per hour.

4 To begin, Sklar cites evidence that a low minimum wage violates federal law. **5** She explains that the Fair Labor Standards Act, passed in 1938, guarantees citizens the right to work and maintain a minimum standard of living. She defines a minimum standard of living as one in which citizens are not forced to choose between necessities and are able to provide themselves with food and shelter. **6** This point is effective because food, water, and shelter are generally recognized by government officials and scientists alike as necessary for life. It is logical that full-time work should provide for these minimum essentials.

Next, Sklar reinforces her claim with evidence that geography does not eliminate the problem with the current minimum wage. **7** She states that a recent study found that "there is no county in the country where a full-time worker making minimum wage can afford a one-bedroom apartment" for less than 30% of his or her income. **8** This evidence is effective because it shows that the problem is prevalent throughout the country and not only in particular areas, cities, or states.

Finally, Sklar responds effectively to a counterargument that raising the minimum wage will raise unemployment. **9** She cites unemployment rates, economic experts, state-specific statistics, and university research studies to refute this counterclaim. **10** The extent and variety of this evidence overwhelmingly undercuts the counterargument.

In conclusion, Sklar suggests that a strong economy is based on a financially secure, and even profit-sharing, workforce. **11** Her recommendation of raising the minimum wage to $10.00 per hour, which equates to a yearly salary of $20,800, is not extravagant. It is fair, and it is the right thing to do.

2 The writer demonstrates varied sentence structure with this complex sentence. This variety creates fluency throughout the response.

4 The writer establishes a point-by-point organizational structure and uses transitional devices to show the logical relationships among ideas.

6 The writer shows a logical progression and development of ideas closely tied to the thesis.

7 The writer integrates text evidence with fluidity.

9 The writer correctly applies standard English conventions by using commas in a series.

11 After summarizing the main ideas, the writer leaves readers with a final thought.

 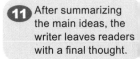

UNIT 4 EDITING

LESSON 1, pp. 122–123

1. C; DOK Level: 1; **Language Assessment Target:** W.3. The correct spelling of the plural of *employee* is *employees*. *Company* stays singular because it agrees with the singular verb *believes*.

2.1 D; DOK Level: 1; **Language Assessment Target:** W.3. The correct plural form of *policy* is *policies*. The plural is required in the sentence because the word *various* indicates more than one policy.

2.2 B; DOK Level: 1; **Language Assessment Target:** L.2.1. *Miami Heat* is the name of a specific team. It should be capitalized because it is a proper noun. Both words in the name must be capitalized. Furthermore, *Miami* is always capitalized because it is the name of a specific city and, therefore, a proper noun.

2.3 C; DOK Level: 1; **Language Assessment Target:** W.3. The correct plural form of *way* is *ways*. It is a word ending in *y* preceded by a vowel.

2.4 A; DOK Level: 1; **Language Assessment Target:** W.3. *League* is a collective noun, meaning that it is singular in form but plural in meaning. *Leagues* is the plural form of the collective noun meaning "more than one league." However, in the context of this paragraph, the author is referring to only one league: the NBA. Therefore, answer A is correct because both *league* and *weighs* are singular.

LESSON 2, pp. 124–125

1. B; DOK Level: 1; **Language Assessment Target:** L.1.3. The subject pronoun *they* replaces *Jonathan and Alison* in the sentence. The best placement is in the second reference to Jonathan and Alison. *Them* is an object pronoun. *She* is incorrect because the female pronoun does not include *Jonathan* and thus changes the meaning of the sentence.

2.1 D; DOK Level: 1; **Language Assessment Target:** L.1.3. The sentence requires the possessive pronoun *my* because the writer is expressing her own appreciation. *Mine* is the incorrect form of the possessive because a noun is not being replaced in the sentence. Answer A is incorrect because a possessive, not a subject, pronoun is needed. Answer C is incorrect because a possessive, not an object, pronoun is needed.

2.2 C; DOK Level: 1; **Language Assessment Target:** L.1.3. The noun to which the pronoun refers, *customer*, is singular. Therefore, a singular pronoun is needed. To avoid gender bias, use *his or her*. Answer A is incorrect because it is not possessive. Answer B is plural, and answer D, although not grammatically incorrect, is incorrect in context, implying that the bank has only female customers.

2.3 C; DOK Level: 1; **Language Assessment Target:** L.1.3. The possessive pronoun *His* is correct because the secretary works for Mr. Jamie Parks. *His* agrees in gender with *Mr. Parks*. The context of the passage might allow for the writer to refer to her own secretary, but that reference would require the use of the pronoun *my* rather than *mine*. *Mine* is grammatically incorrect because a noun is not being replaced. There is no context for the use of the plural *their*.

2.4 B; DOK Level: 1; **Language Assessment Target:** L.1.3. The subject pronoun *I* is correct because the pronoun is part of the subject of the sentence, *Emily Rider and I. Me, her,* and *him* are object pronouns.

LESSON 3, pp. 126–127

1. A; DOK Level: 1; **Writing Assessment Target:** W.3. The word *yesterday* indicates that the action took place in the past. Therefore, the verb should be in the past tense: *dropped*. Answers B, C, and D are not past-tense verbs.

2.1 B; DOK Level: 1; **Writing Assessment Target:** W.3. The sentence predicts that the customer *will find* the phone technologically advanced in the future, as soon as the customer begins to use it. This event will take place in the future. The other answer choices are not future-tense verbs.

2.2 D; DOK Level: 1; **Writing Assessment Target:** W.3. The Cytech phone has the standard features now, so the present tense *has* is correct. *Has* also is consistent with the tense of the verb *want* in the sentence; customers *want* these features, and the phone *has* them. Although answer C is present tense, it is the wrong form of the verb.

2.3 C; DOK Level: 1; **Writing Assessment Target:** W.3. The context indicates that the scientists did the work in the past (it took two years), so *spent* is the correct answer. *Spent* is consistent in tense with *designed* in the following sentence: the design was done by scientists in the past. Answers A, B, and D are not past-tense forms.

2.4 A; DOK Level: 1; **Writing Assessment Target:** W.3. The information will come in the mail in the future (within a few days), so the future tense, *will receive,* is correct. Answers B, C, and D are not future-tense verbs.

LESSON 4, pp. 128–129

1. B; DOK Level: 1; **Writing Assessment Target:** W.3. Ravi will have completed five hours of driving by lunchtime, indicating an action that will be completed at a specific time in the future. The future perfect *will have driven* is correct. The other answer choices are not future-tense verbs.

2.1 C; DOK Level: 1; **Writing Assessment Target:** W.3. The dealer placed the mark-up on the car in the past, and the mark-up continues into the present. The present perfect *has placed* is correct. *Have* is the correct tense but does not agree with the subject.

2.2 A; DOK Level: 1; **Writing Assessment Target:** W.3. The phrase *By the end of this year* indicates a time in the future that something will occur, so the future perfect *will have received* is correct.

2.3 B; DOK Level: 1; **Writing Assessment Target:** W.3. The rebates are currently being offered by the manufacturer, and the offers are ongoing. The present progressive *is offering* should be used.

2.4 D; DOK Level: 1; **Writing Assessment Target:** W.3. The decision about which extras are worth purchasing happened in the past but continues into the present. The present perfect tense *have decided* is correct.

Answer Key

LESSON 5, *pp. 130–131*

1. D; DOK Level: 1; Language Assessment Target: L.1.1. *You're* should be changed to *your* because the possessive is required. The sentence refers to the friends and family of *you*. *You're* is a contraction for *you are* and is incorrect. *It's* is the correct contraction for *it is*. *Friends* is not possessive and is written correctly.

2.1 B; DOK Level: 1; Language Assessment Target: L.2.3. The sentence requires the possessive to show that the position formerly belonged to Pat Charles. The last name *Charles* is a singular noun. The possessive is formed by adding an apostrophe and –*s*: *Pat Charles's former position.* Answer A is incorrect, although it is often used incorrectly. Answer C shows no possessive, and answer D makes the word plural.

2.2 A; DOK Level: 1; Language Assessment Target: L.2.3. The possessive is required to show that the writer belongs to the company as its new sales correspondent. The name of the company *Thomas Building Supplies* (which appears in the return address in the letter) includes the plural noun *Supplies*. The possessive is formed by adding an apostrophe after the *s*: *Supplies' main sales correspondent.* Answer B shows no possession. Answer C treats the word as a singular, and answer D places the apostrophe incorrectly.

2.3 D; DOK Level: 1; Language Assessment Target: L.1.1. In this sentence *it's* should be used as a contraction for *it is*: *it's my pleasure*. *Its* is the possessive form. *Its'* is a misspelling of the possessive with the apostrophe in the wrong place. *It* is grammatically incorrect because the verb *is* is missing.

2.4 B; DOK Level: 1; Language Assessment Targets: L.1.1, L.2.3. The letter refers to a specific company, so the singular form of the noun, *company,* is correct. The possessive is needed in this sentence because the company "possesses" its events. The possessive is formed by adding an apostrophe and –*s*: *company's events.* The possessive pronoun *your* is correct. *You're* is the contraction meaning "you are."

LESSON 6, *pp. 132–133*

1. B; DOK Level: 1; Language Assessment Target: L.1.1. Answer B is correct because *passed* is the correct past-tense form of the verb *pass*. *Past* refers to a time gone by. The other frequently confused words are used correctly in the sentence.

2.1 C; DOK Level: 1; Language Assessment Target: L.1.1. The correct answer is the number *two* (2). Answer A is the preposition, not a number. Answer B is a misspelling and creates the word *tow*, which means "pull." Answer D means "excessively" or "also."

2.2 D; DOK Level: 1; Language Assessment Targets: L.1.1, L.1.3. The possessive pronoun *their* is correct. The medical treatment belongs to them. The homonym *there* refers to a place. The homonym *they're* is a contraction for *they are*. *Thair* is a misspelling.

2.3 B; DOK Level: 1; Language Assessment Target: L.1.1. The response team is *here* to serve you, meaning the team is "in this place" to serve you. The homonym *hear* means "listen." Answers A and C are incorrect in the context of the letter.

2.4 C; DOK Level: 1; Language Assessment Target: L.1.1. The conjunction *than* is used to make a comparison: *you are more than just another customer. Then* refers to time, as in "at that time" or "after that time." *Then* can also refer to consequence, meaning "therefore." Answers B and D are incorrect in the context of the letter.

LESSON 7, *pp. 134–135*

1. A; DOK Level: 1; Language Assessment Target: L.1.7. The singular verb *plays* is correct because it agrees with the singular subject Ana. *Playing* is the incorrect form of the verb. *Team* and *company* should remain singular.

2.1 B; DOK Level: 1; Language Assessment Target: L.1.2. The verb *are* agrees with the plural subject *policies*. Although the verb *were* agrees in number, it is the wrong tense. The company's policies are not past policies; they are current. Answers A and C are singular and, therefore, incorrect.

2.2 C; DOK Level: 1; Language Assessment Target: L.1.2. The company *Office Supply* is a singular subject. The verb *monitors* agrees in number. The other answer options are plural.

2.3 A; DOK Level: 1; Language Assessment Target: L.1.7. The compound subject *business machines and furniture* takes a plural verb, *require.* The verb should be in the present tense because the policy is currently in place. *Required* is the past tense. *Requiring* is the incorrect form of the verb.

2.4 D; DOK Level: 1; Language Assessment Target: L.1.7. Two subjects are connected by *or* (*Office Supply associates or the store manager*). The singular verb *is* is correct because it agrees with the closer subject, *store manager. Are* and *were* are plural. *Be* is the incorrect form of the verb.

LESSON 8, *pp. 136–137*

1. C; DOK Level: 1; Language Assessment Target: L.1.4. *Try and* is an improper construction. *And* should be changed to *to*. The other answers are grammatically incorrect and make no sense in context.

2.1 D; DOK Level: 1; Language Assessment Target: L.1.4. *Used to* is the correct construction for the expression that means "familiar with." Answer A omits the *d*, and the meaning changes so that the phrase makes no sense in the sentence. Although answer B sounds correct when pronounced, it is not standard written English. Answer C makes no sense in context.

2.2 D; DOK Level: 1; Language Assessment Target: L.1.4. Writing *are never going to* avoids a double negative in *not never* and avoids the use of *gonna*, which is slang. *Ain't*, too, is incorrect.

2.3 A; DOK Level: 1; Language Assessment Target: L.1.4. Answer A is correct because it avoids a double negative. Answers B and D create double negatives, and answer C includes *ain't*, which is incorrect.

2.4 **B; DOK Level:** 1; **Language Assessment Target:**
L.1.4. Writing *city is* avoids the repetition of a pronoun in answer A. The other options are grammatically incorrect.

LESSON 9, *pp. 138–139*
1. **D; DOK Level:** 1; **Language Assessment Target:** L.2.1.
Answer D is correct because *Thai* is a proper adjective (based on *Thailand*) that must be capitalized, and *Noodles* is part of the title of an article.

2.1 **A; DOK Level:** 1; **Language Assessment Target:**
L.2.1. The names of holidays should always be capitalized: *New Year's Day.* Each first letter is capitalized. Also, the first letter of the first word in the sentence is capitalized. Answers B, C, and D reflect incorrect sentence and proper-noun capitalization.

2.2 **C; DOK Level:** 1; **Language Assessment Target:**
L.2.1. Because *president* as it is used here does not refer to one specific person, there is no need to capitalize it, but the names of countries should always be capitalized: *president of the United States.* The word *the* is not capitalized when part of this country's name.

2.3 **D; DOK Level:** 1; **Language Assessment Target:**
L.2.1. The names of the days of the week and the months of the year are always capitalized: *Monday in May.*

2.4 **B; DOK Level:** 1; **Language Assessment Target:**
L.2.1. *Dr.* is an abbreviated professional title that should be capitalized when it accompanies a person's name, as it does in this sentence. The first, middle, and last names of a person are always capitalized. The abbreviation *Jr.* (for *junior*) is capitalized when written as part of the name. The correct answer is *Dr. Martin Luther King, Jr.*

LESSON 10, *pp. 140–141*
1. **C; DOK Level:** 1; **Language Assessment Targets:**
L.2.2, L.2.4. The sentence represents an incomplete thought. The punctuation is correct, and the sentence has a verb. Therefore, a subject must be added: for example, *Bo and Madison went to the gym on Thursday.*

2.1 **B; DOK Level:** 1; **Language Assessment Targets:**
L.2.2, L.2.4. The first sentence, *Have you applied for a credit card or a bank loan recently?*, asks a question and should end with a question mark. The other answer options do not include proper end punctuation, and answer A is missing a verb for the next sentence, thus creating a fragment.

2.2 **C; DOK Level:** 1; **Language Assessment Target:**
L.2.2. The sentence should read: *A credit score is based on one's credit history.* This sentence has a subject, *credit score;* a verb, *is based;* and expresses a complete thought. Answer A adds neither a subject nor verb and, therefore, does not correct the fragment. Answers B and D do not correct the fragment because they are missing verbs.

2.3 **D; DOK Level:** 1; **Language Assessment Targets:**
L.2.1, L.2.2, L.2.4. The two sentences should read: *One's credit score is not a stable number. It can go up or down.* The phrase *can go up or down* is a fragment. It does not specify what can go up or down. You must add a subject, the pronoun *it*, which refers to *credit score.* Answer A does not add the necessary subject. Answer B is incorrect because part of the verb is missing. Answer C would be correct if *it* began with a capital letter.

2.4 **B; DOK Level:** 1; **Language Assessment Targets:**
L.2.2, L.2.4. The two sentences should read: *Finally, you should know that a closed account does not disappear. That account may still affect your credit score.* The phrase *May still affect your credit score* is a fragment. You need to add a subject to make the meaning clear (think: *what is doing the affecting?*). Answer A incorrectly places a question mark at the end of the first sentence. Answer C does not add a subject. Answer D does add a subject but omits part of the verb.

LESSON 11 *pp. 142–143*
1. **B; DOK Level:** 1; **Language Assessment Target:**
L.2.4. The phrase *Mike and Tom* adds a description to *two brothers.* It is an interrupting phrase that should be set off by two commas: *My two brothers, Mike and Tom, came with me to the baseball game last weekend.* The commas are incorrectly placed in the other answer options, even if the sentence were interpreted to mean two brothers in addition to two other people, Mike and Tom.

2.1 **D; DOK Level:** 1; **Language Assessment Target:**
L.2.4. The sentence begins with the introductory phrase *As a frequent user of the City Transit System.* As a rule, a comma belongs after an introductory phrase to set it off from the rest of the sentence: *As a frequent user of the City Transit System, I am disappointed with the proposal to discontinue Bus Route 97, which provides direct service from Midtown to the Warehouse District.* Answers A and B have incorrectly placed commas. Answer C is missing the comma.

2.2 **C; DOK Level:** 1; **Language Assessment Target:**
L.2.4. The adjectives *quickest* and *easiest* describe the noun *way.* When two or more adjectives describe the same noun, a comma usually separates them: *It is the quickest, easiest way for her to travel to these places.* Answer A is missing the comma. The commas are incorrectly placed in answers B and D.

2.3 **B; DOK Level:** 1; **Language Assessment Target:**
L.2.4. Commas separate items in a series. In this sentence, the items include *buy groceries*, *pick up medication*, and *see her doctor.* A comma should be used after each of the first two items to help the reader understand that three different elements make up the series: *If the proposal were approved, my mother would have to walk several miles each way to buy her groceries, pick up medication, or see her doctor.* Answer A is missing the comma after *medication* and has a misplaced comma after *or.* Answer C is missing the comma after *groceries.* Answer D has an extra comma after *or.*

2.4 **A; DOK Level:** 1; **Language Assessment Target:**
L.2.4. The compound sentence contains two parts, each of which is a complete sentence on its own. The two parts are usually separated by a connecting word, such as *and* or *but,* and a comma usually appears after the word before the connecting word: *Now it will take longer for many people in Midtown to get to their jobs, and it will cost more money for them to do so.* The comma is incorrectly placed in answer B. Answer C has an extra comma placed after *and.* Answer D is missing the comma.

Answer Key

UNIT 4 *(continued)*

LESSON 12, *pp. 144–145*
1. D; DOK Level: 2; **Reading Assessment Targets:**
L.1.6, L.1.8, L.2.4. The three sentences are short, choppy
sentences that can be combined to create one longer, more
polished sentence. Answer D is the best choice because
it improves the flow, gets rid of extra words, and keeps all
content without repeating needlessly. Answer A omits key
content. Answer B repeats the subject and verb. Answer C
omits and alters content.

2.1 B; DOK Level: 2; **Reading Assessment Targets:**
L.1.6, L.1.8, L.1.9, L.2.4. The best way to combine the ideas
is to separate each example of an emergency (a fire, an
earthquake, etc.) with a comma to create a series. The
sentence should read *An emergency may include a fire, an
earthquake, or a hurricane.* Answer A unnecessarily repeats
the subject and verb. Answer C uses a pronoun for the
subject and repeats the verb. Answer D is wordy, using an
unnecessary signal word, pronoun, and verb.

2.2 D; DOK Level: 2; **Reading Assessment Targets:**
L.1.6, L.1.8, L.1.9. Answer D combines the ideas without
unnecessary words and shows the relationship of the ideas
(cause and effect). Answers A and B needlessly repeat
the phrase *Having an escape route.* Answer C does not
logically connect the two ideas.

2.3 B; DOK Level: 2; **Reading Assessment Targets:**
L.1.6, L.1.8, L.1.9. Answer B is correct because it is the
clearest and most concise way to phrase the sentence(s).
The semicolon is correct, and the connecting word *therefore*
shows a cause-and-effect relationship. The comma after
therefore is used correctly. Answer A adds unnecessary
repetition. Answers C and D create sentence fragments.

2.4 B; DOK Level: 2; **Reading Assessment Targets:**
L.1.6, L.1.8. Answer B combines the ideas most
smoothly without repeating words: *The card should have
information about emergency contacts, medical conditions,
medication, and the names of family members.* Answer
A is grammatically incorrect because it is missing the
conjunction *and* after the comma. Answers C and D repeat
unnecessary words.

LESSON 13, *pp. 146–147*
1. C; DOK Level: 2; **Language Assessment Targets:**
L.2.2, L.2.4. The sentence is a run-on because *Everyone
had a great time at the show* and *we're going to see the
band play again next month* are both complete thoughts that
are combined without correct punctuation. The most logical
connecting word to use in this case is *and: Everyone had
a great time at the show, and we're going to see the band
play again next month.* Answer A creates grammatical error.
Answer B does not correct the run-on sentence by inserting
a comma. Answer D uses a connecting word that does not
make sense in context.

2.1 C; DOK Level: 2; **Language Assessment Targets:**
L.2.2, L.2.4. To avoid a run-on sentence, add a connecting
word, or separate the sentence into two sentences with
a period. The comma and connecting word *however*
do not make sense. Separating the sentences makes
the most sense: *Do not delay. Report all minor injuries
to the department manager and the Human Resources
Department.*

2.2 A; DOK Level: 2; **Language Assessment Targets:**
L.2.2, L.2.4. Answer A is correct because *however* is
surrounded by two complete ideas, or sentences. The
semicolon preceding the word and the comma following
it are correct punctuation for combining the sentences.
Answers B and D create run-on sentences. Answer C
shows the semicolon in the wrong place.

2.3 D; DOK Level: 2; **Language Assessment Targets:**
L.2.2, L.2.4. To avoid a run-on sentence, combine the two
sentences with a comma and connecting word. *And* is a
more logical connecting word than *but* (answer C) in the
sentence. Answers A and B create run-on sentences.

2.4 C; DOK Level: 2; **Language Assessment Targets:**
L.2.2, L.2.4. Answer C is correct because it creates two
complete sentences. Answers A and B create run-on
sentences. Answer D creates two new sentences, but an
incorrect comma follows the subject.

LESSON 14, *pp. 148–149*
1. D; DOK Level: 2; **Language Assessment Target:**
L.1.5. The phrase *nearly over* is confusing because it
should describe the game. However, the way the sentence
is written, *nearly over* modifies the people, *we,* who are
attending the game. To correct the misplaced modifier,
place *the game was* before *nearly over.* The finished
sentence should read *Although the game was nearly over,
we left early because the Colts were losing.* Answers A, B,
and C do not correct the misplaced modifier.

2.1 B; DOK Level: 2; **Language Assessment Target:**
L.1.5. The phrase *Like many other classic dishes* modifies
the noun *lasagna,* which is the subject of the sentence.
Lasagna should appear after the phrase: *Like many other
classic dishes.* In answers A and C, the phrase modifies the
wrong word. In answer D, the subject is missing, and the
introductory phrase modifies nothing.

2.2 B; DOK Level: 2; **Language Assessment Target:**
L.1.5. The adverb *often* modifies the verb *use* and should
be placed before it in this sentence: *For the filling, people
often use tomato sauce and ground meat.* Placing *often* in
a different position changes the meaning of the sentence
or creates confusion. In answers A, C, and D, *often* is a
misplaced modifier.

2.3 A; DOK Level: 2; **Language Assessment Target:**
L.1.5. *First* functions as an adverb in the sentence,
modifying the verb *boil.* It also indicates sequence and
should be placed at the beginning of the sentence: *First,
boil the noodles in a large pot until they are barely softened*
In answers B, C, and D, *first* is a misplaced modifier.

2.4 B; DOK Level: 2; **Language Assessment Target:**
L.1.5. Answer B is the only choice in which the introductory
phrase modifies the understood subject *you.* Answers A and
D actually say that the ingredients prepare for baking, and
answer C says that the layers prepare for baking.

LESSON 15, pp. 150–151

1. D; DOK Level: 2; Language Assessment Target: L.1.7. Answer D is correct because *who* is the correct subject pronoun and makes sense in the sentence. The pronoun that needs to be replaced is not the subject of the sentence but of the verb *is calling*. Answer A is incorrect and makes no sense in the sentence. Answer B is a subject pronoun but makes no sense in the sentence. Answer C is incorrect because the pronoun must be a subject pronoun; *her* is an object pronoun.

2.1 B; DOK Level: 2; Reading Assessment Target: L.1.7. Answer B correctly completes this sentence because it is part of the subject of the sentence and uses the subject pronoun *I*. Answer A is incorrect because *me* is an object pronoun. Answer C is incorrect because a subject pronoun should not follow the word *of*. The author is referring to herself and other students. Answer D is incorrect for the same reason as answer A, in addition to misplacing the first-person pronoun.

2.2 C; DOK Level: 2; Reading Assessment Target: L.1.3. Answer C is correct because *this* does not stand alone. Answer A is incorrect because *this* has no antecedent. Answer B is incorrect because *which* causes a sentence fragment. Answer D is incorrect because *which* has no antecedent and causes a sentence fragment.

2.3 A; DOK Level: 2; Reading Assessment Target: L.1.7. Answer A is correct because an object pronoun must follow *including*. Answer B is incorrect because an object pronoun, not a subject pronoun, is needed. Answers C and D create mistakes in pronoun use and add unnecessary words to the sentence.

2.4 B; DOK Level: 2; Reading Assessment Target: L.1.3. In this sentence, *who* introduces a part of the sentence that explains why the supervisors and teachers would be helpful. Answer B is correct. Answer A is incorrect because *whom* is an object pronoun, and the subject pronoun is needed here as the subject of the verb *can provide*. Answer C is incorrect because the author is giving more information about specific people, so *whoever* is inappropriate. Answer D is incorrect because *they* does not introduce a part of a sentence that tells about another part, and its use would create a run-on sentence.

LESSON 16 pp. 152–153

1. B; DOK Level: 1; Language Assessment Target: L.1.7. Answer B is correct because the compound subject (*a pencil, a piece of cheese, and a phone*) follows the verb. Do not be misled by the word *pocket*, which directly precedes the verb; *pocket* is not the subject. Answers A and D are incorrect because they do not affect subject-verb agreement. Answer C changes the tense of the verb, but it is still singular and thus incorrect.

2.1 D; DOK Level: 1; Language Assessment Target: L.1.7. In this compound subject with a neither/nor construction, the subject closer to the verb, *supervisor*, is singular. Therefore, the singular *has* is correct. Answers A and B are plural forms, and answer C is an incorrect verb construction.

2.2 B; DOK Level: 1; Language Assessment Target: L.1.7. The subject (*Mr. Sanchez's work ethic, his willingness… and his can-do attitude*) is compound and takes the plural verb *have made*. The other answer options are singular.

2.3 C; DOK Level: 1; Language Assessment Target: L.1.7. The subject, *suite*, is singular and takes the singular verb *was*. Answers A and B are plural. Answer D is in the wrong tense because the mastering already has occurred.

2.4 C; DOK Level: 1; Language Assessment Target: L.1.7. The subject, *I*, is singular and takes the singular verb *am*. The aside, *as well as my colleagues*, does not make the subject compound. Answers A and D are plural. Answer B is the incorrect form of the singular.

LESSON 17, pp. 154–155

1. A; DOK Level: 2; Language Assessment Targets: L.1.6, L.1.8. The two equal ideas presented in the sentence are (1) *Garage bands write their own songs* and (2) *these bands perform the songs they have written*. An effective revision of the sentence places these two ideas in parallel structure by using the verbs *write* and *perform* to describe the garage bands' actions: *Garage bands often write and perform their own songs.* The other answer options do not have parallel structure and do not improve the awkward sentence construction.

2. C; DOK Level: 2; Language Assessment Target: L.1.6. The gerund and the infinitive (verb forms that act as nouns) *saving* and *to have* are not parallel in form. Changing *to have* to *having* makes the sentence parallel in structure: *Sure, most people would like saving energy and having more money in their pockets.* It also would be correct to use *to save energy and to have more money.* Answer A repeats the subject unnecessarily without making *saving* and *to have* parallel. Answers B and D do not include both *saving* and *having* and thus create confusing sentences.

3. D; DOK Level: 2; Language Assessment Targets: L.1.6, L.1.8. The phrase *as well as their families* is subordinated in this sentence. People are busy with two things: work and families. These should be given equal status in the sentence by using parallelism: *However, they're busy with their work and their families.* Answer A does not make sense. Answer B may seem parallel because of needless repetition, but *working* and *families* are still not parallel, and the sentence is needlessly repetitive. *Working* should be changed to *work*. Answer C changes the meaning of the sentence.

4. A; DOK Level: 2; Language Assessment Targets: L.1.6, L.1.8. Answer A is the most concise and accurate way of wording these sentences. The combined sentences contain a clear series of parallel items and all the information that is necessary. Answers B, C, and D contain needless repetition and reflect a lack of parallelism. Answer D also creates a run-on sentence.

5. C; DOK Level: 2; Language Assessment Target: L.1.6. Changing *to wash* to *washing* creates parallelism: *If you have a small load of dishes, washing them by hand is more efficient than washing them in the dishwasher.* Answer A is awkward and does not make sense. Answers B and D do not reflect parallelism.

Answer Key

LESSON 18, *pp. 156–157*

1. B; DOK Level: 1; **Language Assessment Target:** L.1.9. The transition *in contrast* should be used at the beginning of the second sentence because it helps show the difference between Juanita and her twin sister. The transition words in answer A indicate sameness, which is incorrect because the sisters are different. Answer C indicates cause and effect, which makes no sense in context. Answer D indicates time, which also makes no sense in context.

2.1 A; DOK Level: 1; **Language Assessment Target:** L.1.9. The transition *for example* should be used because it helps connect the idea of what to wear to an interview with an example of what to wear: *For example, if others will be wearing suits, then you should wear a suit. Afterward* is used to make time transitions. *In addition* indicates more information. *Otherwise* is used to make a transition about a restriction or condition.

2.2 C; DOK Level: 1; **Language Assessment Target:** L.1.9. The transition *therefore* should be used because it helps suggest a cause-and-effect relationship: *Women should choose something simple and subtle that does not attract attention. Therefore, they should avoid bright or unusual nail polish colors. First* and *finally* show transitions in time. *Similarly* is used to show likeness, not cause and effect.

2.3 D; DOK Level: 1; **Language Assessment Target:** L.1.9. The transition *likewise* should be used because the information in the second sentence is similar to the information in the sentence that precedes it: *Likewise, too much cologne or perfume may cause discomfort to those around you.* The other answer options include transition words that show contrast, not similarity.

2.4 B; DOK Level: 1; **Language Assessment Target:** L.1.9. The transition *but* helps provide contrast and qualify the importance of appearance: *Your appearance should make a nice impression, but it should not distract the interviewer.* The other answer options point out similarity, not contrast.

LESSON 19, *pp. 158–159*

1. B; DOK Level: 2; **Writing Assessment Target:** W.2; **Language Assessment Target:** L.1.9. Sentence 4 introduces the idea that tattoo art developed in different cultures, and sentence 6 provides an example of one of the places, Japan, where tattoo art developed. Therefore, sentence 6 should follow sentence 4.

2. B; DOK Level: 2; **Writing Assessment Target:** W.2; **Language Assessment Target:** L.1.9. Sentence 6 introduces the idea that a person's voice makes a personal connection, and sentence 5 provides a detail to support that idea: *A person's voice offers expression that an e-mail cannot convey.* Therefore, sentence 5 should follow sentence 6.

3. A; DOK Level: 2; **Writing Assessment Target:** W.2; **Language Assessment Target:** L.1.9. Sentence 9 belongs at the beginning of paragraph B because it is a topic sentence that introduces the broad idea of how telephones enhance communication among family members. The other sentences in the paragraph provide examples and details to support this idea.

4. C; DOK Level: 2; **Writing Assessment Target:** W.2; **Language Assessment Target:** L.1.9. Although sentence 10 discusses an issue related to cell phones, the topic of monitoring children's cell phone use is not related to the broader idea of the paragraph: that cell phones enhance communication among family members. Therefore, sentence 10 should be removed because it destroys the unity of the paragraph. Placing it elsewhere in the paragraph would not alter the fact that it does not support the main idea.

5. D; DOK Level: 2; **Writing Assessment Target:** W.2; **Language Assessment Target:** L.1.9. Sentence 14 summarizes the ideas of the paragraph and should follow sentence 17. The introductory phrase *In these ways* signals that this sentence is summarizing ideas that have been stated about how telephones provide access to emergency services. Placing the sentence anywhere but after sentence 17 would not improve the organization.

LESSON 20, *pp. 160–161*

1. B; DOK Level: 1; **Language Assessment Targets:** L.2.2, L.2.4. A semicolon is one way to combine sentences. In this fused sentence, adding a semicolon after *meeting* corrects the problem. The other answer choices create punctuation errors.

2.1 D; DOK Level: 1; **Language Assessment Target:** L.2.4. *Customer-focused* should contain a hyphen because it is a combined idea modifying *airline*. The words should not be placed in quotation marks because they are not a quotation. The sentence should read *At Eastern Airways, we pride ourselves on being a customer-focused airline.* Answer A is incorrect because the hyphen is misplaced, and it is missing in answer B.

2.2 B; DOK Level: 1; **Language Assessment Target:** L.2.4. Writers often use parentheses to set aside parts of a sentence that are not necessary for understanding the meaning of the sentence but provide extra information. The words *including your fishing gear* should be placed in parentheses. The sentence should read *We are deeply sorry that your luggage (including your fishing gear) did not arrive in time for the beginning of your vacation in Florida.* Answer A is missing the second parenthesis. Answers C and D create errors.

2.3 A; DOK Level: 1; Language Assessment Target:
L.2.4. The writer provides a direct quotation from Mr. Harvey's letter to the airline, and it should be placed in quotation marks. The statement is not a paraphrasing of what the writer said. In addition, the end quote appears in the sentence, signaling that there should be an initial quotation mark. The correct sentence should read *In your letter to us, you wrote, "Giving me $100 to buy a few items of clothing was no compensation for not having my clothing and fishing gear for three days and having to purchase and rent replacements with my own money."* The other answer choices do not include the needed quotation mark.

2.4 C; DOK Level: 1; Language Assessment Target:
L.2.4. A colon is used to introduce a list preceded by a complete idea. In this sentence, the items offered by the airline as compensation are a list. The sentence should read *We would like to provide you with the following compensation: reimbursement for the clothing you had to purchase, reimbursement for your fishing gear rental charges, and a voucher worth $400 toward the purchase of a future flight on Eastern Airways.* The other answer options have incorrect punctuation.

UNIT 4 REVIEW, *pp. 162–169*
1.1 C; DOK Level: 2; Language Assessment Target:
L.1.2. Answer C is correct because the subject comes after the verb. *Many* is plural and needs a plural verb. Answer A is incorrect because the verb is singular. Answers B and D are incorrect because the changed subject is still plural and needs a plural verb.

1.2 D; DOK Level: 2; Language Assessment Target:
L.1.5. The modifier *only* belongs before *the food* to indicate that the cats eat nothing but the food they find in the neighborhood. The other answer options misplace the modifier and change the meaning of the sentence.

1.3 B; DOK Level: 1; Language Assessment Targets:
L.1.1, L.1.2. Answer B is correct because the correct *too* is used to mean "excessively." Answer A is incorrect because *to* should be *too*. Answer C is incorrect because the object pronoun *them* is used incorrectly. Answer D is incorrect because the number *two* is used incorrectly instead of *too*.

1.4 A; DOK Level: 1; Language Assessment Targets:
L.1.1, L.1.3. Answer A is correct because *Every pet owner* is singular and requires a singular pronoun. *His or her* is correct because it is singular and avoids gender bias. *Their* is plural, *there* is a homonym of *their*, and *he or she's* is the wrong case. Furthermore, *she's* is not a word.

2.1 D; DOK Level: 1; Language Assessment Targets:
L.2.1, L.2.2. The two ideas should be written as separate sentences. Answer D is correct: *We at Ann Arbor Bank wish to take this opportunity to thank you for your continued business over the years. These are difficult economic times.* Answers A and C are run-on sentences. The ideas are illogically connected with the word *because* in answer B.

2.2 C; DOK Level: 1; Language Assessment Target:
L.2.1. *December* is a proper noun and should be capitalized. The other answer choices show incorrect capitalization.

2.3 B; DOK Level: 1; Language Assessment Targets:
L.2.1, L.2.4. Answer A is incorrect because a comma is needed before *who*. Answer C is incorrect because the proper noun *Saturdays* needs to be capitalized. Answer D is incorrect because *Saturdays* should be capitalized.

2.4 B; DOK Level: 2; Language Assessment Targets:
L.1.6, L.1.8, L.1.9. To avoid repetition and wordiness, the two ideas should be combined into one sentence: *We thank you for your business and look forward to serving you in the future.* The subject is repeated needlessly, and two sentences are written in answer A. Incorrect punctuation is used in answer C. The connecting word in answer D, *subsequently*, does not make sense in the context of the sentence.

3.1 D; DOK Level: 1; Language Assessment Targets:
L.1.1, L.2.2, L.2.4. The verb *read* followed by a semicolon should end the first part of the sentence, and the connecting word *however* followed by a comma should begin the second part. The semicolon is incorrect after *however* in answer A. The homonym *reed* is incorrect in answers B and C. In addition, answer C is a run-on sentence.

3.2 A; DOK Level: 1; Language Assessment Targets:
L.2.2, L.2.4. A colon should follow *size* because a colon introduces examples and lists: *The information that follows relates to the serving size: 100 calories in one serving, 200 calories in two servings, 300 calories in three servings, and so on.* A comma or a semicolon cannot introduce the examples in this sentence. The punctuation is missing in answer D.

3.3 B; DOK Level: 1; Language Assessment Target:
L.2.4. The sentence contains a series, so a comma should follow *vitamins* and *calcium*. In addition, the parenthetical phrase is set off from the sentence as a whole. The phrase is introduced with a comma so another comma belongs at the end of the parenthetical phrase: *The "good" ingredients, such as vitamins, calcium, and iron, are listed last.* The other answer options do not have correct punctuation.

3.4 A; DOK Level: 1; Language Assessment Targets:
L.1.6, L.2.4. The phrase *vitamin C, for example* belongs in parentheses to set it off from the rest of the sentence. Using parentheses maintains parallel structure with the way in which *(calcium, for example)* is set off in the sentence: *Depending on the type of item, the food may be high in some good nutritional areas (calcium, for example) and low in others (vitamin C, for example).* The other answer options do not have correct punctuation.

4.1 C; DOK Level: 1; Language Assessment Targets:
L.1.1, L.1.3, L.1.4. Answer C is correct because the collective noun *city*, meaning "city government or officials" is singular and takes the singular verb *tries*. It also is followed correctly by *to*, not *and*, and uses the possessive *its*. The other answer choices have incorrect forms, and answer D introduces an error in subject-verb agreement.

Answer Key

UNIT 4 *(continued)*

4.2 D; DOK Level: 1; Language Assessment Targets:
L.2.3, W.3. The phrase *city's claims* requires an apostrophe because the claims belong to the city. Because the passage discusses one city, the singular form of the possessive is correct. The plural of *study* is *studies*. The correct sentence should read *Despite the city's claims, studies have shown that red-light cameras do not necessarily reduce the risk of accidents in the intersections at which they are placed.* The other answer choices do not reflect the proper possessive form of *city* or the correct spelling of *studies*, nor should *studies* be possessive as in answer B.

4.3 B; DOK Level: 2; Language Assessment Targets:
L.1.5, L.1.7. The plural subject of the sentence is *accidents*, and the verb *result* must agree with the subject in number. Therefore, *result* is correct, eliminating answers A and C, which have singular verbs. The modifier *rarely* should be placed before *result* because *rarely* describes the frequency of the results: *Because accidents caused by an improper right turn rarely result in serious injuries or fatalities, claims that the cameras have been installed primarily for safety seem suspect.* Placing *rarely* in a different position in the sentence creates a misplaced modifier and makes the sentence confusing. For these reasons, answer B is correct.

4.4 A; DOK Level: 2; Language Assessment Target:
L.1.5. The subject, *the city,* must follow the introductory phrase to avoid creating a dangling modifier. Answer A is correct: *If truly concerned with improving safety, the city could apply other practices.* The other answer options all include dangling modifiers because the introductory phrase does not modify the word that follows it.

5.1 C; DOK Level: 1; Language Assessment Targets:
L.1.3, L.1.7. *Ron Taylor and me* is the compound object of the preposition *from* in this sentence. *Myself* is incorrect because it is used only when the subject and object are the same. In this sentence the subject is *many of you*, and the object is *Ron Taylor and me*. The pronoun *I* is a subject pronoun and cannot be used as an object by itself or as part of a compound object. Answer D is incorrect because the first-person pronoun does not belong first in a compound subject or object.

5.2 D; DOK Level: 1; Language Assessment Targets:
L.1.3, L.2.2. Answers A and C use pronouns without clear antecedents indicating what *this* and *that* refer to. Answer B creates a sentence fragment. Answer D contains no unclear pronoun reference and, therefore, is correct.

5.3 B; DOK Level: 1; Language Assessment Target:
L.1.7. The subject pronoun *who* should be used in this sentence. *Who* takes the place of the keynote speaker, *Susan Jeffrey. Whom* is an object pronoun. *That* and *which* are pronouns that take the place of things, not of people.

5.4 A; DOK Level: 2; Language Assessment Targets:
L.1.5, L.1.7. The form of the verb should be the singular *was* because the sentence uses a *neither/nor* construction, and both subjects are singular collective nouns. The modifier *entirely* belongs before *satisfied* because *entirely* modifies *satisfied* (the satisfaction was incomplete). The correct form of the sentence should read *Neither the pro-drilling faction nor the anti-fracking faction was entirely satisfied with her conclusions.* The other choices reflect incorrect subject-verb agreement or a misplaced modifier.

6.1 D; DOK Level: 1; Language Assessment Target:
L.1.4. The sentence should be written *Banking is no longer the same as it used to be. Use to* is not standard English when it refers to something that was habitual or practiced over a period of time in the past. Therefore, answer A is incorrect. Answers B and C contain incorrect forms of the verb in this sentence.

6.2 B; DOK Level: 1; Language Assessment Targets:
L.1.1, L.1.3. The possessive pronoun *their* is correct in the sentence. The customers possess the money. *There* is a homonym for *their* that means "that place." *They're* is also a homonym and is a contraction of *they are. They* is a subject pronoun, and its correct possessive form is *their.*

6.3 A; DOK Level: 1; Language Assessment Target:
L.1.7. The word *each* is always singular and, therefore, needs a singular verb. The intervening phrase *of these features* does not affect subject-verb agreement. The context of the sentence is the present tense, so answer A is correct. The other answer choices are either past tense or plural verbs.

6.4 D; DOK Level: 1; Language Assessment Targets:
L.2.1, L.2.2, L.2.4. *Do you want to learn more or get started* is a question and complete sentence. It should end with a question mark. *Go* should be capitalized because it begins the next sentence: *Do you want to learn more or get started? Go to our Web site and click "Online Banking" at the top of our home page.* A period is incorrectly used to end the sentence in answer A. Answers B and C are run-on sentences.

7.1 B; DOK Level: 2; Language Assessment Target:
L.1.5. *After receiving management approval* modifies *Purchasing*, which is the department that received the approval and then bought the laptops. Answer B is correct because the modifier precedes the noun it modifies. Answers A, C, and D reflect misplaced modifiers—neither the truck nor the laptops received management permission.

7.2 C; DOK Level: 1; Language Assessment Target:
L.1.4. Answer C is correct because it is the only answer choice that contains no double negative. Double negatives reflect nonstandard English.

7.3 D; DOK Level: 2; Language Assessment Targets:
L.1.1, L.1.3, L.1.7. The subject pronoun *whoever* means "whatever person." *Whomever* is an object pronoun. The possessive pronoun *their* indicates ownership of the property. *There* is a homonym for *their* meaning "at that place." The correct form of the sentences should be written *Although the laptops are company property, we expect employees to treat them as they would treat their own property. Whoever checks out a laptop is responsible for the security of confidential company information on the laptop and for the laptop's safekeeping.*

7.4 **B; DOK Level:** 2; **Language Assessment Targets:**
L.1.9, L.2.2, L.2.4. The two ideas in the sentence should
be connected with the clause *as you will be able* because
the new computers enable the accessing of information.
However shows contrast and does not logically connect the
ideas. *Subsequently* indicates sequence in time and does
not make sense in the sentence. A comma splice is created
in answer C.

8. **C; DOK Level:** 1; **Language Assessment Target:**
L.1.9. *Therefore,* which indicates a cause-and-effect
relationship, makes the most sense as a transition word to
begin sentence 4. The writers compiled information to help
consumers or as a result of consumers' confusion. *Finally*
makes a final point. *Similarly* indicates that a comparison
will follow. *On the other hand* shows contrast.

9. **D; DOK Level:** 2; **Language Assessment Target:**
L.1.8. Sentence 7 and sentence 8 are repetitious because
both include the idea of exchanging photos electronically.
The two sentences are already combined, so answer D is
correct. Moving the sentence elsewhere in the paragraph
would not eliminate wordiness and repetition.

10. **A; DOK Level:** 2; **Language Assessment Target:**
L.1.9. Sentence 10 belongs at the beginning of the
paragraph because it introduces the idea of getting a
camera with a zoom. Sentence 9 refers to *this feature,*
but a feature has not yet been mentioned. Therefore, the
sequence of ideas does not flow logically. Sentence 11
refers to *even more zoom features,* suggesting that it should
come last in the paragraph. Answer C is incorrect because
the sentence contains important information. Answer D is
incorrect because the sentence is not related as closely to
the information in paragraph B as it is to the information in
paragraph C.

11. **D; DOK Level:** 2; **Language Assessment Targets:**
L.1.6, L.1.8. The sentence does not reflect parallelism
because the sentence suggests two actions but phrases
the actions in different forms. Answer D is the best choice
because it eliminates wordiness—needless repetition—and
shows parallel structure: *Once the memory card is full, you
must transfer or delete pictures before you can take more.*
Answers A and B are not parallel. Answer C is parallel
but wordy.

Index

A

Adjectives, 14, 138, 142, 148–149
Adverbs, 148–149
Analogies, 38–39, 74–75
Anecdotes, 64, 113
Antecedents, 124, 150
Apostrophes, 124, 130–131, 142
Appeals
   to emotions, 62–64, 66, 68–70, 77, 82
   to ethics, 64, 70
   to logic, 64
Appropriate language, 60
Argument analysis
   analyzing elements of persuasion,
     62–63
   analyzing rhetorical devices, 74–75
   analyzing structure, 72–73
   analyzing visuals and data, 66–67
   classifying valid and invalid evidence,
     70–71
   comparing opposing arguments,
     96–97
   determining author's purpose, 60–61
   identifying evidence, 64–65
   identifying faulty evidence, 68–69
   See also **Persuasive texts**
Articles, capitalization in titles, 138
Asides, 152
Audience, 19, 60–62, 64, 74, 78, 82–83,
   91–93, 96, 98
   addressing in extended responses,
     104, 106
Author's perspective, 14–15, 76, 80 –81
Author's point of view
   comparing opposing viewpoints,
     96–97, 100
   determining, 14–15, 24, 62
Author's purpose
   comparing, 78, 80–82, 96–97
   determining, 14, 18–19, 22, 60–61

B

Bandwagon appeals, 68–69
Biased arguments, 68, 70
**Body, developing for extended
   responses**, 104, 106–109
Books, capitalization in titles, 138
Burroughs, Augusten, 94
Bylines, 14

C

Capitalization, 122, 138–139, 140
Categorizing, 8–9

Cause and effect
   identifying in fiction, 28–29
   identifying in nonfiction, 10–11
   inaccurate relationship, 68
   signal words for, 10, 28, 156
Characters, 32, 34–36, 40, 48
Charts, 66, 78
Choppy sentences, 144–145
Claims
   comparing opposing arguments, 72–73
     96–97
   definition, evidence supporting, 62–65,
     70
   developing, 98–99
   visuals and data supporting, 66–67
Climax, 32
Collective nouns, 122, 152
Colons, 160
Column headings, 66
Commas
   between adjectives, 142–143
   combining sentences, 140, 142–145
   confusing apostrophe and comma, 142
   in dialogue and quotations, 142
   following introductory or descriptive
     phrase and clause, 142–143
   following transition words, 156
   in series, 142–143
Comma splices, 146–147
Common adjectives, 138
Common nouns, 138
Comparing and contrasting
   arguments, 96–97, 100
   in fiction, 30–31
   in nonfiction, 12–13
   texts, 76–77
   texts in different formats, 78–79
   texts in different genres, 82–83
   texts in similar genres, 80–81
Complete idea, 140, 146
Compound sentences, 144–145
Compound subjects, 134–135, 144,
   152–153
Conclusion,
   developing for extended responses,
     104–105
   in persuasive texts, 62, 72
Conclusions, drawing
   from multiple texts, 84–85
   from nonfiction texts, 20–21, 24
   in fiction, 46–47
Conjunctions
   combining sentences, 142–147
   signals for parallel structure, 154–155
Connecting words, 140, 144–147
Connotations, 18–19, 26
Content Topics
   comparison and contrast, 12
   forms of *be, have, do*, 134
   misuse of *they*, 124
   plot elements, 32
   point of view, 40
   purpose of news article/editorial, 82
Context clues, using, 26–27
Contractions, 130, 132–136

Contrasting. *See* **Comparing and
   contrasting**
Counterclaims, 62, 96–97
Credibility, 64

D

Dangling modifiers, 148–149
Data, analyzing, 66–67
Days of the week, 138–139
Definitions, 18, 26
Descriptions
   of characters, 34
   as supporting details, 2
Diagrams, 12, 30, 66, 78
Dialogue, 40, 142
Dictionary, 18, 128
Double negatives, 136
Drafting extended responses, 106–109
Drawings, 66

E

Editing
   apostrophes, 124, 130–131
   capitalization, 138–139
   commas, 142–147, 156
   extended responses, 110–111
   frequently confused words, 132–133
   modifiers, 148–149
   nouns, 122–124, 130, 138, 152
   paragraph organization, 158–159
   parallelism, 154–155
   pronouns, 40, 124, 125, 130, 132,
     150–153
   punctuation, 130–131, 140, 142–147,
     156, 160–161
   run-on sentence correction, 146–147
   sentence combining, 142–146
   sentence fragment correction, 140–141
   standard English, 136–137
   subject-verb agreement, 134–135,
     152–153
   transitions, 156–157
   verbs with helping verbs, 128–129
   verb tenses, 126–127
Editorials, 82
Enumeration, 74–75
Evidence
   analyzing in opposing arguments,
     96–97
   classifying valid and invalid evidence,
     70–71
   comparing and contrasting, 100–101
   gathering for extended response,
     100–101
   identifying faulty evidence, 68–69
   identifying in persuasive texts, 64–65
   supporting claims, 62, 64, 106
   use in persuasive writing, 62

Index

Nouns, 122–124, 130, 138–139, 152

O

Object pronouns, 124, 150–151
Onomatopoeia, 38
Opinions, 14, 62, 64
Opposing arguments, comparing for extended responses, 96–97
Opposing viewpoints, 62, 70, 72
Order of events, 6–7
Order of importance structure, 72
Outlines, 102

P

Paragraph organization, 158–159
Parallelism, 74–75, 80–81, 154–155
Parentheses, 160–161
Participles, 128–129
Parts of speech. *See* **Adjectives; Adverbs; Conjunctions; Modifiers; Nouns; Prepositional phrases; Pronouns; Verbs**
Past participles, 128–129
Past perfect tense, 128–129
Past tense, 126–127, 128
Periods, 140–141
Personification, 38–39
Persuasion, elements of. See Persuasive texts
Persuasive texts
analyzing elements of persuasion, 62–63
analyzing rhetorical devices, 74–75
analyzing structure of arguments, 72–73
analyzing visuals and data, 66–67
classifying valid and invalid evidence, 70–71
determining author's purpose, 60–61
identifying evidence, 64–65
identifying faulty evidence, 68–69
See also **Extended response questions**
Photographs, 64, 66, 78
Phrases
interrupting, 142, 152
introductory, 142–143
prepositional, 148, 152
Planning extended responses, 102–103
Play titles, 138
Plot elements, analyzing, 32–33
Plural nouns, 122–123, 130–131
Plural subjects, 134–135
Poem titles, 138
Points, defining for extended responses, 100–101

Points of view
first-person, 40–41
of narrators, 40–41
omniscient, 40
See also **Author's point of view**
Possessive nouns, 130–131
Possessive pronouns, 124–125, 130–131
Possessive words, 130–131
Predictions, making, 48–49, 84–85
Prepositional phrases, 148–149, 152
Present participles, 128–129
Present perfect tense, 128–129
Present tense, 126–127
Prior knowledge
using to determine meanings, 26
using to draw conclusions, 20, 46
using to make inferences, 16
Pro/con structure, 72
Pronoun-antecedent agreement, 124
Pronouns
agreement with antecedent, 124–125
capitalization of *I*, 138
indefinite pronouns, 150–152
indicating point of view, 40
possessive pronouns, 124–125
subject and object pronouns, 124–125, 150–151
who/whom/that/which, 150–151
Proper adjectives, 138
Proper nouns, 122–123, 138–139
Punctuation
apostrophes, 124, 130–131, 142
colons, 160
commas, 140, 142–145, 156
end marks, 140–141
hyphens, 160–161
parentheses, 160–161
quotation marks, 160–161
semicolons, 144–147, 160–161

Q

Qualifying statements, 74–75
Question marks, 140–141
Question types on GED® Test, vi–vii
drag-and-drop, 7, 17, 25, 51, 55, 57, 69, 71, 77, 81, 87, 89, 93
drop-down, 123, 125, 127, 129, 131, 133, 135, 137, 139, 141, 143, 145, 147, 149, 151, 153, 157, 161, 162–168
extended response, 99, 101, 103, 105, 107–109, 111, 113, 115, 117
fill-in-the-blank, 27, 31, 37, 47, 51, 53, 73, 75, 89, 91, 93, 113
Quotation marks, 160–161
Quotations, 4, 142

R

Reading comprehension
analyzing characters, 34–35
analyzing plot elements, 32–33
analyzing setting, 36–37
analyzing style and tone, 18–19
applying ideas, 48–49
categorizing, 8–9
comparing and contrasting, 12–13, 30–31
determining author's point of view, 14–15
determining main idea and details, 2–3
determining narrative point of view, 40–41
determining sequence, 6–7
drawing conclusions, 20–21, 46–47
identifying cause and effect, 10–11, 28–29
interpreting figurative language, 38–39
making generalizations, 22–23
making inferences, 16–17, 42–43
summarizing, 4–5
synthesizing information, 24–25
theme, 44–45
using context clues, 26–27
Refutation/proof structure, 72
Regular verbs, 126–127
Relevant evidence, 70–71
Reliable evidence, 70–71
Repetition, 18, 74–75, 81, 89, 110, 154–155
Resolution, 32
Reviewing extended responses, 110–111
Rhetorical devices, analyzing, 74–75
Rising action, 32
Rock, Chris, 120
Run-on sentence correction, 146–147

S

Sandwich structure, 72
Scare tactics, 68
Semicolons, 144–147, 160–161
Sentences
combining, 142–145
correcting fragments, 140–141
correcting run-ons, 146–147
revising extended responses for structure of, 110
topic sentences, 2, 158–159
Sequence, determining, 6–7
Setting, analyzing, 36–37
Signal words
for cause and effect, 10, 28, 156
for comparing and contrasting, 12–13, 30
connecting related sentences, 144–145
for sequences, 6
for tense, 126
See also **Transitions**